THE SOVIET UNION
AND THE
DEVELOPING NATIONS

# The Soviet Union
# and
# the Developing Nations

*Edited by*
ROGER E. KANET

The Johns Hopkins University Press

Baltimore and London

The Johns Hopkins University Press, Baltimore, Maryland 21218
The Johns Hopkins University Press Ltd., London

Library of Congress Catalog Card Number 73-15530
ISBN 0-8018-1501-0
Manufactured in the United States of America

Library of Congress Cataloging in Publication Data will be
found on the last printed page of this book.

To My Parents,
Edith M. and Robert G. Kanet

# CONTENTS

Notes on Contributors     ix

Preface     xi

1. The Soviet Union and the Colonial Question, 1917–1953
   *Roger E. Kanet*     1

2. Soviet Attitudes toward Developing Nations since Stalin
   *Roger E. Kanet*     27

3. The Soviet Union and Africa
   *Arthur Jay Klinghoffer*     51

4. The Soviet Union and Southeast Asia
   *Justus M. van der Kroef*     79

5. The Soviet Union and South Asia
   *Bhabani Sen Gupta*     119

6. The Soviet Union and the Middle East
   *John C. Campbell*     153

7. The Soviet Union and Latin America
   *Roger Hamburg*     179

8. Soviet Economic Relations with the Developing Nations
   *Elizabeth Kridl Valkenier*     215

9. The Soviet Union, the United Nations, and the
   Developing States
   *Richard W. Mansbach*     237

10. The Sino-Soviet Split and the Developing Nations
    *Jan S. Prybyla*     265

Index     295

# NOTES ON CONTRIBUTORS

JOHN C. CAMPBELL is a Senior Research Fellow at the Council on Foreign Relations. He has been a member of the Policy Planning Council of the Department of State (1967–1968) and, since 1964, a member of the Governing Board of the Middle East Institute. Since 1967 he has been the Vice President of the Middle East Institute. Included among his numerous publications dealing with the Middle East, the Soviet Union, and Eastern Europe are: *Defense of the Middle East: Problems of American Policy* (1958; rev. ed., 1960); *Tito's Separate Road: America and Yugoslavia in World Politics* (1967); and *The West and the Middle East* (with Helen Caruso) (1972).

ROGER P. HAMBURG is Associate Professor of Political Science at Indiana University at South Bend. His publications include articles on Soviet policy in Latin America and Soviet politics and have appeared in *Journal of Inter-American Studies, Asian Studies, Studies in Comparative Communism,* and *Polity.*

ROGER E. KANET is Visiting Associate Professor of Political Science at The University of Illinois (Urbana) and Associate Professor of Political Science at The University of Kansas (on leave). During the academic year 1972–1973 he was a Joint Senior Fellow at the Research Institute on Communist Affairs and the Russian Institute of Columbia University. He is editor of *The Behavioral Revolution and Communist Studies* (1971), coeditor (with Ivan Volgyes) of *On the Road to Communism: Essays on Soviet Domestic and Foreign Politics* (1972), and compiler of *Soviet and East European Foreign Policy: A Bibliography of English and Russian Language Publications* (1974).

ARTHUR JAY KLINGHOFFER is Associate Professor of Political Science at Rutgers University (Camden) and a member of the Graduate Faculty of Political Science, Rutgers University (New Brunswick). His publications include *Soviet Perspectives on African Socialism* (1969) and numerous articles on Soviet and African affairs in such journals as *Africa Report, African Affairs,* and *Mizan.*

RICHARD W. MANSBACH is Associate Professor of Political Science at Rutgers University (New Brunswick). His publications include (with R. F. Hopkins) *Structure and Process in International Politics* (1973) and articles in *Comparative Politics* and *International Organization.*

JAN S. PRYBYLA is Professor of Economics at The Pennsylvania State University. He has also taught at the National War College and Air University. Among his numerous publications on both Chinese and Soviet domestic and foreign economics are *World Tensions: Conflict and Accommodation* (with Elton Atwater and Kent Forster) (1967; rev. ed., 1972); *From Underdevelopment to Affluence* (coedited with Harry Shaffer) (1968); *Comparative Economic Systems* (ed.) (1969); and *The Political Economy of Communist China* (1970).

BHABANI SEN GUPTA is Professor and Head of the Division of Disarmament and Security Studies, Schools of International Studies, Jawaharlal Nehru University (New Delhi). He has been a Senior Fellow at the Research Institute on Communist Affairs, the East Asia Institute, and the Southern Asia Institute, all of Columbia University. Among his numerous publications are *The Fulcrum of Asia: Relations Among China, India, Pakistan, and the USSR* (1970) and *Communism in Indian Politics* (1972). His articles have appeared in *China Quarterly, Pacific Community, Orbis, Problems of Communism,* and *Asian Survey.*

ELIZABETH KRIDL VALKENIER is a Fellow at the Russian Institute of Columbia University. She has written on the ideological, diplomatic, and economic aspects of Soviet relations with the developing nations for such publications as *World Politics, Survey, Orbis,* and *Europa-Archiv.* She has recently completed a social history of nineteenth-century Russian art which will be published by Princeton University Press.

JUSTUS M. VAN DER KROEF is Charles A. Dana Professor and Chairman, Department of Political Science, University of Bridgeport (Connecticut). He has been a Senior Fellow at the Research Institute on Communist Affairs of Columbia and has been Visiting Professor at universities in Singapore, the Philippines, and Ceylon. He is the author of numerous books and articles on Southeast Asia, including *The Communist Party of Indonesia: Its History, Program, and Tactics* (1965); *Communism in Malaysia and Singapore: A Contemporary Survey* (1967); and *Indonesia since Sukarno* (1971). His articles have appeared in such journals as *Problems of Communism, Studies on the Soviet Union,* and *Studies in Comparative Communism.*

# PREFACE

During the past decade numerous articles and monographs have been written that describe and analyze Soviet relations with the developing nations. An obvious question arises, then: "Why write yet another volume dealing with Soviet policy in this area?" The answer is related to the editor's conviction that, in spite of the outpouring of English-language studies of Soviet policy toward the states of Asia, Africa, and Latin America, a need still exists for a general treatment of Soviet policy which brings together material written from a common perspective. The studies published to date can be divided into several categories. First of all, there are both articles and books that deal with specific aspects of Soviet policy—for example, relations with the Arab countries, economic assistance, or policy during the Indian-Pakistani war. Although valuable, these studies usually do not provide a general treatment of overall Soviet policy toward the developing nations. A second group of studies, which also includes articles and monographs, provides the general overview, but adds little in the way of specific detail. In addition, authors who have done detailed research in a specific area—for example, Soviet policy toward Africa—tend to generalize to the broader areas of relations with all developing nations. A final category, which is very small, consists of readers that bring together articles on various aspects of Soviet relations with the developing nations. Usually, however, these are reprints of articles originally written for publication separately, and there is little relationship among the questions asked or the approaches employed by the several authors.

Hopefully, the reader will find that the present volume does not suffer seriously from the above-mentioned problems. All but one of the articles were prepared specifically for this book by persons who have specialized on the topic they are examining, and, although some of the authors have strayed from the general format that was originally planned, the articles do possess more unity than is usually the case in multi-authored studies.

The purpose of the present volume is to provide the reader with both a general overview of Soviet policy toward the developing nations and more detail on various aspects of that policy. The first two articles present a broad survey of Soviet doctrine concerning the colonial question and the developing nations; the next five articles analyze Soviet policy in five geographic regions of the world; and the final three articles examine the importance of Soviet economic policy in relations with the developing nations, Soviet policy toward the developing states in the United Nations, and the importance of Sino-Soviet competition in the developing nations.

The editor wishes to express his apprecation to the Graduate School of The University of Kansas for financial assistance that facilitated the preparation of the manuscript; to Miss Kristyne Hadel, who typed—and retyped—most of it; and to the Research Institute on Communist Affairs, Columbia University, where the manuscript was finally completed. In addition, he wishes to thank his wife and daughters, who continue to exhibit patience in spite of his physical and mental absences.

# THE SOVIET UNION
## AND THE
## DEVELOPING NATIONS

# 1

## THE SOVIET UNION AND THE COLONIAL QUESTION
### 1917-1953

*Roger E. Kanet*

In the past two decades, the Soviet Union has shifted its policies toward the newly independent nations of Asia and Africa, as well as toward the nations of Latin America, from almost total isolation to rapidly expanding involvement. For example, Soviet trade with the developing nations increased more than eleven times from 1955 to 1970,[1] and the Soviets now have diplomatic relations with most of the nations of Asia and Africa and with half of the nations of Latin America.[2] This increased Soviet activity in the Southern Hemisphere is indicative of the major changes that Soviet policy toward the developing nations has undergone in the years since Stalin's death. From a position of almost total isolation from Asia, Africa, and Latin America, the Soviet Union has evolved into one of the major actors in these parts of the world—recent treaties signed with the Egyptian Arab Republic and India and the Soviets' support for India in the December 1971 war with Pakistan are partial indicators of that increased involvement and influence. The Soviets have been quite successful in achieving some of their policy goals in the developing world—in particular, the reduction of Western influence and the augmentation of Soviet power. Before proceeding with a discussion of recent Soviet policy toward the developing nations, however, I will examine the historical and theoretical bases of Soviet relations with the states of Asia, Africa, and Latin America.

Soon after the Bolsheviks came to power in Russia in 1917, they developed a strategy for the colonial areas that was based on Lenin's

[1] From 261.8 million rubles to 1.98 billion. For several years, 1965-1968, total trade increased only very slowly. In 1969, however, trade jumped 20 percent, and in 1970 it increased an additional 15.7 percent. See U.S.S.R., Ministerstvo Vneshnei Torgovli, *Vneshniaia torgovlia S.S.S.R.* (Moscow: Vneshtorgizdat), for the years 1955 and 1965-1968; see also *Vneshniaia torgovlia*, no. 5 (1971), p. 56.

[2] As of October 1971, the Soviet Union had diplomatic relations with twenty-five of thirty-three non-Communist developing nations in Asia, including the Middle East; in thirty-two of forty-one independent African nations; and in twelve of twenty-four Latin American nations, excluding Cuba. See U.S., Department of State, *Soviet Diplomatic Relations and Representation*, Research Study, RSES-45, November 8, 1971.

1

evaluation of the role of imperialism in the maintenance of the capitalist system. In 1918 and 1919, revolution was sweeping Europe, and Lenin and his lieutenants envisaged the imminent success of the Bolshevik Revolution throughout Europe. The Bolsheviks controlled European Russia, and sister parties held power for a short time in Budapest and Munich. The Spartacists attempted to seize Berlin, and throughout Germany left-wing groups revolted.[3] But there was unrest outside Europe. Throughout the Middle and Far East the nationalist struggle for independence was gaining ground, and, almost immediately after coming to power, the Soviet government appealed to the peoples of colonial Asia, to the former subjects of the tsar, and to the subjects of nominally independent Asian states:

> Moslems of Russia, Tatars of the Volga and the Crimea, Kirghiz and Sarts of Siberia and Turkestan, Turks and Tatars of Trans-Caucasia, Chechens and Mountain Cossacks! All you, whose mosques and shrines have been destroyed, whose faith and customs have been violated by the Tsars and oppressors of Russia! Henceforward your beliefs and customs, your national and cultural institutions are declared free and inviolable! Build your national life freely and without hindrance. It is your right. Know that your rights like those of the peoples of Russia will be protected by the might of the revolution, by the Councils of Workers', Soldiers', and Peasants', Deputies![4]

The Bolsheviks called upon the Muslims of the East—among whom the Persians, Turks, Arabs, and Hindus (sic) were mentioned specifically—to overthrow the imperialist rulers of their nations. All the secret treaties entered into by the tsarist government were declared null and void, including those concerning Russian annexation of Constantinople and the partition of Persia.[5]

At this time the Bolsheviks were still confident that the social revolution in Europe would soon be successful, and they established an international agency, the Comintern, to coordinate the various revolutionary movements throughout Europe.[6] The colonial question played a very

---

[3] For detailed analyses of the period see Franz Borkenau, *World Communism* (Ann Arbor: University of Michigan Press, 1962), pp. 108ff.; Edward H. Carr, *The Bolshevik Revolution, 1917–1923* (London: Macmillan & Co., 1953), 3: 165ff.; and Julius Braunthal, *Geschichte der Internationale* (Hannover: Verlag J. H. E. Dietz, 1963) 2: 180ff.

[4] "Appeal of the Council of People's Commissars to the Moslems of Russia and the East," December 3, 1917, reprinted in *Soviet Documents on Foreign Policy, 1917–1939*, ed. Jane Degras (London–New York–Toronto: Oxford University Press, 1951), 1: 16.

[5] *Ibid.*, pp. 16–17.

[6] V. I. Lenin, *Polnoe sobranie sochinenii*, 5th ed. (Moscow: Politizdat, 1958–1965), 50 (1965): 227–30.

insignificant role in this founding conference, and the only mention of the colonies was contained in the Manifesto of the Comintern prepared by Trotsky, in which he argued that the "emancipation of the colonies is conceivable only in conjunction with the emancipation of the working class in the metropoles. . . . If capitalist Europe has violently dragged the most backward sections of the world into the whirlpool of capitalist relations, then socialist Europe will come to the aid of liberated colonies . . . in order to facilitate their transition to a planned and organized socialist economy."[7]

The view expressed by Trotsky differed greatly from that of Lenin, who emphasized the importance of the national liberation movements in the colonies for the proletarian movement in Europe. However, it was not until the second congress of the Comintern, in July 1920, that the colonial question was dealt with in any detail and that Lenin's views were accepted by the Communist movement. At this congress Lenin argued that "all Communist parties must give active support to the revolutionary movements of liberation" carried on by the national bourgeoisie.[8] This position was strongly attacked by various delegates to the congress, including the Indian Communist M. N. Roy.[9] The major point in dispute concerned the extent to which, if at all, the Communists should cooperate with the nationalists. To Lenin the most important factor was the weakening of the Western nations, which could be accomplished, at least in part, by disruption in their colonial empires. In speaking of the creation of alliances with the nationalists, he went so far as to argue that "Communists may find it necessary to make great concessions with the view of rapidly removing the . . . distrust and prejudices" against all members of the ruling nations.[10]

Even before the national and colonial question had been discussed at the congress, Lenin, in his report "The Present World Situation and

---

[7] Communist International, *Kommunisticheskii Internatsional v dokumentakh . . . 1919–1932*, ed. Bela Kun (Moscow: Partiinoe izdatel'stvo, 1933), p. 57. A few days after the completion of the congress, one of the Soviet leaders, Bukharin, spoke with cynical frankness about the slogans for colonial liberation: "If we propound the solution of the right of self-determination for the colonies, for the Hottentots and Bushmen, the Negroes, the Indians, etc., we lose nothing by it. On the contrary we gain; for the national gain as a whole will damage foreign imperialism. . . . The most outright nationalist movement, for example, that of the Hindus, is only water for our mill, since it contributes to the destruction of English imperialism." *VIII s"ezd Rossiiskoi Kommunisticheskoi Partii (Bol'shevikov), 19–23 marta, 1919: Stenograficheskii otchet* (Moscow–Petrograd: Knigoizdatel'stvo "Kommunisticheskii Internatsional," 1919), p. 128.

[8] Kun, ed., *Kommunisticheskii Internatsional*, p. 128.

[9] See Communist International, *Protokoll des II: Weltkongresses der Kommunistischen Internationale* (Hamburg: Verlag der Kommunistischen Internationale, 1921), pp. 148–49.

[10] *Ibid.*, pp. 230–32.

the Tasks of the Comintern," had outlined a new relationship between the social revolution in Europe and the nationalist movements in Asia. The second congress would be marked by the "union of the revolutionary proletariat of the advanced capitalist countries . . . with the oppressed masses of the Eastern colonial countries."[11] The theses which Lenin proposed at the congress set out two completely different sets of tactics which the Communist movement should take in backward and colonial states. The more important of the two—since the Communist world revolution, which the other set presupposed, did not occur—called for: (1) support for national revolutionary movements; (2) struggle against the clergy and all other reactionary elements, including Pan-Islamism; (3) support for the agrarian movement against the landowners; (4) the formation of temporary alliances, but not mergers, with the bourgeois-democrats in backward areas; and (5) opposition to attempts of the imperialists to create dependent puppet regimes under the guise of independent states.[12] In the discussion on the colonial question at the congress, Lenin pointed out that "the overwhelming mass of the population in backward countries consists of peasants," and that "it would be utopian to believe that proletarian parties, if indeed they can arise in these backward countries, could pursue Communist tactics and a Communist policy without establishing definite relations with the peasant movement and without giving it effective support." However, Lenin was aware of the dangers represented by those parts of the national bourgeoisie which worked "hand in glove with the imperialist bourgeoisie," and he warned the Communists to support only those liberation movements that were "genuinely revolutionary and when their exponents do not hinder our work of educating and organizing the peasantry and the broad mass of the exploited in a revolutionary spirit." If these conditions were not fulfilled, he said, the Communists would have to "combat the reformist bourgeoisie in the colonies."[13] As will be seen later, the changes that occurred in Soviet policy toward the developing nations in the 1950s and 1960s did not take Lenin's strictures into account. The Soviets recommended that local Communist parties be dissolved and that their membership join the nationalist parties.

Another major point which Lenin brought out in the discussions at the second congress was the possibility of economic development in the backward areas by-passing the entire stage of capitalism. According to Lenin, it would be "wrong to assume that the capitalist stage of

---

[11] *Ibid.*, pp. 37–38.
[12] For a discussion of these points, see Branko M. Lazitch, *Lénine et la IIIe Internationale.* Paris: Editions de la Baconnière, 1951, pp. 163ff.
[13] *Protokoll des II: Welkongresses,* pp. 139–40.

development is inevitable for the backward nations," if a victorious revolutionary proletariat, supported by the Soviet government, carried on systematic propaganda to organize peasant soviets. The Communist International had the task of providing the theoretical guidelines that would help the "backward countries pass to the Soviet system and, after passing through a definite stage of development, to Communism, without passing through the capitalist stage of development."[14]

The colonial doctrine developed by Lenin was an attempt to provide new answers for the problems presented by backward areas that lacked capital accumulation and an organized proletariat and that thus did not fit into the Marxist model. In the development of his doctrine, Lenin departed from Marx's position on a number of basic points. First of all, he argued that it was necessary to support peasant revolutionary movements in the colonial states, and that the revolution could not triumph without their support. Marx and Engels, however, had maintained that the peasants constituted a backward class that represented the most tenacious vestiges of private property. Any alliance between the proletariat and the peasantry was doomed to failure, they said.[15]

A second question on which Lenin differed from his mentors concerned the possibility for a backward nation, which has not known capitalist modes of production, to skip the entire capitalist stage of development and proceed immediately to socialism. Lenin argued that, with the rise of socialism in the industrially developed nations, backward areas would be able to skip capitalism by relying on aid from the socialist states. In this way he freed the Communist movement from Marx's laws of economic development by encouraging the establishment of socialist states in colonial areas, which were still primarily prefeudal. State power would be used to by-pass whole stages of economic development.

Lenin's impact on the Marxist doctrine of colonialism was great. While Marx was interested mainly in the modes of economic production and the political conclusions he could draw from such a study, Lenin concentrated on the means necessary for the attainment of political power. He was willing to accept support from any source whatsoever in the struggle for the overthrow of capitalism. He told his followers that the Bolsheviks "would be very poor revolutionaries if, in the great proletarian war for emancipation and socialism, [they] did

[14] *Ibid.*, p. 142.
[15] For Marx's views, see "The Eighteenth Brumaire of Louis Bonaparte," in Karl Marx and Frederick Engels, *Selected Works in Two Volumes* (Moscow: Foreign Languages Publishing House, 1962), 1: 334. Engels also dealt with this question in "The Peasant Question in France and Germany," *ibid.*, 2: 423ff.

nòt know how to utilize *every* popular movement against *each separate* disaster caused by imperialism in order to sharpen and extend the crisis."[16] In spite of the great importance he placed on the colonial revolution, Lenin still believed, as late as 1916, that the revolutionary struggle in Europe was "infinitely more . . . a hundred times more significant politically than a blow of equal might delivered in Asia or Africa."[17] However, after the revolution failed to materialize in Europe, he changed his opinion concerning the importance of the colonial areas, as I have already noted. In the last article he wrote before his death, Lenin argued:

> In the last analysis, the outcome of the struggle will be determined by the fact that Russia, India, China, and so forth, account for the overwhelming majority of the population of the globe. And it is precisely this majority that, during the past few years, has been drawn into the struggle for emancipation with extraordinary rapidity, so that in this respect there cannot be the slightest shadow of a doubt concerning the final victory of socialism which is fully and absolutely assured.[18]

In spite of setbacks in Europe, the spirit of revolutionary optimism still prevailed at the second Comintern congress, and the national and colonial question was placed at the center of discussion. In fact, adherence to the theses on colonialism, which were approved at the congress, was made a condition for entry into the Communist International. However, very few of the delegates were from colonial areas, and not a single delegate represented Africa.[19]

In the summer of 1920, the Communist policy of supporting ultra-left-wing radical movements in the colonies was still being followed, although signs of a change to the new tactics of supporting bourgeois nationalists were evident. In July of that year, the Executive Committee of the Communist International issued an appeal "to the oppressed masses of Persia, Armenia, and Turkey," inviting them to attend a congress of peasants and workers in Baku at the beginning of September in order to discuss "the question of how the forces of the European proletariat can be united with your forces for the struggle against the common enemy." The appeal enumerated the evils perpe-

---

[16] V. I. Lenin, *Selected Works*, vol. 5 (London: Lawrence & Wishart, 1936), p. 305.

[17] *Ibid.*, p. 304.

[18] "Luchshe men'she, da luchshe," in V. I. Lenin, *Sochineniia*, 4th ed. (Moscow: Politizdat, 1941–1951), 33 (1951): 458.

[19] Of the total of 218 delegates (of whom 167 had a vote), only 13 were from Asia (7 of these had a vote) and 10 were from what is now Soviet Central Asia. *Protokoll des II: Weltkongresses*, pp. 780–88.

trated by colonial governments in the Near East and then called on the peasants and workers of the area to organize, to arm themselves, and to unite with the Russian workers' and peasants' Red Army in order "to defy the French, English and American capitalists . . . be free of your oppressors . . . [and] have the opportunity in free alliance with the Workers' republics of the world to take care of your own interests." The appeal concluded: "Every year you make a pilgrimage across deserts to the Holy Places. Now make your way across desert and mountain and river to meet together, to deliberate together, how you can join in brotherly union and live as free and equal men."[20]

When the congress met in Baku, it was still assumed that the revolution would break out in the West and that the underdeveloped nations of the East could arrive at Soviet-type governments without passing through the stage of capitalism. Delegates and self-appointed delegates arrived at Baku from disturbed areas all over Asia—1,891 delegates in all, representing a wide variety of political opinion (only two-thirds called themselves Communists), but all in some sort of national or social revolt against the established order.[21] During the course of the congress, G. E. Zinoviev, one of the organizers of the meeting, made an impassioned appeal for "all of toiling humanity living in Asia and Africa" to follow the Communists. "The European proletariat," he cried out, "cannot help seeing now that the course of historical development has bound together the toilers of the East to the workers of the West. We must conquer or perish together."[22] However, the Soviet leaders of the congress still placed greater importance on the European revolution than they did on the revolutionary movements in the East, for the East was to follow the Russian example and "set up soviets of the laboring peasants" even in areas "where there are no urban workers."[23] Not much room remained for independent development along lines which fit local conditions. But, until such soviets could be established, the workers would have to "create a Red Army in the East . . . arm and organize uprisings in the rear of the British . . . [and] poison the existence of every British officer who lords it over Turkey, Persia, India, China."[24]

[20] *Izvestiia*, July 3, 1920, translated in *The Communist International, 1919–1943: Documents*, ed. Jane Degras (London–New York–Toronto: Oxford University Press, 1956), 1: 106–9.

[21] See G. D. H. Cole, *A History of Socialist Thought*, vol. 4: *Communism and Social Democracy, 1914–1931* (London–New York: Macmillan & Co. and St. Martin's, 1958), pp. 347–48. A list of the delegates in attendance was published in *Pervyi s"ezd narodov Vostoka, Baku 1–8 sentiabria 1920g.: Stenograficheskie otchety* (Petrograd: Izd Kommunisticheskogo Internatsionala, 1920), p. 5.

[22] *Ibid.*, pp. 12, 31–32.

[23] *Ibid.*, pp. 40, 184–86.

[24] *Ibid.*, pp. 47–48.

Karl Radek, one of the representatives of the Comintern, attempted to remove any suspicions that the delegates might have about the durability of the friendship and support of Soviet Russia for their revolutionary movements by assuring them that

> a permanent peace between the country of the workers and the exploiting countries is impossible. The Eastern policy of the Soviet government is, therefore, no diplomatic manoeuvre, no pushing forward of the peoples of the East into the firing-line in order, by betraying them, to win advantages for the Soviet republic. . . . We are bound to you by a common destiny; either we unite with the peoples of the East and hasten the victory of the Western European proletariat, or we shall perish, and you will be slaves.

Radek then concluded with an appeal to the memory of the great Asiatic conquerors of the Middle Ages and "the spirit of struggle which once animated the peoples of the East when they marched against Europe under the leadership of their conquerors."[25]

In spite of Radek's protestations of permanent Soviet support for the oppressed nations of Asia, Soviet leaders soon moderated their support for revolutionaries throughout the area as a corollary of their attempt to improve relations with independent Asian governments as well as with the governments of Europe. The collapse of the revolutionary movement in Central Europe and the retreat of the Red Army from Poland marked the beginning of a more moderate Soviet and Comintern policy. The world revolutionary movement receded, and the Soviet government began to emphasize the importance of attaining friends on the diplomatic level. In early 1922, the Soviet government signed diplomatic agreements with Turkey, Persia, and Afghanistan and extended political and military support to the Kemalist government in Turkey.[26] Earlier, in 1921, the New Economic Policy was adopted in the Soviet Union with the aim of rejuvenating the devastated Russian economy, partially by using private capital to assist in the reconstruction of Russia. The new foreign policy even sought foreign capital to aid in this reconstruction. The primary foreign policy goals of Lenin's government became credits, trade, and diplomatic recognition. Lenin himself stated that "at the present time trade relations, and not only diplomatic victories, are necessary for us."[27] Connected with the Soviets desire for the establishment of trade relations with the capi-

[25] Ibid., pp. 70, 72.

[26] For partial texts of the agreements, see Degras, ed., Soviet Documents on Foreign Policy, 1: 233–42.

[27] Lenin, Sochineniia, 4th ed., 32 (1950): 157. See also George F. Kennan, Russia and the West under Lenin and Stalin (Boston-Toronto: Little, Brown & Co., 1961), p. 183.

talist nations was the development of more peaceful relations with Great Britain, which appeared the most likely prospect for increased trade. In the words of a Soviet commentator, "Peace with England was extremely important for the public economy of our country. It opened the possibility of large-scale export of Soviet raw materials and the import of English products, especially machinery."[28] Moscow's bid for expanded foreign trade, even tied as it was to the demand for credits, found relatively ready acceptance in the West. First Great Britain and Germany, then the other nations of Europe, and finally the United States established commercial relations with the new Soviet republic.

As Soviet Russia sought a *modus vivendi* with the capitalist world, it had also to moderate the position of the Comintern toward the colonial and semicolonial states. The basic policy of the Soviets in the period immediately following 1921 was to seek collaboration with all types of nationalist governments throughout Asia and to attempt to extend Soviet influence over these governments. The policy was to move forward only gradually and unobtrusively, so that it would not destroy the opportunities for profitable economic relations with the capitalist nations. As soon as the trade agreement was reached with the British, Soviet leaders reduced Comintern support to nationalist movements, for they did not wish to jeopardize the new source of material for the economic reconstruction of Russia.[29] This represents an excellent example of Comintern policy being dictated by the demands of internal Soviet economic requirements and of the secondary and dependent position of Soviet anticolonial policy in relation to Soviet policy in Europe.

The result for the colonies was a drop in Comintern interest in the colonial question. At the third congress of the Comintern, for example, a number of speakers from Asia complained that the colonial question was being ignored.[30] At the fifth congress, in 1924, Ho Chi Minh, then a young delegate from Vietnam, condemned the existence of Westernism in the Comintern, and other Asian delegates criticized the lack of attention to the colonial and semicolonial states. John Pepper, an American delegate, complained that the "congress has become one-sidedly a German Congress, or at best a Central European Congress. So far it has been too little of a world congress."[31] Instead of support-

[28] Nikolai L. Rubinshtein, *Vneshniaia politika Sovetskogo gosudarstva v 1921–1925 godakh* (Moscow, 1953), p. 16.

[29] See Carr, *The Bolshevik Revolution*, 3: 467–68.

[30] See Demetrio Boersner, *The Bolsheviks and the National and Colonial Question, 1917–1928* (Paris: Librairie Minand; Geneva: Droz, 1957), p. 106.

[31] *Ibid.*, p. 153; and *International Press Correspondence*, 4, no. 47 (1924): 483. The latter publication, usually referred to as *Inprecorr*, appeared weekly until shortly before World War II.

ing the most radical movements, the leaders of the Comintern now opted for the policy of a united front with social democrats in Europe and more limited activities in the colonial areas. In Asia, Communists were told to cooperate with all types of nationalist movements.[32]

Beginning in 1925 and 1926, Soviet leaders began to reconsider their policy toward the national bourgeoisie and to deny the progressive character of various nationalist movements. The Comintern now admitted that the Indian bourgeoisie was not as revolutionary as most Communists—with the major exception of Roy—had believed.[33] By 1927, the government of Kemal Attaturk of Turkey, which had maintained proper, and even friendly, relations with the Soviets, was called an oppressor of the working class, and the Turkish Communists began a major propaganda campaign against the government.[34]

The major blow to the Communist policy of supporting national liberation movements, however, was the destruction of the Chinese Communist party by Chiang Kai-shek's Kuomintang. During the mid-twenties the Communists had worked closely with the Chinese nationalists and had gained great influence within the KMT. Once Chiang Kai-shek had consolidated his position, however, he turned on the Communists and in the spring of 1927 ordered a raid on the Soviet headquarters in Canton. A few months later he expelled the Communists from the Kuomintang, and in December he suppressed the Canton commune that had been established by the Chinese Communists.[35]

By 1927, the whole policy of the united front in Europe and support for nationalist movements in colonial areas was in disrepute. Nowhere had expectations been fulfilled, and Communists throughout Asia had been persecuted, exiled, and killed. China, the main focus of Comintern colonial policy, had proved to be a disaster. Probably the major reason for the failure of the Comintern policy in Asia was the weakness of the local Communist parties vis à vis the dominant nationalist forces and the basic antipathy of the latter to the goals of the Com-

---

[32] Kun, ed., *Kommunisticheskii Internatsional*, pp. 321–22; and *Inprekorr* (German ed.), 2, no. 2 (1932): 9, reprinted in *The Communist International*, ed. Degras, 1: 326–27.

[33] Communist International, *Ein Jahr Kampf und Arbeit: Tätigkeitsbericht der Exekutive der Kommunistischen Internationale, 1925–1926* (Hamburg: Verlag der Kommunistischen Internationale, 1926), pp. 334–38. For Roy's opposition, see Boersner, *The Bolsheviks*, pp. 267–71.

[34] "Kemalism on the Road to Capitalist Development," *Communist International*, 4, no. 11 (1927): 223–27.

[35] See Harold R. Isaacs, *The Tragedy of the Chinese Revolution*, rev. ed. (Stanford, Calif.: Stanford University Press, 1951), pp. 102–3; and Xenia J. Eudin and Robert C. North, *Soviet Russia and the East, 1920–1927* (Stanford, Calif.: Stanford University Press, 1957), pp. 299–310.

munists. As M. N. Roy had predicted, the nationalists had been willing to use the support of the Communists in order to accomplish certain goals. When, however, the nationalists had consolidated their positions, and when the Communists began to press for the implementation of more radical social and economic policies, cooperation between the two groups became impossible. In such a situation the relative weakness of the Communists resulted in their defeat at the hands of the nationalists. In the period 1927–1928 the Comintern initiated an abrupt shift in its policy in Asia to a militant line which virtually excluded all support for local nationalist movements.

The "United Front from Below," as the new policy was called, required a significant shift in relations with independent Asian countries. In early 1928, the news organ of the Comintern carried an article which pronounced the final demise of the "united front" that had characterized Soviet policy during the past five or six years. The author cautioned his readers to remember "that the united front was never intended to obliterate existing differences or to find a half-way policy between reformism and Communism." He then spoke of the efforts of reformists to subvert the united front policy and condemned the incorrect application of united-front tactics in some states.[36] The new policy aimed at appealing to the rank and file of the socialist movement in the West and the masses of the population in colonial areas rather than to their leaders.

At the sixth congress of the Comintern, in 1928, the new policy was endowed with official sanction. The national bourgeoisies were accused of betraying their own countries and of having sought a rapprochement with the imperialist powers which had led to a "decline in the influence of the national bourgeoisie over the masses of the people, to the sharpening of the revolutionary crisis, to the unleashing of the aggrarian revolution of the widest masses of the peasants and to the creation of favorable conditions for the hegemony of the proletariat in the struggle for full national liberation."[37]

The September 1, 1928, theses on the colonial question reiterated the need for unity between the socialist world revolution and the laboring masses of the colonies, which were "struggling against imperialist slavery." However, no mention was made of the national bourgeois leadership. The Comintern program prescribed the creation and development of Communist parties in the colonial areas and rejected all collaboration with nationalist movements. It ignored the fact that

[36] A. Lozovsky, "Results and Prospects of the United Front," *Communist International*, 5, no. 6 (1928): 142–43.

[37] Communist International, *Stenograficheskii otchet VI: kongressa Kominterna* (Moscow: Gosudarstvennoe izdatel'stvo, 1929), 3: 162.

attempted Communist revolutions in Indonesia and China had been brutally suppressed.[38]

The ultrarevolutionary line adopted by the Comintern in 1928 was largely the result of internal Soviet politics and the problems confronting international communism. First, it was used to attack Bukharin, who was identified with the previous moderate line of the Comintern—in spite of his revolutionary speeches of 1928—and to purge the Comintern of all foreign Communists who might defend Bukharin. Second, it represented a furious attack against the socialist parties that the Communists had failed to take over and that might be critical of the methods being used in the Soviet Union to attain the proposed industrialization. Third, this revolutionary mood in international affairs would help sustain the élan needed within the U.S.S.R. to fulfill the tremendous tasks outlined by the plan for rapid industrialization. After 1928, Stalin was more interested in manipulating foreign Communist parties for the more immediate purposes of consolidating his own political position in the Soviet Union and of maximizing the long-term power position of the Soviet Union in international affairs than he was in spreading a social revolution throughout the world. World revolution was put off into the distant future.[39]

During the ten years immediately following the establishment of the Soviet government, only one real attempt had been made to form an organization to foment revolution in the colonies. Like many other organizations sponsored by the Soviets, this one also depended upon the vagaries of Soviet policy. In the early twenties, a League for the Liberation of the East was established at the Baku congress, but a shift in Soviet policy prevented it from ever becoming more than a plan. Not until 1927, at the instigation of the Soviet members of the Comintern Colonial Presidium, did the Comintern call for a world-wide anti-imperialist conference, which would appeal to all those who opposed imperialism and not only to representatives of the colonial peoples themselves. According to George Padmore, who was then a member of the Comintern, the Soviet leaders did not wish to focus attention on their role in calling the congress, so the task of organizing it fell to the German Communist party.[40] The Soviet Communists made every effort

---

[38] See Communist International, *Protokoll: Sechster Weltkongress der Kommunistischen Internationale, Moskau, 17. June 1. September 1928* (Hamburg: Verlag Karl Hoym Nachfolger, 1929), 4: 159–160; and Kun, ed., *Kommunisticheskii Internatsional*, pp. 30–31.

[39] For a discussion of this question, see Borkenau, *World Communism*, pp. 274–75; and Leonard Schapiro, *The Communist Party of the Soviet Union* (New York: Random House, 1964), pp. 266ff.

[40] George Padmore, *Pan-Africanism or Communism? The Coming Struggle for Africa* (London: Dobson; New York: Roy, 1956), p. 323.

to hide their part in the congress by operating through a committee of distinguished politicians, writers, scientists, and artists, which included Albert Einstein, Henri Barbusse, Mme. Sun Yat-sen, George Lansbury (a leader of the British Labour Party), Paul Henri Spaak, and Nehru.[41]

The primary purpose of this Anti-Imperialist League, which was established before the collapse of united-front tactics, was to create a broad-based organization to fight colonialism. However, the general shift in Soviet and Comintern policy soon turned the League into a battleground between the Communists and their former allies. The Communist press began demanding that the League obtain leadership which would "protect it from many dangers and errors" and "guide it along the path of real revolutionary struggle."[42] By 1928, the Communists had assumed complete control of the League, and those non-Communists who did attend meetings were condemned for retaining "illusions regarding the reformist leaders, and their role in the proletarian class struggle." They did not exhibit the proper enthusiasm for "making use on an international scale of the experience acquired in the proletarian class struggle in the Soviet Union."[43] After the shift in the Comintern line in 1928, the League lingered on for a few more years, but it lost its real value with the defection of the non-Communist membership. By the mid-thirties, the League had ceased to exist and, with another shift in Soviet policy in 1934–1935, new antiwar and anti-facist organizations took its place. The Anti-Imperialist League was merely one in a series of relatively short-lived front organizations which the Communists established to support Soviet foreign policy. Once the goal had been attained or, more often, the policy was changed, these organizations were abandoned or disbanded.

Throughout the early thirties, the Comintern retained its ultra-left-wing bias. In 1931, for example, the Comintern journal published an article that condemned the Indian National Congress and Gandhi for capitulating to imperialism and for collaborating with the imperialist bourgeoisie.[44] The Communists saw in the Depression of the early thirties the verification of their predictions of a great crisis for capi-

[41] League against Imperialism, *Das Flammenzeichen vom Palais Egmont: Offizielles Protokoll des Kongresses gegen Koloniale Unterdrückung und Imperialismus, Brussell, 10–15. Febr. 1927* (Berlin: Neuer Deutscher Verlag, 1927), pp. 250ff. See also Rolf Italiaander, *Schwarze Haut im roten Griff* (Dusseldorf-Venna: Econ Verlag, 1962), pp. 27–31; and Padmore, *Pan-Africanism or Communism?* pp. 323–24.

[42] "Under the Control of the Struggling Masses," *Communist International*, 4, no. 4 (1927): 46.

[43] Willi Munzenberg, "The Cologne Meeting of the League against Imperialism," *Inprecorr*, 9, no. 5 (1929): 78.

[44] G. Safarov, "The Treachery of the National Congress and the Revolutionary Upsurge in India," *Communist International*, 8 (1931): 258–64.

talism in the West, for the "temporary stabilization of capitalism" had disintegrated and a new round of wars and revolutions was on the way.[45] However, the rise of the Nazis in Germany and the resulting danger to the security of the Soviet Union had a profound effect on Soviet policy in Europe and in the colonies. Revolution was de-emphasized in both areas, and security against the Nazi menace was sought. As the Soviet government sought the support of the Western democracies against Germany, its interest in colonial affairs waned.[46] Once again, support for revolution gave way before the demands of Soviet foreign policy. The colonial question lost its immediate importance for Soviet leaders, and so the Comintern dropped its policy of anticolonial agitation.

Perhaps one of the most significant examples of the decrease in support for revolutionary activities was the demise of the Negro International. In 1930, an International Trade Union Committee of Negro Workers had been formed in Hamburg under the direction of George Padmore. The purpose of the organization was to coordinate revolutionary activity in Africa and the West Indies. However, with the rise of the Nazis in Germany the subsequent destruction of the German Communist party, as well as the shift in Soviet policy, Soviet interest in the Negro International disappeared. In an open letter to the head of the American Communist party in 1935, George Padmore accused the Comintern of liquidating the organization "simply in order not to offend the British foreign office which has been bringing pressure to bear on Soviet diplomacy."[47] Although Padmore's total list of accusations is exaggerated, the basic complaint that the Comintern was willing to sacrifice the revolutionary aspects of the organization in the interests of Soviet foreign policy was correct. The new "popular front" demanded less revolutionary agitation, and, therefore, the Negro International was no longer important.[48]

During the period of the popular front, the most significant development concerning Africa was the Italian invasion of Ethiopia. This war placed the Soviet Union in a rather difficult position for a number of reasons. First of all, Soviet Russia was still tied to Italy by the non-aggression pact of 1933, and the Soviet leaders, agreeing with the

---

[45] See the Comintern theses, "The International Situation and the Tasks of the Communist International," in *Kommunisticheskii Internatsional*, ed. Kun, pp. 769–93.

[46] From 1933 on, articles on colonialism published in *Inprecorr*, a publication of the Comintern, almost disappeared.

[47] George Padmore, "An Open Letter to Earl Browder," *Crisis*, 42 (1935): 302.

[48] For an excellent discussion of the Negro International, see Italiaander, *Schwarze Haut im roten Griff*, pp. 42–74; see also Roger E. Kanet, "The Soviet Union and Sub-Saharan Africa: Communist Policy toward Africa, 1917–1965" (Ph.D. diss., Princeton University, 1966), pp. 142–55.

leaders of France, did not wish to drive Italy into an alliance with Hitler. Second, Soviet trade with Italy had become rather important—in 1934 more than 5.0 percent of Soviet imports came from Italy, and more than 4.5 percent of Soviet exports were sold to that country. In addition, more than 22.0 percent of Italian petroleum imports in 1934 came from the U.S.S.R.[49] Max Beloff points out that the Soviet leaders were not in a position to ignore the economic aspects of Soviet-Italian relations, because of their importance for the Soviet economy.[50] In October 1935, in accordance with the recommendations of the Assembly of the League of Nations, the Soviet government announced that it was applying certain sanctions against Italy, and, from December 1935 until March 1936, total trade between the two states dropped almost one-third from that of the previous year.[51] But the Soviets did not place an embargo on oil deliveries, and in February and April 1936 they sent large shipments to Italy.[52] In other words, needs at home moderated policies the Soviets might have taken in support of an African nation against a strong European state. The announcement in the United States of Soviet oil shipments—some directly to Italian troops in Africa—had a disastrous effect on Negro membership in the Amercan Communist party and led to condemnations of Soviet policy in the Negro press in the United States.[53]

Throughout the Second World War, Soviet support for liberation movements in the colonial areas was almost nonexistent, unless such a movement was connected to the successful conclusion of the war. An example of the lack of Soviet interest in revolution in the colonial areas can be seen in a wartime Communist publication which called for the solution of labor problems in the copperbelt of Northern Rhodesia: "It is vitally important from the standpoint of the war against fascism that all difficulties and obstacles in the way of the maximum production of this vital war metal [copper] should be speedily eliminated." References to working conditions or African rights and wages were absent from the account.[54]

By the end of the war, the Communists were beginning, very gradually, to revive their revolutionary propaganda and to set up small cells

[49] Arnold Toynbee, *Survey of International Affairs, 1935* (London: Oxford University Press, 1936), 2: 221ff., 431.

[50] Max Beloff, *The Foreign Policy of the Soviet Union, 1929-1941* (London: Oxford University Press, 1947) 1: 200.

[51] Great Britain, Royal Institute of International Affairs, *Documents on International Affairs, 1935* (London: Oxford University Press, 1937), 2: 244-45.

[52] Toynbee, *Survey for 1935*, 2: 441.

[53] *New York Times*, September 8, 1936, p. 1; *ibid.*, September 14, 1935, p. 1. For the reaction of the American Negro press, see Padmore *Pan-Africanism or Communism?* p. 307n; and *idem*, "An Open Letter to Earl Browder," p. 305.

[54] See *World News and Views*, 23, no. 38 (1943): 303, 366-67.

of Communists from which to spread their influence in the colonial areas. The end of World War II opened up a new era for the Soviet Union and for the world Communist movement. The former was now the strongest land-power in Europe and her power extended far to the west of her prewar borders. Communist parties in Italy and France were strong and envisaged a rapid victory in their states. In Asia and, to a lesser extent, in Africa, nationalist groups were active. In Europe the minimal cooperation that had existed between the Soviet Union and its Western allies during the war rapidly deteriorated during late 1945, and, by spring 1946, both the United States and the Soviet Union had apparently given up any idea of compromise on the questions that divided them. A little more than a year later Soviet policy, under the guiding hand of Stalin, took an unrelenting stand against all cooperation with the West. In a speech before the inaugural session of the Communist Information Bureau in September 1947, Andrei Zhdanov divided the world into two antagonistic camps—one of "peace, socialism and democracy" and the other of "capitalism, Imperialism and war."[55]

In the light of the worsening international situation, it was not surprising that the Soviet attitudes toward colonial areas underwent a major change also. In late 1945 and 1946, Soviet and other Communists still praised the nationalist movements and their leaders in Asia. In late 1945, one British Communist could even see some positive aspects in British colonial policy in Africa.[56] Even when the Communist press renewed its attack on colonialism in 1946, this did not require a break with the nationalists in the colonial areas. According to A. A. Guber, the Soviet Union strongly supported a united front "from above" in Indonesia, for the unification of the various levels of the population gave the revolutionary movements in the colonies a special strength.[57] Throughout Southeast Asia the Communists had been able to forge alliances with various segments of the population during the period of Japanese occupation, and after the war they retained their contracts with these nationalist movements against the returning colonial rulers.[58]

---

[55] Andrei Zhdanov, "The International Situation (Report to a Meeting of the Cominform), September 1947," *For a Lasting Peace, For a People's Democracy,* November 10, 1947, p. 2.

[56] See Desmond Buckle, "Administrative Reform in Kenya," *World News and Views,* 25 (1945): 245.

[57] A. A. Guber, *Natsional'no-osvoboditel'noe dvizhenie v Indonezii* (Moscow, 1946), p. 4, cited in Ruth T. McVey, *The Soviet View of the Indonesian Revolution* (Ithaca, N.Y.: Modern Indonesia Project, Southeast Asia Program, Department of Far Eastern Studies, Cornell University, 1957), p. 14.

[58] For a good study of communism in Southeast Asia in the early postwar years, see Charles B. McLane, *Soviet Strategies in Southeast Asia* (Princeton: Princeton

A leading spokesman for the more optimistic view of developments in the colonial areas was the Soviet economist Evgenii Varga. In 1946 he spoke about the change in the relationship of many colonial areas toward their mother countries. No longer were all of the colonies economically indebted to the metropoles; in some cases the opposite was true. Varga argued that it followed that the changed economic conditions would be accomplished by changed political relations. A new upsurge had developed in the anti-imperialist movement in Asia, and it was based on three factors: the strengthening of the native bourgeoisie and the proletariat, the military training that native troops had received during the war, and the availability of these troops for a struggle against the colonial rulers. Varga's views left open the possibility of recognizing the evolutionary progress of colonial states toward independence.[59] During 1947, however, violent attacks against Varga's theory began to appear in Soviet journals as the Soviets began gradually returning to a policy which opposed cooperation with the national bourgeoisie. According to V. Vasil'eva, the economic prerequisites for independence were lacking in the colonial areas, and the possibility for a peaceful transition from colonial status to independence was precluded.[60] Evgenii Zhukov wrote a strong denunciation of Varga's theory in which he condemned the Indian national bourgeoisie, and by implication all non-Communist nationalists, for being anti-national and willing to compromise with the imperialists.[61]

In his speech at the initial session of the Cominform, Zhdanov called for a more aggressive policy in the colonies, a policy which backed the new view of international affairs as a struggle between two world blocs:

University Press, 1966). See also Malcolm D. Kennedy, A Short History of Communism in Asia (London: Weidenfeld & Nicholson, 1957); and John H. Kautsky, Moscow and the Communist Party of India (New York: John Wiley & Sons; Cambridge: Massachusetts Institute of Technology Press, 1956).

[59] Evgenii Varga, Izmeneniia v ekonomike kapitalizma v itoge Vtoroi Mirovoi Voiny (Moscow: Gospolitizdat, 1946), pp. 219–26. At this time, E. M. Zhukov, who later joined in the condemnations of Varga's theories, saw in the U.N. trusteeship system a possible means for liberation without revolution. The United Nations could help guarantee gradual development of social, economic, political, and educational advancement toward self-government or independence. E. M. Zhukov, "Porazhenie iaponskogo imperializma i natsional'no-osvoboditel'naia bor'ba narodov Vostochnoi Azii," Bol'shevik, 1945, nos. 23–24, p. 86.

[60] V. Ia. Vasil'eva, "Ekonomicheskoe razvitie Kolonii v gody Vtoroi Mirovoi Voiny," Mirovoe Khoziaistvo i mirovaia politika, no. 5 (1947), p. 64. In May 1947, a meeting was held in Moscow to discuss Varga's book, during which most of the comments were extremely critical. See Frederick C. Barghoorn, "The Varga Discussion and Its Significance," The American Slavic and East European Review, 7 (1948): 227ff.

[61] E. M. Zhukov, "K polozheniiu v Indii," Bol'shevik, 1947, no. 7, p. 6.

World War II aggravated the crisis of the colonial system, as expressed in the rise of a powerful movement for national liberation in the colonies and dependencies. This has placed the rear of the capitalist system in jeopardy. The peoples of the colonies no longer wish to live in the old way. The ruling classes of the metropolitan countries can no longer govern the colonies on the old lines. Attempts to crush the national liberation movement by military force now increasingly encounter armed resistance on the part of the colonial peoples and lead to protracted wars (Holland in Indonesia, France in Vietnam).

Although Zhdanov did not openly condemn the bourgeoisie in the colonies, he did emphasize the leading role the Communists must play in the "struggle against the new American expansionist plans."[62]

A few months after Zhdanov's speech to the Cominform, Zhukov applied this new thesis on world affairs to the colonies and observed that there had been an upsurge of revolutionary activity in the colonies which was being led by the working class. He called for a broad revolutionary front, led by the Communists against the imperialists and those sections of the national bourgeoisie that were connected with foreign capital—namely, the "comprador and big bourgeoisie." However, the Communists were to unite with all truly revolutionary segments of the population, including the middle bourgeoisie.[63] John Kautsky argues that this was the first clear statement of a Neo-Maoist strategy that came from Moscow. This new strategy combined a direct appeal to all "patriotic" elements of society with a struggle against foreign imperialism. The Communist party must stand at the head of this anti-imperialist alliance. For two years, from 1947 to 1949, there were no clear guidelines for Communists in the colonies, however, for the CPSU itself was split into two different groups. Besides those who called for the Neo-Maoist strategy, there were those who advocated a return to a complete "left" policy, which would eliminate all cooperation with the bourgeoisie, including the middle and lower segments. By mid-1949, however, the Neo-Maoist position had won out.[64]

[62] Zhdanov, "The International Situation," pp. 2, 4.

[63] E. M. Zhukov, "Obostrenie Krizisa Kolonial'noi sistemy," *Bol'shevik*, 1947, no. 23, pp. 57, 55. In a later article Zhukov explained that the real distinction between the big and middle bourgeoisie was the question of their "attitude toward the Soviet Union." The criterion for the progressive strata of the bourgeoisie, therefore, was its pro-Soviet and anti-American attitude. E. M. Zhukov, "Narodno-osvoboditel'naia bor'ba v kolonial'nykh i polukolonial'nykh stranakh posle Vtoroi Mirovoi Voiny," *Voprosy ekonomiki*, 1949, no. 10, p. 93.

[64] Kautsky, *Moscow and the Communist Party of India*, pp. 8–13, 27–28, 55–56, 89–91. See also Gene D. Overstreet and Marshall Windmiller, *Communism in India* (Berkeley and Los Angeles: University of California Press, 1959), pp. 242ff.; and McVey, *The Soviet View*, pp. 32ff.

For the next six years or so, Communist attitudes toward bourgeois nationalist leaders were extremely hostile. In an address to the Academy of Sciences in June 1949, Zhukov stated that bourgeois nationalism in the colonies had already gone over to the imperialist camp. After discounting the "rotten notions of the possibility of some sort of 'third,' middle road between Communism and capitalism," he condemned the national bourgeoisies for attempting to deceive the masses into believing that they had attained independence, although they had merely aided the imperialists to "replace open, crass forms and methods of colonial rule with more refined and secret forms," such as dominion status and the establishment of treaty relationships on the basis of the formal equality of the participants. The truth was, according to Zhukov, that the big bourgeoisies who ruled the newly "independent" states were merely acting as agents for their imperialist masters.[65] Gandhi, Nehru, Sukarno, and other nationalist leaders were accused of antidemocratic policies and were called everything from lackeys of the imperialists to betrayers of their nations.

In the Soviet view, only a revolutionary movement founded on the broad base of the patriotic masses could ever attain true independence. The movement must be led by the working class and its vanguard, the Communist party, in order to sharpen the conflict with the imperialists. In 1950, an editorial in the official journal of the Cominform quoted a long passage from a speech by Liu Shao-chi in which he had argued that the "path taken by the Chinese people is the path that should be taken by the peoples of many colonial and dependent countries in their struggle for national independence and People's Democracy."[66] The gist of the editorial was that China offered the model for a successful independence movement based on an alliance of workers, peasants, intelligentsia, and the national bourgeoisie, an alliance led by the working class.[67] However, in a speech delivered in 1951, Zhukov stated that he doubted the efficacy of viewing the "Chinese revolution as a kind of pattern for the popular-democratic revolution in other countries." He pointed out that most of these states were unlikely to have the

---

[65] E. M. Zhukov, "Voprosy natsional'no-osvoboditel'noi bor'by posle Vtoroi Mirovoi Voiny," *Voprosy ekonomiki*, 1949, no. 9, pp. 57–58.

[66] "Mighty Advance of the National Liberation Movement in the Colonial and Dependent Countries." *For a Lasting Peace, For a People's Democracy*, January 27, 1950, p. 1. The speech had been made in November 1949 to a trade union conference of Asian and Australian workers; it was printed in *Wen-hui Pao* (Shanghai), November 25, 1969.

[67] This model was declared applicable even to Africa, where there definitely was no sharp division of classes. See I. Lemin, "Uglublenie Krizisa kolonial'noi sistemy i imperialisticheskoe sopernichestvo v Afrike," in *Imperialisticheskaia bor'ba za Afriku i osvoboditel'noe dvizhenie narodov: Sbornik statei*, ed. V. Ia. Vasil'eva et al. (Moscow: Izd. Akademii Nauk SSSR, 1953), p. 31.

"most important advantage of the Chinese revolution—namely, a revolutionary army."[68]

The logical extension of the Soviet attitude to the newly independent states of South and Southeast Asia was a policy of nonrecognition and subversion. Rather than recognize the new governments and attempt to reach agreements with them based on common hostility toward Western Europe and the United States, the Soviet regime encouraged local Communist-led movements to rebel against their national governments.[69] As a result of this policy, the Soviet Union, in spite of its protestations of support for national liberation movements, was unable to make any real progress in influencing developments in Asia until after the death of Stalin and the initiation of a radically new appraisal of events in the area. The wave of Communist-inspired insurrections occurred not only in territories still under colonial rule, like Indochina and Malaya but also against nationalist regimes in Burma and Indonesia. In Burma, the Communists first welcomed the independence which was to come in January 1948. However, the new line that came from Moscow required a condemnation of the Anglo-Burmese agreements that brought about independence, and within three months the new government was involved in a major struggle against the Communist-inspired revolt that had broken out.[70]

In Indonesia, where a government more favorable to the Communists was in power until January 1948—in those areas controlled by the nationalists—Soviet attitudes did not change quite so rapidly, and, as late as May 1948, the Soviets still spoke favorably of the nationalist government. Not until the return of the Indonesian Communist Muso from Moscow in the summer of 1948 did the Communists withdraw their support from the government.[71] Finally, in September, the Communists issued a call to arms, but the Sukarno government was able to suppress the revolt.

For Stalin and the executors of his foreign policy there was no room

---

[68] *Izvestiia Akademii Nauk SSSR, Seriia istorii i filosofii*, 9, no. 1 (1952): 81.

[69] This is not the place to go into the argument concerning the importance of the February 1948 Conference of Youth and Students of Southeast Asia Fighting for Freedom and Independence, which met in Calcutta under the sponsorship of the World Federation of Democratic Youth and the International Union of Students. Whether or not Soviet representatives at this meeting called for violent uprisings, it seems clear that the Soviets did support them and indicated this to the Communists throughout the area. See Ruth T. McVey, *The Calcutta Conference and the Southeast Asian Uprisings* (Ithaca, N.Y.: Modern Indonesia Project, Southeast Asia Program, Department of Far Eastern Studies, Cornell University, 1958).

[70] See Kennedy, *Communism in Asia*, pp. 440ff.; and McLane, *Soviet Strategies in Southeast Asia*, pp. 371ff.

[71] McLane, *Soviet Strategies in Southeast Asia*, pp. 401–7; and McVey, *The Soviet View of the Indonesian Revolution*, pp. 29, 58ff.

for nonaligned states. Professor Ivan Potekhin, who later became one of the most famous Soviet Africanists, outlined the Stalinist theory of colonial revolution in 1950. According to the theory, "the solution of colonial slavery is impossible without a proletarian revolution and the overthrow of imperialism."[72] The only type of revolution that Moscow was willing to accept was that based on the Chinese model. The refusal to recognize the existence of the new force of nationalism that was struggling against the old colonial empires cost the Soviet Union the friendship of a number of potential anti-Western allies. Such an alliance was impossible until, after Stalin's death, his successors abandoned the attempt to force the new states into the Soviet camp before recognizing their independence.[73]

I have already noted that the Soviet Union supported attempts to overthrow national governments throughout Southeast Asia in the period after 1947. In the following pages, I will briefly summarize the basic strategies the Soviets followed in the developing nations in the late 1940s and early 1950s. Basically, Soviet policies toward these states were closely connected to the attitudes that have already been discussed. Until 1947, the policy advocated by the Soviet leaders for the Communist movements in Asia was primarily a reflection of the course in Western Europe, where relatively strong Communist parties continued to hope for power for themselves and for advantages for the Soviet Union through parliamentary action and cooperation with non-Communists. The adaptation of this policy in Asia meant, primarily, cooperation with nationalist movements. By 1947, however, the situation in Western Europe had changed significantly. Communists had been maneuvered out of positions of influence in France and Italy and the United States had reassessed its role in Europe and had decided that its interests required continued U.S. involvement. This, in turn, resulted in the new Soviet doctrine of a hostile world divided into two permanently antagonistic camps and a break between the Communists and their non-Communist allies. In Asia, the change in policy resulted

[72] I. I. Potekhin, "Stalinskaia teoriia kolonial'noi revoliutsii i natsional'no-osvoboditel'noi dvizhenie v tropicheskoi i iuzhnoi Afrike," *Sovetskaia etnografiia*, 1950, no. 1, p. 24.

[73] Although a number of factors indicate that the Soviet leadership was beginning to appreciate the potentialities of the trend toward neutralism before Stalin's death, there was no significant change in policy before 1953. For the argument that Soviet policy began to change much earlier, see Marshall Shulman, *Stalin's Foreign Policy Reappraised* (Cambridge, Mass.: Harvard University Press, 1963). See also Leland G. Stauber, who adds that Soviet policy was making a "progressive reorientation toward increasing support for nationalist governments" before Stalin's death. "Recent Soviet Policy in the Underdeveloped Countries: The Significance of the 'National Democracy' Doctrine of 1960" (Ph.D. diss., Harvard University, 1964), p. 52.

in a withdrawal of Communist support from nationalist movements and newly independent governments.

In Latin America, Soviet and Communist strategy followed a pattern which was quite similar to that in Asia, although the Soviets showed much less interest in the area. In the years immediately following the war, the Communists attempted to establish front organizations throughout Latin America and, in general, worked with left-wing elements within the various states. There was also a tendency to attempt to work within the framework of the existing political systems. After 1947, however, with the change of line in Moscow, Latin American Communist parties turned violently against the United States and against governments and groups friendly to the U.S.[74]

In Africa, where nationalist movements were much later in starting, Communist activity took a somewhat different path—or, rather, did not make the shifts that Communist policy elsewhere in the world made in 1947 and 1948. During World War II, Communist study groups had been formed in a number of cities in French West Africa, although they were extremely small and disorganized. One of the most important problems facing the Communists was the relative lack of support for any movement that called for rapid and complete independence. As late as the mid-1950s, the African delegates to the Assembly of the French Union were interested more in the equal treatment of Africans and the development of full citizenship rights than in independence.[75] Those Africans who referred, even indirectly, to eventual independence, such as Souron Mignan of Dahomey in 1946, were definitely in a minority. Even the "radical elements" of African leadership in French Africa, represented by Gabriel d'Arboussier, argued that they sought merely the full application of the French Constitution in Africa, for "we remain convinced that union with the people of France is the best and least costly means to assure the emancipation of Black Africa."[76]

The most important political development in the French colonies in Africa in the immediate postwar period was the formation of a united

---

[74] See Rollie E. Poppino, *International Communism in Latin America: A History of the Movement, 1917–1963* (New York: The Free Press of Glencoe, 1964), pp. 163ff.; and U.S., Congress, Senate, *United States–Latin American Relations: Soviet Bloc Latin American Activities and Their Implications for United States Foreign Policy*, prepared for the Subcommittee on American Republics Affairs of the Committee on Foreign Relations by the Corporation for Economic and Industrial Research (Washington, D.C.: Government Printing Office, 1960), p. 15.

[75] See Michael Crowder, "Independence as a Goal in French West African Politics, 1944–1960," in *French-speaking Africa: The Search for Identity*, ed. William H. Lewis (New York: Walker, 1965), pp. 19–20.

[76] For the remarks by Apithy, see France, *Journal Officiel: Debats de l'Assemblée Nationale Constituante*, 1946, 4: 3802. For the remarks by d'Arboussier, see France, *Journal Officiel: Debats de l'Assemblé de l'Union Française*, 1950, 1: 233.

African political movement, which was established at a meeting in Bamako, French Sudan, in October 1946. The French Communists were quick to see the advantages that a united African political movement would offer them, and Raymond Barbé and a group of French Communists were present at the Bamako conference and were influential in organizing the fledgling political movement, the *Rassemblement Démocratique Africain* (RDA).[77] The African delegates who went to Paris after the first elections of 1946 found in the French Communists their strongest and most consistent allies. In response to a question about the ties of the RDA with the Communists, Houphouet-Boigny, the leader of the party, replied:

> It is correct to say that we are connected with the Communist Party, but that does not mean that we are Communists. It is likely that I, Houphouet, a traditional chief, an African doctor, a big landowner and a Catholic, should be a Communist? But our connection with the Communist Party is valuable to us in that we have found in it a French Parliamentary group that welcomed us in friendly fashion, while others paid no attention to us. . . . Each time that we, the R.D.A., defend a project, we can count on the 183 votes of the Communist Party. If, in exchange we loan our votes to the Communist group, what is that to us?[78]

The major areas in which the Communists assisted the African cause were those of extending constitutional rights to Africans and eliminating the hated system of forced labor that had been prevalent in West Africa.[79] The alliance between the RDA and the PCF was truly advantageous for the Africans, for, as Houphouet-Boigny pointed out, it gave them strong, influential allies in Paris. However, the Communists were not satisfied with the amount of control they exercised within the African movement and, in 1948, they made a move for even greater influence in the RDA—at the very time that Communists in Asia were breaking all ties with nationalist parties.[80]

[77] Richard Adloff, *West Africa: The French-speaking Nations Yesterday and Today* (New York: Holt, Rinehart, Winston, 1965), p. 192.

[78] Quoted by Georges Monnet in the French Union Assembly on February 9, 1950. *Journal Officiel: Debats de l'Assemblée de l'Union Francaise*, 1950, 1: 225.

[79] Virginia Thompson and Richard Adloff, *French West Africa* (Stanford, Calif.: Stanford University Press, 1957), pp. 54-56, 33-34.

[80] Raymond Barbé, "L'Orientation et la direction des organizations politiques en Afrique noire," circular no. 144, July 20, 1948, printed in *Journal Officiel: Debats de l'Assemblée de l'Union Francaise*, 1950, 1: 255-58. The letter was read into the record in its entirety on July 10, 1950, by the Communist deputy Donnat after Georges Monnet had read sections of it the day before. See also Virginia Thompson and Richard Adloff, *The Emerging States of French Equatorial Africa* (Stanford, Calif.: Stanford University Press; London: Oxford University Press, 1960), pp. 4, 48.

Even though the Communists did not break with the nationalists in West Africa, as they did in most of Asia, they were unable to increase their control over the RDA. In fact, as Communist influence in France lessened, so did the reasons for continued contact between the RDA and the PCF. Also, the refusal of the French Communists to take a strong position in favor of African independence alienated some of the more radical Africans, who, by 1950, were beginning to demand some form of autonomy. The Communists, however, continued to argue that the French Union was the most favorable framework for realizing the strivings of the colonial peoples of Africa:

> The collapse of the French Union would bring upon you [the colonial peoples] an apparent independence, as the prelude to the pressing rule of the powers among whom the trusts rule as masters, among whom racist ideas are current, and by whom Negroes are lynched. Therefore, remain in the French Union with us. It will be what we together make of it and nothing can be strong enough to hinder the workers and republicans of France, in union with your democratic and national forces, from making of it a real, brotherly and progressive Union.[81]

In his open letter to the head of the French Communist party, the noted African poet and sometime Communist Aimé Césaire condemned the Communists for viewing the colonial revolution as merely a "part of a more important whole" to which the revolutionary movement must be subordinated.[82]

During 1949 and 1950 it became clear to the African leaders of the RDA that their association with the Communists was no longer profitable. The colonial administration began to clamp down on the more militant members of the party, and in 1950 all public meetings of the RDA in Africa were banned after the outbreak of riots in Ivory Coast.[83] In the light of these new difficulties, Houphouet-Boigny and the vast majority of the party broke with the Communists in October 1950 and began to follow more moderate policies. Only a small group, led by d'Arboussier, refused to sever ties with the Communists. Once again a

---

[81] Remarks of Etion Fajon at the congress of the PCF in Strassbourg, June 26, 1947, printed in *Humanité*, June 27, 1947, and cited in Fran Ansprenger, *Politik im schwarzen Afrika: Die modernen politischen Bewegungen im Afrika französischer Prägung* (Cologne-Opladen: Westdeutscher Verlag, 1961), p. 88.

[82] Aimé Césaire, *Lettre à Maurice Thorez* (Paris: Présence Africaine, 1956), p. 8.

[83] Victor D. Dubois, "The Independence Movement in Guinea: A Study in African Nationalism" (Ph.D. diss., Princeton University, 1962), p. 45; and Ernest Milcent, *L'A.O.F. entre en scène* (Paris: Bibliotheque de l'Homme d'Action, 1958), pp. 49, 54.

policy of supporting a bourgeois nationalist movement had failed, and the Communists now switched to more radical demands for the dissolution of the French Union and independence for all overseas territories.[84]

Before concluding this examination of Soviet strategy in the developing nations in the years preceding the death of Stalin, I will examine, at least briefly, Soviet policy toward those nations that border directly on the Soviet Union—Turkey, Iran, and Afghanistan. This was an area of traditional Russian interest and one of strategic importance for the Soviet government. Even before the end of World War II the Soviets began making territorial demands on the government of Turkey and supported break-away governments in northern Iran. On March 19, 1945, the Soviet government denounced the Soviet-Turkish Treaty of Friendship, Neutrality, and Nonaggression of 1925, which was to expire in November 1945, as "no longer in accord with present conditions." Before the Soviets would reconsider a renewal of the treaty, they demanded the return of Kars and Ardahan, two small pieces of territory in Eastern Anatolia that they had ceded in 1921, and a revision of the Montreaux Convention of 1936, which gave Turkey control over passage into and out of the Black Sea. In June 1945, the Soviet foreign minister presented an additional demand—a Soviet base in the Dardanelles on Turkish territory.[85] These Soviet demands, along with the guerrilla war in Greece, were important factors in the decision of the United States to create a defense system against the Soviet Union. They were also instrumental in the creation of an American-Turkish alliance aimed at the Soviet Union. Not until the 1960s, when the Soviets changed their approach toward the developing nations, did the Soviet government make any headway in improving relations with the Turkish government and in lessening U.S. domination in Turkey.

Developments in Iran immediately after the war followed a pattern similar to that in Turkey. Soviet troops that had been in the northern part of the country during the war supported rebellions and the establishment of "autonomous republics" in Azerbaijan and among the Kurds. Not until the United Nations took up the question of the with-

---

[84] See George Chaffard, *Les carnets secrets de la décolonisations* (Paris: Calmann-Levy, 1965), pp. 126–27; and Virginia Thompson and Richard Adloff, *The Malagasy Republic: Madagascar Today* (Stanford, Calif.: Stanford University Press, 1965), p. 89.

[85] See Ivar Spector, *The Soviet Union and the Muslim World, 1917–1958* (Seattle: University of Washington Press, 1959), p. 204; and George Lenczowski, *The Middle East in World Affairs,* 2nd ed. (Ithaca, N.Y.: Cornell University Press, 1956), pp. 484–85.

drawal of Soviet troops and the United States threatened to intervene in the dispute did the Soviets withdraw their troops. As a result of Soviet actions, Iran formed one of the major areas of U.S. support in the Middle East during the 1950s.

Afghanistan represents a somewhat different example from that of both Turkey and Iran. The Soviets made no territorial demands on the Afghan government, nor did Soviet troops attempt to occupy any part of the country. In general, Soviet-Afghan relations in the late forties were quite correct. Minor boundary differences were solved by a Soviet-Afghan boundary commission in 1948, and in 1950 the Soviet and Afghan governments concluded a trade agreement.[86] During the 1950s, Afghanistan became one of the first developing nations to accept large-scale Soviet economic and technical assistance.

In evaluating the success of Soviet strategy in the developing nations in the last years of Stalin's rule, one would have to say that the Soviet Union wasted an excellent opportunity to find allies and friends throughout Asia and Africa. Most of the areas of these two continents either had just acquired independence or were witnessing a rise in nationalist demands for freedom. The leaders and people saw in Western Europe, and to a lesser degree in the United States, their primary enemies. However, instead of attempting to court the friendship of these nations, the Soviets antagonized them by condemning their leaders and supporting rebellions against their governments. Not until the middle-fifties did a significant shift in this policy take place.

[86] Lenczowski, *The Middle East in World Affairs*, pp. 222–23.

# 2

## SOVIET ATTITUDES TOWARD DEVELOPING
## NATIONS SINCE STALIN

*Roger E. Kanet*

The death of Stalin in the spring of 1953 found Soviet relations with most of the newly independent states of Asia and the Middle East extremely strained. As has been noted, the Soviets viewed the leaders of these states as mere puppets of the Western colonial powers and therefore incapable of formulating and implementing an independent policy—either domestic or foreign. In 1952, however, there had been stirrings of change in Soviet policy. The Soviet-supported Communist revolutionary movements in Southeast Asia had failed, and gradually Soviet support for them was dropped. At an economic conference held in Moscow in April 1952, the beginning of a Soviet reconsideration of relations with the developing nations was voiced when the president of the Soviet Chamber of Commerce stated that the Soviet government wanted to increase its trade relations, especially with the developing nations. He also outlined a list of the products the Soviet Union wished to trade and indicated that any problems involved in reaching agreements could be facilitated.[1] It is clear from the account of the meeting that there were those in the Soviet Union who wished to increase the contacts of the Soviet government with the developing nations. They recognized that the states which had obtained their independence since the end of World War II were areas of potential Soviet influence, but that the rigid and hostile policy which the Soviet government had followed since 1947 had actually isolated it from these areas. Although no changes in Soviet policy were introduced before Stalin's death, the new ideas and attitudes laid the groundwork for the more flexible Soviet approach toward the new states that appeared soon after Stalin's death. The most dramatic sign of the new importance of the developing nations for Soviet leaders was the extended trip of Khrushchev and Bulganin throughout South Asia in 1954. On every possible occasion they emphasized the friendship of the Soviet Union for those nations that advocated a neutralist position in international affairs.

By 1955, Soviet writers had begun to revise the Soviet doctrine on

---

[1] Comité de contribution au developpement du commerce international, *Rencontre internationale de Moscou* (Paris, 1952) pp. 67–72, cited in Louis Kawan, *La nouvelle orientation du commerce extérieur soviétique* (Brussels: Centre National pour l'étude des Pays à Regime Communiste, 1958), pp. 61–62.

27

national revolution, the role of the bourgeoisie in the revolution, and the possibility of true independence in states not ruled by Communist governments. In an article in *Sovetskoe vostokovedenie*, the Soviet journal for Asian studies, S. N. Rostovskii argued:

> The people of this huge continent [Asia] have entered into the advance-ranks of history. The Asian countries have been transformed from the tools of the imperialists' policy into states which are beginning to follow an independent international policy. The idea of freedom, democracy, progress, socialism, has seized tens of millions of people. The extreme rear of imperialism—the colonies—has now, to a considerable degree, become its front line.[2]

In a book published in 1957, the Soviet economist Evgenii Varga summarized the changed attitudes of the Soviets toward the developing nations:

> In the course of the last twenty years there has been the widespread tendency among us to think that the victory of the peoples of the colonies in the national liberation struggle is only possible when the proletariat, with the Communist Party in the vanguard, plays the leading role in the struggle. The experience of the post-war years has shown that this view is false. . . . Of course the bourgeoisie is of less consequence in the anti-imperialist struggle than the proletariat, or even the peasantry, for individual strata of the bourgeoisie in the colonies have common interests with the imperialist bourgeoisie for the exploitation of the workers. On the other hand, the national industrial bourgeoisie suffers greatly under the economic policies of the imperialists who hinder the industrialization of the colonies.

Varga argued that the experiences of the past years had proved that, during the period of struggle for national liberation, the tendency of the bourgeoisie to enter into compromises with the imperialists becomes inconsequential, for "an important part of the colonial bourgeoisie strives for the complete independence of its country, often even to the detriment of its own immediate material interests."[3]

In 1956, Evgenii Zhukov, the same Soviet Asian specialist who condemned Varga's views in the late 1940s, explained that the collapse of the colonial system was a "complex and many-sided process" which proceeded in different ways in different countries. In some the path

[2] S. N. Rostovskii, "Novaia mezhdunarodnaia obstanovka v Azii," *Sovetskoe vostokovedenie*, 1955, no. 1, pp. 26–27.

[3] E. Varga, *Osnovnye voprosy ekonomiki i politiki imperializma (posle Vtoroi Mirovoi Voiny)*, 2nd ed. (Moscow: Gospolitizdat, 1957), pp. 339–40.

went directly to full political and economic independence, as in the popular democracies, while in others the process was much longer and the leading position was held by the national bourgeoisie, as in India, Egypt, and Indonesia. Even though these countries were not people's democracies and were ruled by the bourgeoisie, it would have been

> the greatest mistake to minimize the world-historical significance of the process of the decomposition of the colonial system only because it has brought in its wake non-socialist sovereign states. . . . Whatever the form of national liberation of the colonies and semi-colonies might be . . . this liberation is a blow to imperialism and, consequently, necessarily does not strengthen, but weakens, the world capitalist system.[4]

These statements by Soviet writers represented quite a change in the Soviet attitude toward the governments that had come to power in Asia and Africa since World War II. However, the Soviets had not changed their doctrine merely for the sake of academic accuracy, for they were still far from accurate in their characterization of the developing nations. Once Stalin's pervading influence in policy-making disappeared, concrete political considerations, based on developments in Asia and Africa especially, forced the Soviets to re-evaluate their attitudes toward these areas. If the Soviets wished to participate in the movements occurring in the developing nations, they would have to change the views which had kept them isolated from the nationalist leaders of these states.

### The Theory of Peaceful Coexistence and the Role of the Developing Nations

At the Twentieth Party Congress in 1956, First Secretary Nikita Khrushchev stated that peaceful coexistence was "the general line" and "a fundamental principle of Soviet foreign policy" and not merely a tactical move. This meant, he added, that the competition between the capitalist and socialist systems would be carried on in the economic sphere. "And this is natural, for there is no other way in present-day conditions. Indeed, there are only two ways: either peaceful coexistence or the most destructive war in history. There is no third way."[5]

---

[4] E. Zhukov, "Raspad kolonial'noi sistemy imperializma," *Partiinaia zhizn'*, 1956, no. 16, pp. 41–43.

[5] N. S. Khrushchev, quoted *Current Soviet Policies II: The Documentary Record of the 20th Communist Party Congress and Its Aftermath*, ed. Leo Gruliow (New York: Praeger, 1957), pp. 36–37. Already in August 1953, Prime Minister Malenkov had stressed the urgent need for reducing international tensions, lest they lead to a nuclear war, *Pravda*, August 9, 1953, p. 3.

According to the new formulation, the economic basis for wars, inherent in capitalism, still remains, but at the present time, "the situation has changed radically. Now there is a world camp of . . . peace forces [that] have not only the moral but also the material means to prevent aggression."[6] The basic characteristics of peaceful coexistence, according to the Soviets, include: (1) the possibility of states with different social systems living side by side in peace, in order to avoid the danger of war and the annihilation of the human race; (2) economic competition between the two systems as the means for deciding the final victory of the struggle between communism and capitalism; and (3) a sharper ideological struggle because the world of today is the battleground in the bitter contest of the ideologies of communism and capitalism.[7]

The essence of the doctrine of peaceful coexistence is that the socialist system is so much stronger than the capitalist system that it will be able to keep the latter's warlike propensities in check and thus will attain eventual victory by peaceful means. It is not a state of tranquility, but one of development and struggle, and it presumes the revolutionary transformation of society and accelerates the disintegration of imperialism, according to Soviet writers.[8] Not only does it not weaken the revolutionary movement within the capitalist world, but, on the contrary, it promotes its successful development toward socialism.

The Soviets fit the developing nations into this policy of peaceful coexistence by calling them, together with the socialist states, a worldwide "peace zone." According to Khrushchev, the leaders of the neutralist states have realized that the participation of their countries in military blocs increases the danger that they will be dragged into a war by the aggressive forces of the capitalist West.[9] In a speech to the Indonesian Parliament in 1960, Khrushchev explained that the good relations between the Soviet Union and many of the neutralist states were based on a common interest in world peace.[10] Actually, early Soviet interpretations of the value of the "peace zone" and of neu-

[6] N. S. Khrushchev, quoted in *Current Soviet Policies II*, ed. *Gruliow*, p. 37.

[7] See N. S. Khrushchev, *Predotvrashchenie voiny—pervostepennaia zadacha* (Moscow: Izd. lit. na izostrannykh iazykakh, 1963), p. 69; *idem, For Victory in Peaceful Competition with Capitalism* (Moscow: Izd. lit. na inostrannykh iazykakh, 1960), pp. 259–60; and Otto Kuusinen, ed., *Fundamentals of Marxism-Leninism*, 2nd ed. (Moscow: Foreign Languages Publishing House, 1963), p. 471.

[8] See, for example, D. Aleksandrov, and O. Nakropin, "Mirnoe sosushchestvovanie i sovremennost'," *Mirovaia ekonomika i mezhdunarodnye otnosheniia*, 1961, no. 12, p. 32.

[9] N. S. Khrushchev, quoted in *Current Soviet Policies II*, ed. Gruliow p. 37.

[10] N. S. Khrushchev, *O vneshnei politike Sovetskogo Soiuza 1960 god* (Moscow: Gospolitizdat, 1961), 1: 147.

tralist foreign policy for the Soviet Union were predicated on the assumption that these nations would soon align themselves with the Soviet Union. According to Khrushchev, speaking at the Twenty-second Party Congress in 1961,

> These countries are often called neutralist, though they can be considered neutral only in the sense that they do not belong to any of the existing military-political alliances. But the majority of these countries are *by no means neutral when it comes to the fundamental question of the day—the question of war and peace.*[11]

When the Communists first proposed the new doctrine on the value of neutralism in the mid-1950s, they made few distinctions among types of neutralism, for they hoped that by supporting the position of the nonaligned states they would be able to forge some sort of an alliance with these countries. This new Soviet position represented an invitation to countries outside the Communist world to join an expanding peace zone by instituting and strengthening policies of nonalignment. It also included a positive evaluation of the role of nationalist leaders and nationalism in the world revolutionary process. Three basic characteristics of the early Soviet evaluation of the developing nations were: (1) an emphasis on the importance of the anticolonial movement for international affairs; (2) a great optimism concerning developments in the Third World and the impending collapse of capitalism; and (3) a lack of detailed information or ideological formulations concerning domestic developments in the Third World.[12]

The main reason for the oversimplified Soviet view of the developing nations—a view that changed significantly in the 1960s—was a lack of knowledge and experience in these areas. Related to this was an attempt to develop broad general propositions that would apply to the historical process in all developing nations. Also, the Soviet preoccupa-

---

[11] "Report of the Central Committee of the Communist Party of the Soviet Union," *Pravda*, October 18, 1961, translated in Leo Gruliow, ed., *Current Soviet Policies IV: The Documentary Record of the 22nd Communist Party Congress*, ed. Leo Gruliow (New York: Columbia University Press, 1962), pp. 48–49 (italics in the original). See also Walter Markov, "Zur universalgeschichtlichen Einordnung des akrikanischen Freiheitskampfs," in *Geschichte und Geschichtsbild Afrikas*, vol. 2, of *Studien zur Kolonialgeschichte und Geschichte der nationalen und kolonialen Befreiungsbewegung*, ed. Walter Markov (Berlin, 1960), p. 22, where the author argues that a policy of neutralism is merely a transitional stage, for in the long run there can be no neutral zones with respect to the Communist bloc among the developing states.

[12] See, for example, C. P. Zadorozhnii, *OON i mirnoe sosushchestvovanie gosudarstv* (Moscow: Gospolitizdat, 1958), p. 10; and G. M. Gak, "Warksistsko-leninskaia teoriia revoliutsii i sovremennoe istoricheskoe razvitie," *Voprosy filosofii*, 1958, no. 5, p. 11.

tion with the international implications of the anticolonial movement did not favor an emphasis on realistic analyses of domestic socio-economic conditions.[13]

One could say that Soviet policy and ideology concerning the developing nations in the late 1950s were based on a minimum amount of factual information and a large amount of Marxist theory—theory which the rapidly increasing knowledge of Soviet diplomats and scholars has proved to be inaccurate or inapplicable in Asia, Africa, and Latin America. The increase in Soviet contacts and knowledge led eventually not only to shifts in Soviet policies but also to changes in Soviet theoretical statements about the developing world.

By the late 1950s, it had become evident that initial Soviet optimism about trends in the Third World were unfounded. With the exception of Cuba, no developing nation had taken the socialist path of development—at least not in Soviet terms—and none had aligned itself fully with the Soviet Union in international affairs. David Dallin summarized the dilemma facing the Soviet leadership as follows:

> Although the process of decolonization continued and the number of independent nations was growing, and although "neutralism" was often preferred by the new governments, all Soviet efforts to assume the role of guide and create a real alliance between the Soviet bloc and the "neutralists" and thus, in an evolutionary way, enlarge the number of "socialist" states were in vain.[14]

The failure to fulfill original Soviet hopes led to a refinement of Soviet theory and policy on neutralism. Communist theoreticians began speaking more of the two sides of neutralism—the positive side, which must be exploited, and the harmful side, which must be opposed.

One of the major attempts by the Soviets to fill the theoretical void concerning developing nations was the enunciation of the doctrine of the state of national democracy at the Congress of the Eighty-one Communist Parties in Moscow in November 1960 and its elaboration at the Twenty-second Party Congress a few months later. In presenting the idea of a state of "national democracy," the Soviets set forth the objectives they hoped would be implemented in the developing nations. The major characteristics of this new type of state were to include: (1) the refusal to join military blocs or to permit foreign military bases on its territory; (2) a major effort to decrease Western eco-

---

[13] See the excellent survey of Soviet analyses by R. A. Yellon, "The Winds of Change," *Mizan*, 9 (1967): 51–57, 155–73.

[14] David J. Dallin, *Soviet Foreign Policy after Stalin* (Philadelphia: Lippincott, 1961), p. 523.

nomic influences in its economy; (3) the granting of democratic rights and freedoms to progressive political parties, labor unions, and other social organizations, including the Communists; and (4) the introduction of major social changes, especially agrarian reforms, in the interests of the people.[15]

Although the new doctrine was an innovation in Communist theory, it did not represent a basic change in Soviet policy, but rather a doctrinal implementation of the conclusions of the Twentieth Party Congress of 1956. The new theory represented a response to the real problems facing Soviet policy in the former colonies. According to the classical Communist theory of national liberation, the struggle for independence takes place in two stages. During the first of these, colonial peoples attain their independence from their foreign rulers and from the domestic feudal class in a revolution that is both national and "bourgeois-democratic." During the revolutionary process the national bourgeoisie turns to the workers and peasants for support against the colonial rulers, thereby creating the conditions for the development of powerful class organizations and, eventually, the conditions for the second, socialist, stage.[16]

The whole theory represented an attempt to pave the way for the gradual development of the necessary prerequisites for a socialist society in states in which the proletariat is extremely weak. The task of the local Communists during the transition period represented by this type of state was to increase their power and gradually gain control of the alliance of workers, peasants, democratic intelligentsia, and a part of the national bourgeoisie. In his report on the Conference of the Eighty-one Communist Parties, Khrushchev clearly indicated that this was the role which local Communists had to play:

> The correct application of Marxist-Leninist theory in the liberated countries consists precisely in seeking the forms which will take cognizance of the peculiarities of the economic, political and cultural life of the peoples to unite all the sound forces of the nation, *to ensure the leading role of the working class in the national front,* in the struggle completely to eradicate the roots of imperialism and the remnants of feudalism, and to clear the way for the ultimate advance towards socialism.[17]

[15] B. Ponomarev, "O gosudarstve natsional'noi demokratii," *Kommunist,* 1961, no. 8, pp. 45–45.

[16] The discussions that were held in Leipzig in May 1959 were published as "The National Bourgeoisie and the Liberation Movement," *World Marxist Review,* 2, no. 8 (1959): 61–81, and no. 9 (1959): 66–81.

[17] N. S. Khrushchev, "For New Victories for the World Communist Movement." *ibid.,* 4, no. 1 (1961): 21 (italics added).

The Soviet hope obviously was that the transition from a state of "national democracy" to socialism would take place without violence. According to one Soviet writer, one function of the national-democratic state is that it "eases the carrying out of the future socialist changes in a peaceful, bloodless way and makes it possible to avoid an armed struggle and civil war, and in this the state of national democracy differs from the dictatorship of the proletariat."[18]

Nationalism, which in its European form was strongly condemned, came to be viewed as a progressive force in Asia and Africa. It had "become a banner rallying them [the oppressed nations] against imperialism, colonialism and neocolonialism and it would be a mistake to underestimate the part it played in national liberation and the forming of young states."[19] However, Soviet writers have increasingly distinguished between the progressive aspects of "state nationalism," which is an instrument in the struggle against tribalism, and a type of "tribal nationalism," which they see developing even among the educated classes, and which is used by the imperialists in order to further their goals of continued domination.[20]

The new Soviet doctrine contained a number of innovations in Communist theory. First of all, the Communists were willing to let the national bourgeoisie play out its progressive role, so long as it was unaligned with the West and strove for economic independence and social reform. Also, the role assigned to the trade unions represented a change in attitude, for never before in Marxist-Leninist theory had it been argued that the trade union could perform the tasks usually assigned to the Communist party. An additional innovation was the view that a peaceful road to power was possible for the Communists.

However, even those governments which the Soviets called progressive in the early 1960s—such as those of Guinea, Mali, the U.A.R., Ghana, and Algeria—did not permit the creation or functioning of open Communist parties, and African and Asian leaders began claiming that they were developing their own brands of socialism. The Soviets, rather than antagonize their new friends, did not push the idea of independent Communist parties and even acknowledged that these states were building socialism. Rather than speak of states of national democracy, the Soviets began to refer to "revolutionary-democratic" states and to recognize that non-Communist governments were actually initiating policies the Soviets themselves had earlier thought only a

[18] G. Starushenko, "The National-Liberation Movement and the Struggle for Peace," *International Affairs*, 1963, no. 10, p. 5.

[19] M. Dzhunusov, "The National Question: Two Ideologies, Two Policies," *ibid., 1966*, no. 10, p. 40.

[20] L. Etinger, "Natsionalizm v Afrike," *Aziia i Afrika segodnia*, 1968, no. 8, pp. 10–11.

Communist regime was capable of introducing. Soviet writers began to argue that the Communists need not form independent parties, but should cooperate with the single-party nationalist regimes which had been established throughout Asia and Africa.

Beginning in 1963, the Soviets revised their attitudes toward non-Communist, one-party regimes in the Third World, as well as toward the socialism advocated by the nationalist leaders of Africa and Asia. In an article published in 1962, Professor Ivan Potekhin, the dean of Soviet African scholars until his death two years later, had condemned the negative aspects of attempts on the part of African and Asian leaders to seek a "third way." According to him, "African Socialism," although it contained "sincere efforts of progressive individuals to find the transition to socialism which fits in with the special conditions of African reality," was also "used as a means to deceive the working masses in the interests of capitalist development."[21] Another Soviet specialist on developing nations was more blunt in his denunciation of ideas of a "third way": "There is not and cannot be any 'third path' and experience shows that the African peoples are not looking for one."[22] In this period, although the Soviets were willing to develop economic and political ties with one-party regimes, they were extremely critical of these governments' political and ideological positions.[23] By late 1963, however, comments concerning these regimes became much more favorable. The reasons for this change in attitude are easy to find. According to the "national democracy" doctrine, only the working class and its vanguard were considered capable of initiating the social revolution that was required for the development of truly independent

[21] Ivan I. Potekhin, "Nekotorye problemy Afrikanistiki v svete reshenii XXII s"ezda KPSS," Narody Azii i Afriki, 1962, no. 1, p. 15.

[22] G. Mirskii, "Whither the Newly Independent Countries," International Affairs, 1962, no. 12, p. 25.

[23] See, for example, Khrushchev's statement at the Twenty-first CPSU Congress in 1959, quoted in Current Soviet Policies III: The Documentary Record of the Extraordinary 21st Communist Party Congress, ed. Leo Gruliow (New York: Columbia University Press, 1960), p. 60. Three years later Khrushchev voiced a strong Soviet complaint about the treatment of Communists in developing nations:

> Unfortunately, truths which are fully obvious to us Communists are not always acceptable to many leaders of the national-liberation movement. . . . Under contemporary conditions the national bourgeoisie has not yet exhausted its progressive role. However, as contradictions between the workers and other classes accumulate, it reveals more and more an inclination for agreement with reaction. Leaders who really hold dear the interests of the people and of the toiling masses will have to understand sooner or later that only by relying on the working class . . . can victory be achieved. . . . Either they will understand this, or other people will come after them who will understand better the demands of life.

Pravda, May 19, 1962, pp. 2–3.

states. However, some of the very regimes that banned the activities of local Communist parties also initiated radical measures of nationalization of "both domestic and foreign capital and were willing to rely on the support of the Soviet bloc in any ensuing conflict with the Western powers."[24] The question which the Soviet leadership must have asked itself was: "Why wait for the development of strong local Communist parties, if non-Communist nationalist governments were willing to carry out much of the program advocated by the Soviets?"

In an article published in *Kommunist,* the theoretical organ of the CPSU, R. Ul'ianovskii outlined the new policy to be followed by local Communist parties. Rather than call for the formation of strong Communist organizations, he argued that "the most consistent and best trained Marxist-Leninist elements should play the role of friend and assistant" of the nationalist leaders.

> Upholding the principles of Marxist-Leninist doctrine, Marxists must be flexible and shrewd, in order not to antagonize the masses. They must constantly seek to find their allies among those social strata and groups which at the moment do not fully accept the theory of scientific socialism, but who today make partial use of it and may fully arm themselves with it tomorrow.

Ulianovskii added that the question concerned the initial approach to the building of socialism, not its detailed construction or completion.

> If the working people of an economically underdeveloped country, without a formed working class, had to wait for the possibility of forming a national proletarian dictatorship in order to begin the transition to socialist development, this would mean that it was necessary to develop capitalism rapidly, in order that a working class might be created on the basis of capitalist industrialization and, subsequently, a Marxist-Leninist party might be formed on this base.[25]

Actually, before the shift in Soviet attitudes and policies toward the nationalist, one-party regimes in Africa and Asia occurred, Soviet scholars had begun to question the foundations of the "national democ-

---

[24] Richard Lowenthal, "Russia, the One-Party System, and the Third World," *Survey,* January 1966, pp. 46–47. In this article Lowenthal presents an excellent analysis of the recent shifts in Soviet doctrine. See also John H. Kautsky, "Soviet Policy in the Underdeveloped Countries: Changing Behavior and Persistent Symbols," in *Communism and the Politics of Development* (New York: John Wiley & Sons, 1968), pp. 145–62.

[25] R. Ul'ianovskii, "Nekotorye voprosy nekapitalisticheskogo razvitiia osvobodivshikhsia stran," *Kommunist,* 1966, no. 1, pp. 113–14.

racy" doctrine. First of all, the question of class structure in the developing nations was raised. Already in 1958, and again in the early sixties, Professor Potekhin admitted that classes, as defined in Marxist-Leninist terms, did not exist in Africa.[26] In published studies of the class structure in the Middle East and North Africa, two young Soviet economists, Gordon and Fridman, argued:

> An underestimation of the depths of the real socio-political differences between the modern proletariat, which is connected with large-scale capitalistic ownership on the one hand, and the majority of agricultural and artisan-handcraft workers on the other, will lead to an oversimplified understanding of the problems of the formation of the working class in Asia and Africa. An unconditional unification of all elements of the army of hired labor into an entity embracing almost one-half of the gainfully employed population would in reality be an admission that the proletariat has already become the most numerous class of society. Such an approach could produce an incorrect evaluation of the degree of capitalist development and arrangement of the class forces.[27]

Besides re-evaluating the position of the workers, Soviet writers began to take a closer look at the role of the military and the intellectuals in the developing nations. Georgii Mirskii, a scholar at the Institute of World Economics and International Relations, called for more detailed study of the intelligentsia and the army, from whose ranks had come the "revolutionary and national democrats" in the developing area. Mirskii argued that the revolutionary leaders who ruled in such states as the U.A.R., Ghana, Guinea, and Mali could not be called members of the bourgeoisie, but represented progressive elements of the intelligentsia and the army, and that the men who made up the class were truly striving to build the foundations for future socialism.[28]

[26] See, for example, I. I. Potekhin, *Afrika smotrit v budushchee* (Moscow: Izd. vost. Lit., 1960), pp. 18–19.

[27] L. Gordon and L. Fridman, "Osobennosti sostava i struktury rabochego klassa v ekonomicheski slaborazvitykh stran Azii i Afriki (na primere Indii i OAR)," *Narody Azii i Afriki*, 1963, no. 2, pp. 3–22, translated in *The Third World in Soviet Perspective: Studies by Soviet Writers on Developing Areas*, ed. Thomas Thorton (Princeton: Princeton University Press, 1964), pp. 180–181. For a later study by the same authors, see "Rabochii klass osvobodivshikhsia stran," *Mirovaia ekonomika i mezhdunarodnye otnosheniia*, 1965, no. 12, pp. 75–87; and 1966, no. 1, pp. 27–39.

[28] G. I. Mirskii, "Tvorcheskii marksizn," p. 65. Later Communist writings re-emphasized the potentially progressive nature of the military in developing nations. See, for example, A. Iskenderov, "Problems and Judgments: The Army, Politics, and the People," *Izvestiia*, January 17, 1967, p. 2, translated in *Current Digest of the Soviet Press*, 19, no. 3 (February 6, 1967): 9–10. Tigani Babiker, a Sudanese journalist on the staff of *Problems of Peace and Socialism*, argued that the new

In addition to reconsidering their views of the class structure and leadership of the nationalist regimes in the Third World, Soviet theoreticians began to analyze the economic policies of these leaders. According to the "national democracy" doctrine, only the active influence of the Communists would lead to the introduction of socialist programs in the developing nations. Domestic "progressive" forces were urged to bring pressure on their governments to initiate radical internal reforms. However, even without the existence of legal Communist parties, a number of African and Asian regimes did decide to select the noncapitalist path of development. For example, in discussions held in Moscow by the Institute of World Economics and International Affairs and published in its journal in 1964, Soviet scholars admitted that some developing nations had undertaken economic reforms which were aimed at both foreign and domestic capital. In these states—especially Burma, the U.A.R., and some African nations—the state sector of the economy was growing at the expense of the private sector. According to G. Akopian, "in a number of liberated countries of Asia and Africa not only have the principles of socialism been proclaimed, but the first practical steps to the realization of these principles have been made."[29] One Soviet writer went so far as to say: "If the conditions for proletarian leadership have not yet matured, the historic mission of breaking with capitalism can be carried out by elements close to the working class."[30]

Not only did the Soviets reassess the class structures of the developing nations and the role of the nationalist leaders in economic and political development, but they also shifted their attitudes toward the nationalist versions of socialism which have been expounded throughout Africa and Asia. As noted above, as late as 1962, Professor Ivan Potekhin had strongly condemned those who proposed a "third path" for the new states. However, later Soviet writing on the noncapitalist path of development emphasized the progressive influence of such doctrines. After speaking of the great differences between scientific socialism and the various forms of national socialism, R. Avakov noted:

---

generation of African military officers is drawn from the petty bourgeoisie and workers and peasants, has fought against colonialism and is, therefore, "more likely to be imbued with hatred of imperialism, to find friends among the younger people, presently active in the revolutionary struggle, and to be more amenable to revolutionary ideas." Tigani Babiker, "At the Cairo Seminar," *World Marxist Review*, 9, no. 1 (1967): 54.

[29] "Sotsializm, kapitalizm, slaborazvitye strany." *Mirovaia ekonomika i mezhdunarodnye otnosheniia*, 1964, no. 4, pp. 117, 119; and 1966, no. 6, p. 75. See also K. Ivanov, "National-Liberation Movement and Non-Capitalist Path of Development," *International Affairs*, 1965, no. 5, p. 61.

[30] G. I. Mirskii, "The Proletariat and National Liberation," *New Times*, 1965, no. 18, pp. 8–9.

However, all this cannot hide the fact that in the socialist doctrines of a nationalist type there are definite revolutionary and progressive beginnings. The existence of principles found at the heart of these doctrines can assist national progress, the development of revolutions of liberation, and their transition to the stage of national democracy.[31]

Another Soviet writer argued that the ideology of a developing state is not the most important factor in evaluating its progressive nature. "Actually the real content of any revolution is determined . . . solely by the objective socio-economic content of the changes (chiefly in settling the question of ownership of the means of production) which the revolution brings about."[32] Revolutionary practice in such states as the U.A.R., Burma, and Mali (before the overthrow of Modibo Keita in 1968) was said to be ahead of the development of ideological doctrine: "Social and economic reforms in these countries are often deeper and more radical than the theories 'elucidating' them."[33]

Since the Soviet reassessment of the nationalist regimes led to the conclusion that some of these regimes were truly progressive, even though they had banned local Communist organizations, the Soviets decided that their interests would be better served by not calling for independent Communist movements; instead, local Communists would operate inside the single-party regimes. In late 1963 and early 1964, even before the new doctrines had been fully enunciated, the Algerian Communist party supported the establishment of a non-Communist, one-party state in Algeria. Ben Bella was declared a "hero of the Soviet Union," and the local Communists accepted positions within the nationalist government.[34] In April 1965, the Egyptian Communist party officially dissolved itself and declared that Nasser's single party was the only organization capable of carrying out the revolution in the U.A.R.[35] Obviously the leaders in Moscow had decided that the best means to maintain and increase Soviet influence in the Third World— at least in the "revolutionary" countries—was by infiltrating nationalist parties with individual Communists. This course was followed in Algeria and the U.A.R., as well as in Guinea, Ghana (until the 1966

[31] "Sotsializm, kapitalizm, slaborazvitye strany," "*Mirovaia ekonomika i mezhdunarodnye otnosheniia, 1966,* no. 6, p. 66.

[32] Ivanov, "National-Liberation Movement," p. 65.

[33] V. Tiagunenko, "Sotsialisticheskie doktriny obshestvennogo razvitiia osvobodivshikhsia stran," *Mirovaia ekonomika i mezhdunarodyne otnosheniia,* 1965, no. 8, p. 85.

[34] See Lowenthal, "Russia, the One-Party System, and the Third World," pp. 50–52; and V. Kaboshkin and Iu. Shchepovskii, "Alzhir: Ot natsionalnogo osvobozhdeniia k sotsialnomy," *Kommunist,* 1963, no. 16, pp. 115–19.

[35] "Party Dissolved by Reds in Cairo," *New York Times,* April 26, 1695, p. 16.

overthrow of Nkrumah), and Mali (until the overthrow of Keita in 1968). European and African Communists have been sent to staff training schools for party and labor leaders which have been constructed with Soviet aid. Soviet and East European economic and technical advisers have played important roles in the economic planning in these countries.

However, even though the Soviets have been relatively successful in implementing this new program, they have found that the instability of the domestic political situation in many developing nations is a threat to the continued success of their policy. In less than a decade, four of the leaders to whom the Soviets had given large-scale economic and political support were overthrown by military coups—Ben Bella, Keita, Nkrumah, and Sukarno. The Soviets now realize the weakness of a policy which is based largely on favorable relations with a single charismatic leader and they are encouraging the development of "vanguard" parties that will be able to institutionalize the revolutionary policies of individual leaders, even if the leader himself were to disappear. The Communist interpretation of Nkrumah's overthrow emphasizes the "absence of a well-organized vanguard party capable of rallying the masses to the defense of their gains."[36] Georgii Mirsskii has written of the necessity for the Egyptians leaders "to train a new cadre of officials and extend the political education of the masses." He argues that a mass party like the Arab Socialist Union, although it has played a positive role in Egyptian life, "cannot act as a politically conscious vanguard. Socialist development is inconceivable without a party, without ideological work among the masses. That is precisely what the Egyptian revolution lacks, for from the very outset its leaders came from the middle strata, which had no social platform, and were inspired solely by the ideals of 'pure' nationalism."[37]

Since the proletariat is extremely weak in most African and Asian countries, "socialist consciousness" must be stimulated from the outside, with the cooperation of the international proletariat—that is, of the Soviet Union and other Communist countries. Developing nations should look to the example of other backward regions which have

[36] Thierno Amath, "Some Problems of Tropical Africa," World Marxist Review, 9, no. 8 (1966): 33. One Soviet writer points to the examples of Mali and the U.A.R., which were attempting to create vanguard parties inside the mass parties that have existed for a number of years. N. Gavrilov, "Africa: Classes, Parties, and Politics," International Affairs, 1966, no. 7, pp. 43–44.

[37] G. I. Mirskii, "United Arab Republic: New Stage," New Times, 1965, no. 48, p. 4. See also his discussion of the need for vanguard parties as the only means to "wrest the masses from the stronghold of nationalist, religious, patriarchal, feudal, and bourgeois ideas and concepts." G. I. Mirskii, Armiia i politika v stranakh Azii i Afriki (Moscow: IMO, 1970), p. 219.

made the transition from feudalism to socialism, such as Soviet Central Asia and Mongolia.[38] A major thrust of Soviet policy in the "progressive" states of the Third World has become support for "revolutionary" regimes. No longer do the Soviets call for freedom for Communist party activities as a sign of a progressive regime, as they did when the doctrine of "national democracy" was in vogue.[39] According to the more recent view, the only political prerequisites for progressive regimes are internal democracy for progressive elements (not necessarily Communists) and a strengthening of ties with the socialist countries.[40]

However, although most Soviet writers have emphasized the progressive nature of the "revolutionary democracies" during the past few years, the importance of these countries in the anti-imperialist movement, and the gains that the noncapitalist path of development has made in the creation of the prerequisites for socialism throughout Asia and Africa, a number of Soviet scholars have questioned the assumptions underlying such optimistic statements. These questions have been based on increasing empirical data concerning conditions in the developing nations and the continuing failure of Soviet expectations to be fulfilled.

Gordon and Fridman criticized the view which lumped the "modern proletariat" and "the majority of agricultural and artisan-handcraft workers" into one group, for "such an approach could produce an incorrect evaluation of the degree of capitalist development and arrange-

---

[38] G. F. Kim and P. Shastiko, "Proletarskii internatsionalizm i natsionalno-osvoboditelnye revoliutsii," *Pravda*, September 14, 1966, p. 4.

[39] See Khrushchev, "For New Victories," p. 21; and A. Sobolev, "National Democracy—The Way to Social Progress," *World Marxist Review*, 6, no. 2 (1963): 45. Two recent examples of Soviet reactions to the suppression of local Communists concern President Sadat's expulsion of ex-Communists from important posts in the Egyptian government and the Arab Socialist Union in the spring of role in the abortive coup of July 1971. In Egypt, the Soviets saw the dismissal of Sabry and his associates as an "event . . . of a strictly domestic character," although some criticism was voiced. See *Pravda*, June 5, 1971, p. 4. Apparently the retention of good relations with Sadat's government far outweighed, for the Soviets, the importance of the dismissal and trial of Egyptian "leftists." In the Sudan, on the other hand, the execution of Communists was strongly condemned by the Soviet press. See *ibid.*, July 27, 28, and 31, 1971. The probable reason for the difference in these Soviet reactions was that the prospects of maintaining harmonious relations with the Sudanese government after the coup were very bleak.

[40] I. Pronichev, "Nekapitalisticheskii put' razvitiia i ego mesto v istoricheskom protsesse," *Mirovaia ekonomika i mezhdunarodnye otnosheniia*, 1966, no. 12, pp. 7–8. A more recent and more explicit statement of this point was made by Y. Seleznyova: "Close alliance and cooperation with the Soviet Union and other Socialist countries . . . is an important condition for their [developing nations following a noncapitalist path] success." Y. Seleznyova, "Developing States and International Relations," *International Affairs*, 1968, no. 5, p. 72.

ment of class forces."[41] Other writers have also argued that the class structure and other conditions in the developing nations are not nearly so favorable for a proletarian revolution as most earlier Soviet writers had assumed.[42]

Other Soviet writers—especially since Khrushchev's removal from power—have seriously questioned general Soviet conceptions of the developing nations. First of all, some have questioned whether the national liberation movement will automatically turn into a socialist movement, as most earlier writers assumed. N. A. Simoniia has argued that the existence of the Communist camp can aid bourgeois leaders in the Third World as well as aid the revolutionary democrats. He maintains that domestic social policy and the leadership of the workers is essential for the creation of socialism. In most of the developing nations, this is not the case, and "one cannot speak of 'growing into socialism' as the dominant or general tendency in the development of national liberation revolutions."[43] Another writer has maintained that "it is premature to regard the countries developing the non-capitalist way as already being at the stage of socialist construction also because the political situation in many of them continues to be unstable."[44]

These are among the frankest statements of the trend toward realism in Soviet writing on the developing nations since Khrushchev's fall. However, the trend actually began before Khrushchev's removal from power, as the Soviets acquired more information about actual conditions in the Third World. As I have noted, the emphasis in most Soviet writing until 1964 was on the international importance of the national liberation movement as a part of the world revolutionary process. However, by 1964, even Khrushchev had begun to de-emphasize the priority granted to developing nations in Soviet policy and to speak of the construction of socialism and communism as the "primary international duty" of the socialist states.[45]

---

[41] Gordon and Fridman, "Osobennosti sostava i struktury rabochego klassa," pp. 180–81.

[42] See, for example, I. P. Iastrebova, ed., *Rabochii klass Afriki* (Moscow: Nauka, 1966), pp. 29–30.

[43] Simoniia points out that, of the seventy-six states in Asia and Africa, only four have elected communism, and no more than seven are following a non-capitalist path of development. N. A. Simoniia, "O kharaktere natsional'no-osvobo-ditelnykh revoliutsii," *Narody Azii i Afriki, 1966,* no. 6, p. 14. For the earlier view, see Kim, who argued that "the national liberation movement" is a "constituent part of the world struggle of progressive forces for socialism and communism." G. F. Kim, "Oktiabr'skaia revoliutsiia i istoricheskie sub'by narodov Asii i Afriki," *Voprosy istorii,* 1962, no. 11, p. 21.

[44] B. Nikolayev, " 'Third World': Choice of Path," *International Affairs,* 1970, no. 7, p. 36.

[45] See *Pravda,* September 29, 1964, p. 1. Throughout 1965 and 1966 the Soviet press and Soviet ideologues continually referred to the international duty of

Along with the new tendency to de-emphasize the role of the developing nations in Soviet priorities has come a realization among some writers that "scientific socialism" is not winning in Afro-Asia. They have pointed out that the noncapitalist path of development is not the same as the socialist path, but a lower stage of development, and that the most progressive of the developing nations are merely at the lower level.[46] In a recent analysis of the class struggle in the developing nations, D. Zarine noted the passivity of the semiproletarian groups in the countryside, the narrow-mindedness and chauvinism of the rural petty bourgeoisie, and the inadvisability of relying on "sudden action by the revolutionary forces or the carelessness of the reactionaries" to bring about rapid social revolution. According to Zarine, the "most important and difficult task of the revolution there is to prevent imperialist intervention."[47] This is far from the optimism expressed by most Soviet writers ten years ago.

Although a number of Soviet writers have criticized the optimism of the official Soviet line on developing nations during the past decade, the majority still emphasize the progressive aspects of events in the "revolutionary democracies."[48] In spite of the numerous changes in emphasis in Soviet writings on the Third World, one thread has remained constant—the desire to expand Soviet contacts with, and influence in, the newly independent nations. This desire has been expressed not only by increased diplomatic and economic relations but also by the shifts in theoretical statements as outlined in the present study. The Soviets have been unwilling to antagonize leaders who are favorable to them by calling for the expansion of local Communist activity, but have rather called upon local Communists to work within the framework of existing political units. The Soviets have also shown that they are aware of the discrepancies between Marxist-Leninist dogma and the realities of the Third World and have modified dogma

building communism in the Soviet Union. See, for example, the editorial entitled "Zhiznenno neobkhodimoe delo," *Kommunist*, 1965, no. 5, p. 16; and a *Pravda* editorial of October 27, 1965, entitled "Vyshnii internatsional'nyi dolg stran sotializma."

[46] See G. I. Mirskii, "On Non-capitalist Path of Development of Former colonies," *Pravda*, January 31, 1965, p. 5, translated in *Current Digest of the Soviet Press*, 17, no. 5 (February 24, 1965): 14. See also I. Pronichev, "Nekapitalisticheskii put'razvitiia i ego mesto v istoricheskom protsesse," *Mirovaia ekonomika i mezhdunarodnye otnosheniia*, 1966, no. 12, pp. 9–14.

[47] D. Zarine, "Classes and Class Struggle in Developing Countries," *International Affairs*, 1968, no. 4, pp. 51–52.

[48] See, for example, the article by Seleznyova, "Developing States and International Relations," p. 72, in which the author argues that the noncapitalist path "is regarded as a means for creating certain socio-material conditions which will pave the way for the transition to Socialism. This is the political, economic and ideological goal of progressive regimes."

to fit more closely with reality. Their initial optimism has been tempered, and they now fear the revival of "reactionary influences" throughout much of the Third World. After more than fifteen years of concerted activity throughout Asia and Africa—and a shorter period in Latin America—the Soviets look upon significant success in the expansion of their influence, but they have not achieved—nor are they likely to achieve—their stated goal of creating a Communist commonwealth throughout the developing nations.

## The Soviet Conception of Development

As has been noted, the basic Soviet prescription for development in the Third World calls for progressive revolutionary democracies. In determining their policies toward various types of countries in the developing areas, Soviet leaders have used as criteria the relative strength of various classes in these countries and the policies followed by their leaders. In accordance with these they have developed a number of typologies of developing nations that differentiate according to three basic factors: (1) the class or classes that are in power; (2) the type of foreign policy that is pursued; and (3) the nature of the domestic policies that are implemented. Writing in 1961, A. A. Arsumanian listed three fundamental types of developing nations. First of all, there are states with reactionary governments that belong to Western alliances or are tied to the European Economic Community. A second set of states includes all those that have national bourgeois governments and are unaligned with any political or military bloc. The third type of state is the "national democracy."[49]

At a conference on developing nations held in Moscow in 1962, R. Avakov and G. Mirskii presented a much more detailed classification. Using the same criteria as Arsumanian, they found six types of developing nations. First, there are those states with relatively well-developed capitalist relationships in which the national bourgeoisie maintains a dominant position; this group includes such states as India, Ceylon, Lebanon, Tunisia, and Mexico. The second group of states is characterized by less-developed capitalist relations and the sharing of political power between bourgeois and feudal elements; representative states are Iraq, Morocco, Nigeria, and Somalia. The states in both of these groups pursue a policy of nonalignment and seek the development of independent economies.

A third category is composed of states that are ruled by elements of the proimperialist bourgeoisie, either alone or together with fedual

---

[49] A. A. Arsumanian, "Krizis mirovogo kapitalizma," *Mirovaia ekonomika i mezhdunarodnye otnosheniia*, 1961, no. 12, pp. 12–13.

landowners. Formal independence exists, but no attempt is made to attain real political or economic independence. Examples of this category are the Philippines, Malaya, Thailand, and many Latin American countries. A special group of countries is constituted by national or revolutionary democracies, where the class structure is characterized by the lack of developed capitalist relations and the virtual absence of a national bourgeoisie or feudal class. However, an incipient proletarian class does exist, and the class configuration is such that those forces that favor a noncapitalist path of development are growing stronger. Representatives of this category have been Ghana (until 1966), Guinea, Mali (until 1968), Algeria (since 1965), and others. The class structure of the fifth group of states, in which the former French colonies in Africa, the Malagasy Republic, and the Congo (Kinshasa) can be included, displays most of the features that characterize the revolutionary democracies. The main difference, however, is that in these states the influence of imperialism remains strong, and power is held by circles that largely pattern their policies on those of the West.

One final group of states is constituted by feudal countries with a small proletariat, low capitalist development, and almost no national bourgeoisie; these include Nepal, Yemen, Ethiopia, and Afghanistan. In spite of their feudal class struggle, these states follow a neutralist policy in international affairs.[50]

Another Soviet writer has attempted to deal with the question of the criteria that should guide Communists in distinguishing one type of liberation movement from another, or one type of state from another. He argues that the major criteria are the outlook of the movement in question and its desire or willingness to cooperate with the Soviet Union and other socialist states in international affairs, as well as the social and economic factors that characterize the movement.[51]

Although the Soviets have formulated these classifications of developing nations largely on the basis of their relations with the Soviet Union itself and the domestic policies of the new states, the Soviets have been willing to deal with almost any type of government. For example, Turkey only a few years ago was considered a reactionary outpost of imperialism. Now the Soviets speak of the common interests of the two countries as a "factor making for stability and the strengthening of peace in the Middle East."[52]

[50] R. Avakov and G. I. Mirskii, "O klassovoi strukture v slaborazvitykh stranakh," *ibid.*, 1962, no. 4, pp. 76–77.

[51] K. Ivanov, "National-Liberation Movement and Non-Capitalist Path of Development," *International Affairs*, 1965, no. 5, pp. 57–58.

[52] G. Nikolayev, "Soviet-Turkish Relations," *ibid.*, 1968, no. 11, p. 40.

So far I have said very little about the Soviet view of economic development in the Third World, although this is a focal point in Soviet policy. Included in the Soviet doctrine of the state of revolutionary democracy is the necessity for economic policies that increase the role of the state in the economy. The basic Soviet prescription for economic development has been largely a result of Soviet experience, with its emphasis on the development of heavy industry. The official party handbook on Marxism-Leninism, published in 1963, argued that the developing nations "cannot simply repeat the usual course of capitalist development," because the Western states built up their economies through the exploitation of their colonies. Also, the masses of the people "will not tolerate the 'classical' capitalist course with its painful primitive accumulation and bitter sufferings of the working sections of the people."[53] Soviet authors argue that, by building up the state sector of the economy in the developing nations, their isolation from the world capitalist system can be furthered, along with their political "neutrality." The strengthening of the state sector of the economy also assists the development of economic independence from the West and represents the logical continuation of the struggle against imperialism, for it offers a direct means to attack the position of the imperialist monopolies.

The primary emphasis in early Soviet recommendations for economic development was on the development of heavy industry. Since most of the economic problems that beset the developing nations were seen as the result of colonialist exploitation, which prevented the colonies from developing a modern industrial complex, full industrialization was viewed as the only means to improve the lot of the population. One Soviet economist condemned those who warned against too much industrialization for wishing "to perpetuate the economic backwardness of the underdeveloped countries and their dependence on imperialism."[54] A few years later, however, another Soviet economist recognized that many of the new states were not yet able to develop a complete industrial complex and would have to rely on imports of industrial products from the Soviet Union and even from the West.[55] More recently, other authors have emphasized the necessity for most developing nations to begin with the processing of raw materials rather than the development of heavy industry. In 1965, V. S. Baskin also

---

[53] Kuusinen ed., *Fundamentals of Marxism-Leninism*, pp. 418–19.

[54] G. Skorov, "Nekotorye ekonomicheskie voprosy raspada kolonial'noi sistemy," *Mirovaia ekonomika i mezhdunarodnye otnosheniia*, 1958, no. 4, p. 57.

[55] R. Ul'ianovskii in a discussion entitled "Sotsializm, kapitalizm, slaborazvitye strany," *ibid.*, 1964, no. 4, pp. 122–23.

cautioned that economic advance would be possible only with "the simultaneous and balanced development of industry and agriculture."[56] Other Soviet writers have supported the development of small handicraft production as a means of getting industrialization started.[57]

One question that has been much discussed in the Soviet journals deals with the scarcity of capital. Although the Soviets have condemned Western investments and economic assistance as methods of neocolonialist domination of the African economies, they have also admitted that at present the needs of these states prevent them from renouncing "a purposeful use of the private sector in solving the serious technical and economic tasks of building up the productive forces" of the country.[58] The leaders of the developing nations "have every right to demand from the Western countries a real increase in the size of financial and technical assistance, granted at low interest rates . . . with long periods for repayment." This is now possible because the policy of the Communist countries of granting ready aid has forced the capitalists to follow a program that is more in line with the real demands of the developing nations.[59]

Because of the small size of the markets in most developing nations, industrial development, and economic development in general, will require the creation of regional cooperation, according to the Soviets. "It is clear that if the developing countries are to boost their economy they must pool their natural resources, finances, technical know-how and skilled personnel." The major detriments to regional cooperation are the lack of intra-African trade and the competitive, rather than complementary, nature of the various economies.[60] Although many Soviet economists favor the development of regional groupings, there are still those who view organizations such as the West African Common Market as means to assist the imperialists in dominating the

[56] V. S. Baskin, "Problemy razvitiia promyshlennosti," in *Nezavisimye strany Afriki*, ed. N. I. Gavrilov (Moscow, 1965), pp. 57–59. See also the argument in favor of this type of development presented by R. Andreasian and A. El'ianov, "Razvivaiushchiesia strany: Deversifikatsiia i strategiia promyshlennogo razvitiia," *Mirovaia ekonomika i mezhdunarodnye otnosheniia*, 1968, no. 1, p. 33.

[57] O. Ul'rikh, "O gosudarstvennoi ekonomicheskoi politike v slaborazvitykh stranakh," *Mirovaia ekonomika i mezhdunarodnye otnosheniia*, 1962, no. 4, p. 98.

[58] V. Kondrat'ev, "Gana: vybor puti i preobrazovanie ekonomiki," *ibid.*, 1965, no. 5, p. 54. See also E. E. Obminskii, *Vneshneekonomicheskie razvivaiushchikhsia stran* (Moscow: IMO, 1970), pp. 17, 56.

[59] V. S. Baskin, "Voprosy ekonomicheskoi i tekhnicheskoi pomoshchi stranam Afriki," in *Nezavisimye strany Afriki*, ed. Gavrilov, pp. 195–96.

[60] A. Kodachenko, "Economic Cooperation between Developing Countries," *International Affairs*, 1966, no. 12, pp. 40–41.

African economies.[61] Another problem related to the development of industry in Africa and Asia is the lack of skilled manpower. Soviet technical assistance is seen as an important means to train the specialists needed by the economy.[62]

As I have already noted, Soviet economists have become aware of the necessity of developing agriculture as well as industry, and have acknowledged that a lack of attention to this sector of the economy has led to serious problems in a number of developing nations. Although most Soviet authors in the late fifties and early sixties called for large-scale programs of land distribution as the only means to solve the agricultural problems of the developing nations, more recently they have recognized the need for caution and the potential danger of a drop in the production of food and cash crops. According to two Soviet economists, "in those cases when the working of the land is being done in large sectors, at least by extensive methods, mechanical copying of the same approach [the transfer of land to the peasants] would be fraught with serious economic consequences."[63] Increasingly, Soviet economists are pointing to the need for most developing nations to develop their agricultural sectorss rather than heavy industry. The choice of what industry is to be developed should be based on the processing of local foodstuffs and raw materials. In fact, Soviet economic assistance is increasingly geared toward the development of just such types of industries.[64]

A problem closely related to agricultural development in Africa is the population explosion. Overpopulation, long ignored by Soviet writer as a myth of the Neo-Malthusians, is now acknowledged as an important factor that slows down economic progress. One Soviet demographer, Ia. Guzevatii, has developed the concepts not only of relative overpopulation but also of "absolute overpopulation."[65] The

[61] K. Karpovich, "Obshchii rynok Zapadnoi Afriki," *Aziia i Afrika segodnia*, 1968, no. 2, p. 8. Kodachenko, however, argues that such a view of regional groups as mere tools of the European powers is a gross oversimplification, for the economic cooperation of the developing nations is aimed at changing the existing dependence of the African economies on the former colonial powers. Kodachenko, "Economic Cooperation," p. 39.

[62] See V. G. Solodovnikov, "Africa's Objective Difficulties and Contradictions," *International Affairs*, 1967, no. 5, p. 67.

[63] Andreasian and El'ianov, "Razvivaiushchiesia strany," p. 32. See also V. G. Rastiannikov, "Prodovol'stvennaia problema v razvivaiushchikhsia stranakh Azii i Severvoi Afriki," *Narody Azii i Afriki*, 1967, no. 1, pp. 28–42, 219–23. For the earlier views, see M. Maksimov, A. Maslennikov, and V. Rastiannikov, "Agrarnyi vopros na Vostoke," *Mirovaia ekonomika i mezhdunarodnye otnosheniia*, 1959, no. 5, pp. 28–41.

[64] See *Mizan Newsletter*, 5, no. 7 (1963): 10.

[65] Ia. Guzevatii, quoted in *Literaturnaia gazeta*, November 23, 1965. For more recent discussions, see S. Bruk and V. Kozlov, "Demografiia i 'Tretii Mir,'" *Aziia i Afrika segodnia*, 1968, no. 4, pp. 5–10; and M. Sidorov, "Demograficheskie problemy Indiia," *ibid.*, pp. 11–15.

recommendation given is largely the same as the one given in the West: increased agricultural production, the introduction of methods of birth control, and the development of industry.

The Soviets strongly recommend planning as an essential part of economic development in Asia and Africa. Planning, according to the CPSU handbook, "facilitates more expedient utilisation of national resources for the purpose of sspeedily overcoming the former colonial backwardness."[66] However, Soviet writers are now indicating an increased interest in planning for a mixed, rather than a purely state-controlled, economy. According to N. Shmelev, the developing nations need to combine centralized planning with the use of market stimuli in order to strengthen their economies. Soviet economists are increasingly interested in results rather than merely in the growth of the state sector.[67]

One major area of Soviet recommendations for economic development still remains to be discussed—economic relations with the industrialized nations of the Northern Hemisphere. As I have noted, the Soviets argue that the economic and technical assistance they and the other Communist states of Europe can offer is essential to development. According to them, long-term trade agreements guarantee the developing nations a stable market and fairer prices for their products. They also permit the new states to conserve foreign currency.[68] Besides, the Soviets alone are supposedly disinterested in the assistance they grant.

Most Soviet authors still view Western trade, investment, and assistance, as a detriment to African economic development, for it ties the African economies to the capitalist world market. The policy recommended to overcome such a dependence on the West has been nationalization, combined with extreme caution in accepting Western financial aid. As has been seen, however, the Soviets have become much more realistic in their appraisals of the possibility of such policies in Africa. Indiscriminate nationalization is now condemned for its negative implications for production, and African governments are advised to control Western capital investments and economic assistance rather

---

[66] Kuusinen, ed., *Fundamentals of Marxism-Leninism*, pp. 418–19.

[67] N. Shmelev, "Razvivaiushchiesia strany: Formirovanie khoziaistvennogo mekhanizma," *Mirovaia ekonomika i mezhdunarodnye otnosheniia*, 1968, no. 8, p. 60. See also the papers from a conference on industrialization sponsored by the Institute of World Economics and International Relations, "Problemy industrializatsii razvivaiushchikhsia stran," *ibid.*, 1967, no. 4, pp. 106–27; and no. 5, pp. 93–108.

[68] For a discussion of the weakness of these claims, see Roger E. Kanet, "Soviet Economic Policy in Sub-Saharan Africa," *Canadian Slavic Studies*, 1 (1967): 578–84.

than refuse them.[69] Mali was even criticized for frightening away prospective Western investors and for thereby creating additional problems for the development of its economy.[70]

In conclusion, I wish to point to the increased realism in Soviet attitudes concerning developments in the developing world and the lessening of Soviet optimism. I have already noted that Soviet scholars have been willing to modify their position on such issues as the role of national varieties of socialism, means of achieving economic development, and the like. They have also indicated an increased pessimism concerning the prospects for socialist development. One writer has stated that "it would be utopian to expect rapid changes for the better in the economy, living standards and culture."[71] This statement should be compared with much more optimistic views, expressed in the late 1950s, that the developing nations would soon join the Communist camps.[72] It is now pointed out that the national liberation movement does not automatically develop into a socialist one, that initial policies leading toward socialism do not necessarily mean the successful development of socialism.[73] Soviet scholars are much more interested in the specifics of economic development, the possibilities of mixed economies, and the development of agricultural production than they are in advocating fully socialist policies.

Since I have dealt almost exclusively with the writings of Soviet scholars in this paper, it should be noted that Soviet-decision-makers seem to share the attitudes I have outlined. Soviet policy in Africa, Asia, and Latin America has been extremely pragmatic over the past fifteen years, and the Soviet government has been willing to develop diplomatic relations and grant economic assistance to all sorts of governments. In their economic assistance programs, the Soviets have begun to support the development of light industry rather than the huge showpieces of the late 1950s. In many respects, the politicians have led the scholars in reorienting Soviet policies and attitudes.

[69] See, for example, the statement of V. L. Tiagunenko, who argued that "the countries of Asia, Africa, and Latin America . . . have to satisfy a considerable part of their needs through the imperialist countries." "Aktual'nye voprosy nekapitalistcheskogo puti razvitiia," *Mirovaia ekonomika i mezhdunarodnye otnosheniia*, 1964, no. 11, p. 17.

[70] L. V. Goncharov, quoted in S. D. Zak and Iu. V. Il'in, "Itogi i perspektivy sotsial'no-ekonomicheskogo razvitiia molodykh puverennykh gosudarstv," *Narody Azii i Afriki*, 1966, no. 5, p. 229.

[71] Y. M. Zhukov, "Contemporary Pace of the Development of National-Liberation Revolutions," *International Affairs*, 1967, no. 5, p. 53.

[72] See, for example, C. P. Zadorozhnii, *OON i mirnoe sosushchestvovanie gosudarstv* (Moscow, 1958), p. 10.

[73] See Simoniia, "O kharaktere natsional'no-osvoboditel'nykh revoliutsii," pp. 14–21; and D. Zarine, "Classes and Class Struggle in Developing Countries," *International Affairs*, 1968, no. 4, pp. 51–52.

# 3

## THE SOVIET UNION AND AFRICA

*Arthur Jay Klinghoffer*

Prior to the upsurge of African nationalist movements and the acquisition of the political independence by most African states, the Soviets viewed Africa as a relatively insignificant appendage of the imperialist camp. However, the rise to power of Nikita Khrushchev and the proliferation of newly independent African states brought about a reassessment of Soviet attitudes. Africa came to be depicted as a major battleground in the East-West conflict and as the focal point of the historical clash between capitalist and scientific-socialist ideologies. The Soviets were particularly concerned with furthering the radicalization of African nationalist leaders and with steering the African states toward domestic socialism and external friendliness with the Communist world community.

This approach suffered some severe setbacks as three of the African leaders viewed as most "progressive" and favorable to the Soviet cause—Ahmed Ben Bella of Algeria, Kwame Nkrumah of Ghana, and Modibo Keita of Mali—were overthrown in military insurrections. In addition, Khrushchev's removal from power brought a greater realism and pragmatism to bear on Soviet policy toward Africa. Ideological considerations became less significant and the overall importance of Africa in the context of Soviet foreign policy was minimized. The Soviet's past failures to increase their influence and their more circumspect foreign aid program (brought about by the greater emphasis placed on the domestic Soviet economy) were important factors, as was their loss of patience with African political instability and economic mismanagement. Another crucial ingredient was the Soviet Union's growing preoccupation with Egypt. As Soviet activities in Egypt grew following the 1967 Arab-Israeli war, involvement in most other parts of Africa was correspondingly reduced.

At present, the Soviets are keeping a low profile in Africa. They eschew revolutionary rhetoric, enter into economic agreements only when they appear financially advantageous, and present a sober and businesslike diplomatic image. They seem concerned about practical matters, particularly those with geopolitical relevance, such as the use of port facilities and overflight and landing rights. Although still wary of the Western role in Africa, they are becoming increasingly perturbed by the Chinese diplomatic offensive, which has accelerated since the Peking government gained admission into the United Nations. The new triangular polarization may present certain problems for dialecticians, so the Soviets simplify the matter by often perceiving collusion between China and the Western powers.[1]

## I

Soviet interaction with the African states was minimal prior to Khrushchev's advent to power in 1955. Because almost all of Africa was under colonial rule, the Soviets attempted to develop African Communist parties which would lead the struggle for national liberation. The Communist International was active in this regard during the 1920s and early 1930s and was instrumental in the creation of a Negro International in 1930. The latter organization met with limited success in spreading revolutionary ideas among African and American blacks, and it suffered from harassment by the European colonial powers. Actually, the largest Communist party in Africa at the time was the multiracial party in South Africa. Communist parties were rather weakly developed throughout black Africa. This was particularly true during the popular front period of 1935–1939, when fear of Nazi Germany led the Soviets to seek accomodation with the colonial powers. Communist activities in the African colonies were greatly curtailed and were not really given new impetus until after World War II. However, the Communist International was no longer in existence, and primary responsibility for the dissemination of Communist views in Africa was given to the French and British Communist parties. The former assisted and helped organize the Rassemblement Démocratique Africaine, the major international political grouping in French-speaking Africa, but the RDA leader, Félix Houphouët-Boigny of the Ivory Coast, turned against the Communists in 1950, and their influence waned. The British Communists had even less success in developing Communist parties or in gaining leverage within African nationalist movements. In fact, the influence among English-speaking Pan-Africanists which they had built up during the thirties was declining.

During the late Stalinist years, Soviet theorists adhered to a rigid two-camp analysis of world power relations. There were only the capitalist and imperialist blocs; neutralism was not recognized. The African colonies were seen as reserves of the imperialist camp, and even the nationalist leaders who were seeking political independence for their states were viewed negatively. They were deemed to be members of the national bourgeoisie, who would develop capitalism once they were

---

[1] See Evgeny Tarabrin, "Peking's Manoeuvres in Africa," *New Times*, 1972, no. 6, pp. 18–20.

in power. They were prone to collaborate with the imperialists, and it was believed that only the proletariat of each country, led by the Communist party, could successfully overthrow the colonial rulers. The leading Soviet Africanist, Ivan Potekhin, wrote: "Stalin's theory of colonial revolution proceeds from the fact that the solution of the colonial question, the liberation of oppressed peoples from colonial slavery, is impossible without a proletarian revolution and the overthrow of imperialism."[2] Leading African nationalists, such as Kwame Nkruham and Jomo Kenyatta, were not considered "progressive," and Soviet comments on Nasser following the Egyptian officers' takeover of 1952 were not particularly favorable. As late as 1953, Potekhin described Nkrumah's government in the pre-independent Gold Coast as "a screen concealing the actual rule of English imperialism."[3] Nkrumah was considered a representative of the big bourgeoisie.

The Soviet approach was to stress the revolutionary role of the proletariat and the organizational abilities of the African Communist parties and not to support non-Communist nationalist movements. Little attempt was made to win over the nationalist leadership while Stalin was alive, but, after his death in 1953, Malenkov did move to improve relations with Third World states. He expanded Soviet aid and trade programs in these areas, but his steps were small compared with what was to follow.

## II

Although the Stalinist coolness toward African nationalism was replaced by a more cordial attitude during the years of Malenkov's ascendancy in the Soviet Union, it was not until Khrushchev's rise to power in February 1955 that there was a major Soviet effort to woo the African nationalist leaders. The Soviets recognized that many of these leaders were anti-Western as a result of their colonial experiences and that the neutralism they professed was a positive step, since it led away from Western control and influence. In addition, the Soviets hoped that the African states would limit Western access to their minerals and other vital resources and thereby put a cramp in the capitalist economic system.

Khrushchev immediately set out to accelerate the process of change in Soviet policy toward the Afro-Asian world, and in March 1955 the

[2] Ivan Potekhin, "Stalin's Theory of Colonial Revolution and the National Liberation Movement in Tropical and South Africa," *Sovetskaiia Etnografiia*, 1950, no. 1, translated and reprinted in *The Third World in Soviet Perspective*, ed. Thomas Thorton (Princeton: Princeton University Press, 1964), p. 32.

[3] Ivan Potekhin, "Ethnic and Class Composition of the Population of the Gold Coast," *Sovetskaiia Etnografiia*, 1953, no. 3, p. 113.

Soviet Union replaced its neutralism in the Arab-Israeli dispute with support for the Arab cause. For the first time, the Soviets began to vote at the United Nations on behalf of the Arab states rather than abstain.[4] In addition, after an initial attempt to upstage the neutralists by calling a meeting at New Delhi that resulted in the creation of the Afro-Asian People's Solidarity Organization, the Soviets eventually warmly praised the efforts of the Afro-Asian leaders at the Bandung conference, held in April 1955. This was the first major conclave of Afro-Asian states, and the Soviets recognized that cooperation among former colonial areas could be a strong and useful weapon in the struggle against the capitalist world.[5] The Soviets therefore tried to gain the good will of these states and claimed that the nationalists (national bourgeoisie) could indeed lead the national liberation movements in their countries and secure independence from the colonialists.

The Twentieth Congress of the Communist Party of the Soviet Union (February 1956) featured Khrushchev's "secret speech" and the initiation of the anti-Stalin campaign, but it was also noteworthy for its revision of Soviet African policy. The new themes of peaceful coexistence, parliamentary transition to socialism, and the noninevitability of war were considered relevant to Africa, and a "peace zone" concept, according to which the Communist and Afro-Asian states were considered aligned against imperialism, was introduced.

Also significant was the attack on Stalinist attitudes toward Africa and a call for the revitalization of Soviet African studies. "Dogmatism and blind acceptance" were attacked, as were "subjective-idealist views on the role of personality in history." The major emphasis was on the contradiction between the nationalists (national bourgeoisie) and the imperialists. It was claimed, rather accurately, that Stalin failed to realize that the nationalist leaders had the support of their people and were actually at odds with the Western powers; they were not imperialist puppets.[6]

The Soviet Union supported Egypt during the 1956 Suez war, but did not become directly involved militarily. The Soviet's posture during the crisis was beneficial to their image in the Muslim countries of Northern Africa, but interest in sub-Saharan Africa was also shown. Ghana's achievement of independence in 1957 was received rather

---

[4] For a good analysis of Soviet policy toward the Arab states during the mid-fifties, see Oles Smolansky, "The Soviet Union and the Arab East, 1947–1957" (Ph.D. diss., Columbia University, 1959).

[5] See E. M. Zhukov, "The Bandung Conference of African and Asian Countries and Its Historical Significance," *International Affairs*, 1955, no. 5, pp. 18–32.

[6] "The Twentieth Congress of the C.P.S.U. and the Problems of Studying the Contemporary East," *Sovetskoe Vostokovedenie*, 1956, no. 1, translated and reprinted in Thornton, ed., *op. cit.*, pp. 80–84.

cooly, since Kwame Nkrumah's Convention People's party was considered to be representative of the national bourgeoisie and to be aligned with British interest. However, the Soviets became extremely optimistic about developments in black Africa when Guinea attained independence in 1958 as Sékou Touré's Parti Démocratique Guinéen showed by its abrupt break with France that it was indeed a radical and "progressive" party.

On September 28, 1958, the French colonial areas participated in a referendum on the issue of whether they wished to join the new French Community. De Gaulle appealed for a "yes" vote and even campaigned in Guinea on behalf of his cause, but Sékou Touré preferred immediate independence to membership in the French Community and therefore called upon his people to vote "no." The Guineans overwhelmingly supported Touré, and Guinea became the only French colony to refuse membership in the French Community. When Guinea won its independence, France immediately countered with economic and diplomatic pressure, but the government of Sékou Touré firmly held its ground and turned toward the Communist world for economic aid. This defiance of France endeared Guinea to the Soviet Union, and Sékou Touré became the idol of the Soviet Africanists. However, it must be pointed out that Touré's close relationship with the Soviet Union was due as much to pragmatism as to ideological proclivity. Guinea lacked capital and trained personnel, and the United States refused to support her for fear of offending France.

The Soviet Union and Guinea had no trade relations in 1958, but economic relations grew rapidly, and, in 1961, 28.3 million rubles in goods were exchanged. Guinea had become the Soviet Union's largest trading partner in Africa, with Soviet exports to Guinea greatly exceeding her imports.[7] By 1960, 44.2 percent of Guinea's imports came from Communist states and 22.9 percent of her exports went to these states.[8] Guinea was also the recipient of Soviet credits, with 35 million dollars offered in August 1959 and an additional 21.5 million in September, 1960.[9]

Although the Soviets did not become disillusioned with the "progressivism" of Sékou Touré, they did become somewhat discouraged with their policy of trying to win nationalist leaders over to more pro-Communist positions. They saw some favorable signs in Ghana, but, in

[7] Alexander Erlich and Christian Sonne, "The Soviet Union: Economic Activity," in *Africa and the Communist World*, ed. Zbigiew Brzezinski (Stanford: Stanford University Press, 1963), p. 61.

[8] *Ibid.*, p. 72.

[9] Kurt Müller, "Soviet and Chinese Programmes of Technical Aid to African Countries," in *The Soviet Bloc, China, and Africa*, ed. Sven Hamrell and Carl Gosta Widstrand (London: Pall Mall Press, 1964), p. 116.

general, as the African rush to independence gathered momentum in 1959, the Soviets became rather pessimistic about the efficacy of their tactic of wooing nationalist leaders instead of organizing Communist parties to overthrow them. Since numerous African states were to gain independence in the next few years, the Soviets decided that a reassessment of their policy was definitely in order.

During this period of reshaping attitudes, the Soviets accentuated the importance attached to Communist parties and proletarian revolution and lessened the significance of nationalists possibly coming over to Communist positions. Chinese criticism of the Soviets for losing their revolutionary fervor may have had some influence upon this new analysis, but developments in Cuba probably had a more direct effect. Castro came to power on January 1, 1959, and his socialist program and revolutionary zeal were viewed somewhat askance by Soviet analysts because his model seemed to provide an alternative to Communist revolution in Latin America. Castro had a charismatic hold upon many Latin American revolutionaries, and yet he denied that he was a Communist; he considered the established Latin American Communist parties to be too reformist and bourgeois. Castro was an example of a nationalist leader who advocated socialist programs, but he was not a Communist and could not be controlled by the U.S.S.R. The Soviets did not regard him favorably during his first year in power, for they preferred working through Communist parties in the less-developed world.

In 1959 and 1960, the Soviets encouraged the creation of African Communist parties and helped strengthen those that were already in existence.[10] In the fall of 1959, a new journal entitled *The African Communist* was founded in London. It was the organ of the Communist party of South Africa but was intended to have a continental scope. It generally adopted a pro-Moscow attitude in issues related to the Sino-Soviet dispute.

While the Soviets were re-evaluating their approach toward Africa, they fell back upon the old tactic of stressing Communist, proletarian revolutions, but a new direction was found in 1960 and the policy of the U.S.S.R. was greatly changed. Again, events in Cuba seem to have had a significant effect.

Cuban-American relations deteriorated during 1960 and the new Soviet evaluation of Castro was most favorable. Castro was now deemed to be a nationalist leader who could lead his country on into the socialist stage of development, and his course therefore became the model for Asia, Africa, and Latin America. He did not actually declare

[10] See Arthur Jay Klinghoffer, *Soviet Perspective on African Socialism* (Cranbury, N.J.: Fairleigh Dickinson University Press, 1969), pp. 166–67 and 199–200.

that his revolution was "socialist" until April 1961, but the Soviets perceived that he was headed in that direction.

The new Soviet analysis was first presented by E. M. Zhukov in a *Pravda* article of August 26, 1960.[11] He averred that members of the national bourgeoisie must lead the nationalist movements during their early stages and that they are capable of carrying out progressive reforms. He described what was later to be the concept of "national democracy" but this concept was not officially announced until after the Moscow conference of Communist parties in November and December 1960.

According to the concept of "national democracy," or "the national democratic state," a coalition of classes, including the national bourgeoisie, may lead a country toward socialism. Nationalist leaders were to be encouraged to carry out "progressive" reforms, and many allusions in Soviet writings indicated that the model for this concept was Castro.[12] "National democracies" were to fight imperialism, reject military blocs and military bases on their soil, and maintain political and economic independence. However significant the nuances of theoretical interpretation, the main point was that the Soviets again looked upon the African nationalist leaders with optimism and began to court those states which were considered to be building "national democratic states." Countries cited in this category were Guinea, Ghana, Mali, Algeria, Egypt, Burma, and Indonesia, with the Congo (Brazzaville) and Syria being recent additions, and with Indonesia, Ghana, and Mali being removed from the list following the military overthrow of their respective governments in 1965, 1966, and 1968.

The development of cordial relations with leftist African states reached its climax in October 1961 when delegates from the ruling parties of Guinea, Ghana, and Mali attended the Twenty-second Congress of the Communist Party of the Soviet Union. This was the first time that representatives of non-Communist parties were invited to attend a congress of the CPSU, and the delegates were even permitted to make speeches. Acknowledging that the three invited parties were not Communist, the Soviets praised them on the ground that they were "anti-imperialist" and "democratic." The rulers of Guinea, Ghana, and Mali were all to receive Lenin Peace Prizes: Touré in 1961, Nkrumah in 1962, and Keita in 1963. All three countries were members of the Casablanca bloc of African states, other members being Egypt, Algeria, and Morocco. The Soviet Union favored these African states

---

[11] E. M. Zhukov, "Significant Factor of Our Times," *Pravda*, August 26, 1960, pp. 3–4. An English translation in abridged form appears in *Current Digest of the Soviet Press*, 12, no. 34 (September 21, 1960): 18–19.

[12] See Klinghoffer, *op. cit.*, pp. 212–13.

because of their leftist proclivities. With the creation of the Organization of African Unity in 1963, the Casablanca bloc was disbanded.

During the late Khrushchev period, 1962–1964, the Soviets stressed
the radicalization of African nationalist parties rather than the development of African Communist parties. African Communists were encouraged to work within the nationalist parties so as to steer them
further leftward, and it was believed that African nationalist leaders of
bourgeois-democratic origin could eventually become Marxist-Leninists
and "scientific socialists." Again, Fidel Castro appeared to be the
model. On December 1, 1961, Castro for the first time declared himself
a "Marxist-Leninist," and in March 1962 the Soviets began publishing
articles discussing the possibility of the transformation of other nationalist leaders. Castro was specifically mentioned as a leader who had
undergone this metamorphosis. By 1963 the Soviets had begun to apply
the term "revolutionary democrat" to those people in Africa who were
considered "progressive." This group was said to include the petty
bourgeois intelligentsia, students, and some military officers, and it was
claimed that "revolutionary democrats" could proceed from capitalist
to socialist ideology. World Marxist Review relayed the Soviet interpretation to the world's Communist parties when it declared: "If a
revolutionary democrat or a member of the national bourgeoisie is
willing to take one step forward, it is the duty of the Marxists to help
him take two. . . . There is, then, the possibility that many revolutionary democrats will come over to the positions of scientific socialism,
to the positions of the working class."[13]

Although African Communists were expected to increase their influence within the nationalist parties, they were to keep their own
organizational base as an alternative source of strength. This was particularly evident in the more conservative African states, but less so
in those that showed signs of "progressivism," such as Guinea, Ghana,
Mali, and, late in 1963, the Congo (Brazzaville). African Communist
parties are not very strong, and some are fragmented into various
groups. However, some sort of Communist party seems to exist in
Somalia, the Malagasy Republic, Zambia, Zanzibar (now part of Tanzania), Lesotho, Algeria, Morocco, Tunisia, Sudan, Nigeria, the Republic of South Africa, Egypt and Libya. Many Communist parties in
Africa are outlawed including those in all Arab states, but the Soviet
Union has stressed cordial relations with African states at the expense
of the Communist parties. For example, at certain times when the
Soviet Union enjoyed close relations with Egypt, Egyptian Communists

---

[13] A. Sobolev, "National Democracy: The Way to Social Progress," World
Marxist Review, 6, no. 2 (1963): 41–42. See Mikhail Kremnev, "Africa in Search
of New Paths," ibid., no. 8, pp. 72–76.

were forced to remain in jail. The Soviets therefore subordinated the concept of overthrowing African governments through the use of African Communist parties to the more immediate task of increasing Soviet influence within the existing state structures.

After Nikita Khrushchev's fall from power in October 1964, Soviet policy toward Africa was marked by even greater flexibility as to whom to accept as a friend. Ideology became insignificant in determining policy positions as the Soviets adopted the practical course of dealing with almost any type of African government which was in power. The hope that certain African leaders could build socialist societies and move closer to the Soviet Union began to fade as the military overthrow of Ben Bella, Nkrumah, and Keita diminished Soviet optimism. The views of men such as Senghor and Nyerere were accepted with much less criticism than previously when the U.S.S.R. sought to improve relations with Senegal and Tanzania, but the policy of forging bonds of friendship went far beyond the bounds of socialist-oriented states. Diplomatic relations were established with states of all political persuasions, and cordial ties were developed with such nonrevolutionary and "nonprogressive" states as Morocco, Zaire (Congo-Kinshasa), Ethiopia, Upper Volta, Nigeria, and the Ivory Coast (although diplomatic relations with the Ivory Coast were broken off in 1969). The diplomatic offensive was not confined to Africa, however, for the U.S.S.R. also improved relations with Turkey, Iran, and Pakistan. Because the Soviets viewed Africa more in the practical terms of furthering Soviet strategic interests than in the unrealistic ideological terms of encouraging states to advance toward socialism, the U.S.S.R. became more directly involved in African affairs, as experience with Egypt and Nigeria has shown.

At the Twenty-third Congress of the Communist Party of the Soviet Union, held in March and April 1966, the emphasis was on development of the Soviet economy. It was declared that the chief international task of the U.S.S.R. was to build up its own economy so that it could then aid the world revolutionary struggle.[14] Soviet policy toward Africa was affected, as uneconomical prestige projects were de-emphasized and Soviet economic relations with the African states came to be based primarily upon mutual economic need and efficiency. African economic advancement was considered to be more important than ideological purity, and it was recognized that some aspects of capitalism in the African economic systems might be beneficial at this stage of development. Industrialization continued to be emphasized as a prime requisite, but it came to be viewed more as an element of

[14] See "Pointers from the 23rd CPSU Congress," *Mizan,* 8, no. 3 (1966): 95–99.

economic growth than as a means of reducing African dependence upon the Western industrial states.

As a concomitant of economic progress, the Soviets stressed political stability. Radical political programs were not particularly encouraged, for the Soviets realized that they might lead to instability or military takeover. The lessons of Ghana and Mali certainly had an effect upon Soviet thinking, but the Soviets became reconciled to military take-overs even before the coups in Ghana and Mali. The military was obviously rising to a position of prominence in numerous African states, and the Soviets did not particularly look askance at this development, for they admired the stability which military rule could bring. Military leaders were even recognized as "revolutionary democrats" when they carried out reforms that were considered to be "progressive."[15]

The increasing Soviet practicality in dealing with the African states was accompanied by changes in ideological interpretation. Because military regimes were accepted with a certain cordiality, and non-socialist economic practices were approved as long as they helped advance the economy, a new theoretical framework had to be devised. The "liberal" Soviet analysts, who had stressed the "progressive" reforms in Africa and who believed that many African leaders were embarking upon the path to socialism, had to be discredited because their prophecies had failed to materialize. Following the fall of Krushchev, these analysts lost much of their stature, but it was not until 1966 that a new school of thought rose to prominence.

N. A. Simoniia led the new group of analysts in arguing that the immediate prospects for socialism in Africa were not very bright because the proletariat builds socialism and the proletariat was not then in control of the African states.[16] One of the implicit assumptions of Simoniia's interpretation is that one must permit capitalism to exist for a while in order to help create a proletarian class.

Simoniia maintained that the Soviets had been overoptimistic in looking for elements of socialism in Africa, for he averred that contemporary developments in Africa were still part of the bourgeois-democratic revolution. Capitalist economic systems predominated in Africa, and Simoniia therefore called for sobriety and patience when intrepreting the evolution of the African states.

A similar and extremely pessimistic analysis of the prospects for

---

[15] The military in Egypt, Libya, Sudan, and Algeria in particular was viewed favorably, but the assessment of the military in sub-Saharan Africa also was increasingly positive. For a positive assessment of the January 1972 military coup in Ghana, see Yuri Tsaplin, "Ghana Seeks a Way," *New Times*, 1972, no. 15, pp. 12–13.

[16] N. A. Simoniia, "On the Character of National Liberation Revolutions," *Narody Azii i Afrika*, 1966, no. 6, pp. 3–21.

socialism in Third World states was given by Vladimir Lee. He maintained that some capitalist development must precede socialist construction, and that the transition to the latter is "lengthy" and "gradual." He went on to declare that nationalization is often "hasty" and "ill-timed," that some capitalism should be permitted to exist alongside the state economic sector, and that loans from "imperialist countries" should be accepted.[17] Lee concluded with a rather gloomy assessment of the situation: "The national liberation revolution today is developing along difficult and thorny paths. . . . Lenin taught the fighters against imperialism not to get panic-stricken and despondent in the face of temporary, though grave, setbacks. He taught them to take a sober view of miscalculations and draw the necessary lessons from their defeats."[18]

In tracing Soviet attitudes toward Africa during the years since the death of Stalin, the tendency has been toward greater realism and less reliance upon outmoded ideological dogmas. The Soviet Union has come to behave more as a great world power seeking influence and strategic economic and military position and less as the center of a revolutionary movement aimed at overthrowing African governments and installing Communist regimes.

## III

When approaching Africa, the Soviets are faced with their traditional tactical dilemma: should they help organize Communist-led revolutions against the nationalist leaders, or should they attempt to cooperate with these leaders? Such a problem has existed since the early years of the Comintern as the Soviets have attempted to devise appropriate tactics for dealing with such nationalists as Sun Yat-sen, Chiang Kai-shek, Ataturk, Gandhi, and Nehru. When stressing the tactic of revolution, the emphasis is on strengthening Communist parties, furthering people-to-people contacts (in order to increase mass support for the Communists), and encouraging united fronts from below. People-to-people contacts may be extended through the dissemination of Communist propaganda, radio broadcasts, indoctrination of Third World students who are enrolled in Soviet schools, and through the development of Communist front organizations for journalists, students, women, peace activists, or trade unionists. United fronts from below are based upon influencing rank-and-file members of nationalist movements to align with the Communists, even though there is no mutual

---

[17] Vladimir Lee, "The National Liberation Movement Today," *International Affairs*, 1969, no. 12, p. 42.
[18] *Ibid.*, p. 46.

agreement between the Communists and the nationalist leadership. When emphasizing cooperation with nationalist leaders, the accent is on economic aid, trade, diplomatic exchanges, strategic interest, and diplomatic support on major world issues and at the United Nations. This last tactic is often accompanied by a united front from above, an alliance between the local Communist and nationalist leaders. However, in the African context, such united fronts from above have rarely occurred, because African nationalist leaders have been able to suppress local Communist parties while at the same time forming close ties with the Soviet Union. The Soviet leadership has generally closed its eyes to such a situation because the diplomatic and strategic interests of the Soviet Union are considered much more important than the fate of African Communist parties.

The tactical pendulum has often swung to extremes, such as the revolutionary fervor of the late Stalin period and the cordial Soviet ties with the African nationalists Touré, Nkrumah, and Keita in the early sixties. The recent emphasis has been on establishing warm state-to-state relations and on minimizing the prospects for Communist revolution in Africa. However, it must be pointed out that these two tactical alternatives do not preclude some middle range of Soviet and African Communist party activity. For example, the Soviets could play a double game, wooing a nationalist leader while at the same time planning his overthrow. In addition, the Soviets could encourage the radicalization of African nationalist parties, striving to push them toward a more pro-Soviet orientation. This tactic was prominent in the early sixties and was initiated on two levels. At the upper level, the Soviets attempted to influence the leaders of "national democratic states" through flattery (Lenin Peace Prizes), economic aid, and diplomatic support on colonial issues, while, at the lower level, African Communists were advised to participate in nationalist political parties and to try to steer them further to the left.

Placed in a chronological perspective, the tactic of fomenting Communist-led revolutions was emphasized during the Stalin period, but Khrushchev's rise to power brought about a major tactical shift. He advocated cooperation with African nationalist leaders, in the hope that this would turn them against the West and secure their diplomatic support. There was some congruence of views on the issues of colonialism, white-ruled African states, and the rather nebulous peace theme, and the Soviets had some success in rallying African states (particularly those which were to organize the Casablanca grouping in 1961) behind their diplomatic bandwagon. Not completely satisfied with their partial success, however, the Soviets began to re-emphasize the revolutionary potential of African Communist parties for a brief period in 1959–1960, but they soon returned to the previous, government-to-government approach. They paid particular attention to states which had adopted socialist economic programs and which espoused radical Marxist ideologies and apparently hoped to secure diplomatic and ideological allies. This did not necessarily indicate a desire to gain new adherents to the Communist world community, but the Soviets would perhaps have been agreeable to such a move on the part of Ghana or Algeria, with the Cuban experience serving as precedent. In any case, the Soviet Union suffered a rude shock when the governments of Ben Bella, Nkrumah, and Keita were overthrown, and Soviet optimism was obviously dampened. African states came to be viewed as unstable and incapable of radical socialist reforms, and the Soviets began to advocate political stability and economic growth, even if carried out by means which had previously been considered to be ideologically unorthodox.

Seeing the search for allies as almost chimerical in the rapidly changing African political arena, the Soviet Union became primarily concerned with pure strategic interest. Largely disregarding the existence of military rule or of clearly nonsocialist economic programs, the Soviets began to seek beneficial economic agreements, port facilities, overflight rights, naval bases, and an advantageous military position. Such policies, however, led to a more direct involvement in African affairs, which was not necessarily beneficial. The enormous commitment to Egypt, in terms of weaponry, advisers, and front-line personnel (pilots and missile crews), resulted in an economic drain on the Soviet economy, as well as in the ignominy of expulsion in July 1972. However, the Soviets have succeeded in restraining the Egyptian military and have virtually secured naval-base rights in three Egyptian ports.

Soviet involvement in Nigeria has been somewhat less direct but only slightly more successful. The Soviet Union supplied arms and advisers for the struggle against Biafra and was also instrumental in recruiting Egyptian pilots for the Nigerian air force. The Soviets hoped to increase their influence in Africa's most populous state, champion the cause of African territorial unity against secessionist tendencies, restrict the flow of Nigerian oil to Western states, and prevent Biafran oil from falling into the hands of French or Portuguese interests. They also sought to discredit both the United States and Great Britain, since each refused to provide military assistance (although Britain then reversed its position and supplied armaments and ammunition). The Soviet Union correctly selected the eventual winner of the Nigerian-Biafran war and certainly emerged with more influence than before, but Nigeria has not changed its moderate foreign policy and is still economically linked with both the United States and Great Britain.

Although Soviet-Nigerian relations are proper, the Soviet Union has neither gained any political leverage nor acquired any significant strategic rights.

Viewed in geopolitical terms, Africa has never held a position of high priority in Soviet policy, for the Soviet Union has concentrated on its own strategic position in Europe and Asia. However, as the Middle East has become a major focal point of Soviet foreign policy, the Soviets' strategic interest in Africa has grown. The Arab-Israeli dispute and the closing of the Suez Canal have led to increased Soviet concern with the strategic possibilities evident in the Arab states of North Africa, as well as in the African states adjacent to the Red Sea. The Soviet Union has developed close relations with Egypt, Algeria, and Somalia, and it even maintains cordial relations with the Ethiopian and Moroccan monarchies. Although supported by many of the militant Arab states, the Eritrean secessionist movement in Ethiopia has not been supported by the U.S.S.R. Also, despite Nimeiry's suppression of the Sudanese Communist movement, the Soviets have attempted to maintain a political foothold in Sudan.

The Soviets' push toward the Suez area includes the extension of economic and military aid, an increase in trade ties, and an expansion of the Soviet naval presence in the Mediterranean, Red Sea, and Indian Ocean areas. The U.S.S.R. has extensive port facilities in Egypt and Algeria which can be used to service the Soviet fleet, and the Soviets may seek similar port rights in Sudan. The closing of the Suez Canal has greatly inhibited Soviet geopolitical ambitions, since ships now must sail around Africa in order to reach the Indian Ocean.[19] If the Suez Canal were to reopen, the Soviet Union would probably increase its trade with India and seek greater influence in the Persian Gulf area. In addition, the U.S.S.R. might begin to import oil from Iraq via the sea route through the Suez Canal, and shipments of equipment to North Vietnam might also pass through this area more easily than over the land route across China or through Siberia to Vladivostok and then by ship to North Vietnam.

Big power competition is evident in Africa, and the Soviets particularly fear the challenge of the Chinese. The Chinese claim that the main focus of world revolution should be Africa, Asia, and Latin America, because the "countryside" of the world will fall to the Communist cause before the "cities" (the industrialized states). They emphasize the conflict between the national liberation movement and

---

[19] For an analysis of the effect of the Suez Canal Closure on the U.S.S.R., see Gary Sick, "The U.S.S.R. and the Suez Canal Closure," *Mizan*, 12, no. 2 (November 1970): 91–98; and Yevgeny Primakov, "Why the Suez Canal Must Be Reopened: A Russian View," *New Middle East*, July 1972.

imperialism, and their activities in Africa provide a threat to Soviet interests. The Chinese deny the Soviets' contention that the U.S.S.R. is partially an Asian power, and therefore they attempted to prevent Soviet participation in the ill-fated "Second Bandung" conference, which was scheduled to be held in Algeria in 1965. They have also carried their anti-Soviet campaign into the Afro-Asian People's Solidarity Organization, and internecine Communist strife within that organization has been the outcome. Being nonwhite, the Chinese try to use this fact to their advantage in Third World countries, and the Soviets are forced to claim defensively that the U.S.S.R. is a multinational state and that Africans can indeed have friends of the white race.

The Chinese have not been capable of providing as much economic aid as have the Soviets, and their espousal of revolution has not been popular with African nationalist leaders. Chou En-lai irritated many African officials when he declared that Africa was ripe for revolution, for these leaders realized against whom such revolutions would be directed. This fear of Chinese intentions led to a reduction of Chinese influence in Burundi, Mali, Somalia, and Guinea. Since the end of the Cultural Revolution, however, the Chinese have increased their economic aid programs (witness the Tanzania-Zambia railroad project) and moderated their image by reducing their revolutionary fervor and by furthering cordial government-to-government relations. Their new approach is similar to that of the Soviet Union, and direct competition is inevitable, particularly in Somalia, Sudan, and Ethiopia.

The Soviets perceive the United States to be a neocolonial threat that is interested in economic control and military bases. They portray the U.S. as an ally of British, French, Belgian, and Portuguese colonialism, and they castigate it for attaching political strings to its economic aid. The Soviets usually gain a propaganda advantage by pointing out that the United States has not taken a strong stand against the governments of South Africa and Rhodesia or against Portuguese practices in Angola, Mozambique, and Guinea (Bissau). A theme used to influence many Islamic states in Africa is that the United States is basically pro-Israeli and anti-Arab.

The original Soviet goal of spreading communism in Africa is no longer realistic, for most Africans do not desire communism, and the Communist world has itself broken up into nationalistic entities. As recent reunification efforts in Germany, Korea, and Vietnam have shown, the force of nationalism has been able to bridge the gap between Communist and capitalist ideologies. In addition, the examples of China and Yugoslavia show that even Communist-ruled states need not align themselves with the Soviet Union. Thus, the Soviet Union has come to emphasize strategic, rather than ideological, interest, but in so doing it has come closer to the United States in terms of practice. Direct involvement in Nigeria and Egypt, the search for naval bases and overflight rights, and the strong Soviet naval presence in the Mediterranean have changed the Soviet image from that of ideological *bête noire* of colonialism to practitioner of superpower Realpolitik. Libya and Suden have already demonstrated their mistrust, and Sadat's expulsion of Soviet advisers from Egypt was the most telling blow. The Soviets' actions have become similar to those of the imperialist powers they have always condemned, and perhaps the Africans will begin to place more credence in the Chinese charge that the Soviets are big power chauvinists and collaborators with the imperialists.

## IV

The Soviet Union seeks proper state-to-state relations with most African states and maintains diplomatic relations with all but nine: the Republic of South Africa, Lesotho, Swaziland, Botswana, Malawi, Liberia, the Ivory Coast, Gabon, and Niger. Cultural agreements have been concluded with almost every African state, and the Soviets strongly support many African positions at the United Nations, particularly those dealing with colonialism and the extension of technical and economic assistance programs in Africa.

The Soviet Union provides as much military aid to Africa as it does economic aid. The bulk of this military aid is concentrated in North Africa and the eastern horn area, with Egypt, Algeria, Sudan, and Somalia being the major recipients. The Soviets furnish 300 military advisers for Somalia and had 14,000 in Egypt before almost all of them were expelled in July 1972. Advisers were also active in Sudan until the summer of 1971, but their role has been somewhat reduced by the Sudanese authorities in retaliation for a Communist-supported, abortive attempt at revolution. Soviet military aid to sub-Saharan African states has been minimal, with the only major program being carried out in Nigeria during the Biafran war. The Soviets sided with Nigeria and sold jet planes and other equipment to the government.[20] They also provided military advisers and helped recruit Egyptian pilots. In addition to its military assistance agreements with the African states, the Soviet Union also helps arm the nationalist movements that operate in Portuguese territories, assisting FRELIMO in Mozambique, MPLA in Angola, and PAIGC in Guinea (Bissau).

[20] See Arthur Jay Klinghoffer, "Why the Soviets Chose Sides," *Africa Report*, 13, no. 2 (1968): 47–49. See also Chris Osakwe, "The Soviet Union and the Biafran Question: A Case Study" (Paper presented at the Annual Meeting of the African Studies Association, Philadelphia, November 8–11, 1972).

Soviet economic relations with African states grew in the late fifties as Khrushchev pursued a policy of encouraging close contact between the U.S.S.R. and the African nationalist leadership. Abundant credit was extended, but not many outright grants were made. The credits carried low interest rates and were to be repaid in commodities. However, less than half the credits were actually drawn upon by the African states, for their economic development plans were not yet well organized. Furthermore, the African states had difficulty in providing their own funds for the economic improvements which had to be effected in conjunction with the construction of Soviet-financed projects.

Following Khrushchev's removal from power, the Soviet economic aid program became less ideological and more financially conservative. Whereas the "progressive" African states had received almost all of the Soviet aid while Khrushchev was in power, the new leadership furthered contacts with the more moderate African leaders and extended aid to Ethiopia and Kenya. Prestige projects, such as stadiums, received less emphasis as the accent was put on sound and necessary projects. Credit was provided much more warily, but the total credit granted to the African states remained relatively constant.

The Soviet aid system was always re-enforced by those of the East European Communist states. During the period 1954–1970, the U.S.S.R. provided $1,044,000,000 in credits and grants to the African states (excluding Egypt), while her East European allies added an additional $443,000,000.[21] Algeria and Guinea have been the major recipients. The Chinese were not very active on the economic front, but since the Cultural Revolution they have emerged as significant competition for the Soviets. The Tanzania-Zambia railroad project is the largest aid project ever undertaken in Africa by a Communist state, and more than $400,000,000 has been provided. This comprises more than half of all Chinese aid to Africa since 1954. In terms of technical assistance, the Soviet Union had 4,000 technicians in Africa (excluding Egypt) in 1970, the East European states had 3,000, and the Chinese had 7,000. Most of the Chinese were involved with the construction of the Tanzania-Zambia railroad.[22]

Since the Soviet Union trades mostly with other Communist states, its trade with Africa amounts to only 2 percent of its total trade. Also, since many African states are still economically linked with the former colonial powers, only 4 percent of Africa's trade is with the Soviet

[21] U.S., Department of State, Bureau of Intelligence and Research, *Communist States and Developing Countries: Aid and Trade in 1970,* 92nd Cong., 1st sess., September 22, 1971, p. 2.
[22] *Ibid.,* p. 10.

Union. However, the volume of Soviet-African trade is clearly increasing. The Soviet Union's major African trading partners are Algeria, Sudan, Morocco, Ghana, and Nigeria. It should be noted that the last three states are generally moderate rather than "progressive." The Soviets maintain a slightly favorable trade balance because they export more than they import. They have particularly favorable balances with Libya, Morocco, and Guinea, while they have deficits with Nigeria and Ghana. However, these deficits are counteracted by favorable balances between the East Euroepan nations and these two states.

Although the Soviets seek to influence African governments through state-to-state contacts, they are also strongly concerned about developing a good image and gaining some Communist adherents among the African people. Radio Moscow directs more than one-third of its foreign broadcasts at sub-Saharan Africa, and the Soviets have attempted to create front organizations that are sympathetic to their interests. The World Federation of Trade Unions has not met with much success in Africa, but the Afro-Asian Peoples' Solidarity met with much success in Africa, but the Afro-Asian Peoples' Solidarity Organization did influence many politicians and intellectuals during the late fifties and early sixties. It then declined in importance as it became factionalized by the Sino-Soviet conflict and other issues.

The largest Communist program aimed at influencing Africans is in the area of education. Africans comprise half of all Third World students in the Soviet Union and Eastern Europe, the largest contingents being from Sudan, Nigeria, Kenya, Algeria, and Somalia.[23] Of the 11,000 Africans who are studying at universities in the Soviet Union and Eastern Europe, more than half are in the Soviet Union. Most Africans in the U.S.S.R. attend Lumumba University in Moscow. It was founded in 1960 and serves primarily Third World students. African students are basically engaged in academic programs. Although many technical training courses did exist in the U.S.S.R., they are being phased out, for the Soviets now prefer to send technical instructors to Africa to perform on-the-job training. As of 1970, only 210 Africans were receiving technical training in Communist countries, 145 of them in Eastern Europe.[24] The Chinese have not been active in the educational field, because their own universities were disrupted during the Cultural Revolution. Now that these universities have reopened, Sino-African educational programs may be developed.

[23] U.S., Department of State, Bureau of Intelligence and Research, *Educational and Cultural Exchanges between Communist and Noncommunist Countries in 1970*, 92nd Cong., 1st sess., August 30, 1971, p. 17.
[24] *Ibid.*, p. 19.

## V

Nikita Khrushchev used the term "creative Marxism" to describe his ideological pronouncements because he adapted, and often bent, Marxist formulas in order to make them more relevant to contemporary events. Practicality was the keynote, and ideology often became an explanation rather than a guide to action. Brezhnev and Kosygin have followed in Khrushchev's footsteps, and post-Stalinist ideological interpretations of African affairs have therefore been expressed in terms that gracefully complement the Soviet policy of gaining the support of nationalist leaders.

Of course, Soviet theoreticians do not always agree, and there is a fundamental dichotomy between the "conservatives" and the "liberals." The former adhere more strongly to the concept of proletarian leadership during the transition to socialism and therefore are somewhat skeptical about the "progressivism" attributed to the nationalist leaders by the "liberals." The "liberals" look for positive signs in the statements and actions of African political leaders and tend to believe that these leaders and their parties, rather than the Communist parties, now command the support of their people and are capable of building socialism. Although disagreements between the Soviet "conservatives" and "liberals" appear in scholarly and theoretical journals, there is still a basic "line" which all Soviet political officials and academicians follow. The "line" is usually set by the Communist party leadership, and it is expounded upon by some key theorists who write for the scholarly journals, for the party journal, *Kommunist*, or for the party newspaper, *Pravda*. The line sets the tone and general guidelines for the discussion; the "conservatives" and "liberals" debate only the fine points and differ somewhat in emphasis. When approaching the subject of Soviet ideological interpretation, the present study addresses itself to the "line" of the Communist party of the Soviet Union.

The Soviets have consistently maintained that, although there may be an "African road to socialism," there is no such thing as "African socialism." The paths to socialism may vary because of national peculiarities, and the African states may therefore have unique methods of achieving socialism. However, it is affirmed that there are no variations upon socialism and that all socialist systems are based upon "Marxism-Leninism," or, as it is often called, "scientific socialism." Socialism is the same throughout the world, and African peculiarities may affect only the transition to socialism, not socialism itself.[25]

[25] See Ivan Potekhin, *Africa: Ways of Development* (Moscow: Nauka Publishing House, 1964); and *idem*, "On 'African Socialism,'" *International Affairs*, 1963, no. 1, pp. 71–79.

Although they have never accepted the idea of "African socialism," Soviet spokesmen have gradually approved of many of its aspects, such as the compatibility between religion and socialism. Even the views of the moderate Léopold Senghor, president of Senegal, have been looked upon favorably in recent years as Soviet friendship toward certain African leaders has led to a coming to terms with the "African socialist" concepts of these men.[26]

Beginning with the Twentieth Congress of the Communist Party of the Soviet Union in February 1956, Nikita Khrushchev emphasized the concept of "different roads to socialism," and it has remained an integral part of the Soviet analysis of African affairs ever since. Khrushchev was primarily concerned with the growing restlessness in the Communist world, especially in China, for all Communist states were supposed to follow the Soviet model of socialist development. He was also interested in improving relations with the renegade Communist government of Yugoslavia, so his formulation of "different roads to socialism" was therefore intended as a signal to the Communist world that differences in national programs of development would be tolerated. In a tactical move aimed at the Communist parties that were not in power, Khrushchev discussed the "peaceful transition to socialism." Communist parties were to participate in elections and reduce their revolutionary image, and these tactics were to complement the Soviet foreign policy of "peaceful coexistence" with the capitalist world.

Although not specifically directed at Africa, the concept of "different roads to socialism" had an effect as African socialist programs became more readily acceptable. The tribal and cultural values of the African peoples were seen as relevant to the building of socialism, and an "African road to socialism" was recognized. However, as previously mentioned, a system of "African socialism" was not.

The concept of "different roads to socialism" added some flexibility and realism to the Soviet analysis, but it was still maintained that only the working class could lead the building of a socialist society. This was rather far removed from the African context, where the size of the working class (proletariat) was minute, and it was not until the introduction of the concept of the "national democratic state" in 1960 that the Soviets acknowledged that nonproletariat elements could initiate the transition to socialism.

The Soviets emphasize the negative consequences of colonialism when discussing Africa's unique identity. They recognize a spiritual rebirth, which has arisen as a reaction to the colonial policy of treating

[26] See Robert Legvold, "The Soviet Union and Senegal," *Mizan*, 8, no. 4 (1966): 161–70.

Africans as inferiors, and they favor the new concentration on African history and culture. They also maintain that Africa was much further advanced before the colonial period than Western writers are willing to concede. Africa's uniqueness is seen as directly relevant to the method of building socialism in Africa.

However, Soviet theorists claim that racial concepts are not a factor in African uniqueness. Marxism-Leninism recognizes a class struggle throughout the world, not racial solidarity, but of course the Soviets are anxious to play down racial differences, since the Soviet Union is basically a "white" power. In addition, the Soviets fear that the Chinese are trying to use an antiwhite racial theme in order to rally the Afro-Asian peoples to their side.

The concept of "Negritude," most fervently espoused by Léopold Senghor, has been consistently attacked by the Soviets, although these attacks have become muted in recent years as Soviet-Senegalese relations have improved. According to this concept, blacks and whites are basically different phychologically: blacks are "intuitive"; whites are "analytical and logical." Color creates one's consciousness. The Soviets decry what they consider to be "anti-racial racism" and aver that class, not color, determines consciousness.[27] The concept of "African personality," put forth by Nkrumah and others, was not similarly attacked, probably because the Soviet Union maintained cordial relations with Ghana and did not want to cause any antagonisms.

The Soviet Union generally adheres to the orthodox Marxist position that religion is the "opiate of the masses" and that it is based upon superstition rather than scientific validity. Atheism is favored, and the Soviet government attempts to limit religious influence. It is believed that, once people are educated with the ideas of dialectical materialsm, religion will die out as a result of its conflict with scientific reality. However, when discussing Africa, Soviet theorists take a different approach. They still point out negative aspects of religion in Africa, but, so as not to offend many of the religion-oriented African leaders, the Soviets have come to maintain that religion and socialism are indeed compatible. Many Soviet articles have discussed the religious aspects of African socialism in states such as Mali or Algeria and have concluded that Islam is not an obstacle to achieving socialism.[28]

The Soviets tend to oppose pan-national movements because they emphasize the solidarity of a nationality group or racial group and

---

[27] See O. Vadeev, ed., *Meeting with Africa* (Moscow: Izdatel'stvo Politicheskoi Literatury, 1964), p. 170; and Ivan Potekhin, "Pan-Africanism and the Struggle of the Two Ideologies," *International Affairs*, 1964, no. 4, pp. 48–54.

[28] Iu. Bochkarev, "Communists are Doughtiest Fighters for National Independence," *Kommunist*, 1963, no. 5, translated in Joint Publication Research Service no. 18768, pp. 24–25.

thereby reject the concept of class struggle. Therefore, Pan-Africanism is viewed unfavorably when it refers to a racial concept. Soviet writers condemn it when it refers to an international alliance of Negroes or to the solidarity of black Africans. However, they do appraise Pan-Africanism positively when it does not concern itself with race.[29]

Pan-Africanism has developed into a geographical concept which incorporates both the Arab northern part of Africa and the primarily Negro south. The Soviets laud this development, as they do the idea of Pan-African economic cooperation. If the Africans cooperate more among themselves, they will rely less upon the Western powers for their economic needs.[30] Also, in the same area of diplomacy, Pan-Africanism may refer to African solidarity against colonialism and neo-colonialism and thus serve to reduce Western influence.

The Soviet attitude is therefore ambivalent; it supports Pan-Africanism only when it does not include the idea of racial identity. Class struggle is de-emphasized by African leaders who favor Pan-African unity, but the Soviets find solace in the thought that Pan-Africanism developed as a reaction against colonial control and feelings of superiority.

Because the Soviets claim that Marxist-Leninist "scientific socialism" is the only kind of socialism, they must therefore present reasons why so many Africans have arrived at supposedly incorrect interpretations which they believe to be socialist. Although they recognize the influence of both nationalism and tribalism, the Soviets minimize these factors and stress the inroads made by bourgeois ideology. This ideology was introduced to Africa from the outside and was well received by the petty bourgeoisie and small capitalist class. Colonialism and the education of many Africans in England and France led to the dissemination of these ideas.

Another explanation for mistaken interpretations of socialism is the fact that few Africans are proletarians. However, this contradicts the Soviet theory, particularly emphasized in the concepts of "national democracy" and "revolutionary democracy," that nonproletarians may become "scientific socialists." More meaningful to Soviet writers is their claim that true socialists must support the Soviet Union and other socialist (Communist) states in the international arena. The views of an African socialist are much more palatable if this person is pro-Soviet. One prominent Soviet spokesman attacked those African leaders "whose vows of dedication to socialism are merely a screen for reac-

---

[29] Ivan Potekhin, "Africa Shakes Off Colonial Slavery," *International Affairs*, 1959, no. 2, pp. 87–88.

[30] See V. Korochantsev, "Africa's Regional Associations," *New Times*, 1972, no. 2, pp. 18–19.

tionary pro-imperialist activities. Some even contrive to combine such vows with hostility toward the socialist countries."[31]

Western propaganda is another reason cited for the failure of Africans to become "scientific socialists." A fear of communism is instilled in the people, partly through religious missions, which play an active role in spreading this Western propaganda. Also, many of the African claims of socialism not only are based on a poor understanding of the subject but often are merely cover-ups for capitalist exploitation. Many African leaders realize that the masses desire socialism, and they therefore use socialist slogans to placate the people while continuing to exploit them. This interpretation leads to an ideological problem: Why should the African masses desire socialism if most Africans are not proletarians? The Soviets have difficulty answering this question in terms of class structure.

Although African socialist ideas are still rather widespread, the Soviets maintain that "scientific socialism" is acquiring ever more adherents. Nkrumah and Keita claimed to be "scientific socialists" before they were overthrown, but there is really a fundamental difference between public espousal and action. Neither of these men accepted all of the tenets of Marxism-Leninism, particularly in the area of the relationship between religion and socialism.

Soviet writers maintain that, prior to the colonization of Africa, the people lived in primitive-communal and feudal societies. Class differentiation was proceeding rapidly, and the African socialist assertion that African society was classless is vehemently disputed.

Viewed in terms of the Marxist-Leninist pattern of historical development, African societies advanced from tribalism to nationality to nation, with their economic structures changing from communal to feudal to capitalist.[32] The next step would be toward socialism, but no African state is yet considered to be socialistic.

During the communal period of development, tribes are organized along kinship lines. There are no social classes, and each tribe has a common language and culture. As feudalism becomes prevalent, tribes amalgamate into nationalities, each of which has a common language, territory, and culture, but not a common economy. There is class differentiation and possibly slavery. As feudalism develops into capitalism, nationalities are converted into nations, and private property dominates the economy. Soviet theorists affirm that there were no nations

[31] Karen Brutents, "The October Revolution and Africa," *ibid.*, 1962, no. 45, p. 10.

[32] Ivan Potekhin, "De quelques questions méthodologiques pour l'étude de la formation des nations en Afrique au du Sahara," *Présence Africaine,* no. 17 (December 1957–January 1958), pp. 60–75.

in Africa until the end of the nineteenth century and that African society today is a melange of communal, feudal, and capitalist elements.[33]

The Soviets strongly disagree with those African socialist leaders who maintain that there is no class struggle in Africa. They insist that class struggle is an objective law of historical development and that Africa may not be excepted from its influence. They reject themes of national, or racial, unity, as well as the concept that all Africans are brothers, and they claim that, although class formation in Africa has not been completed, Africa is indeed racked by class struggle. They believe that many African leaders who exploit their people use the theme of no class struggle in order to prevent people from realizing that they are being exploited. As Nikita Khrushchev once asserted: "Many of the leaders of the countries that have won their national independence are trying to pursue a kind of fence-sitting policy, which they call non-class, are trying to ignore the class structure of society and the class struggle, which are matters of fact in their countries."[34]

Soviet theorists maintain that the African bourgeoisie is small and underdeveloped, and that the proletariat is further developed than one would suspect from Africa's historical advancement, because of the impact of colonialism. Since members of the foreign bourgeoisie owned most of the industry, the growth of the African bourgeoisie was held back, but an African proletariat did burgeon. This interpretation is used to support the Soviets' contention that the capitalist stage in Africa may be of short duration and that the prospects for socialism are therefore bright.

Despite this analysis of African class development, the proletariat is still extremely small in most African nations, and Soviet hopes for the building of socialism in Africa run counter to the Marxist-Leninist dictum that a large proletariat is a necessary concomitant of the advent of socialism. Another area in which the Soviets experience doctrinal difficulties concerns the one-party state. They would like to justify one-party rule in states such as Guinea or Egypt, but, according to Marxist-Leninist interpretation, a one-party state features an absence of class struggle.

## VI

Doctrines which rarely change lie at the heart of ideology, and they have a greater effect on long-term strategy than on short-term tactics. The Soviets adhere to certain Marxist-Leninist doctrines—namely, that

[33] *Ibid.*
[34] Nikita Khrushchev, "Speech in Sofia," *Pravda*, May 20, 1962, pp. 1–3; excerpts of the speech were translated in *Current Digest of the Soviet Press*, 14, no. 20 (June 13, 1962): 7.

there is a definite progression of historical stages which inevitably leads to communism; that economics is at the base of society and determines all aspects of the superstructure, including the political; that history has developed out of the conflict between various socio-economic classes; and that imperialism and capitalism are always seen in opposition to the Soviet regime. On the basis of this analysis, Soviet ideologists can easily perceive possible friends and possible opponents, and the main thrust of their policy is to further the cause of communism and defeat the forces of imperialism and capitalism. For example, Soviet aid to African states is never given to the private economic sector; it is given to the state sector, because this furthers socialist development.

Ideology often leads to distortion and excessive optimism. The view that history always favors the cause of communism and that the main struggle of our time is between socialism and imperialism leads to the perception of anti-Western sentiment as necessarily pro-Communist and to a general nonrecognition of important indigenous factors which are not relevant to ideological conflict. However, ideology may beneficially affect Soviet policy-makers, as, for instance, in terms of economic influence in Africa. It is realistically understood that those nations which accentuate state and cooperative ownership of property tend to lean more toward the Soviet camp, while those which have "neocolonial" economic systems do not.

Since Stalin's death, many Soviet misconceptions about Africa have been eliminated as ideology has come into closer contact with reality. Rigid class distinctions are no longer upheld, for it is now recognized that nonproletarians can desire to build a socialist society. Flexible terms such as "revolutionary democrat" and "progressive intelligentsia" are now common, and they imply that ideology can cross class lines. In addition, the positive aspects of the role of the national bourgeoisie have been accepted because members of this class are now deemed capable of gaining political independence and of initiating the transition to socialism. National differences in socialist construction are also a factor in the revised Soviet interpretation.

Despite increased Soviet realism, some misconceptions based upon ideological interpretation still remain. Too much emphasis is placed upon class analysis, and factors such as race, tribe, region, identity, and personal charisma are not given proper regard. Race is certainly a factor in Chad and Sudan—as tribe is in Kenya, regionalism is in Nigeria, and charisma is in the appeals of Kenyatta or Touré—but Soviet observers tend to avoid these factors and to stress a class analysis of African politics. The Soviets are also too rigid in maintaining that the Africans must take either the capitalist or the socialist path.

Perhaps there can be a synthesis of these two systems. The theme of the objective laws of historical development is also too confining and submerges much of Africa's uniqueness. Another area of negative ideological consequences concerns the role of the African proletariat. Although Soviet ideologists realize that many "progressive" reforms may be carried out by nonproletarian elements, they nevertheless pay undue regard to the proletarian class. Its size, organization, and class consciousness are constantly discussed, but the growth of socialism in Africa is not really dependent upon the growth of the miniscule African proletariat, and a class analysis of African society is not particularly insightful. Paradoxically, the Soviets relate the size of the proletariat to the advent of socialism but then look toward Africa for its advent rather than toward the more industrialized states of Western Europe and North America. Another inconsistency involves the possibility of by-passing a stage of historical development. While maintaining that capitalism may indeed be by-passed, the Soviets insist in their dialogue with the Chinese that socialism may not.

Soviet ideology has been eroding as outdated tenets have had to be revised in the light of a changing international situation. Ideology has become more flexible and more attuned to political realities, and its role as a determinant of policy has decreased as it has evolved as a reflection of practical national interest. Socialist agricultural programs instituted in Guinea are viewed positively because Guinea is considered a "progressive" state, while similar programs instituted in Israel are roundly criticized. The Soviet Union's relations with the various states have a great effect upon ideological interpretation, and ideology has therefore ceased to be "scientific" and has become pragmatic.

The Soviet Union presents itself to Africa as an anticolonial, antiracist, anti-imperialist power which does not seek military bases, does not intervene militarily, supports the national unity of the African states, and gives economic aid devoid of political strings. It has a certain advantage over most Western states because it was never an African colonial power and did consistently oppose European colonialism in Africa (although it should be pointed out that the Soviet Union was interested in securing a trusteeship over Libya after World War II). The Soviet model of socialism, which features state ownership of the basic sectors of the economy and collective ownership of much of the agricultural sector, is more relevant to Africa than the American system of free enterprise capitalism and the multinational structure of the Soviet Union is widely admired in Africa.

Viewed within the Soviet theoretical framework, Africa must inevitably become socialistic because socialism is a scientifically necessary stage in historical progression. Therefore, when looking at long-term prospects in Africa, the Soviets are generally optimistic and patient. They now realistically acknowledge that the advent of socialism in Africa lies in the distant future and that the immediate task is not to get African states to move into the Soviet orbit but to turn them against the West.

The prime Soviet objective in Africa is to spread its influence and thereby decrease Africa's reliance on the Western powers. Once the Western presence is removed, the next step will be to bring the African states into the Soviet orbit. Working with the existing governments is fundamental to this approach, and the Soviets have the capability to do so effectively because of their ability to supply economic and military aid and because of their noncolonial past.

Among the successes in the Soviet approach toward Africa has been the support of African neutralism, especially during the surge toward independence in the 1950s. At this time, the United States was generally unwilling to accept neutralism, and pressures were put on African states to lean more toward the West. Acceptance of neutralism and the formulation of a "peace zone" concept were greatly beneficial to the Soviets, for their image in Africa became more favorable. Another notable success has been the ability to replace the revolutionary, Communist, Soviet image with one of willingness to give aid to nationalist governments and to advocate stability and peace. African Communists were detrimentally affected by this new Soviet approach, but the Soviets' influence certainly increased as a result of its inception in the mid-fifties.

The Soviet Union now envisions Africa in rather practical terms, but certain failures in approach had to be overcome after the initial period of overoptimistic zeal. The possibility that many African leaders would become Communists was seriously over-rated, and the ability of "progressive" African states to institute radical socialist economic programs was exaggerated. Attempts to introduce ideological formulations into the African context were also found to be overdrawn, for the Africans were much more concerned with practical needs.

Viewed in the context of the East-West, Communist-capitalist struggle, the Soviet Union has profited by its actions in Africa. Western influence (which at one time was direct control) has decreased, and socialism has begun to compete with the capitalist remnants of the colonial economic order. However, the East-West conflict is not particularly relevant to Africa. Soviet influence had to increase, for the Soviets had none during the years of colonialism, and the initiation of socialist programs in many African states had little to do with Soviet entreaties and more to do with the economic needs of developing societies. Africa may become anti-Westernized and socialized, but it is unlikely to become sovietized or communized.

# 4

## THE SOVIET UNION AND SOUTHEAST ASIA

### Justus M. van der Kroef

### Soviet Policy and the Southeast Asian Setting

At the close of November 1971 a spokesman for the "Malaysia-Soviet Friendship Society" in Kuala Lumpur announced that a counterpart, the "Soviet-Malaysia Friendship Society," had just been formed in Moscow, headed by U.S.S.R. Minister of Oil and Refineries V. Fedorov.[1] This was but the latest development in a steadily warming relationship between the two countries which had begun with the establishment of the Soviet trade commission in the Malaysian capital in September 1967, and of an exchange of ambassadors in May the following year. Malaysia's avowed interest in the future politico-military "neutralization" of Southeast Asia, to be discussed presently, has considerably endeared her to the Russians,[2] and there is perhaps no country in Southeast Asia today where the graph of official cordiality with Moscow registers such a quiet but steady rise as in Kuala Lumpur.

The fact that this is happening in a country such as Malaysia, which as recently as 1964 still rebuffed Moscow's overtures to establish diplomatic relations, and where the government's resources are increasingly being mobilized to crush a domestic Communist guerrilla insurgency which has assumed many of the trappings of a "national liberation" movement (along the Thai-Malaysian border, and in the Borneo state of Sarawak), is no longer particularly remarkable. The Philippines, for example, with an equally serious insurgency and with an underground, Moscow-oriented Communist party (there is also a more active Maoist branch, with its own "New People's Army"), formally began reassessing the possibility of concluding diplomatic and commercial ties with Communist nations, especially in Eastern Europe, as early as the middle of 1970. By the middle of February 1972, the first steps had been taken toward forming relations with Yugoslavia and Rumania. President Ferdinand Marcos also announced that Philippine trade was

---

[1] Bernama dispatch, Kuala Lumpur, Malaysia, November 29, 1971.

[2] V. L. Kudriavtsev, vice chairman of the Soviet Committee of the Afro-Asian People's Solidarity Organization, declared as early as March 1971, during an official visit to Malaysia, that the U.S.S.R. welcomed Malaysia's call for the "neutralization" of Southeast Asia: "The Soviet Union greets all the efforts for non-alignment and neutralization of the region if they are directed towards all the countries equally. . . . Your [that is, Malaysia's] policy corresponds with that of our government's." Bernama dispatch, Kuala Lumpur, March 4, 1971.

79

now formally open with all Communist nations, including the People's Republic of China and the U.S.S.R. Padre Faura circles were speculating that, despite opposition among some (by no means all) Philippine military leaders, an exchange of embassies with the Soviet Union was the next logical step and only a matter of time,[3] the more so because recent visiting Philippine trade missions in Moscow had come back with encouraging reports.

On the basis of the Malaysian and Philippine examples, one might speculate on the possible emergence of a new pattern in Moscow's relations with Southeast Asia. In this pattern, visiting trade missions not only increasingly accustom public opinion in the relevant Southeast Asian nation to the conclusion of formal diplomatic ties with the Soviets in an environment where the old protectors, such as the United Kingdom and the U.S., can no longer be relied upon and where the Chinese shadow looms ever larger, but also—beyond the exchange of embassies—open up new choices, which, through the press of circumstance, may actually have to be made, as mutual "friendship" societies and ongoing exchanges nudge thinking toward the formation of formal treaties of friendship and assistance, in the manner of the August 1971 Soviet-Indian pact. Thus far, however, I hasten to add, the scenario has had only limited application. And, in some states of Southeast Asia, despite the existence of diplomatic ties, formidable obstacles to cordial relations with the U.S.S.R. remain.

Thailand is an obvious case in point. Diplomatic relations between Bangkok and Moscow are seemingly perpetually well below the freezing point (in part an aftereffect of Thai anger over an initial Soviet attempt to keep Thailand out of the United Nations in 1946). This is so despite a periodic realization in leading Thai political circles that excessive dependence on the U.S. and the hostility from the People's Republic of China both counsel the desirability of new foreign policy approaches, including that toward the Soviet Union. But twice Thailand's military leaders have all but nullified such new moves, and ostensibly for the same reason: the threat of Communist subversion, in which little distinction is made between Moscow and Peking. In 1962 it seemed that Thai-Soviet exploratory talks to accelerate trade would soon bear fruit. But in the next two years the growing evidence of a China-backed Communist underground resistance movement in Thai-

---

[3] On the changing position of the Philippine government toward Communist nations, see, for example, *Far Eastern Economic Review*, September 19, 1970, and January 29, 1972; and *New York Times,* January 25 and February 13, 1972. On March 16, 1972, Mrs. Imelda Marcos, wife of the Philippine president, reported that Soviet Premier Alexei Kosygin, during discussions with her in Moscow the day before, had assured her of "any and all manner of aid" to the Philippines.

land, as well as the Bangkok government's increasing readiness to undergird the developing American military commitment in Vietnam, contributed to a near obliteration of future trading overtures. In subsequent years Thai-Soviet trade was negligible.

The advent of the Nixon administration also accentuated a foreign policy re-evaluation in Thailand, and Thai Foreign Minister Thanat Khoman soon came to be associated not just with a concept of progressive disengagement from American policies but even with a possible future "neutralization" of Southeast Asia of the kind that currently has won Moscow's qualified praise. On December 25, 1970, Thailand and the U.S.S.R. signed a trade agreement promising to expand trade and commercial relations "on the basis of equality." Planned Soviet purchases of Thai tin and rubber would be matched by Soviet exports of machinery. During most of 1971, as the impact of Nixon's planned visit to Peking was being felt, there was also considerable speculation that even Sino-Thai relations were moderating, although Thai Premier Thanom Kittikachorn warned his visting Malaysian opposite number, Tun Abdul Razak, in Bangkok in June 1971 that Thailand could not be neutral, because "Communist China is carrying out a war of insurgency against our country."[4] Then, in a bloodless coup on November 17, 1971, a military-dominated "National Executive Council" (NEC), led by premier Thanom, seized control in Bangkok, ousting Thanat Khoman and emphasizing the Chinese and domestic Communist insurgent threat to Thailand. Once again the likelihood of improved relations with the U.S.S.R. diminished considerably.

Yet, Soviet comment on Thai developments has remained fleeting and in any case quite restrained. For example, on November 27, 1971, the Association of Southeast Asian Nations (ASEAN), whose membership included "the Special Envoy of the National Executive Council of Thailand," as well as the foreign ministers of Indonesia, Malaysia, the Philippines, and Singapore, issued a declaration proclaiming the region to be "a zone of peace, freedom, and neutrality." Soviet commentators contented themselves with pointing out (1) that, despite this declaration, Thailand intended to remain in SEATO, (2) that Thailand also persisted in participating in the "American armed aggression" in Indochina, and (3) that, given other ambiguities of ASEAN, only future events could confirm the sincerity of the declaration's signers.[5]

Distrust of an eventual Sino-American rapprochement may yet bring

---

[4] *Bangkok Post*, June 17, 1971; and *New Nation* (Singapore), November 12, 1971.

[5] B. Vetin in *Pravda*, December 27, 1971; V. Kudriavtsev in *Izvestiia*, January 7, 1972. References to the Soviet press throughout this article are drawn from *Current Digest of the Soviet Press* unless otherwise indicated.

Bangkok's NEC eventually to embrace a position similar to Thanat
Khoman's and to that of the minor Thai parties which have been calling for a complete severance of Bangkok's ties with SEATO and the
implementation of a more independent foreign policy. For the foreseeable future, however, the NEC's hard-line anticommunism seems to
preclude little more than minimal diplomatic formalities in Thai-Soviet
relations, although there is growing recognition of the need for
improvement.

Elsewhere in Southeast Asia, Moscow also could do little better
than the same relatively cold and/or quiescent formality. The severe
strain in Sino-Burmese relations of 1967–1969, attendant upon Peking's
baffling effort to export her "Great Proletarian Cultural Revolution" to
Burma's half a million Chinese minority, did not cause Ne Win's government to swerve from its officially resolute, and on the whole consistent, "nonalignment" in favor of the U.S.S.R. or the U.S. Nor did the
Soviets then seek to exploit the upsurge of anti-Chinese sentiment
among the Burmese. By early August 1971, Sino-Burmese relations had
sufficiently recovered, however, for Premier Ne Win to make a state
visit to Peking. The following November a new Chinese trade-and-
commodity loan agreement with Burma went still further in restoring
the erstwhile *pauk phaw* ("cousinly") relationship between the two
nations. By this time the impact of the new twenty-year Soviet-Indian
nonaggression treaty (signed about the same time that Ne Win was in
Peking) had also begun to accentuate Rangoon's fears that both Moscow and Peking would intensify their efforts to influence Burma, and
that, like it or not, Burma might become a pawn in a possible Sino-
Soviet power struggle in South and Southeast Asia.[6] A Burmese accommodation with Peking (which is actively backing Burmese Communist
and tribal insurgents), if only because of China's proximity, is, however, as unlikely at the moment as an open turn toward the U.S.S.R.,
unless no other alternatives remain. Yet here too one now senses a
new interest in greater amicability.

Then there is the U.S.S.R.'s increasingly embarrassing position in
Cambodia. It may be recalled that in early January 1970 Cambodia's
chief of state, Prince Norodom Sihanouk, began a fruitless tour of
major world capitals—including Paris, Moscow, and Peking—in the
hope that pressures might there be brought to bear on the North
Vietnamese and Cambodian Communists to "scale down their presence
in Cambodia," a presence which was increasingly jeopardizing Sihanouk's attempt to preserve his country's neutrality.[7] Sihanouk's mission

---

[6] *New York Times*, February 14, 1972.
[7] Douglas Pike, "Cambodia's War," *Southeast Asian Perspectives*, March 1971,
p. 10.

was a failure (certainly the Soviets gave him no encouragement at the time), and by March 18, 1970, he had been deposed and flown into exile in Peking, as meanwhile the new government of Lon Nol assumed power in Phnom Penh. Very shortly the new Peking-based Cambodian "National Union" government (headed by the exiled Sihanouk), its political arm (the "National United Front of Kampuchea"), and various Hanoi-associated Cambodian "liberation forces" began their campaign against Phnom Penh, where the continuing U.S.S.R. diplomatic mission was in the ever more uncomfortable position of finding itself the only embassy of a major Communist power being "protected from Communist attack by South Vietnamese and American forces."[8]

To be sure, within weeks of the Lon Nol coup, Moscow had sharply reduced its technical assistance personnel and program (Soviet loans and grants to Cambodia had amounted to about $20 million in the period 1946–1970), had "issued vague statements in support of the Cambodian revolution," and had recalled its ambassador.[9] But, even though subsequent emissaries of the "National United Front of Kampuchea" visited Moscow informally, and according to Soviet sources "conveyed profound gratitude from Prince Norodom Sihanouk to the Soviet people for their support of Cambodia's just cause,"[10] Soviet diplomatic relations with the Phnom Penh government were not broken. It must be supposed, however, that the Soviet government had had ample occasion to reflect on the frequent past warnings of Sihanouk's ambassadors in Moscow and other Communist capitals, in the days when the prince was still in office, that continuing North Vietnamese encroachment on Cambodian territory inevitably would bring an avowedly anti-Communist, and certainly an anti-Hanoi, government to power in Cambodia. To add to Moscow's embarrassment, by the close of 1971, the irrepressible Sihanouk had begun to polarize Cambodia's position still further by sharply attacking the continued presence of the Russians in Phnom Penh ("Is it honorable for them to brush shoulders with the diplomatic representatives of Seoul, Saigon, and Taipei?") and by attributing racist motives to Soviet policy ("I think the Russians consider themselves white, and they do not want yellow people to become too strong").[11] The Soviets' reply to Sihanouk ("Prince Norodom Sihanouk's pronouncements remind one a great deal of the anti-Soviet hogwash disseminated by Peking's propaganda")

[8] T. D. Allman in *Mirror* (Singapore), July 20, 1970.
[9] *Ibid.*
[10] Vasiliy Kharkov commentary, Radio Moscow in English to South Asia, January 27, 1972, 1100 GMT, Foreign Broadcast Information Service (hereafter cited as FBIS).
[11] See the interview of Norodom Sihanouk by Alessandro Casella in *Far Eastern Economic Review*, December 25, 1971, p. 20.

seemed to undo whatever limited effect Moscow's past, guarded praise of the "National Front of Kampuchea" had had.[12]

In early February 1972 a *Pravda* editorial, "Solidarity with the Peoples of Indo-China," confined itself largely to reiterating Moscow's support for the demands of Hanoi and its Laotian and Cambodian allies that all American bombing of "the territory of the Democratic Republic of Vietnam (D.R.V.), South Vietnam, Laos and Cambodia" cease at once and that all American forces be withdrawn "from Indochina."[13] This position was also said to be in accord with the general policy of giving "all possible support" to "the peoples of Indochina" in their struggle against "the aggression of American imperialism" and of promoting a "political settlement in the area" as formulated in the spring of 1971 by the Twenty-fourth Congress of the Communist Party of the Soviet Union and as subsequently "reaffirmed" at the Prague meeting of the political consultative committees of the Warsaw pact powers.

But the Soviets' "all possible support" still has not included the closing of their Phnom Penh embassy. To a significant degree the Soviet quandary in Cambodia reflects the historic ambivalence of Moscow's commitments to the Indochina problem in general, and to the Vietnam war in particular. Although as early as 1947 and the foundation of the Cominform, Moscow had described the developing struggle in Indochina as an example of a "national liberation" movement in colonial areas, and, although an exchange of diplomatic recognition with Hanoi had occurred late in January 1950 (within two weeks after a similar exchange with Peking), the Vietnam question did not loom large in the foreign policy concerns of Stalin's final years.[14] This was in keeping with what has been termed—perhaps exaggeratedly—the "virtual neglect of Southeast Asia under Stalin," which stemmed from a preoccupation with European affairs and with support for the Chinese Communists, and which in turn reflected an essentially rigid "two-camp" foreign policy perception, with Communists in the world lining up against anti-Communists, thus seemingly leaving little room for more subtle and varied approaches in the "gray" areas of international poli-

[12] See *Literaturnaia Gazeta*, January 12, 1972; Kharkov Commentary, January 27, 1972, FBIS; and the April 8, 1971, CPSU "message to Indochina" in *Vietnam Courier* (Hanoi), no. 317 (April 19, 1971), p. 6.

[13] Radio Moscow in English to North America, February 9, 1972, 2250 GMT, FBIS.

[14] Allan W. Cameron, "The Soviet Union and Vietnam: The Origins of Involvement," in *Soviet Policy in Developing Countries*, ed. W. Raymond Duncan (Waltham, Mass: Blaisdell, 1970), pp. 174–76. I have relied heavily on Cameron's perceptive analysis in the present paragraph. See also Donald S. Zagoria, *Vietnam Triangle* (New York: Pegasus Books, Western Publishing Co., 1967), esp. pp. 36–38.

tics.[15] Even after Stalin's death the Soviets' preoccupation with European affairs, and, in Asia, with securing for the People's Republic of
China a pre-eminent position, tended to impel the Soviets toward support for a cease-fire and a negotiated settlement of the Vietnam conflict, specifically at the 1954 Geneva conference, despite the grave misgivings and contrary wishes of many D.R.V. leaders. In the months and
years immediately following the Geneva accords, it also seemed that
Moscow was becoming all but insensitive to the obvious failure to implement the Geneva provisions on the reunification of the two Viet-
nams, that it was counseling restraint on DRV leaders, and that it was
going so far as to propose, in January 1957, that North and South
Vietnam be admitted as separte states into the United Nations.[16]

Within three years, however, a number of factors caused Moscow's
interest in the D.R.V.'s struggle to heighten dramatically. Since the
advent of Khrushchev, Soviet political theorists had begun to show a
new sophistication (which experience would occasionally sour) in dealing with the self-styled non- or anticapitalist and/or socialist development planning of Third World nations. A more positive flexibility of
attitude on Moscow's part toward the developmental aspirations of
new nations seemed to be reflected in increasing theoretical experimen-
tation by Soviet writers with such concepts as "national democracy"
and "revolutionary democracy," which were used to denote the political
leadership and governments of Ghana, Algeria, Burma, and other
"progressive" nations.[17] This relative flexibility persisted, despite the
effects of the 1956 rebellions in Poland and Hungary and of the growing doctrinal dispute with Peking (indeed, the latter may well have
accentuated it in some cases). At the February 1956 Twentieth Party
Congress, Khrushchev had affirmed the concept that various countries
might follow different roads to socialism, while the 1960 Moscow statement stressed the importance of taking account of "national peculiarities" and "specific historical conditions" in the "creative application"

---

[15] John R. Thomas, "Soviet Russia and Southeast Asia," *Current History*,
November 1968, p. 275. Stalin's last years (1950–1953) were marked by frustration and reversals in his cold war strategy, as a result of which he began moving
toward more varied, moderate, and flexible tactics in promoting Soviet influence
in international affairs. These tactics foreshadowed Soviet reliance on long-term,
"noncapitalist" modes of economic and political development in the new Southeast
Asian nations and an emphasis on an equally long-term, more "moderate" course
for local Communist parties instead of reliance on militant confrontation and
rebellions. See Charles B. McLane, *Soviet Strategies in Southeast Asia: An
Exploration of Eastern Policy under Lenin and Stalin* (Princeton: Princeton Press,
1966), pp. 464–73.
[16] Cameron, *op. cit.*, pp. 198–202.
[17] See David Morison, "Africa and Asia: Some Trends in Soviet Thinking,"
*Mizan*, September–October 1968, pp. 167–68.

of "socialist" revolutionary principles.[18] By 1967 (three years after Khrushchev was deposed), and afterward, authoritative Soviet writers were still elaborating on the significance of "the non-capitalist road" undertaken by "previously backward countries" in their evolution toward socialism.[19] Such theoretical and strategic concerns were accompanied by a steadily rising Soviet interest in, and warmth toward, a number of Southeast Asian regimes, a development which was reflected in mounting Soviet economic and military assistance to some states of the region and which in turn also interacted with growing Soviet involvement in the Vietnam crisis.

A good example of this process is Indonesia. No diplomatic relations existed between Djakarta and Moscow before 1954, and initial credits from Communist nations (including a Soviet credit of $100 million in 1956) met with considerable domestic Indonesian opposition.[20] Shortly, however, Indonesia's political climate changed. The failure of constitutional and parliamentary democracy; the rise of Sukarno's ever more authoritarian "guided democracy" and, concurrently, the rise of the PKI, or Indonesian Communist party; Indonesia's increasingly anti-Western policy and militant confrontation with Dutch-held New Guinea and subsequently with the Malyasian Federation—all these generally sat well with Moscow. On the occasion of Khrushchev's visit to Indonesia in February 1960, an additional $250 million in Soviet economic aid to the Djakarta government was arranged, and by January 1961 Indonesia had obtained a $400–$450 million Soviet arms credit, possibly the largest single military aid package ever handed over by Moscow.[21] Meanwhile, the adaptability of the Indonesian Communists to the Sukarnoist policies of militant and revolutionary nationalism won the PKI particular praise in the Soviet press.[22]

### The U.S.S.R. and Hanoi

Moscow's changing outlook on the Southeast Asian scene was apparently well appreciated in Hanoi, where initial reaction to the Sino-Soviet split was conditioned by the historical Vietnamese distrust of China and by a new willingness to ignore earlier Soviet disinterest:

[18] Alvin Z. Rubinstein, ed., *The Foreign Policy of the Soviet Union*, 2nd ed. (New York: Random House, 1966), pp. 36–28, 283; and "The 1960 Moscow Statement," *China Quarterly*, January–March 1960, p. 33.

[19] N. A. Simoniia in *Aziia i Afrika segodnia*, 1967, no. 9, p. 4, cited in Morison, "Africa and Asia," p. 168.

[20] Guy J. Parker, "General Nasution's Mission to Moscow," *Asian Survey*, 1 (1961–1962): 13.

[21] *Ibid.*

[22] Michael Kovner, "Soviet Aid Strategy in Developing Countries," *Orbis*, Fall, 1964, pp. 629–30.

Before the National Assembly, on December 23, 1959, President Ho Chi Minh praised "the leadership role played by the Soviet Union in the domain of science and peace," without making any reference to China. Similarly, on the celebration of the fifteenth anniversary of the army, the prime minister spoke in the same terms of the Soviet Union, making only brief mention of the military aid granted by China. Again, on January 1, President Ho Chi Minh in his traditional speech, in the presence of the diplomatic corps, praised Premier Khrushchev and the Soviet Union while making no allusion to China.

Until May 1959, however, the talk and speeches and writings were always of the "fraternal socialist camp led by the Soviet Union, and aided by the Republic of China." During the following twenty months the formula employed was solely "the fraternal socialist camp led by the Soviet Union."[23]

Concurrently, Soviet trade with North Vietnam doubled in 1959, compared to 1957, and Russian exports to Hanoi in 1962 were again twice what they had been in 1959.[24] With little question, by the close of 1961 the Soviets saw Southeast Asia in general, and the Vietnam question in particular, as a vital sector of their widening global doctrinal and strategic conflict with Peking, which compelled the substitution of ardent wooing of Southeast Asian regimes for erstwhile majestic near indifference.

In his well-known report to the Moscow Congress of Eighty-one Parties in January 1961, Khrushchev served notice that he would not be outdone by the Chinese in full-throated support for national liberation movements in the Third World, and he singled out Vietnam (along with Algeria) as an example of "national liberation wars," which would be "inevitable" and which would have to be waged "as long as imperialism exists, as long as colonialism exists."[25] Khrushchev's subsequent fall from power would only intensify this formal Soviet commitment, notwithstanding growing uneasiness among his successors that D.R.V. leaders were exhibiting obvious expertise in playing Peking off against Moscow as the Sino-Soviet dispute went on. After renewed promises of providing the required aid to the Hanoi government, made in February 1964, and a subsequent assurance, made by Premier A. N. Kosygin during his sojourn in Hanoi in early February 1965, that the U.S.S.R., "along with its allies and friends," would take "additional measures to protect the safety and strengthen the defense of the

---

[23] Jean Lacouture, *Vietnam between Two Truces* (New York: Random House, 1966), pp. 47–48.
[24] Cameron, *op. cit.*, p. 203.
[25] *Pravda*, January 25, 1961.

D.R.V.," visits by North Vietnamese delegations to Moscow for the implementation of Soviet aid agreements began to become regular occasions. At the same time, however, the U.S.S.R. remained interested in
keeping the level of the Vietnam conflict down, and there is some evidence, for example, that Kosygin, shortly after returning from his February 1965 trip to Hanoi, renewed efforts to settle the Indochinese
question by means of an international conference without preconditions.[26] Early in 1966 the Soviets again appear to have pressured Hanoi
into negotiating with the U.S. According to some observers, the Soviets'
concern over Hanoi's seeming inflexibility in pursuing the war, aggravated by a rumored drift of some D.R.V. leaders toward Peking's doctrinal and tactical position in her ever more bitter clash with Moscow,
was particularly apparent during Aleksandr Shelepin's visit to Hanoi in
January 1966, although the communiqué issued at the end of Shelepin's
stay again reiterated the Russians' "full support" for the position of the
D.R.V. and the National Liberation Front of South Vietnam.[27]

Whatever qualms over D.R.V. policies Soviet leaders may have felt
in private, however, they were well aware that they could not afford
to be outflanked by Peking in issuing open and unequivocal assurances
of assistance to Hanoi. There is little question that Peking was constantly trying such outflanking maneuvers. Commemorating the fifteenth anniversary of the Sino-Soviet Mutual Assistance Pact, the
Chinese sent Moscow a message which declared that, "confronted by
the common foe," the Soviet and Chinese peoples and those of the
socialist bloc had to "rally staunchly" and stand together and "reso-
lutely" help "the armed struggle of the Vietnamese people and the
Indochinese peoples against American imperialism."[28] Peking's bitter
repudiation of Moscow's invitation to attend the CPSU's March 1966
congress contained the charge that the Soviets were collaborating with
the U.S. "to sell out the Vietnamese people." This accusation echoed a
similar Chinese charge made in connection with the March 1965
"consultative meeting" of world Communist parties held in Moscow.[29]

Shortly, however, the convulsions of the "Great Proletarian Cultural
Revolution" within China itself are known to have caused considerable

[26] See John Gittings, "The Soviet Initiative on Vietnam: A Missed Opportunity?"
*Viet-Report* (New York), November–December 1965, pp. 18–22.

[27] Rodger Swearingen and Hammond Rolph, *Communism in Vietnam: A Documentary Study* (Chicago: American Bar Association, 1967), pp. 169–71; and
"Vietnam: The Soviet Dilemma," *Mizan*, September–October 1966, pp. 200–22.

[28] *Pravda*, February 14, 1965.

[29] Editorial Departments of *Renmin Ribao* and *Hongqi*, *A Comment on the
March Moscow Meeting* (Peking: Foreign Languages Press, 1965), pp. 10–11;
and *Idem, Letter of Reply Dated March 22, 1966, of the Central Committee of
the Communist Party of China to the Central Committee of the Communist Party
of the Soviet Union* (Peking: Foreign Languages Press, 1966), p. 3.

alarm in Hanoi over the reliability of Peking's friendship. And, in any case, the Soviets' military supplies, not China's, had by then become an indispensible dimension of Hanoi's own ongoing war efforts. In 1965 alone, Soviet party leaders claimed to have supplied Hanoi with weapons and other war material worth $550 million, including aircraft, antiaircraft artillery, rocket installations, tanks, coastal artillery, as well as training for pilots, tank personnel, and so on.[30] A peak of $720 million in Soviet aid to the D.R.V. was reached in 1967, and, since then, according to an authoritative estimate made near the close of 1971, Hanoi has been getting an average of about half a billion dollars worth of diversified Russian help a year, about half of which has been considered economic aid.[31] Through the years, however, this expenditure, interspersed with periodic visits back and forth by official delegates to Moscow and Hanoi, has not altered the relatively independent position of the D.R.V. in the Sino-Soviet conflict. The Soviets have not been able to induce the North Vietnamese openly to take sides against Peking (nor, for that matter, have the Chinese succeeded in making the D.R.V. into an Asian Albania). From time to time, in recent years, there has been evident disappointment and skepticism within the Kremlin itself and among authoritative Soviet writers about the policies of "revolutionary democrats" in the new nations generally, and, by implication, of Soviet aid (both economic and military) to them.[32] It may be surmised that such skepticism has had implications even for Soviet considerations of assistance to the D.R.V. Officially, however, there can be no question of continuing Soviet devotion to the D.R.V. cause.

Moscow supported Hanoi in rejecting all American peace overtures that fell short of the D.R.V.'s own seven-point proposal of July 1, 1971 (which demanded not only a total American military withdrawal from Indochina, but also cessation of all American support for the government of President Nguyen Van Thieu of South Vietnam).[33] Evidently agreeing with the preponderant North Vietnamese official views that the dynamic of the Nixon policies, also in the context of pre-

---

[30] New York Times, March 24, 1966.
[31] Ibid., November 13, 1971. Subsequent estimates have slightly scaled down the amount of Soviet aid to Hanoi. According to these new estimates, total Soviet military-economic aid to the D.R.V. was $705 million in 1967, $415 million in 1970, and again $415 million in 1971. Military aid alone amounted to $505 million in 1967, $70 million in 1970, and $100 million in 1971. Chinese Communist military aid to Hanoi was $145 million in 1967, $85 million in 1970, and $75 million in 1971. Ibid., April 13, 1972.
[32] See, for example, David Morison, "U.S.S.R. and Third World: I. Ideal and Reality," Mizan, October 1970, pp. 7-25.
[33] See, for example, the commentary of Viktor Maevskii on the Paris peace talks on Vietnam in Pravda, January 19, 1972.

vailing antiwar sentiment in the U.S., pointed to an inevitable and total American accommodation of the D.R.V. position as only a matter of time, the U.S.S.R., at the close of January 1972, reiterated its policy on the solution of the Indochina problem thus: "A full and unconditional withdrawal of troops of the United States and its allies from Indochina, an end to acts of aggression against the DRV, an end to all military actions in Indochina, to interference in the internal affairs of South Vietnam, Laos and Cambodia, is the only realistic road to a settlement of the Indochina conflict started by the United States."[34]

Meanwhile, further Soviet-Vietnamese cooperation was to be implemented. At the conclusion of the visit of Soviet President N. V. Podgorny to Hanoi, a joint statement was released, dated October 7, 1971, which said that agreement had been reached on the drafting of the "long range development of economic cooperation and of trade, cultural, scientific, and technological and other relations between the two countries." The same statement's assertion that the Vietnamese expressed their "warmest and most heartfelt sentiments" for the Soviet Union, together with the general tones of fulsome praise in the statement for the "remarkable achievements" of the "fraternal Soviet people in every field over the past 54 years," appeared to some observers to reflect a new outreach by Hanoi to Moscow, an outreach which resulted from North Vietnam's uneasiness over the recent thaw in Sino-American relations and concern that in a new international system of multiparity the D.R.V.'s position might well become progressively less secure. Without a doubt, future Chinese assurances to Hanoi will minimize, but probably not wholly dissipate, this new concern. Because of this, because of Russia's slowly lengthening diplomatic and military shadow elsewhere in South and Southeast Asia, and because of its steady supply of aid and military hardware to Hanoi, the U.S.S.R. is today in a relatively better position to influence the D.R.V. than it was a decade ago. How Moscow influenced Hanoi, if at all, into accepting the January 27, 1973, cease-fire agreement on Vietnam, and its repetition and amplification in the June 13, 1973, agreement, still is a matter of speculation. In the course of 1973, Soviet spokesmen repeatedly affirmed their support for Hanoi's continuing struggle, although little is known about new Soviet assurances of aid to the D.R.V. in the latter's policy to establish Communist hegemony over all of Indochina.

The Soviets' post-Stalin policy of greater flexibility and emphasis on the tactical opportunities afforded by an alliance with radical nationalism and with "revolutionary democrats" who are charging their own

---

[34] Radio Moscow, Tass International Service in English, January 28, 1972, 1847 GMT, FIBS.

gradualist "road" to socialism gives no certain assurance of success, however. Among directly neighboring states in Southeast Asia, the Kremlin's leaders can find clear object lessons of that. Indeed, in this respect the Philippines and Indonesia afford useful comparisons.

## Soviet-Philippine Relations

Before the upsurge of the Hukbalahap guerrilla war in the late 1940s and early 1950s, Soviet interest in the Philippines was relatively slight. The Kremlin seemed content to let the American Communist party play the more important role in directing the early Philippine radical left and the fledgling PKP (Partido Komunista Ng Pilipinas, or Communist party of the Philippines); the latter was not formally established until August 1930.[35] At the PKP's first congress, held in early May 1931, greetings were addressed to the Soviet Communist party ("the model bolshevik section in the Communist International . . . the only Fatherland of the international proletariat and of all oppressed peoples").[36] But neither the Pan-Pacific Trade Union Secretariat nor the American Communist party, Moscow's principal conduits and lines of communication and influence with the soon to be badly riven and underground PKP, appears to have given much realistic information to the Kremlin on the Philippines' real revolutionary class potential, for each overstressed the importance of trade union radicalism, rejected the Philippine bourgeoisie as an ally, and misjudged the explosive force of such peasant insurgent movements in the thirties as that of the Sakdalistas.[37]

Neither during World War II nor during the critical early postwar years, when the revived PKP sought to involve itself in parliamentary politics, including the 1946 and 1949 Philippine presidential elections, was there much Soviet concern with, let alone a grasp of, Philippine Communist tactics. In 1950, the PKP's decision to proceed with an all-out revolutionary battle against the Philippine government at first brought little or no reaction from Moscow other than an early denial that the U.S.S.R. was in any way involved in the widening unrest in the Philippines.[38] The quarrels within the leadership of the HMB

[35] Renze L. Hoeksema, "Communism in the Philippines: An Historical and Analytical Study of Communism and the Communist Party in the Philippines and Its Relations to Communist Movements Abroad" (Ph.D. diss., Harvard University, 1956); Antonio S. Araneta, Jr., "The Communist Party of the Philippines and the Comintern, 1919 to 1930" (Ph.D. diss., Oxford University, 1966).

[36] S. Carpio, "First Congress of the Communist Party of the Philippines," *International Press Correspondence* (*Inprecor*), June 25, 1931, p. 603.

[37] McLane, *op. cit.*, pp. 113–31, 183–84.

[38] Alfredo B. Saulo, *Communism in the Philippines: An Introduction* (Manila: Ateneo Publications, 1969), pp. 44–56; McLane, *op. cit.*, pp. 424–25.

(Hukbong Mapagpalaya ng Bayan, or "People's Liberation Army," the successor to the wartime Hukbalahap) and the arrest of PKP General Secretary José Lava and other party leaders in 1950–1951, the implementation in 1952 of a new, less militant party tactic which placed more emphasis on quiet burrowing into trade unions, the seemingly successful land reform measures of the late President Ramon Magsaysay, and the formal outlawing of the PKP and HMB by the Philippine "Anti-Subversion" Act of 1957 all seemed to provide little occasion for comment in the official Soviet media beyond vague and routine encomiums of the Philippine "people's" struggle and denunciations of American imperialism. Subsequent Soviet analyses in the later fifties, however, like the one by the Soviet specialist on the Philippines, G. I. Levinson, displayed considerably more insight into the complex social structure of the Philippines and the role of American capital in the Philippine economy, and showed sympathy for the nationalist and "bourgeois democratic" currents that were stirring Philippine society.[39]

In the subsequent decade, a gradual confluence of intellectuals, radicalized students and youth (often unemployed), left-wing trade unions, and the more ideological remnants of the Huks (much, if not most, of the Huks' activity had degenerated into mere banditry and organized crime) emerged, and the Philippines rapidly appeared to be moving toward the kind of relatively broad-based, militant, anti-American nationalism that had already been viewed as a potential ally by the Soviets in other parts of the world.[40] The harried and seemingly almost leaderless PKP underground identified with, and sought to amplify, this united-front tactic, initiating or encouraging marches and demonstrations that embraced "workers, peasants, students and other youth, unemployed, business and professional groups, religious organizations neighborhood associations, nationalist groups and others."[41] Projecting a nationalist image, the PKP also encouraged and infiltrated a variety of groups, such as the "Movement for the Advancement of Nationalism" (founded in February 1967, and initially with some appeal among Philippine intellectuals), the radical Kabataang Makabayaan youth front, and the new, urban, trade union–based Socialist party, all of which articulated the PKP-approved demand for the establishment of a "national democracy" in the state.[42] The PKP de-

[39] G. I. Levinson, *Die Philippinen-Gestern und Heute* (Berlin: Akademie Verlag, 1966).

[40] Justus M. van der Kroef, "Communist Fronts in the Philippines," *Problems of Communism*, March–April 1967, pp. 65–75.

[41] Jorge Maraville, "Philippines: Results, Difficulties, Prospects," *World Marxist Review*, December 1970, p. 21.

[42] See, for example, Movement for the Advancement of Nationalism, *Basic Documents and Speeches of the Founding Congress* (Quezon City, the Philip-

fined the "national democratic" state as one in which political power "is shared by an alliance of the workers, peasants, the petty bourgeoisie and the progressive national bourgeoisie."[43] Also contributing to the upsurge of the new radical nationalism was an increasingly and widely felt public sense of "immiseration" (authoritative estimates in 1966 indicated that 3.0 million out of a total work force of 11.2 million were unemployed, and that more than 78 percent of Philippine households were earning less than 2,000 pesos, or $400, per year) and government corruption and incompetence. In addition, Huk banditry and guerrilla activity had resumed, and was centered in part around a radical "New People's Democratic Force" (Bayung Fuerza Democratica Ding Memalen) and allegedly also around a revival of the Huks erstwhile "Stalin University," a principal Communist training center in barrio Saguin in Pampanga province.[44]

All these developments elicited a significant and growing Soviet interest in the Philippines, an interest which focused on the allegedly widespread social and economic inequalities in the country and on Philippine bondage to U.S. military and financial interests.[45] Soviet writers took particular note of the rise of anti-American nationalism and of the support for it by a significant segment of the Philippine bourgeoisie. The Philippine Nacionalista party, in part because of the representation within it of restive petty bourgeois elements, particularly drew a measure of sympathetic Soviet consideration. Curiously, Soviet concern with the emergent radical Philippine left, including the PKP, remained slight however, and the principal target of Russian attention seemed to be the radicalizing changes within the national bourgeoisie, changes which Soviet commentators appeared to believe were steadily

---

pines: Phoenix Press, 1967); and José Ma. Sison, *Struggle for National Democracy* (Quezon City, the Philippines: Progressive Publications, 1967). Sison was general secretary of the Movement for the Advancement of Nationalism and played an active role in a number of Communist front groups in the 1960s before becoming identified with organized Philippine Maoism. See also "Manifesto of the Socialist Party of the Philippines" and "Program of Kabataang Makabayan," *Progressive Review* (Quezon City, the Philippines), 1965, no. 6, pp. 68–73, and 1967, no. 10, pp. 46–50, respectively; and Frances L. Starner, "Communism and the Philippine Nationalist Movement," *Solidarity* (Manila), February 1971, pp. 9–26. See *New York Times*, October 4, 1971, for a report on the "national democracy" demands of the Socialist party and the Kabataang Makabayan.

[43] Francisco Balagtas, "The Philippines at the Crossroads," *World Marxist Review*, November 1971, p. 42.

[44] Napoleon G. Rama, "Who Are Sabotaging the Land Reform Programs?" *Philippines Free Press*, July 9, 1966, p. 68; Edward R. Kiunisala, "Hearing on the Huks," *ibid.*, August 27, 1966, p. 83; Edward R. Kiunisala, "Inside Huklandia," *ibid.*, September 3, 1966, p. 6.

[45] P. H. "The Soviet Union and the Philippines: Prospects for Improved Relations," *Mizan*, May–June 1968, pp. 96–99. Data in this and the following paragraph have been drawn primarily from this informative article.

driving a wedge between Washington and Manila and which correlatively were making for closer Philippine ties with Eastern Europe and the U.S.S.R. It need not be emphasized that this new appreciation of the Philippine bourgeoisie as an ally is in rather marked contrast to the Soviets' failure to appreciate the Philippine bourgeoisie's revolutionary potential in the 1920s and 1930s.

There is little doubt that Soviet expectations of improved relations with Manila were and are quite realistic. Philippine President Marcos promised in an address to the Philippine Congress in January 1972 to establish diplomatic relations with both Peking and Moscow because "today is the era of multiple alignments," and, as already noted, on February 11, 1972, the Philippines removed all trade restrictions with Communist nations, including the People's Republic of China and the U.S.S.R. There has been speculation that as early as 1955 the Soviets may have attempted to sound out Manila on the possibility of future diplomatic ties. But it was not until the sixties that Soviet delegations, in the context of international meetings in Manila—for example, that of the U.N.'s Economic Commission for Asia and the Far East—became more or less regular visitors to the Philippines, and as late as 1965 a Tass request to station a permanent representative in Manila was turned down by the Philippine authorities.[46] Two years later, however, regular discussions began on a preliminary trade agreement between the two states. Philippine commercial delegations, the chairman of the Philippine House of Representatives' Committee on Foreign Relations, cultural groups, and individual Philippine journalists and citizens also began traveling to Moscow, and, as one Philippine press account put it, "their visits earn[ed] for them not stigma as incorrigible anti-Communists might have wished, but some kind of status among their countrymen."[47]

Although, in the dispute between the Philippines and Malaysia over which of the two has rightful control over Sabah (North Borneo), the Soviets have supported Malaysia, this has not thus far greatly affected the slowly rising warmth between Manila and Moscow, largely because the Sabah question has not aroused intense and widespread popular sentiment in the Philippines. More significant in the future pattern of Soviet-Philippine relations is likely to be the position of the still outlawed PKP and its Maoist competitor, the "Re-established" Communist Party of the Philippines, formed at the close of December 1968.[48] Prior

[46] Ibid., p. 99.
[47] Ernesto M. Macatuno, "Tying the Red Knot," Sunday Times Magazine (Manila), July 4, 1971, p. 6.
[48] For a useful analysis of the background of the rise of the Maoist wing of Philippine communism, see Eduardo Lachica, Huk: Philippine Agrarian Society in Revolt (Manila: Solidaridad Publishing House, 1971), pp. 155–89.

to this split the scattered, imprisoned PKP leadership had formally retained a loyalty toward Moscow, although in the sixties Kabataang
Makabayan radicals and Huk cadres, some of whom had covertly
traveled to China, began forming a Maoist nucleus. The Maoist group,
initially led by the former University of the Philippines professor José
Sison, and by the Kabataang Makabayan stalwart Arthur Garcia, formally aligned itself against the "counter-revolutionary revisionist" and
Moscow-oriented PKP, and created its own fighting arm, "the New
People's Army," whose guerilla attacks against government constabu-
lary and village "self-defense" units have been extensively reported and
praised in the People's Republic of China's news media.[49] Meanwhile,
retaining its older leadership (former Secretary General José Lava was
released from prison in January 1970, but is inactive), the original
PKP controls the Socialist party and much of the latter's organized
labor backing. But the PKP's attacks on the "Left adventurist" and
"cowboy ideology" of the Maoist faction have generally struck as little
of a responsive chord among the rapidly radicalizing new Philippine
intelligentsia as has the PKP's continued doctrinaire characterization
of the Communist party of the Soviet Union as "the leading detach-
ment" of the "international Communist movement."[50]

On the other hand, the Soviets do not suffer from the historical and
deep-seated anti-Chinese racial and cultural prejudices that are en-
demic in broad layers of Philippine society, nor are the Russians
charged (as the People's Republic of China is) by Philippine officials
from President Ferdinand Marcos on down with directly aiding the
guerrilla insurgents in Central Luzon.[51] In the present Philippine climate of widening public discontent with, and dissent from, the present
constitutional establishment, the two-party system and its corrupt political ancillaries, the severe social and economic inequalities and excessive dependence upon the U.S. in economic and foreign policies, the
Soviets are exceptionally well situated to enlarge their influence slowly,
steadily, and in a disciplined way, utilizing especially a new and more

[49] On the Philippine Maoist doctrinal position, see Amado Guerrero, *Philippine
Society and Revolution* (Manila: Pulang Tala Publications, 1971). On Chinese
Communist reports on the alleged exploits of "the New People's Army," see,
for example, *Peking Review*, January 14, 1972, pp. 18–19; and Radio Peking, New
China News Agency, International Service in English, December 29, 1970, 1725
GMT, FBIS.
[50] Mario Frunze, "Marxism-Leninism and 'Revolutionary' Quixotism," *Ang
Komunista* (Manila, English ed.), February 1971, p. 13; and PKP message to the
Twentieth Convention of the CPUSA, *Daily World*, February 19, 1972, p. 13.
*Ang Komunista* is the Moscow PKP's "internal bulletin."
[51] See Justus M. van der Kroef, "The Philippine Maoists," *Orbis*, Winter 1973,
pp. 892–926, on the present constitutional emergency in the Philippines following
the Maoist upsurge.

radical Philippine nationalism that finds adherents ranging from the bourgeoisie and professional groups to the industrial and rural proletariats.

## Moscow and Djakarta: Diplomacy under Stress

In noteworthy contrast, present Soviet-Indonesian relations are more than a decade and half past the point which Soviet-Philippine relations seem now to be entering. Indeed, Indonesia could well serve as a textbook illustration of the Soviets' failure to capitalize effectively on radical nationalism and on the policies of "revolutionary democrats" in the Third World. Perhaps this is not remarkable after all, because, throughout their historical relationship with Indonesia and Indonesia's Communists, Comintern and Soviet leaders have had difficulty in defining their ideological and tactical positions, particularly toward the potential or actual allies of the Indonesian Communist party (Partai Komunis Indonesia, or PKI).

For example, although the early founders of the PKI in May 1920 easily committed themselves to adhere to the Comintern, some regarded "nationalism" as "fatal" for the Indonesian proletariat and peasantry (thus disregarding Lenin's directive that under appropriate conditions Communist cooperation with revolutionary nationalist movements should be undertaken, especially in the colonial areas). Meanwhile, other PKI leaders, such as Tan Malaka, sought to explain away Comintern opposition to Pan-Islamism and Islamic nationalism (a powerful force in nascent Indonesia, especially in the native entrepreneurial groups) by asserting that, in practice, support of the Pan-Islamic movement merely meant support for the struggle for national freedom. "The virtually insoluble aspect of the problem," as one early student of the PKI has written about Comintern policies, "was the question: on which side should the national-native non-proletarian groups of the bourgeoisie, landowners and petty-capitalists be brought together."[52] Initial PKI policies, including attacks on other nationalist groups as well as on the Dutch colonial establishment in Indonesia, ambivalent and contradictory party attitudes toward the peasantry, advocacy of the creation of soviets in villages and industrial plants, rapid radicalization of the Indonesian trade union movement, and, in 1926–1927, ill-planned coup attempts in West Java and West Sumatra— all these earned the PKI sometimes severe Soviet criticism and oppro-

---

[52] J. Th. Petrus Blumberger, *De Communistische Beweging in Nederlandsch-Indië*, 2nd ed. (Haarlem: H. D. Tjeenk Willink, 1935), pp. 14, 18, 22–23.

brium; yet, at the same time, tactical directives to the party from Moscow during these years were few and vague.[53]

In the early thirties the banned and underground PKI could not, and did not, participate in the new upsurge of radical nationalist agitation, in part because of Comintern opposition to collaboration with nationalism which lasted until the seventh Comintern congress in 1935. In any case, Comintern leaders had little good to say of Sukarno, Muhammad Hatta, and other prominent nationalist spokesmen, an attitude which did not really change significantly until, at the close of World War II, Sukarno and Hatta took the lead in proclaiming the new revolutionary Indonesian Republic. Then, Indonesia came to be strongly supported by the U.S.S.R. in the United Nations. And Moscow (see A. Zhdanov's celebrated September 1947 speech, which laid down Stalin's hard-line policy of an irreconcilable conflict between the "imperialist" and "anti-imperialist" blocs) now regarded revolutionary Indonesia, one of the two non-Communist nations (the other was Finland) aligned with the U.S.S.R., as leader of the "anti-imperialist" camp. The Kremlin failed to appreciate, however, that the radical left (the Communists included) were losing the political power struggle within the fledgling Indonesian Republic. Another unplanned and soon repressed PKI coup attempt, this one in East and Central Java in September 1948, may have surprised the Soviets as much and as unpleasantly as the abortive 1926–1927 Communist coup had. In this context it is still unclear what the Kremlin had been expecting from the radicalizing effects of the February 1948 Calcutta Conference of Southeast Asian Youth and from the arrival in Indonesia, in August 1948, of a veteran PKI member and Comintern agent Musso, who after the 1926–1927 debacle had spent much of the next two decades in Moscow. Hatta's and Sukarno's swift obliteration of the 1948 coup again earned them the denunciations of Moscow. But Soviet support for the Indonesian Republic (which formally won its independence from the Dutch at the close of 1949) continued, as did Soviet hopes that a once more discredited and disorganized PKI would soon rise again and lead a new "armed struggle," this time against the now independent Indonesian Republic.[54]

In general, Stalin's policies had had little or no success in Indonesia, and certainly they had been of little benefit to the PKI. The latter,

[53] On the PKI's activity in the twenties and its relations with Moscow, see Ruth T. McVey, *The Rise of Indonesian Communism* (Ithaca, N.Y.: Cornell University Press, 1965).

[54] McLane, *op. cit.*, pp. 190–91, 287, 410–15; Henri J. H. Alers, *On een Rode of Groene Merdeka* (N.p.: Uitgeverij De Pelgrim, 1956), esp. pp. 170–97.

while not formally banned after the 1948 coup attempt, was a target of general distrust, if not hostility, among government officials and public alike, and was viewed as an alien element in the new constellation of Indonesian national politics. However, a few Indonesian politicians—among them Sukarno—were prepared to work with, and if possible to utilize, the weakened PKI for their own ends. Most grievous had been the PKI's failure in forging effective united-front tactics. This failure had stemmed in large part from doctrinaire Soviet and Comintern rigidities in colonial class analysis, and especially from Comintern hostility (which lasted until 1935) toward collaboration with the various nationalist (including Islamic) petty bourgeois, entrepreneurial, and emergent professional segments of Indonesian society. (When, in the wake of the decisions of the seventh Comintern congress in 1935, Soviet interest had been aroused in non-Communist nationalist groups in Indonesia and in Communist collaboration with them, the PKI had been driven underground and had lost all significance.)[55] As in the case of the Philippines, all this had resulted, as early as the first years of the twenties, in an over-reliance by the PKI on the growing but organizationally weak and divided trade union movement, and sometimes, too, on excessive expectations from the peasantry, neither of which, not even during the revolutionary war against the Dutch (1945–1949), had been effectively coordinated by anyone or any group in a mass base.

The dynamics of the remarkable rise of the PKI since the early fifties fall outside the scope of these pages, but it should be noted that well before Stalin's death a younger group of PKI leaders, led by the later party chairman, D. N. Aidit, had begun to initiate new tactical directives and organizational reforms which, within little more than a decade, were to help the PKI become the most influential political party on the Indonesian scene.[56] The cornerstone of these tactics was the forging of an effective "national united front," as Aidit put it in March 1954, a front which

unites Indonesian men and women of all political persuasions, religious beliefs and social status and which is clearly founded on the general desire to triumph over the economic crisis which constantly chokes Indonesia, to prevent Indonesia from being dragged into an aggressive alliance with American imperialism, to defend [Dutch-held] West New Guinea as a part of the territory of the Indonesian

[55] McLane, *op. cit.*, pp. 231–35.
[56] Donald Hindley, *The Communist Party of Indonesia, 1951–1963* (Berkeley and Los Angeles: University of California Press, 1964); and Justus M. van der Kroef, *The Communist Party of Indonesia: Its History, Program, and Tactics* (Vancouver: University of British Columbia, 1965).

Republic, to oppose Japanese rearmament, to raise high the banners of democracy and struggle for complete national independence for Indonesia.[57]

In short, cultivation of, and reliance on, an ever more radical, "nativistic" style of Indonesian nationalism by appealing to the broad segments of Indonesian society for whom the achievement of independence from Dutch rule had not brought the expected Nirvana was to be the PKI's major policy and would legitimize the party in Indonesian eyes as a genuinely Indonesian movement, not a foreign-based conspiracy.[58] In this new approach, the PKI was to become eminently successful, and not least because of the instabilities of the domestic Indonesian scene caused by serious, army-backed discontent in the outlying provinces over the rule of Djakarta. This development, in turn, caused Sukarno to rely ever more heavily on the Communists in maintaining his own position. The PKI in the latter fifties demonstrated the advantages to be got for Moscow from its more flexible post-Stalin policy of encouraging "national democratic" regimes in the Third World to seek to find their own path to socialism ("Indonesian socialism" became, in fact, an official state policy under Sukarno).

As early as April 1950, despite Soviet exhortations to the PKI to continue the "armed struggle" against the Hatta government then in power in Djakarta, the U.S.S.R. had indirectly initiated discussions with the Indonesians, looking toward formal establishment of diplomatic relations. Nothing had come of these overtures, largely because of Muslim opposition. But by 1953 the Indonesian Parliament had passed a resolution authorizing the opening of an Indonesian embassy in Moscow by the end of that year, although it was not until March 1954 that such an embassy was in fact opened. Mutual visits by Sukarno and Voroshilov to each others' countries followed in 1956–57, a $100 million Soviet credit was extended, and shortly Soviet-Indonesian trade took a quantum jump: Indonesian exports to the U.S.S.R. grew from 107,123 rupiah in 1955 to 8,619,657 rupiah in 1959, while Indonesian imports from the U.S.S.R. increased from 2,317,734 rupiah in 1955 to 15,994,940 rupiah by November 1958.[59]

[57] "Djalan Ke Demokrasi Rakjat Bagi Indonesia," in the collection of D. N. Aidit's writings, Pilihan Tulisan (Djakarta: Jajasan Pembaruan, 1959), 1: 232.
[58] On this tactic, see, for example, Justus M. van der Kroef, "Indonesian Communisms's Drive to Power," Communist Affairs, March–April 1965, pp. 3–9, idem, "Indonesian Communism's 'Revolutionary Gymnastics,'" Asian Survey, May 1965, pp. 217–32; and idem, "D. N. Aidit," in Leaders of the Communist World, ed. Rodger Swearingen (New York: Free Press, 1971), pp. 48–74.
[59] Willard A. Hanna, Bung Karno's Indonesia (New York: American Universities Field Staff, 1960), pt. 23, pp. 2–3.

Visits to Indonesia in 1959 by a Soviet friendship mission composed of members of the Supreme Soviet of the U.S.S.R. and by vessels of the Soviet Pacific fleet further strengthened Soviet-Indonesian ties and also gave a boost to the prestige of the PKI.[60] A Soviet credit of $250 million came at the time of Khrushchev's journey to Indonesia in February 1960. The following January, during the Moscow visit of the Indonesian chief of staff, General Abdul Haris Nasution, Indonesia formally secured another $400–$450 million military grant concurrently with a separate, additional $250 million in economic credits. Sukarno, meanwhile, began to endear himself to the Kremlin with his own variant of the Zhdanov "two-camp" doctrine by declaring that the socialist powers, along with the Third World nations, now comprised the "newly emerging forces" as they confronted the imperialist and unprogressive "old established forces" of the West, including, by implication, the U.S.[61]

Moscow fully backed Indonesia in its "confrontation" policy against the Dutch over Dutch-held West New Guinea (indeed, the 1961 Soviet military credits were at least partly designed to create the impression that Indonesia was acquiring additional hardware for an extended "confrontation"). Yet the Soviets could not help but have had some qualms over the increasingly destabilizing and economically disorganizing effect which anti-Dutch "confrontation" militancy eventually had on the Indonesian domestic political scene. This concern grew still further as, in the course of 1962–1963, and after the Dutch agreed to surrender West New Guinea to the Indonesians, Djakarta's "confrontation" policies—while virtually ignoring planned economic development and sound fiscal management—continued and intensified, this time being directed against the projected Malaysian Federation. Officially, Moscow sided with Djakarta in describing Malaysia as merely "a new manifestation of the old colonialist policy" of "the British imperialists," as Khrushchev put it at the close of October 1963. And, to a degree, "confrontation" was obviously in Moscow's interest. But covertly there was "waning Soviet sympathy for President Sukarno's foreign adventures which were seen as a drain on the Indonesian economy and a waste of the immense amount of aid which was being poured into the country by the U.S.S.R."[62]

Indeed, the year 1963 and the development of Djakarta's anti-

[60] See the PKI's English language monthly, *Review of Indonesia* (Djakarta), January 1960, pp. 15–18.

[61] Guy J. Pauker, "The Soviet Challenge in Indonesia," *Foreign Affairs*, July 1962, pp. 612–14. On Soviet aid to Indonesia, see also Stephen P. Gibert and Wynfred Joshua, *Guns and Rubles: Soviet Aid Diplomacy in Neutral Asia* (New York: American Asian Educational Exchange, 1970), pp. 32–39.

[62] *Pravda*, October 30, 1963; and P. H., "Soviet Relations with Malaysia and Singapore," *Mizan*, January–February 1968, pp. 29–30. For another hostile Soviet

Malaysia confrontation campaign were to be dramatic turning points in Soviet-Indonesian relations. While Djakarta's attitude toward Moscow formally remained correct, the PKI and a whole constellation of other domestic political factors in Indonesia were rapidly beginning to drive the Sukarno regime into ever-closer partnership with the People's Republic of China.[63]

The PKI, meanwhile, though tactically siding with Peking's militant line, especially in the Third World, formally preferred to remain "independent" in the developing Sino-Soviet split. Thus, Aidit and his associates urged that the split be resolved "in a family spirit," attacked Yugoslav revisionism, but refused to join in criticism of Albania at the Twenty-second Congress of the Communist Party of the Soviet Union in 1961 or in condemning Stalin beyond the Soviet leaders' own criticism of him "in connection with the cult of the individual."[64] Although Aidit continued to find praise for the U.S.S.R. and expressed hope (as on the occasion of Lenin's ninety-fourth birthday celebration in Djakarta in April 1964) for the long life of Soviet-Indonesian friendship, he also declined to send a delegation to the avowedly anti-Peking, International Conference of Communist and Workers' Parties in Moscow in March 1965, on the grounds that not all such parties in the world had been invited. By this time, the PKI seemed more and more to be amplifying Peking's line of revolutionary militancy in the "triple A" region (that is, Asia, Africa, and Latin America), and domestically, and with the covert assistance of Sukarno, it appeared to be launched on an accelerated drive to power.[65]

The culmination of this drive was the Peking-assisted, abortive coup attempt of September 30, 1965, by important PKI leaders, party front groups, and by radical and dissident army and airforce personnel.[66]

view of the creation of Malaysia, see V. S. Rudnev, *Malaiia, 1945–1963* (Moscow, 1963), pp. 104–5, cited in Peter Boyce, *Malaysia and Singapore in International Diplomacy: Documents and Commentaries* (Sydney: Sydney University Press, 1968), p. 251.

[63] I have described the details of this development in "The Sino-Indonesian Partnership," *Orbis*, Summer 1964, pp. 332–56.

[64] *Strengthen National Unity and Communist Unity: Documents of the Third Plenum of the Central Committee of the Communist Party of Indonesia, Djakarta, end December 1961* (Djakarta: Jajasan Pembaruan, 1962), pp. 75–76, 81.

[65] In addition to the sources cited in note 58, see also Justus M. van der Kroef, "The Wages of Ambiguity: The 1965 Coup in Indonesia, Its Origins and Meaning," *Studies on the Soviet Union*, 1972 (special issue on "The Anatomy of Communist Take-overs").

[66] The literature on the 1965 coup is large and growing. For critical summaries, see, for example, Jerome R. Bass, "The PKI and the Attempted Coup," *Journal of Southeast Asian Studies*, March 1970, pp. 96–105; Donald E. Weatherbee, "Interpretations of Gestapu: The 1965 Indonesian Coup," *World Affairs*, March 1970, pp. 305–17; and Justus M. van der Kroef, "Interpretations of the 1965 Indonesian Coup: A Review of the Literature," *Pacific Affairs*, Winter 1970–1971, pp. 557–77.

102    JUSTUS M. VAN DER KROEF

Moscow almost certainly disapproved of the coup attempt, but very shortly, in the bloody aftermath of the coup's failure and the anti-Communist pogrom, the U.S.S.R. began sharply attacking Indonesian "reactionaries" in their campaign against the PKI.[67] Through the proxy of the publications of rival Moscow- and Peking-orientated factions of underground or exiled PKI cadres, both China and the U.S.S.R. voiced their official views on the origins and effects of the new debacle that had now overtaken Indonesian communism, as well as alleged "self-criticisms" of past PKI policies by the respective faction spokesmen.[68] From the Soviet point of view the PKI in the last few years before the coup had been guilty of a "revisionist leftist" policy, "petty bourgeois revolutionism" and "adventurism," of inadequate organization, poor planning, and undue reliance on Sukarno's power and protection.[69] Sukarno's eventual fall from power was the occasion for sharp, retrospective Soviet criticism of the "dangerous adventures" of his policies, such as Indonesia's withdrawal from the United Nations in January 1965 ("many countries, including the U.S.S.R., believe that with all its failings the U.N. is a real international institution for the struggle against imperialism," one Soviet critique put it), and, by the middle of 1966, Radio Moscow greeted with unequivocal approval Indonesia's abandonment of her "confrontation" policy against Malaysia.[70]

Perhaps the Kremlin felt wry satisfaction over the collapse of the Sukarno regime. Even so, and not least because of the debacle which once more had overtaken the PKI (by March 1966 the party had once again been formally banned, and all through the subsequent years arrests of suspected PKI leaders, members, sympathizers, or other alleged coup participants continued), the advent of the militantly anti-Communist regime of President Suharto and its increasing reliance on Western development capital and investment could be interpreted only

[67] See, for example, *Pravda*, October 10 and 26, 1965, and September 29, 1966. See also "The U.S.S.R. and Indonesia," *Mizan*, January–February 1966, pp. 14–22.
[68] Justus M. van der Kroef, "Indonesia's Gestapu: The View from Moscow and Peking," *Australian Journal of Politics and History*, August 1968, pp. 163–76; and Rex Mortimer, "Indonesia: Émigré Post-Mortems on the PKI," *Australian Outlook*, December 1968, pp. 347–59.
[69] See the publication by the underground, pro-Moscow PKI faction, *To Brothers at Home and Comrades abroad Fighting against Imperialism for Independence, Peace, Democracy, and Socialism: For a Sound Indonesian Revolution* (Colombo Ceylon: Tribune Publication, 1967). An excerpt appears in the theoretical journal of the American Communist party under the title "Lessons from the Setback in Indonesia," *Political Affairs* (New York), March 1968, pp. 49–61. See also *Information Bulletin* (Prague), no. 18 (1967), pp. 40–65.
[70] V. Verbenko in *Komsomol'skaia Pravda*, March 19, 1967, cited in "Soviet Relations with Malaysia and Singapore," *Mizan*, January–February 1968, pp. 30–31). For Soviet satisfaction over the end of Indonesia's anti-Malaysia "confrontation," see the same *Mizan* article.

as the culmination of one of the most serious diplomatic defeats sustained by the U.S.S.R. in the post-Stalin era. For, despite the huge Soviet economic and military credits granted between 1956 and 1961, not only had the "revolutionary democratic" Sukarno regime increasingly allied itself with the People's Republic of China, but the collapse of that regime after the 1965 coup had thrust Soviet-Indonesian relations back to the worst moments of the era of coldness and suspicion following the 1948 abortive Communist coup attempt. Ironically, Soviet policy itself—specifically economic, military, and international political aid and encouragement to the Sukarno regime—had initially contributed much to the unpredictable independence in foreign policy and the anti-Western truculence of that regime. Once underway, the latter tendencies, because of domestic political pressures, led to the regime's accelerated radicalization (1963–1965), which the Kremlin was clearly unable to moderate as Sukarno and the PKI, deftly taking up their options, moved more and more into Peking's orbit.

Since the 1965 coup, Soviet-Indonesian relations have gradually improved somewhat, though serious strains persist. Diplomatic ties have not been suspended however, as in the case of Djakarta's relations with Peking in October 1967. As early as November 1966, the Soviets, evidently prepared to make the best of a bad job, agreed to a financial protocol which fixed Indonesia's total indebtedness to the U.S.S.R. at $804 million (including some $523 million in military debts) and set the final date of repayment as July, 1, 1981.[71] According to this agreement, some outstanding Soviet aid projects would be canceled; others, such as the oceanographic facility in Ambon, East Indonesia, would be completed. Complications over the debt repayment schedule; a new barrage of anti-Indonesian Soviet criticism in the course of 1968, which stemmed in part from the Suharto government's intensified drive against underground PKI insurgents; the execution of prominent captured PKI leaders; a student attack on the Soviet embassy in Djakarta on August 24, 1968, in the wake of the Soviets' invasion of Czechoslovakia; and periodic charges by the Indonesian press and political figures alleging Soviet spying in Indonesia—all these formed obstacles to better relations between the two nations.

Some of these obstacles have persisted. Throughout 1971, for example, the correspondents of Tass and *Pravda* in Indonesia, as well as Soviet embassy officials in Indonesia, were accused by several Indo-

[71] On postcoup Soviet-Indonesian relations, see Rodolfo Severino, "Soviet Policy toward the New Order in Indonesia," *Pacific Community*, Autumn 1971, pp. 59–75; Justus M. van der Kroef, "Soviet-Indonesian Relations and the PKI," *ibid.*, Autumn 1970, pp. 311–25; and Robert C. Horn, "Soviet-Indonesian Relations since 1965," *Survey*, Winter 1971, pp. 216–32.

nesian newspapers, mainly those with close army connections, of engaging in espionage. Meanwhile, allegedly anti-Indonesian broadcasts over Radio Moscow, particularly some by a group of Moscow-domiciled Indonesian students opposed to the Suharto regime, further aroused Indonesian ire.[72] At about the same time, circulation in Indonesia of allegedly Soviet leaflets and of a study of Islam by a Soviet diplomat, all of which were said to contain material defamatory and humiliating to Islam, led to a sharp outcry among powerful Indonesian Muslim groups.[73]

On the other hand, Soviet readiness in early 1971 to increase Indonesian rubber purchases and to increase trade generally, Russian offers to sell on "easy terms" spare parts for Indonesian naval vessels and air force planes, Soviet promises of assistance in the completion of the Tjilegon steel project and the Tjilatjap sulphur-phosphate plant, and rumors of new Soviet aid counteracted these adverse developments somewhat. Soviet media today, however, continue to be skeptical and sometimes openly hostile to Indonesian policies, and they particularly excoriate the huge influx of Western development and investment capital, expressing doubt about Indonesia's 1971 general elections, warning that "international imperialism helped by domestic Indonesian reactionaries is doing all to complicate "Soviet-Indonesian relations," and urging Djakarta to return to its erstwhile "nonaligned" international position.[74] Realizing only too well that it cannot afford to have its left flank turned by Peking because of a too obvious desire for a rapprochement with the Suharto government, Moscow (like Peking) also continues to give shelter to a number of anti-Suharto Indonesian radicals, and to support its own faction of underground and exiled PKI cadres (reportedly headquartered in Ceylon). In the pages of the major world media of Moscow-oriented Communist parties, spokesmen for this faction declare that, though Indonesia presently is in the grip

[72] *Antara Daily News Bulletin,* March 25 and 27, 1971; *Straits Times,* October 14, 1971; *Mirror* (Singapore), July 5, 1971; *Far Eastern Economic Review,* July 19, 1971, p. 7, and October 16, 1971, p. 4; and *Duta Masjarakat* (Djakarta), June 14, 1971.
[73] *Antara Daily News Bulletin,* March 2, October 27, and November 2, 1971.
[74] See, for example, M. Muravlev in *Izvestiia,* February 8, 1970; M. Domogatskikh in *Pravda,* December 19, 1970; *Izvestiia,* December 9, 1971 (unsigned article on alleged Indonesian public alarm over the Suharto government's "pro-Western" policies); B. Vetin, "Indonesia before the Election," *New Times,* May 1971, pp. 20–21; V. Viktorov, "Indonesia: Monopolies on the Offensive," *International Affairs* (Moscow), July 1969, pp. 106–7; *idem,* "Indonesia's Hour of Trial," *ibid.,* December 1968, pp. 24–47. On the "reactionary" character of the Suharto government today, see also A. A. Guber *et al., Natsional'no-osvoboditel'noe dvizhenie v Indonezii* (Moscow: Nauka, 1970).

of an "ultra-right" and "military-fascist" dictatorship, "conditions are maturing" for a resurgence of the Communist party.[75]

The latter claim is speculative, but there is no denying the discontent, particularly in intellectual and student circles in Indonesia, with the Suharto regime's often high-handed and authoritarian policies, ranging from allegedy undue pressure and manipulation by the government in winning the July 1971 general elections to excessive obesiance to Washington in foreign policy (even well-known anti-Sukarno journalist supporters of Suharto have begun to characterize Indonesia as "rather like a lackey or a client state of the U.S.").[76] In the context of the new realignments currently taking place among the U.S., the U.S.S.R., the People's Republic of China, and other powers, the inflexible, doctrinaire anticommunism, particularly as exhibited by prominent Indonesian military commanders in charge of domestic security and by Suharto's military "assistants," is viewed by many Indonesians as unrealistic.[77]

### Soviet Collective Security Proposals

It is here, precisely against a background of changing collective security patterns in the area, that new tactical diplomatic opportunities are being opened to Moscow in its search for greater influence in Southeast Asia. Once coolly regarded Soviet initiatives are now being given a second and closer look. An example is the history of the remark made by Soviet Communist party Chairman Leonid Brezhnev in the course of his address to the International Conference of Communist and Workers' Parties in Moscow on June 7, 1969. Brezhnev on that occasion observed that "the course of events is also bringing to the fore the need to create a collective security system in Asia." (There had been earlier speculation in the Soviet press about the need for such a system. And, while there had been no comparable official Soviet ex-

---

[75] Thomas Sinuraja, "On the Situation in the Communist Movement of Indonesia," World Marxist Review, September 1969, p. 32. See also "Urgent tasks of the Communist Movement in Indonesia," Information Bulletin (Prague), 1969, no. 7, pp. 23–42.

[76] Rosihan Anwar in Pedoman (Djakarta), cited in Far Eastern Economic Review, February 19, 1972, p. 23. On the Suharto era generally, see Justus M. van der Kroef, Indonesia since Sukarno (Singapore: Asia Pacific Press, 1971).

[77] Early in March 1972 the deputy chief of the Indonesian government's "Command for the Restoration of Security and Order" (Kopkamtib), General Sumitro, declared that "Communist dangers" were now coming to Indonesia, not only from Moscow and Peking, but also from the Middle East and certain Western nations, including the U.S. He deplored the trend toward radicalism in Western nations, implying that Indonesian youth were being affected by this trend. Antara Daily News Bulletin, March 2, 1972.

pression of concern for Asia's "collective security" needs in the preceding years, one could argue that, for example, Soviet diplomatic concerns for the region, such as the 1966 conference in Tashkent on the Indo-Pakistani problem and interest in the formation of the Asian Development Bank, presaged new diplomatic initiatives as much as did the Soviets' willingness to seek or maintain diplomatic relations with such states as Malaysia and Indonesia, which were known for their strong domestic anti-Communist policies.) Almost immediately denounced by Peking, but further amplified by Soviet spokesmen at the United Nations in the following weeks and in contacts with Asian capitals, the Brezhnev suggestion for some sort of new collective security arrangement in Asia became the subject of considerable speculation and discussion, and particularly so in light of President Richard Nixon's July 1969 "Guam doctrine," which implied a diminution in direct American involvement in future Asian conflicts.[78] What Brezhnev had actually intended became further clouded with seemingly contradictory reports that, initially, Moscow had not demanded abrogation of bilateral defense agreements between Asian countries (such as Thailand, the Philippines, and Japan) and the U.S., but that later the Soviets did envisage the withdrawal of American forces from Asia as a precondition of any new Soviet-approved collective security system.[79]

While Djakarta was at first said to agree with the Soviet proposal in principle and to be studying it, and while, indeed, in October 1969 Moscow was reported assiduously to be "courting" Indonesia to support it, by March 1970, Indonesian Foreign Minister Adam Malik, during a brief stopover in Singapore after five days of talks in Moscow, said flatly that "all Asian countries, including Indonesia, have rejected the Soviet Union's proposals for a regional security arrangement."[80] Continuing, Malik was almost scornful. Moscow really did not have any specific ideas on the matter at all, he said. "All the Russians want to do is to sell the idea, and if given backing of Asian countries they will think out something." Elsewhere in Asia, reaction, at least on the surface, initially appeared to be similarly unresponsive.[81]

[78] See, for example, Peter Howard, "A System of Collective Security," *Mizan*, July–August 1969, pp. 199–204; and Hemen Ray, "Soviet Diplomacy in Asia," *Problems of Communism*, March–April 1970, pp. 46–49. For the Chinese Communist reaction, see especially Radio Peking, New China News Agency, International Service in English, August 15, 1969, 0205 GMT, FBIS. See also the *Malay Mail* (Kuala Lumpur), October 11, 1969.

[79] See, for example, Marian P. Kirsch, "Soviet Security Objectives in Asia," *International Organization*, Summer 1970, p. 467; and *Straits Times* (Kuala Lumpur and Singapore), July 20, 1970.

[80] *Djakarta Times*, October 16 and 22, 1969; *Antara Daily News Bulletin*, October 15, 1969; *Sunday Times* (Singapore and Kuala Lumpur), March 8, 1970.

[81] See, for example, Harald Munthe-Kaas, "Back to the Drawing Board," *Far Eastern Economic Review*, October 9, 1969, p. 84.

Yet, within months of Malik's nearly contemptuous remarks in Singapore, the Brezhnev collective security remark had begun to acquire a new measure of significance, if only as a warning that, whatever the nature of the newly developing Sino-American rapprochement and of the ultimate settlement of the Vietnam question, Moscow meant to have a say in whatever international order and security system came into being in Southeast Asia in the future. The concurrently emergent pattern of Soviet and East European diplomatic and commercial interests in Malaysia and the Philippines re-enforced this Soviet policy. The new framework that was developed to accomodate simultaneously rising Soviet involvement, American disengagement, and the persistent and historical Chinese interest in Southeast Asia appeared essentially to be "neutralization." Such "neutralization" had been speculated upon for many years, and one of its preconditions—the striking of a new balance of forces in the region among the principal powers concerned, including the U.S., the U.S.S.R., and the People's Republic of China—now seemed to be inching toward reality.[82]

### Southeast Asia and "Neutralization"

Malaysia took the lead in propagating the "neutralization" idea. In January 1968 a veteran Malaysian politician and frequent cabinet minister, Tun Ismail bin Dato Abdul Rahman (generally known as a hard-line anti-Communist) suggested in the Malaysian Parliament a comprehensive plan for the neutralization of Southeast Asia, including guarantees by the big powers (among them was named the People's Republic of China) and a "nonaggression treaty" between the Southeast Asian signatory member states. Because of Tun Ismail's eminence his suggestion attracted considerable attention and, significantly, won praise among opposition parties in Malaysia.[83] In October 1969, in the wake of Soviet diplomatic activity on behalf of the Brezhnev proposal, Malaysian Deputy Premier Tun Abdul Razak declared that Southeast Asia required big power assistance, including specifically that of the U.S.S.R., in order to guarantee the region's future security. And, by the middle of April 1970, the Malaysian delegate to a conference of "nonaligned nations" being held in Dar es Salaam publicly expressed the hope that the conference would endorse a neutralization of Southeast Asia under the guarantee of the U.S.S.R., the U.S., and the People's Republic of China.[84]

[82] See, for example, U.S., Congress, Senate, *Neutralization in Southeast Asia: Problems and Prospects*, prepared for the Committee on Foreign Relations (Washington, D.C.: Government Printing Office, 1966).
[83] *Straits Times*, June 12, 1968; and *Daily Express* (Kota Kinabalu, Sabah), June 12, 1968 (editorial, "Guaranteeing Neutrality and Defense").
[84] *Sarawak Tribune* (Kuching), October 13, 1969; and *Eastern Sun* (Kuala Lumpur), April 18, 1970.

Meanwhile, as Indonesian Foreign Minister Malik began calling for the neutralization of "regions around the Indian Ocean," the then Malaysian premier, Tengku Abdul Rahman, was reported to have given "tacit approval" to Russian naval patrols in the Indian Ocean, provided "peace and security" would not be disturbed.[85] At the Commonwealth Heads of Government Conference in Singapore on January 15, 1971, Razak (now premier) made a strong plea for a neutralization of Southeast Asia guaranteed by the U.S., the U.S.S.R., and the People's Republic of China, and particularly stressed the necessity of China's involvement in the plan. Throughout the rest of the year Razak and other Malaysian spokesmen were to repeat this theme.[86] Something of a culmination of this development came at the November 26–27, 1971, Kuala Lumpur meeting of the foreign ministers of the Association of Southeast Asia Nations (ASEAN), which includes Malaysia, Singapore, the Philippines, Thailand, and Indonesia. At this meeting the ASEAN members declared Southeast Asia to be a "zone of peace, freedom, and neutrality" and pledged their mutual efforts to secure respect and recognition for this principle.[87]

Before considering the Soviet reaction to this neutralization concept, it should be noted that the seeming unanimity of the signatories of the Kuala Lumpur declaration is, in some ways, quite misleading, and that, on the whole, the declaration is perhaps best viewed as an expression of a policy hope rather than as a reality. Thailand, where only a little more than a week before the Kuala Lumpur conference a bloodless coup tightened the control of the military, is confronted with a widening Peking- and Hanoi-backed Communist insurgency, so that by the middle of June 1971 Thai Premier Thanom Kittikachorn told the visiting Razak in Bangkok that Thailand could not be neutral, because "Communist China is carrying out a war of insurgency against our country."[88] The Thais are also well aware that the 40,000-man American military presence in Thailand and the use of Thai air bases for strikes in Indochina render "neutralization" illusory. Former Thai Foreign Minister Thanat Khoman, identified with a more accommodating policy toward both Moscow and Peking, has pointed out that neutralization means the withdrawal of all foreign troops—presumably U.S. forces, but also Chinese units now in Burma and Laos—and he has also said that neutralization would not affect Thailand's or Malay-

---

[85] *Bangkok Post,* March 22, 1970; and *Antara Daily News Bulletin,* March 12, 1970.

[86] *Malaysian Digest* (Kuala Lumpur), January 18, May 15, and October 15, 1971.

[87] The full text of the Kuala Lumpur declaration appears in *International Legal Materials,* January 1972, pp. 183–84.

[88] *Bangkok Post,* June 17, 1971.

sia's right to stamp out the Communist insurgents along their borders.[89] Would Moscow or Peking be agreeable to a strenuous anti-
insurgent policy?

In the Philippines, too, "neutralization" has brought second thoughts.
Indeed, hours after the Kuala Lumpur declaration Philippine President
Ferdinand Marcos said that the declaration did not in fact commit the
ASEAN nations involved, and that the declaration should be considered
for approval at a forthcoming ASEAN summit meeting of heads of
state. Reportedly, a Philippine spokesman warned at the Kuala Lumpur meeting that "neutralization" would not mean abandonment of the
Philippine claim to Malaysian Sabah.[90] The Philippine position points
up other patterns of ethnic and boundary disputes among the Southeast Asian states (such as the Thai-Cambodian border question) which
are bound to affect the neutralization concept.

Perhaps Indonesia's position has aroused the greatest controversy,
particularly as regards the U.S.S.R. On the one hand, President
Suharto has often stressed that his nation would not tie itself to any
power bloc and has warned of the possibly adverse effects of a big
power presence in Southeast Asia—views interpreted as leaning toward
a neutralization idea.[91] On the other hand, Foreign Minister Adam
Malik has said that any neutralization is dependent upon the restoration of good relations between Peking and Djakarta.[92] The continuing
strain in Sino-Indonesian relations has already been noted, and, in the
aftermath of Nixon's visit to China, Indonesia appeared to be playing
off this visit—and what it might also portend for Indonesia—against the
Soviets. At the close of Nixon's visit to China, Malik declared that the
Sino-American Shanghai communiqué of February 27, 1972, implied
support for the Kuala Lumpur declaration, since both the U.S. and the
People's Republic of China now appeared to endorse the principle of
noninterference in the internal affairs of other nations. Malik added,
however, that this left only the position of the U.S.S.R. still "undefined"—a statement which prompted an expression of surprise and a
visit to Malik from the Soviet ambassador in Djakarta. Reacting publicly to Ambassador Mikhail Volkov's visit, Malik thereupon declared
that he, Malik, was only observing "things as they are," and thus presumably reiterated the view that, in his opinion, the U.S.S.R. had not
yet made its position known on the neutralization concepts.[93]

[89] Bernama dispatch, Kuala Lumpur, Malaysia, November 28, 1971; and *Far
Eastern Economic Review*, January 29, 1972, p. 4.
[90] *Indonesian Observer* (Djakarta), November 30, 1971.
[91] *Suara Karya* (Djakarta), January 17, 1972; *and Times of India*, February 15,
1972.
[92] *Straits Times*, December 23, 1971.
[93] *Antara Daily News Bulletin*, March 13, 1972.

More appeared to be involved in this *contretemps* than met the eye, however, for, two days before his exchange with Volkov, Malik had had occasion to strain Soviet-Indonesian relations over another matter, the question of passage through the Straits of Malacca. Indonesia, Malaysia, and Singapore, over the objections of the U.S.S.R., Japan, Britain, and the U.S., agreed on November 16, 1971, not to regard these Straits as open international waters, though they recognized their use for international shipping in accordance with the concept of innocent passage. According to Malik, foreign vessels intending to use the Straits would first have to inform the Indonesian, Malaysian, and Singapore governments, and, in any case, some restrictions on the tonnage of vessels passing through would likely be necessary. The need to dredge the Straits, the problem of pollution by the big oil tankers, and the inherent legitimacy of the principle of a twelve-mile limit for their territorial waters claimed by Indonesia and Malaysia have further obscured the controversy. To some observers it appears that Indonesia was ready to use the issue of passage through the Straits of Malacca as a pressure device, particularly against the Soviets and the Japanese, in winning various concessions, possibly including unequivocal commitments by Moscow and Tokyo to a neutralization arrangement.[94]

Even Malaysia, the champion of neutralization, can be faulted for policy inconsistencies. For example, both Malaysia and Singapore, in the face of diminished British military commitments to their defense and tendencies toward a similar disengagement by Australia and New Zealand, labored mightily in the closing years of the sixties to retain some measure of military protection from London, Canberra, and Wellington.[95] Early in November 1971 a new five-power defense arrangement, involving Australia, Britain, Malaysia, New Zealand, and Singapore, went into effect. Under its provisions immediate mutual consultations would take place in order to decide proper countermeasures in the event one of the signatories was attacked. Regular discussions at the senior official level, a five-power naval advisory group, a joint air defense council, and an integrated air defense system for Malaysia and Singapore also were envisaged by the agreement.[96] The actual, day-to-

---

[94] *Ibid.* See also *ibid.*, November 19, 1971, and March 11, 1972; and *New York Times*, March 13, 1972. On March 20, 1972, Malik assured the alarmed Russians, who had sent a roving ambassador, L. I. Mendelvitch, to Djakarta to discuss the matter, that Indonesia would not use force in seeking implementation of its position on passage through the Straits of Malacca. Malik expressed the hope that the Soviets would voluntarily agree.

[95] See, for example, Justus M. van der Kroef, "Australia's New Search for Collective Security," *Orbis*, Summer 1969, pp. 526–55; and *idem*, "The Gorton Manner: Australia, Southeast Asia, and the U.S.," *Pacific Affairs*, Fall 1969, pp. 311–33.

[96] *Sarawak Tribune*, November 2, 1971.

day commitment in military hardware by non-Asian members under this arrangement was minimal, to be sure. But the five-power defense pact was both psychologically and politically highly significant for Malaysia, Singapore, and indeed for Southeast Asia, and for that reason it could hardly be reconciled with the "neutralization" idea.

Despite all these paradoxes and inconsistencies, however, the Kuala Lumpur declaration was a clear indication that the winds of change are blowing in Southeast Asia. The Communist nations, including the U.S.S.R., are well aware of that. "The neutralization plan is merely the Asian urge to stop being pawns," one perceptive observer has written, and it is evident that warnings by SEATO spokesmen regarding the new threat to Southeast Asia posed by Moscow's attempt to widen its influence in the region no longer carry decisive weight.[97] Of necessity, however, the Communist position generally has been equivocal with respect to the neutralization idea. Hanoi's announced opinion, for example, is that ASEAN is a product of U.S. imperialism, but that, even so, the Kuala Lumpur declaration reflects changes in Southeast Asia and in the world that are "favorable to the revolutionary and progressive forces" and that it is thus a setback to "counter-revolutionary" and "imperialist" states.[98]

Similarly guarded optimism has been evident in the Soviets' reaction. In 1969 the Soviet press said that "Malaysia has demonstrated that it strives for peace" and noted that "the progressive Malaysian public" had considerable interest in the idea of an Asian collective security system (presumably a reference to the recent Brezhnev proposal).[99] In an initial report on the Kuala Lumpur declaration, one Soviet commentator in *Pravda* stressed the inconsistencies in the policies of the signatory states (for example, Thailand's and the Philippine's participation in SEATO, and Malaysia's and Singapore's membership in a five-power defense agreement with Britain, Australia, and New Zealand). While admitting that the neutralization proposal was certainly "significant," the same commentator added that clearing "the political atmosphere" in Southeast Asia, now "poisoned by U.S. aggression in Indo-China," by Peking's "aspirations to hegemony," and by the presence of foreign military bases, would be a necessary first step.[100]

Later Soviet writing has generally echoed these themes. In an extended analysis of the possibilities of neutralization in the region, another prominent Soviet political writer on Southeast Asian affairs,

---

[97] T. J. S. George, "The Neutralization Stakes," *Far Eastern Economic Review*, December 11, 1971, p. 18; and *New York Times*, September 8, 1969.

[98] *Nhan Dan* (Hanoi), December 1, 1971.

[99] Y. Popov in *Izvestiia*, August 31, 1969.

[100] B. Vetin in *Pravda*, December 29, 1971.

V. Kudriavtsev, began by noting the effect on the Southeast Asian states of the allegedly weakening position of the U.S. at a time when concern over the "expansion" of Chinese influence is also rising. The old policy of maneuvering among conflicting great power ambitions, Kudriavtsev argued, no longer satisfied the Southeast Asian governments, and hence they desired neutralization. He considered this neutralization tendency worthy of "attention and interest" because it revealed the shattering of the dream that "imperialist powers" can be relied upon to provide protection and guarantee independence. Kudriavtsev too, however, noted the internal inconsistencies in the foreign and defense policies of the Southeast Asian nations, which "do not accord with their professed wish for neutralization." But he also conceded that the demand for neutralization could assist in ending "American aggression" in the Southeast Asian area, for the reason that, among the Southeast Asian nations that desired neutrality, some were obviously getting American military help, and it should be clear to them, Kudriavtsev implied, that the latter must end if the former is to succeed. Only with the removal of these policy paradoxes could conditions within the Southeast Asian nations become favorable "to the creation of a system of collective security in Asia." In other words, the implementation of a Brezhnev-endorsed new security system in Asia now seemed, in effect, to have been made contingent by the Soviets upon the withdrawal of American and other non-Soviet-approved military forces.[101]

From Kudriavtsev's analysis it has become evident that Moscow is intent upon using "neutralization" as a means of diminishing, preferably to the vanishing point, any outside military presence, and Moscow is likely to continue to hold off a complete endorsement of the neutralization idea until it has become satisfied that such foreign military influence in the region has, in fact, sufficiently subsided. The U.S.S.R. will therefore continue to be critical of SEATO. For example, in February 1972, naval maneuvers in the South China Sea, involving units of the U.S., Britain, Australia, New Zealand, Thailand, and the Philippines, elicited sharp Russian comment about the "provocations and acts of aggression" by "America's ruling quarters."[102] But, in respect of the increased interest among the Southeast Asian states in mutual and regional cooperation, Soviet attitudes are beginning to soften somewhat, and are likely to become still more sympathetic. For example, initial Soviet hostility to ASEAN was quite pronounced, and even now

[101] *Izvestiia,* January 7, 1972.
[102] Commentary of Captain Vasiliy Pustov, Radio Moscow in English to South Asia, February 16, 1972, 1500 GMT, FBIS.

serious reservations remain.[103] But Moscow has not been insensitive to trends among ASEAN leaders to make their organization more truly neutral, independent, and free from cold war influences. Malaysian Premier Razak has emphasized that the maturing sense of regional solidarity of Southeast Asia "is not directed against any state outside the region, nor does it adversely affect their interests." Indonesian President Suharto said in Manila in February 1972 that he envisaged ASEAN as the nucleus of a still wider regional organization which could include states with a Communist form of government.[104] ASEAN, Suharto said, should reflect the determination of Southeast Asian nations not to let their "future be determined by the interests or whims of outside powers."

But Djakarta's 1971 agreement to provide training to military personnel of the Lon Nol government in Cambodia, and Djakarta's own acquisition of U.S. and Australian military aid and training services, are likely to speak louder in the Kremlin than Suharto's assurances. As early as November 1970, Soviet media were skeptical that Djakarta's repeatedly announced intention not to join in any military alliances really meant very much in the light of the simultaneous anti-Communist tendencies in Indonesia's foreign policies.[105] Nor was there Soviet enthusiasm for Marcos and Suharto's call at the close of the latter's visit to Manila in mid-February 1972 for Asian nations to begin conducting unspecified "joint maneuvers" in order to raise the "resistance" powers of each state in the region.[106] Yet today the ASEAN states themselves would sharply oppose the characterization, which the U.S.S.R. was wont to make earlier, that their regional organization is essentially an American "imperialist" tool. The real question for the future is the Soviets' patience, and their skill in assisting in the accentuation of existing neutralization dynamics within ASEAN and other Southeast Asian nations. Such skills will be measured to a considerable degree in the Soviets not disparaging or undercutting the future thrust

[103] "Regional Cooperation in Southeast Asia: Soviet Misgivings," *Mizan*, November–December 1967, pp. 252–57.
[104] Address of Tun Abdul Razak, Bonn, April 21, 1971, in *Asia Pacific Record*, May 1971, p. 24; Suharto's speech in *Asian Student*, February 26, 1972.
[105] V. Matveev in *Izvestiia*, November 19, 1970. On Indonesian readiness to undertake military "cooperation" (for example, with India and Malaysia) without committing itself to any military "pact," see also Suharto's remarks in *Antara Daily News Bulletin*, February 14, 1972.
[106] *Nusantara* (Djakarta), February 17, 1972. By the same token, anti-Soviet suspicion is frequently formed by segments of the Indonesian press. The Djakarta weekly *Chas*, which has close ties to the Indonesian military, reported at the close of January 1972 that the Soviets were planning to construct a military base in Portuguese Timor and that the Russians in Djakarta were quietly collecting data about the Indonesian seas. *Berita Buana* (Djakarta), February 1, 1972;

toward regional cooperation in Southeast Asia. There are indications that the Soviets recognize this. On March 21, 1972, CPSU General Secretary Leonid Brezhnev reiterated the desirability of a new collective security system for Asia, a system based not only on renunciation of force, mutual respect for boundaries, and noninterference in one another's domestic affairs, but also on the "extensive development of economic and other cooperation" on the basis of equality and mutual interest. The U.S.S.R. would fully support such a system, Brezhnev said.

### New Soviet Diplomatic Flexibility

Thus it is evident that, while the time is ripe for a new Soviet diplomatic offensive in Southeast Asia, Soviet tactics must remain highly flexible. Such tactics will likely continue to range from massive, direct military assistance for the D.R.V. to careful preservation and—in the context of Chinese political and guerilla pressures, uncertainties over further American commitments, and Japan's economic expansionism—a possible strengthening of fragile diplomatic ties with such states as Indonesia and Thailand. In some parts of the region these ties may well have to be snapped altogther (for example, in Phnom Penh, Cambodia) if Soviet policy positions with respect to such critical and contentious questions as support of "national liberation" movements are to retain any credibility in the face of persistent Chinese Communist criticism. At the Communist-inspired "World Assembly for Peace and Independence of Indochina," held in Paris in February 1972, the Soviets were ultimately compelled by Vietnamese and Laotian Communist delegates to allow a final conference resolution which recognized the Peking-based "Government of National Union of Cambodia" as "the only legal government" that genuinely represented the Cambodian people.[107] The Russians had pressured other delegations to omit any reference to Sihanouk's government-in-exile but had failed. Sihanouk's delegate at the conference complained that he could not understand why certain states had not given de jure recognition to his government—a slap at Moscow. The anomaly of the Soviets' position in Phnom Penh has steadily grown, but with a return of Sihanouk to the Cambodian capital may well disappear again.

Elsewhere, however (for example, in the Philippines), in the near future, brand-new diplomatic ties will have to be made for the first time in history. And, in still other areas of the region (for example, in Burma), existing relations will have to be reviewed in light of new diplomatic and strategic opportunities recently opened in the imme-

---

*Indonesian Current Affairs Translation Service* (Djakarta), February 1972, pp. 95, 103.

[107] Nayan Chanda, "Hard Peace at Versailles," *Far Eastern Economic Review,* February 26, 1972, p. 7.

diate vicinity, such as the August 1971 Soviet-Indian treaty and the new pattern of relations which is developing between the U.S.S.R. and Bangladesh. Russia has been critical of alleged "foreign interference" by the U.S. in Burmese affairs.[108] But, though it is not likely that the Rangoon government's fears of continuing Chinese assistance to tribal insurgents and Communist guerrillas in Northern Burma will cause it to seek treaty bonds with Moscow, in the near future the Soviets can hardly forego the opening presented by Chinese subversion in Burma. The same is likely to be true in Thailand, where the need for stronger relations with Moscow is slowly being recognized.

Concern over China's revolutionary expansionism, and concurrently over the loyalties of younger overseas Chinese, however discounted by occasional Western observers, is a real factor in the policy calculations of those Southeast Asian governments which are inclined to see in the new Nixon détente a tacit American acknowledgment that Southeast Asia falls within the Chinese sphere of influence. Moscow, rather than Washington, is now being viewed as the real countervailing power in Asia, and the 1971 Soviet-Indian treaty is thus seen in some Southeast Asian military and diplomatic quarters as a model which others might well eventually wish to emulate. This is still a minority view, however.

As early as June 1969, Singapore Premier Lee Kuan Yew said that Singapore might welcome Soviet "peacekeeping forces" in Southeast Asia.[109] But, while no one of similar prominence in the region has publicly repeated this thought since, the regular appearance in the Indian Ocean of a Soviet naval squadron and the reported Soviet bargaining with a number of nations in the area (including India, Ceylon, and Mauritius) for permanent docking and refueling facilities have brought official Southeast Asian reactions ranging from very mild protest to usually quiet approval—reactions that are similar, one might add, to reports of new U.S. moves in the area (for example, the construction of the Diego Garcia communications facility, more frequent cruises by U.S. Seventh Fleet units in the Indian Ocean, and construction of a permanent naval facility at Bahrain, in the Persian Gulf). These U.S. moves have brought predictable Soviet (and Chinese Communist) verbal attacks,[110] which, however, can only encourage those

[108] *Statesman* (Delhi), June 23, 1971. Burma's reaction to the "neutralization" of Southeast Asia has been guarded. Little about it has appeared in the Burmese press. After his mid-February 1972 visit to Burma, Malaysian Premier Razak reported that the Ne Win government supported the neutralization concept but would join in a regional plan only "if all other countries are genuinely neutral." *Malaysian Digest*, February 29, 1972.
[109] *Australian* (Sydney), June 19, 1969.
[110] See V. Kudriavtsev in *Izvestiia*, January 18, 1972; and "U.S.-Soviet Scramble for Hegemony in South Asian Subcontinent and Indian Ocean," *Peking Review*, January 14, 1972, pp. 16–17.

among Southeast Asia's leaders who see safety in a neutralized or neu-
tralizing Southeast Asia only if it is carefully watched from the region's
perimeter by *all* the major powers. Meanwhile, nations such as Burma,
which in the past has been almost fetishistic in its efforts to maintain
neutrality, might well be occasionally tempted to adopt a new accommodation with the Kremlin, in the manner of one authoritative Indian
commentator who described the 1971 Soviet-Indian treaty as "a new
and a sophisticated stage in the development of non-alignment" and
"therefore signficant."[111] But one hastens to add that the Burmese have
given no sign, as yet, that they are seeking such an accommodation.

The Soviets have shown, however, that they can wait, and that they
realize nothing is to be gained from precipitate policy moves toward
accommodation. In this regard Soviet relations with Singapore are
something of a model. Independent of Malaysia since 1965, Singapore
waited until 1967 to respond actively to quiet Soviet expressions of
interest in better trade and diplomatic relations. In September 1967,
Inche Othman Wok, Singapore's minister of culture and social affairs,
visited Moscow at the Soviets' invitation; earlier there had been trade
agreements with Bulgaria and Poland. Not until January 1969 did a
Soviet ambassador arrive in Singapore, after Singapore's Foreign Minister S. Rajaratnam had repeatedly stressed that his nation's "international position" demanded a steady widening of consular and commercial ties. Also in 1969, the first significant fruits of Soviet-Singa-
porean economic cooperation became apparent. Plans were announced
for a joint Singaporean-Soviet production of watch parts, in which the
Soviets would contribute technical supervision and equipment and
Singapore would provide the initial funding. Neutralization by means
of "internationalization"—that is, by having as many of the major
powers acquire a stake in the prosperity and stability (and the neutral
"status quo") of the Southeast Asian region—is clearly served by such
joint Singaporean-Soviet ventures. The warm reception accorded Lee
Kuan Yew in Moscow in September 1970 suggests that the Soviets
may see some advantages in such a policy gambit also.

The credibility and effectiveness of the new Soviet presence in
Southeast Asia will obviously involve more than peripheral military
strength or participation in a new international gambit of big power
multiparity in the region. Diplomatic finesse in dealing with the area's
problems will count for as much, if not for more, and there are indications that the Soviets are well aware of it. The Soviets' record in the
Indochinese embroglio is replete with diplomatic initiatives and efforts
(most of which have been only partly revealed thus far) designed to

---

[111] M. S. Rajan, "Indo-Soviet Treaty and Non-Alignment," *Indian and Foreign
Review* (New Delhi), February 15, 1972, p. 13.

alter the course of the conflict in the direction of a political settlement. At the close of January 1972, for example, the Soviet embassy in Phnom Penh appears to have acted as middleman in an unsuccessful peace overture by the Lon Nol government to the D.R.V. (another reason, perhaps, why Moscow has been reluctant to sever ties formally with the Lon Nol regime). The author has been informed by former Indonesian diplomats in Hanoi that Soviet efforts were periodically made from 1969 through 1971 to mitigate, or at least to slow down, accelerating D.R.V. and Neo Lao Haksat drives in Laos, in order not to jeopardize the Nixon disengagement policy. All this was happening, even though Moscow continued to repeat publicly that "every Lao patriot" knows that "the U.S. imperialists" are "the aggressors and the enemy of Laos' peace and independence."[112] Meanwhile, as Hanoi called the Nixon Doctrine "a perfidious counter-revolutionary global strategy aimed at dividing and weakening the revolutionary and progressive forces,"[113] there was little doubt that Moscow also saw tactical opportunities in the domestic American pressures toward disengagement from Asia being exerted upon the Nixon administration.

It is to be noted that there is a significant "de-ideologized" Soviet perception in these new tactical options. Experience with Sukarno, no less than with Sihanouk, has given the Kremlin's current leaders a more sophisticated appreciation of "revolutionary democrats" in the Third World. These days Soviet specialists on the developing nations, especially those in Southeast Asia, "incline towards a pragmatic caution and flexibility,"[114] urging consideration for unique features in particular political economies of the region as they make their anticipated "transition" to socialism. Burma again affords an illustration of this attitude. The initial optimistic Soviet evaluaton of the Ne Win government in the early 1960s soon gave way to caution and skepticism as the Rangoon government's economic policies, like Sukarno's, appeared to be edging ever closer to fiscal disaster and chaos in development.[115] Although Ne Win's doctrinaire socialist economic development policies have scarcely been mitigated, the Soviet position today is a good deal more positive, stressing the extent of Soviet technical assistance to the Burmans, and reflecting Moscow's realistic understanding of the Ne

---

[112] Radio Moscow in Lao to Laos, January 30, 1972, 1400 GMT, FBIS. In March 1972, Chinese Premier Chou En-lai and Prince Sihanouk in Peking charged "unnamed certain powers" (presumably the U.S.S.R. and France) with trying to split Sihanouk's government and create "a third force" in Cambodia which would seek a "political solution" to the Cambodian crisis. *New York Times*, March 20, 1972.

[113] *Nhan Dan* (Hanoi), March 2, 1972.

[114] J. L. S. Girling, "Soviet Attitudes towards Southeast Asia," *The World Today*, May 1973, p. 207.

[115] "Soviet Writers on Burmese Socialism," *Mizan*, May–June 1966, pp. 101–8.

Win polity.[116] Then, too, the fact that the Rangoon government continues to be confronted by Peking-assisted tribal and Communist
guerilla insurgents in its upland border regions has given Soviet commentators the opportunity to fulminate against the "Left-wing extremist clique" and their "Maoist leaders," who, "obeying orders from
Peking," are allegedly subverting Burma.[117]

The current Soviet "pragmatism," while in some respects matching
that of many of Southeast Asia's governing circles (for example, in
Suharto's Indonesia and Lee Kuan Yew's Singapore), cannot be said to
be an unqualified success, however, not least because its implications
are far from clear. With the end of direct U.S. military involvement in
the Indochina conflict, and in the context of the Nixon administration's diplomatic initiatives toward Moscow and Peking, Soviet "pragmatism" is in Southeast Asian Communist circles sometimes seen as a
compliance with the Nixon Doctrine and with the Nixon perception of
a new "multipolar" and "flexible" international order dominated by the
superpowers, in which revolutionary and liberation movements in the
Third World will be all but ignored. The warning, in May 1973 in the
North Vietnamese army paper *Quan Doi Nhan Dan*, that the Nixon
Doctrine was designed to relax tensions among the big powers so
that the U.S. could more easily "repress the small countries" seemed
directed as much to Washington as to Moscow and Peking.[118] On the
other hand, the Soviet view that with the Vietnam peace agreement
and moves toward a normalization of relations in Southeast Asia such
countries as the Philippines would now be in a position to broaden
their relations with the rest of the world and lessen their dependence
on the U.S.[119] is undoubtedly in accord with prevailing Philippine
opinion. A low-keyed, flexible Soviet attitude, benevolently pragmatic
toward the economic policies of the Southeast Asian states, turning its
back on cold war rigidities, and above all ready to assure that there
will be no Russian involvement in "subversive activities,"[120] would
probably go far in creating a new climate in which the nations of
Southeast Asia are prepared to take another look at Moscow's appeals
and interests.

[116] See, for example, A. Ledovsky, "Burma on the Road of Progressive Development," *International Affairs* (Moscow), 1973, no. 3, pp. 45–47.
[117] Radio Moscow (in Chinese) to Southeast Asia, March 27, 1973, cited in
*USSR and Third World*, 3, no. 3 (1973): 138.
[118] *Quan Doi Nhan Dan* (Hanoi), May 25, 1973; and *Far Eastern Economic
Review*, July 2, 1973, p. 15.
[119] *USSR and Third World*, 3, no. 3 (1973): 148.
[120] See, for example, such Soviet assurances to the Indonesian government in
*Antara Daily News Bulletin*, December 23, 1972.

# 5

## THE SOVIET UNION AND SOUTH ASIA

*Bhabani Sen Gupta*

*I*

The Soviet Union today is generally perceived to be the dominant external power in South Asia.[1] Russian popularity has reached its zenith. To the peoples and governments of South Asia, the Soviet Union appears to have succeeded in besting the United States, as well as China, in the competitive intervention that has characterized the politics of this region. Soviet intervention and influence-building in South Asia has proved to be more effective than that of its two great power rivals.

South Asia provides the link among the three types of Soviet involvement in Asian conflict situations, the two others being West Asia (the Middle East) and Southeast Asia. The Soviets' simultaneous involvement in these three areas illustrates the alacrity with which Soviet leaders have made political use of Russia's recently acquired global power apparatus.[2] The three types of involvement have their similari-

---

[1] As James Reston wrote in 1971: "India has won the battle for East Pakistan, but in the larger perspectives of world politics, this is not the main thing. For the Soviet Union has emerged from this avoidable and tragic conflict as the military arsenal and political defender of India, with access for Moscow's rising naval power to the Indian Ocean, and a base of political and military operation on China's southern flank." "Who Won in India?" *New York Times*, December 17, 1971. Indian commentators generally agree with this assessment. "It is obvious in retrospect that India could not have liberated Bangladesh in April–May, as many leaders of public opinion had advocated at that time, and it could not have done so even in November–December in the absence of the treaty of friendship with the Soviet Union." As a result of the war, the position of the Soviet Union "is bound to be strengthened from the Mediterranean to the Straits of Malacca. Even its detractors in the Arab world will revise their views about it, and the Southeast Asian countries will now have greater confidence in its willingness and confidence to protect them against encroachments by China." Girilal Jain, "New Equations in Asia," *Times of India* (New Delhi), December 21, 1971. "In the triangular tussle between the superpowers for world influence, the Soviet Union has scored a deserved victory against its rivals. The growth of Soviet prestige in the area is in more than direct proportion to the loss of faith in American credibility and good sense. The competition between the superpowers for influence in South Asia has been decided unmistakably by America's own behavior." M. J. Desai, "Global Dimensions," *Seminar* (New Delhi), February 1972.

[2] In terms of military aid to Hanoi and the provisional revolutionary government of South Vietnam, the Soviets have played a much greater role than has China. For instance, the Soviet delegate to the unofficial international conference for peace in Vietnam, held in Paris in February 1972, announced that Moscow had supplied "terrible modern weapons" to North Vietnam to combat the United States, and that the U.S.S.R. was the "decisive power" behind the Communist forces. *Times of India*, February 13, 1972.

ties and differences. In the Middle East, the Soviets are backing the party that is, at least in the short run, weaker in the Arab-Israeli conflict. In Southeast Asia, the Russian commitment is to forces that appear to be weak but that are actually strong enough to wrest from the United States a radical reversal of its interventionist policy. In South Asia, the Soviets have consistently backed the forces that are decisively stronger than their opponents, who have enjoyed the backing of the United States or China or both.

Soviet strategies for South Asia can therefore offer a model study of influence-building in an area of competitive intervention by external powers.[3] It is remarkable that the Soviets have not met with major reverses during the decade and a half of active operation of their South Asian policy. To be sure, there have been strains and stresses on Moscow's relations with India, and other nations of the region, but these have not been permitted to distort the progress of influence-building. Even the president of dismembered Pakistan is unwilling to adopt an anti-Soviet posture. In the aftermath of the Indo-Pakistani conflict of December 1971, Soviet leaders seem to be convinced that, given the political and economic problems of truncated Pakistan and the emerging configuration of social forces in the subcontinent, the rulers of Pakistan will have no alternative but to seek Moscow's friendship.

It would be reckless to ascribe the success of Soviet influence-building to a series of lucky accidents or merely to clever manipulation of the contradictions and weaknesses of American and Chinese strategies. Soviet scholars attribute the success to the soundness of their own "model" relative to the U.S. and Chinese "models" in South Asia. The Soviet "model" is based on what one Soviet scholar has termed a sound geopolitical appraisal of the realities in South Asia; its persistent thrust since the death of Stalin has been to build friendly relations with India, by far the largest, strongest, and stablest power in the region. In comparison, according to this scholar, the U.S. "model" has been based on anticommunism, while the Chinese, since 1959, have increasingly built their strategies on antisovietism; the net result of either strategy has been a growing hiatus between these two powers and the "progressive forces" in the region.[4] In other words, while U.S. and Chinese strategies have been largely "negative," Moscow has been able to construct a durable partnership between Soviet communism and

---

[3] Although an illusive term, "influence" can be defined as an actor's ability to induce another actor to do what it wishes and not to do what it does not wish. In the case of the Soviet Union, "influence" also means the capacity to induce a friend like India to adopt certain priorities in domestic socioeconomic policies which correspond to the Soviet concept of progressive social change.

[4] Comments made by Nikolai Sirota, of the Institute of World Economy and International Relations, Moscow, at a seminar at the School of International Studies, Jawaharlal Nehru University, New Delhi, on January 8, 1972.

"progressive bourgeois nationalism" in South Asia. If it is a marriage of convenience, it has proved to be a convenience of long duration.

In effecting this marriage, the Soviets have been favored by South Asia's historical experience. Unlike China, South Asia does not have a historical devil's image of imperial Russia; the British took care to keep their empire insulated against Russian penetration.[5] The Bolshevik Revolution, with its anti-imperialist overtones, made a profound impression on the younger leaders of the Indian nationalist movement, notably Nehru, and in the 1930s a certain emotional and intellectual linkage was established between Soviet communism and Indian nationalism.[6] Remarkably, the linkage survived even the entirely negative Stalinist stance toward the independence of India. Nehru was once shown by a senior civil servant a sheaf of Moscow radio attacks on him and his government. He glanced at the extracts cursorily and said with a wry smile: "The heat is not against us though it looks like it. The heat is against the British. The British have always tried to keep the Russians out of this subcontinent and the Russians cannot believe that the policy has changed. . . . If we can show the world that we are, in fact, an independent country, the world will change its attitude towards us."[7]

In his last years, Stalin himself had begun to relent in his hostility to the newly liberated regimes in South Asia. It was, however, left to his successors, notably Khrushchev, to dramatically reverse the process. When in June 1955 Nehru paid his first visit to the U.S.S.R. as India's prime minister, he was agreeably surprised by the scale of Russian hospitality; he was the first non-Communist leader to be allowed public forums in the U.S.S.R. to express his views directly to the Soviet people. The Soviet media sought to invest Indo-Soviet friendship with the sanction of history, and the Indian journalists who accompanied Nehru were impressed by the industry deployed in a short time to the study of India's political system, social institutions, governmental policies, and problems of development.[8] In November 1955, during their joint tour of India, Khrushchev and Bulganin not only offered Soviet assistance in building heavy industries but also, once again to Nehru's agreeable surprise, publicly announced their support for the Indian stand on Kashmir and to India's claim to the Portuguese enclaves of Goa, Daman, and Dieu. Simultaneously, the Soviet leaders supported

[5] For the two images of Russia which run through contemporary Chinese history, see T. A. Hsiah, "Demons in Paradise: The Chinese Image of Russia," *Annals of the American Academy of Political and Social Science*, March 1965, pp. 28–29.

[6] Jayantuja Bandyopadhyaya, *Indian Nationalism versus International Communism* (Calcutta, 1966), chaps. 5–6.

[7] Quoted in Arthur Stein, *India and the Soviet Union* (Chicago: University of Chicago Press, 1969), p. 26n.

[8] *Hindu,* July 2, 1955.

the Pakhtoonistan movement in the northwest frontier of Pakistan, which had the backing of the Afghan government. Then began a steady process of rehabilitating the ethos of the Indian parliamentary democratic experiment in the eyes of the Soviet people. Gandhi was recognized as a national liberator. Nehru's foreign, as well as *domestic*, policies were evaluated as progressive, to the chagrin and bewilderment of Indian Communists. In 1956 the Soviet leaders administered an effective warning to the Communist party of India (CPI), that if they were forced to choose between Indian communism and progressive bourgeois nationalism, they would choose the latter.[9]

They did not have to make the choice. The CPI, which had grown up in the suburbs of the nationalist movement and under Comintern control, had since 1952 been functioning more or less as a parliamentary party. At the Twentieth Congress of the CPSU in 1956, the theory of peaceful transition to socialism through the parliamentary way was given a strategic dimension, and its acceptance by the CPI muted a major contradiction between Indian nationalism and communism. The theory that peaceful competition between the two rival international systems would lead inevitably to the triumph of the socialist order over the capitalist order was also acceptable to the national liberation leaders in South Asia. How the Twentieth Congress line, as practiced by the CPI, integrated communism with nationalism became evident in the late fifties and early sixties. The dominant group in the CPI sided wholeheartedly with Indian nationalism during the Sino-Indian border conflict. In 1960, Soviet leaders, working closely with the CPI, had the strategic concept of the national democratic state adopted by the conference of world Communist parties, despite Chinese opposition. Unlike the Maoist strategic concept of the new democratic state, the national democratic state (NDS) envisages not a Communist takeover but only a strong Communist partnership of state power in coalition with undefined national or revolutionary democratic forces. To this day, the NDS remains the strategic goal of Soviet communism in South Asia. It is also the strategic goal of the CPI. The Soviets, to put it more concretely, have given the national bourgeoisie to understand

[9] The CPI leadership was still opposing Nehru's domestic policies, while lending qualified support to the anti-imperialistic thrusts of his foreign policy, when mid-term elections were held in Andhra Pradesh, a Communist stronghold. On the eve of the election, *Pravda* came out with an editorial that heaped praise on both the foreign and domestic policies of the Nehru government, and the Congress party circulated several million copies of the editorial in its election campaign. The CPI lost heavily to the Congress party, and then quickly synchronized its watch with Moscow. For details, see Gene D. Overstreet and Marshall Windmiller, *Communism in India* (Berkeley and Los Angeles: University of California Press, 1959), chap. 4; and Bhabani Sen Gupta, *Communism in Indian Politics* (New York: Columbia University Press, 1972).

that they are pushing their societies not toward communism but toward "progressive social change."

For Soviet leaders, idea-milieu linkages with the national bourgeoisies of Third World nations are an essential tactical requirement of influence-building—partly because Communist movements in these nations are still weak, but mostly because the Soviets regard the national liberation movement, with its anti-imperialist overtones, as a natural ally of the world socialist system. The Soviet tactics are, however, to be seen in the context of the two major phenomena that, running parallel, have profoundly influenced the politics of our time. These are the nation-building endeavor of the elites of the newly liberated nations and the influence-building enterprise of the two superpowers. The two phenomena have often meshed and mingled together, more in South Asia than in some other Third World regions. One of the main problems of influence-building is the social base of the political actors of the new nations through whom each superpower must act in order to build its presence. It is a problem that dogs all influence-builders; they have sometimes to clutch at straw men. If one looks at the process of American influence-building in Asia since the mid-forties, one is struck by the relative lack of success of U.S. policy-makers to build influence around local actors who are anchored on a reasonably broad social base of support and recruitment. "Broad-basing the regime" was as much of a problem for the United States in Chaing Kai-shek's China as it has been in the South Vietnam of Diem and Theiu. The Soviets have generally sought to act through viable political systems and actors in the Third World. While they have experienced several notable failures in Africa, they have been quite successful in South Asia.

In cultivating friendly, viable forces, the Soviet Union has persistently tried to satisfy some of the *felt* needs of the power elites of Third World societies. In South Asia, they have come forward to provide aid for industrialization programs in India, for which the Indians could not secure resources either domestically or from Western nations. In Afghanistan, on the other hand, Soviet aid programs have been tailored to the preferences of the king and his council of ministers. The Soviets have given selective support to the geopolitical and strategic interests and aspirations of the elites they have sought to befriend. For instance, they upheld the Indian position on Kashmir and supported the Afghan position on the Pakhtoonistan issue in the mid-fifties, soon after the United States brought Pakistan into its global military alliance system. Since the late fifties, the Soviets have supported the Indians in their border conflict with China. They have fed and strongly backed the anti-imperialism of these elites; the Indian military action against the Portuguese enclaves received firm Russian support.

The Soviets, then, have been able to exploit contradictions among the various South Asian elites as well as contradictions between these elites and the Western powers (and later China). In South Asia one can also discern some success of Moscow's efforts to establish a community of geopolitical interests of the U.S.S.R. and India, and of the U.S.S.R. and Afghanistan. Soviet support for India during the Sino-Indian border crisis led to Indian support for the Soviets following the Ussuri River clash. For political, if not strategic reasons, a community of geopolitical interests grew between Moscow and New Delhi in the sixties and became even stronger in the first years of the seventies.

A peculiar aspect of the Soviets' South Asian strategy is their involvement in the politically sensitive territorial issues that divide the nations of the region. Kashmir and Pakhtoonistan were issues inherited by India, Pakistan, and Afghanistan from the subcontinent's colonial past; they also reflected the clashing geopolitical interests and aspirations of the ruling elites. By supporting India and Afghanistan against Pakistan, the Soviets made it clear even in the mid-fifties that they were not rigidly committed to the boundaries of the nations born of the passing empires. In Kashmir, they supported the status quo that had emerged from the Indo-Pakistani war of 1948; over the question of Pakhtoonistan, they favored redrawing the political map of the area that comprised Pakistan and Afghanistan.

Soviet involvement in the events that led to the dismemberment of Pakistan probably constitutes a landmark in Moscow's attitude toward the Third World nations. To provide an ideological justification for this involvement, the Soviets recognized the Bangladesh movement as a national liberation movement rather than a separatist movement. The implication of this theoretical term of reference cannot possibly escape the ruling elites of those Asian-African nations that have a sizable national minority problem. Basically, however, Soviet involvement is a question of the stability of the Third World regimes. The Soviet Union is apparently unwilling to invest in regimes that lack a strong popular support base. If altering a political map would correspond to the best interest of Soviet power, the Soviets may not be opposed to such an alteration, provided it can be worked out to their satisfaction. In the South Asian region, at any rate, they have been largely responsible for radically redrawing the political map of the subcontinent without anything more than a verbal confrontation with the United States and China. By doing so, they have sought to set the direction of social change in the subcontinent. The emergence of Bangladesh, with its declared adherence to "secularism, democracy, and socialism," has severely undermined the religion-oriented political forces in the subcontinent, and has generally weakened the forces of the right. In each of the three nations of the subcontinent, domestic politics have tended to move toward the left. The Soviet bloc nations have emerged as the principal suppliers of economic and technological assistance to India and Bangladesh.

## II

This remarkable expansion of Soviet influence has to be seen in the context of (1) the status of the U.S.S.R. as a world power; (2) the Soviets' competition-conflict relationship with the United States and China; (3) the interests of the U.S. and China in South Asia; and (4) the state of domestic politics within the South Asian region.

As a superpower, a global power, and a Communist power, the U.S.S.R. still commands the loyalty of by far the major faction of the international Communist movement. In the global configuration of power politics, Moscow seeks to play three roles at the same time. As a superpower, Moscow is locked in a complex rivalry-collaboration relationship with the United States: the two, with their accumulated capability to annihilate civilization several times over, share a common responsibility to deter each other with a seemingly ever-unstable parity of strategic power. From this superpower relationship stems the compulsion not merely to avoid a head-on collision but also to seek areas of détente covering the most explosive points of conflict. Soviet leaders and the Soviet scholarly community reject the concept of covergence of the two rival systems or of their vital interests in the highly inflammable areas of world politics. They are still committed to lead the world to Marxist socialism, for which the decline and fall of American imperialism remains a major precondition. This, however, does not deter them from seeking accommodation with the rival superpower where accommodation is considered necessary to further the interests of the Soviet state. Soviet leaders reject the concept of a permanent division of the world into spheres of influence, although they are not averse to temporary arrangements that may stabilize an otherwise explosive situation. Inherent in the Soviet concept of peaceful coexistence is continuing competition between the two global systems; peace is nonwar, not absence of conflict.[10]

---

[10] An "aggressive" doctrine, Marxism-Leninism is wedded to the fundamental transformation of social systems whereby bourgeois ownership of the means of production is replaced by proletarian ownership. Much of the confusion in contemporary international politics stems from a basic misunderstanding of what the Soviets mean by peace. In 1929, Boris Shaposhnikov, a Soviet military authority, wrote: "If war is a continuation of politics, only by other means, so also peace is a continuation of struggle only by other means." *Mozg Armii* [The Brain of the Army] (Moscow, 1929), 3: 239. The techniques and norms of struggle have changed qualitatively because of the enormously altered character of world politics, but one would be mistaken to believe that the Soviet leaders have ceased to be Communist and have come to mean by peace the continuation of the status quo.

By acquiring the trappings of a global power, the Soviet Union is now in a position to neutralize the global power of the United States in the far-flung areas of the world. Experts may differ on whether air power or naval power is the key to Soviet strategy, but the spectacular expansion of the Soviet navy in recent years has enabled the U.S.S.R. to translate its military power into political action in the different conflict areas of the world. Nowhere is this more evident than in Asia, where the Soviet navy confronts the U.S. Sixth Fleet in the Mediterranean; where the Soviets have been able to keep North Vietnam well supplied with war matériel, despite obstacles placed by Peking to the transit of supplies by land through Chinese territory; and where, during the Indo-Pakistani conflict, a unit of the Soviet Navy trailed a task force of the U.S. Seventh Fleet to the Bay of Bengal. The Soviet Union is now in a position to confront the world's other superpower on a global scale in dealing with local conflicts. This relatively new factor has introduced a qualitative change in the strategy of superpower intervention in local conflicts.

In an age of competitive influence-building by the superpowers, the U.S.S.R. enjoys certain subjective advantages in South Asia that are denied to its two rivals. It also enjoys a number of objective advantages. The first, and the most important, is the low-level American involvement in South Asian affairs. By concluding a military alliance with Pakistan in 1954, the United States created the objective condition by which to bring the Soviet Union and India closer together, but, paradoxically, at no stage did it commit itself to the military defense of Pakistan against an attack from India. In the crucial first days of the 1971 Indo-Pakistani war, Henry Kissinger could only vaguely recall "certain things" he had heard during his visit to Rawalpindi in July about a treaty obligation to go to Pakistan's help in the event of "aggression from any quarter." His musings were apparently unconfirmed by the State Department.[11] In fact, American friendship for Pakistan had begun to lose its credibility in 1962, when the United States provided India with military assistance in the wake of the Sino-Indian border conflict. This, more than anything else, pushed Pakistan

---

[11] According to Jack Anderson, Kissinger told the WSAG meeting on December 4, 1971: "I remember a letter or memo interpreting our existing treaty with a special India tilt. When I visited Pakistan in January 1962 I was briefed on a secret document or oral understanding about contingencies arising in other than SEATO context. Perhaps it was a Presidential letter. This was a special interpretation of the March 1959 bilateral treaty [between the U.S. and Pakistan]." There is nothing in the Anderson documents that suggests that Kissinger's recollection was confirmed by the State Department. In fact, the State Department denied that the United States had any treaty obligation to defend Pakistan outside the SEATO context. *New York Times*, January 6, 1972.

toward close relations with Peking, and later with Moscow. Pakistan got little support from the United States during the 1965 war with India. President Johnson's simultaneous suspension of military and economic aid to both India and Pakistan hurt the latter much more than the former, for, despite the massive volume of military aid, the United States had given Pakistan no more than thirty days' fighting capability.[12] The U.S. played no role in the peace settlement between India and Pakistan after the conflict. This role was played entirely and solely by the U.S.S.R. at Tashkent in January 1966, with reluctant American approval and to the deep, though impotent, resentment of Peking.[13]

During the 1965 conflict the Soviet Union formulated a geopolitical doctrine of intervention in South Asian affairs: it could not remain indifferent to a conflict which broke out in an area "adjacent to the Soviet Union." This was the beginning of the attempt to bring South Asia within the orbit of the security of the Soviet state. Soviet strategy in 1965 was, however, largely influenced by a perception shared with the United States that the real danger to the subcontinent came from Peking. In the U.N. Security Council, therefore, the two superpowers worked together to "demand" a cease-fire and withdrawal of armed personnel to preconflict positions. The Soviets voted for the cease-fire resolution, in spite of the fact that its wording was not entirely to their liking. Moscow's great concern was to keep the Chinese out, and, to do this, it combined repeated pressures on both India and Pakistan to cry for a halt to the fighting with repeated warnings to "third powers" not to intervene.

The contrast with Soviet conduct during the 1971 crisis in the subcontinent is striking. Moscow was now pitted against the United States and China. It operated its own strategy. The objective was to change the Pakistani politics. Because the crisis in Pakistan immediately developed into a crisis between Pakistan and India, the Soviet leaders sided with India right up to the final act: the fourteen-day war that led to the dismemberment of Pakistan.

For six years the Soviets had labored hard to improve their relations

---

[12] The Indó-Pakistani correspondent of *The Times* (London) reported on October 17, 1965: "But the essential factor in Pakistan's military posture is that her stamina in war is limited not by her own capacities but by the Pentagon. Not only the numbers of her front line tanks and aircraft are set in Washington but also the level of supplies for them that can be accumulated. That level is secret but is believed to be in the region of 30 days in war conditions." See also Selig Harrison's dispatch in the *Washington Post,* October 16, 1965, confirming *The Times* report.

[13] For a detailed politico-military analysis of the 1965 Indo-Pakistani war and of the Soviet and Chinese strategies with regard to it, see the present author's *The Fulcrum of Asia: Relations among China, India, Pakistan, and the USSR* (New York: Pegasus, 1970), chap. 4.

with Pakistan, risking, since 1968, a certain misunderstanding with India and a certain strain on Indo-Soviet friendship.[14] Their attitude toward Pakistan, however, cooled off somewhat when, in 1970, President Yahya Khan went back on a commitment he was reported to have made earlier to fall in line with the Brezhnev plan for regional economic cooperation among the U.S.S.R., Afghanistan, Pakistan, and India in the use of the overland trade routes.[15] Moscow probably watched with concern the Chinese use of the roads built in recent years to connect Sinkiang with Gilgit and the flow of Chinese merchandise to the Persian Gulf region through the port of Karachi. The political crisis between West and East Pakistan in 1971 led to a major reappraisal of Moscow's Pakistan policy. Within a week of the March 25 West Pakistani military crackdown on the autonomy movement in East Pakistan led by the Awami League, President Podgorny issued a public message to Yahya Khan on behalf of the Presidium of the Supreme Soviet:

The Soviet people cannot but be concerned by the enormous casualties, by the sufferings and privations that such a development of event[s] brings to the people of Pakistan. Concern is also caused in the Soviet Union by the arrests and persecution of Mujibur Rahman and other politicians who had received such convincing support by the overwhelming majority of the population of East Pakistan at the recent general election. . . . We have been and remain convinced that the problems that have risen in Pakistan can and must be solved politically, without the use of force. . . . We consider it our duty to address you, Mr. President . . . with an insistent appeal for the adoption of the most urgent measures to stop the bloodshed and repressions against the population of East Pakistan and for turning to methods of a peaceful political settlement. We are convinced that this would meet the interests of the entire people of Pakistan and the interests of preserving peace in the area.

This prompt Soviet intervention in an internal crisis in Pakistan must have been preceded by serious reflections on the short- and long-term implications of the crisis on the politics of South Asia. By insisting on a political solution of the crisis, the Soviets apparently tried to influence strongly Pakistan's internal politics. A Pakistan that was politically

[14] Kuldip Nayyar's *Between the Lines* (New Delhi, 1970), pp. 130–68, includes the only inside report of a meeting of Soviet and Indian officials that has been made available so far. It reveals some of the strains on Indo-Soviet relations that followed Moscow's attempts to build a friendly presence in Pakistan.
[15] V. R. Bhatt, "The Great Powers and Pakistan," *Hindustan Times* (New Delhi), July 22, 1971.

balanced between its two wings, and ruled by an Awami League government headed by Mujibur Rahman, would have introduced a certain symmetry in the politics of the subcontinent. The Soviet leaders could not have been indifferent to the fact that in the spring of 1971 the Indian government had deployed some 200,000 armed personnel to flush out Communist radicalism in the West Bengali countryside. From the beginning, then, a major thrust of Soviet intervention in the East Pakistani crisis was to help the bourgeois-democratic forces in Bangladesh emerge and thereby check the area's drift toward extreme radicalism.

The crisis in Pakistan coincided with Henry Kissinger's secret journey to Peking in July and the announcement that President Nixon would be visiting China in 1972. During his brief stopover in Delhi, Kissinger warned the Indian government against taking military action in East Pakistan, and volunteered the counsel that India could not expect U.S. assistance in the event of Chinese action across the northern borders. Pakistan's role in arranging Kissinger's visit to Peking persuaded the Indians that a Sino-American convergence was replacing the Soviet-U.S. convergence in Asia, and that Pakistan constituted an important lever in a new Asian balance of power being sought by Washington and Peking. The Indians perceived that in the latter part of the sixties the U.S. and the U.S.S.R. had struck some kind of bargain over South and Southeast Asia which diffused the danger of a direct conflict between them over Vietnam. It was also about this period that the Americans began to recognize Russia's interest in the Indo-Pakistani subcontinent. The United States acknowledged that Russia had an over-riding stake in the confrontation with China, and allowed the Soviet Union to assume the role of conflict manager in the subcontinent after the 1965 Indo-Pakistani war. For more than five years, Soviet and American policies ran parallel to one another in South Asia; the common aim was to contain China, and in this India was given a role commensurate with its resources and ability.

What altered the situation, according to India, was the sharp worsening of relations between Russia and China which grew out of the armed clash on the Ussuri River. The United States noted with apprehension that the U.S.S.R. was about to emerge as the world's number one military power. If the Soviets could bring China under their control, either by military force or by political means, Soviet hegemony would become unquestionable throughout the entire Eurasian land mass, from the Atlantic coast to the Pacific coast. Thus, there was a compelling need for both the United States and China to contain the might of the U.S.S.R. This was what President Nixon had initiated, and, for the time being at least, the U.S. would join with

China to cut the U.S.S.R. down to size. The United States, Indians now believed, might very well sacrifice some of its regional interests to advance its global interests; this explained Nixon's assurance that the U.S. would respect China's legitimate interests in Southeast Asia. The United States not only did not any longer regard South Asia as mainly a Soviet sphere of influence, but it would do whatever it could to promote and protect Chinese interests in this region.[16]

This Indian elite perception broadly resembled the Soviet's perception of the changing relationship between the U.S. and China. In a mid-1971 article in *Pravda*, Georgi A. Arbatov, director of the U.S.S.R. Academy of Sciences' Institute on the U.S.A., offered an analysis of the diverse forces that persuaded President Nixon to seek a radical reversal of his country's twenty-year China policy. Among these forces Arbatov identified progressive and liberal elements who had always wanted better relations with China, as well as "rabid haters" of the Soviet Union who had been attracted by Peking's anti-Sovietism and who would like to use China to undermine the power and influence of the U.S.S.R. Arbatov visualized two diverse directions in which American policy could move with regard to the U.S.S.R. The U.S. could combine the steps toward improving relations with China "with a turn toward a more constructive position" on issues that stood between it and Moscow. "But there are grounds to expect that events will develop in another direction, in which US policy will remain unchanged, except for relations with China, and its course will, as before, be the main obstacle in eliminating sharp international conflicts."[17]

While Arbatov reserved "definite conclusions" on the "future of American-Chinese relations," the Soviet leaders appeared to have made up their minds to direct the main thrust of their policy in Asia to achieve the strategic objective of isolating and containing Chinese power and influence during the transitional phase in Sino-U.S. relations. An article in *Pravda* toward the end of July 1971 betrayed the Soviets' fear of even a limited Sino-U.S. accord to serve the two powers' parallel interests vis à vis Moscow. "It should be clear," *Pravda* warned, "that all plans to use the contacts between Peking and Washington for some sort of "pressure" on the Soviet Union and the states of the socialist commonwealth are only the result of the loss of an understanding of reality." The article anticipated a Sino-American

---

[16] This outline of Indian perception is based on the present author's analysis of commentaries and editorials in the Indian press from August to October 1972. For a typical presentation of this perception, see Pran Chopra, "Nixon's Pilgrimage at Peking," *Tribune* (Chandigarh), August 6, 1972; and Girilal Jain, "The Triangular Balance," *Times of India*, August 4, 1971.

[17] *Pravda*, August 10, 1971.

"political combination" against the U.S.S.R. and its East European allies. To counter such a combination it suggested a Soviet initiative to woo a string of medium powers, notably Japan in Asia and West Germany in Europe, while at the same time keeping options open to work with the U.S. to resolve specific issues of major conflict.[18]

Nixon's China diplomacy, then, polarized the conflict between Moscow and Peking, and South Asia was the first geopolitical region to reflect the polarization. In the summer and autumn of 1971, Soviet media made it clear that Moscow regarded the "Maoist clique" as its principal adversary as much as Peking perceived the "revisionist leaders of the CPSU" as its number one enemy. The principal theme of a torrent of anti-China polemics was that Maoist China was an arrogant, expansionist power at whose hands neither the territorial integrity nor the political stability of Asian nations was or could be safe.[19]

The image of an emerging Washington-Peking-Rawalpindi axis predictably enhanced the importance of Indo-Soviet friendship for India as well as for the Soviet Union; the crisis in Pakistan, which brought seven million refugees into India in the summer of 1971, added a new dimension to it. On June 20 President Yahya Khan warned that he would "declare war" if "India made any attempt to seize any part of East Pakistan," and that in a war "Pakistan will not be alone." Yahya Khan's threat brought about the Indo-Soviet treaty of peace and friendship, an important landmark in the unfolding of Soviet strategies for South Asia.

[18] The Soviet stance on China hardened sharply after the Ninth Congress of the CPC, which, in Moscow's estimation, heralded the final defeat of the pro-Soviet elements in the Chinese Communist party. *Kommunist*, March 1969, printed a long thesis on Mao's China, which listed formidable charges against the "Maoist clique," the gravest of them being that the "Maoists are stepping up their subversive activities against the socialist countries," trying to set up "illegal groups" to head "the struggle of the people" against the Communist party leaderships. Peking's ultimate objective was to unleash a "clash between the USSR and the socialist countries on the one hand and the forces of imperialism on the other." The article conceded that "the CPC's return to the path of scientific socialism will be a complicated and difficult process, attended by all sorts of unexpected occurances." Moscow and its allies must therefore be ready for a long and difficult struggle against "the theory and practice of militant Maoism."

[19] Among the spate of anti-Chinese polemical writings in the Soviet Union, mention may be made of O. Vladimirov and V. Ryazanov, "50th Anniversary of the Communist Party of China," *Kommunist*, October 1971; E. Nikolaev, "Sensation and Reality," *Izvestiia*, July 28, 1971; I. Alexandrov, "Regarding Peking-Washington Contacts," *Pravda*, July 25, 1971; G. Yakubov, "Conflict in Hindostan and the Provocative Role of Mao's Group," *ibid.*, December 28, 1971; and V. Vasiliev, "Increasing Militarization of Life in China Today," *Soviet Review*, no. 56 (1971). See also Pyotr N. Fedoseev's 5,000-word article in *Pravda*, December 5, 1971, which preceded a three-day conference of Soviet scholars on China at which Fedoseev delivered the keynote address.

## III

In signing the treaty[20] on August 9, the twenty-ninth anniversary of the "Quit India" movement launched by Gandhi against Britain, New Delhi and Moscow entered into a coalition-type relationship in which collaboration for the attainment of shared objectives did not preclude efforts by each to influence the other for the pursuit of its own strategic interests. India's minister for external affairs, Swaran Singh, while presenting the treaty for the Lok Sabha's approval, saw "a rapidly changing and dynamic picture" in the configuration of world forces, and declared that the treaty would "act as a deterrent to any powers that may have aggressive designs on our territorial integrity and sovereignty." Public opinion in India was almost unanimous that the treaty ended India's "loneliness" and gave it a feeling of effective strength. In other words, the security aspects of the treaty made the profoundest impression on the Indian elite. As the *Financial Express* put it, "In the present context of strained relations with Pakistan, and the possibility of armed clash between the two countries and the likelihood of Chinese intervention in support of Pakistan, the assurance of military support from the Soviet Union is of no small significance."[21] However, India needed Soviet support not merely to deter Pakistan and China but also to frustrate U.S. attempts to treat as an Indo-Pakistani conflict what to the Indians was entirely a nationalist revolt in East Pakistan. In the third week of July the U.S. government, with Pakistan's approval, tried to persuade U Thant to post U.N. peace observers on both sides of the East Pakistani border. Indians saw in the move a sinister design to equate India with Pakistan; it was reported

[20] Of the twelve articles of the treaty, Articles 9 and 10 are related to security. "In the event of either Party being subjected to an attack or a threat thereof, the High Contracting Parties shall immediately enter into mutual consultations in order to remove such threat and to take appropriate effective steps to ensure peace and the security of their countries" (Article 9). "Each High Contracting Party solemnly declares that it shall not enter into any obligation, secret or public, with one or more States, which is incompatible with this Treaty. Each High Contracting Party further declares that no obligation be entered into, between itself and and other State or States, which might cause military damage to the other Party" (Article 10). The Indo-Soviet treaty differs substantially from the Soviet-U.A.R. treaty of May 27, 1971. The latter provides for cooperation at the political level "to create the necessary conditions for safeguarding and maintaining the development of their two peoples' social and economic gains." (Articles 2, 6.) The Soviet-U.A.R. treaty is more ideologically oriented, and commits Cairo to certain socioeconomic policies and programs. It provides for elaborate military collaboration (Article 7), and almost commits the U.S.S.R. to come to Egypt's defense in the event of war." "In the event of the emergence of circumstances which, according to the view of both parties, constitute a threat to or a violation of peace, they will contact each other immediately with a view to coordinating their stand to remove the arising threat or to restore peace" (Article 8).

[21] Editorial, August 10, 1971.

in the Indian press that the U.S. was getting deeply involved in East Pakistan on behalf of Rawalpindi, and was planning to send "police experts" there to push through "public safety programs," thereby applying its Vietnam counterinsurgency experience to East Bengal.[22] The Indian government flatly rejected U Thant's scheme for peace observers because it opposed any move "which tends to convey that the problem is not between East Pakistan and Pakistan but between India and Pakistan."[23] The Soviet Union backed India's position, and it took no time for the Indians to realize that, unlike 1965, there was in 1971 little prospect of the two superpowers working together for stability in South Asia.[24]

It soon became clear, however, that India's and the Soviets' strategic objectives in East Pakistan were not the same in the fall of 1971. The question that assailed many Indians was whether the treaty would enable the U.S.S.R. to use India for its global strategic purposes rather than allow India to use the Soviets for its regional strategic objectives. To most Indians it appeared that the Soviets were opposed to any action that might lead to Pakistan's dismemberment, and that they still sought a political solution within the state structure of Pakistan. Indian analysts urged their government to take advantage of the treaty to pursue its own national interests. Thus, a columnist of the *Times of India* said that Indians would be disappointed if they expected the Soviet Union and the treaty to facilitate the establishment of an independent Bangladesh. Within the framework of the treaty, India must strive to pursue its own strategic objectives, even if these differed from those of the Soviet Union. "There is in fact no dearth of examples where smaller and weaker countries—France, Israel, North Vietnam and Pakistan—have effectively used links with the superpowers to advance their national interests."[25] An expert in strategic affairs believed that current developments in Sino-U.S. relations would "result in a strategic stand-off between the United States and China on the one hand and the Soviet Union on the other, thereby restoring to India the full initiative in the subcontinent"; the task for India was only to use that initiative.[26]

[22] *Amrita Bazar Patrika* (Calcutta), July 24, 1971.
[23] *Indian Express* (New Delhi), July 31, 1971.
[24] *Times of India,* July 27, 1971.
[25] *Ibid.,* August 25, 1971.
[26] K. Subramanyam, "Where India Stands in Global Power Equations," *Motherland* (New Delhi), September 28, 1971. Subramanyam, who is director of the Institute of Defense Studies and Analysis, New Delhi, wrote in another article: "In this new [power] game, the U.S. and China have a shared incentive to come together against the Soviet Union. The U.S. justifiably feels that the primary challenge to its security and top position comes not from China but from the Soviet Union. Consequently, the compulsion is greater to curb the power and influence of the Soviet Union. Similarly for China the Soviet Union is the next power standing

In early September, the Soviet Embassy in New Delhi took the un-
usual measure of printing as an advertisement in a mass-circulation
English daily what was undoubtedly intended to be an authoritative
interpretation of the treaty. One-half of the 6,000-word document detailed what the Soviet Union had already done to strengthen the economic defense and cultural base of Indian democracy. In dealing with
the international implications of the treaty, the document played down
its security aspects. The treaty was not a military alliance, it did not
draw India into a military bloc, and therefore it did not injure or limit
India's policy of nonalignment. Nor did it herald the launching of a
Soviet drive for collective security in Asia.

Does the treaty represent the first link in the chain visualized in
the so-called "Brezhneven Plan" for collective security in Asia, as
claimed by some vociferous pseudo-political pundits in the West?
Political analysts here [Moscow] are of the view that an attempt to
put the treaty as a component of a grand Soviet strategy design in
Asia is nothing but a striving to turn the treaty, an act of peace, into
a scarecrow. Those who make such claims only reveal their reactionary outlook and their aversion *to peace and stability and progressive social change* in Asia. In fact, the treaty has a much more
modest objective. It aims to give juridical concretization to a mani-
fold relationship between the two countries and peoples that has
since long become an established fact of contemporary international
life, a relationship to which the Soviet people are used to refer as
traditional.[27]

Between August and October, the Soviet and Indian leaders were
apparently trying to win each to the other's viewpoint. Indians noted
with chagrin the Soviets' reluctance to use the word Bangladesh in any

---

in its way to the top. Before it challenges the U.S. in power terms, it must neutralize the Soviet Union to the extent possible." "Power Growing Out of the Barrel
of a Gun," *Tribune*, July 27, 1972.

Most Indian commentators warned the government in September–October 1971
not to subordinate Indian interests in South Asia to the global interests of the
U.S.S.R. A typical example was: "Consequently it is within the context of superpower rivalries in the region that the significance of the treaty lies. If India can, on
the one hand, drive a wedge between the parallel policies of the United States
and the Soviet Union—which was to keep India weak—and on the other hand
deter China against any adventurist enterprise, the treaty will have been a diplomatic and political breakthrough. If, on the other hand, we find ourselves shoul-
dered into a subordinate role in our relationship with Russia, we will have dealt a
disastrous blow to our sovereign right to make our own independent decisions."
Patwant Singh, "Evolving Power Patterns," *Hindustan Times*, August 22, 1971.

[27] The advertisement appeared in *Indian Express*, September 4, 1971. Curiously,
it attracted little public notice in India. *Times of India* was almost the only major
newspaper to comment on it.

official document. In early October, the Indian government appeared to have made a major concession to the Soviet point of view. Swaran Singh announced at the meeting of the All-India Congress Committee and the policy-making caucus of the ruling party that a political solution of the East Bengali crisis between the Pakistani government and the Awami League would be acceptable to India, even if it were within the framework of a united Pakistan. Both governments moved troops toward the border. The air smelled of war. When the monsoon ended in East Pakistan, the partisan forces increased their activity and apparently succeeded in inflicting considerable damage on vital communication lines and military installations.[28] In a broadcast on October 12, Yahya Khan talked of an all-out war, which led to immediate high-level conclaves in New Delhi. What perturbed Delhi more was Yahya Khan's attempt to assemble an alternative, non–Awami League civilian regime in East Pakistan. Soviet Deputy Foreign Minister Feryubin paid an extended visit to New Delhi. While he was reported to entirely approve of the defensive measures taken by the Indian government, he also urged the imperative need for caution and restraint.[29] Then came Mrs. Gandhi's trip to Moscow, where she held extensive conversations with Soviet leaders. During these talks the two countries evidently came to an agreement on the crucial question of Indian intervention in East Bengal. Mrs. Gandhi, who was scheduled to undertake a tour of Western capitals, including Washington, in November, told the Soviet

[28] The partisan forces were built around the Bengali personnel of the East Pakistani regiment of the Pakistani army who had managed to desert after the Pakistani military crackdown on Bengali nationalists on March 25. The main partisan force was called *Mukti Bahini,* "Liberation Force." A second group was recruited during the summer and autumn from among the youthful followers of the Awami League; called *Mujib Bahini,* it was supposed to be a strongly anti-Communist force. With the help of like-minded people in West Bengal, some leftist elements in East Bengal also raised smaller, politically oriented partisan groups. As far as is known, all of these groups functioned under the overall direction of the chief of the *Mukti Bahini,* Colonel Osmani, a retired officer of the Pakistani army who became commander in chief of the Bangladesh army after liberation. Osmani, of course, operated closely with the Indian army.

[29] *Times of India,* October 5, 1971. In Washington, it may be noted, the main perception of the Soviet role in the subcontinent was one of restraining India from military action. When the treaty was signed, reported the *New York Times* on August 13, "Authoritative United States officials said that they understood the Soviet Union succeeded in dissuading India from formally recognizing East Pakistan as an independent country. . . . According to intelligence reports submitted to President Nixon, . . . the Soviet Union had warned the Indian Government that recognition of Bangla Desh could precipitate a war between India and Pakistan." Even during the Indo-Pakistani war, when the Soviets vetoed three resolutions in the U.N. Security Council, there was no public criticism of Moscow by the U.S. government, although President Nixon "was reliably reported to be irked privately by what he regards as Soviet efforts to obtain unilateral advantages from the war." *Ibid.,* December 14, 1971.

leaders that she would give them from two to three months to bend Rawalpindi to negotiate a political solution with the Awami League. In return, she apparently got an assurance that the Soviets would back her fully if she were compelled to act in East Pakistan. A knowledgeable Indian correspondent located in Moscow summed up the results of the prime minister's visit thus: "In the first place the Soviet side has stopped conveying the impression of ambiguity [on the Pakistan issue] which it did before Mrs. Gandhi's visit to Moscow. In the second place, the Soviet side, in spite of its known and strongly expressed preference for peace, has accepted the idea that, if unavoidable, India can take very firm steps in East Bengal without being concerned about Soviet support at any level—political, economic or otherwise."[30]

In November Mrs. Gandhi returned from her tour of Western capitals without any firm indication that the United States was willing to nudge the Pakistani government toward a settlement with the Awami League. The partisan army in East Bengal was now receiving increasing logistical support from India. Returning to India, the prime minister ordered the army to move inside East Bengali territory to silence the forward Pakistani positions, from which the troops had been firing across the border. The Soviet Union moved toward supporting India in this situation of escalating tension. On November 9, a visiting Soviet dignitary, V. Kudriavtsev, described the struggle in East Bengal as "a national liberation movement with an element of civil war in it."[31] Six days later Mr. Kudriavtsev declared that, in the event of a war between India and Pakistan or any other country, the Soviet Union would play the role it played in the Vietnam War.[32] Meanwhile, a series of articles in *Pravda* blamed Pakistan for the increasing tension, counseled Rawalpindi to build good-neighborly relations with India, and defended the Indian government against the accusation that it was about to attack Pakistan and thus to take advantage of that country's weakness.[33] Toward the end of November, the Soviet ambassador to Pakistan, Rodionov, met Yahya Khan and conveyed his government's "demand" that Yahya Khan come to a political settlement with the Awami League and desist from escalating the crisis in the subconti-

[30] Dev Murarka, "Twofold Gain for India," *Western Times* (Ahmedabad), October 16, 1971.

[31] *Patriot* (New Delhi), November 9, 1971. Mr. Kudriavtsev, who is a political correspondent of *Izvestiia* and a member of the CPSU Central Committee, was heading a parliamentary delegation to India.

[32] *Times of India*, November 16, 1971.

[33] See, for example, Oleg Orestov's article in *Pravda*, November 9, 1971, replying to Joseph Alsop's charge that India was about to boot Pakistan in the groin at a time when the latter was "down."

nent.[34] Almost simultaneously the Soviet ambassador to India, Nikolai Pegov, saw Mrs. Gandhi to assure her of Moscow's support should the United States raise the Indo-Pakistani issue at the U.N. Security Council.[35] On December 1, the joint Soviet-Bulgarian communiqué issued at the end of Kosygin's visit to Sofia mentioned the tension in the subcontinent, thereby indicating that Moscow had begun to enlist the support of the East European states for its line of action.[36] On December 3, *Pravda* carried Mrs. Gandhi's remark that the withdrawal of Pakistani troops from East Bengal would create conditions for the return of the refugees who had taken shelter in India.

Full-scale fighting between Pakistan and India broke out on December 3. Two days later the Soviet government warned all nations to keep away from involvement in the conflict. In a statement issued through *Tass*, it identified as the cause of the conflict Pakistan's refusal to settle East Bengal's demand for autonomy with the elected representatives of the people, and declared that, "in the face of the military threat now overhanging Hindustan, the Soviet Government comes out for the speediest ending of the bloodshed and for a political settlement in East Pakistan on the basis of respect for the lawful rights and interests of its people."[37] At the U.N. Security Council, the U.S.S.R. vetoed two resolutions backed by the United States and China calling for a cease-fire and withdrawal of troops, and fully supported India's position. It backed a Polish resolution which could very well have been drafted in New Delhi. On December 18, the Soviet government issued another statement welcoming India's unilateral offer of a cease-fire on the western front after the surrender of the Pakistani forces in East Bengal, and warned all nations once again not to take any steps that could

[34] *Patriot*, November 26, 1971, quoting the AP in Rawalpindi. The paper also carried a Press Trust of India report from Moscow that the Soviet Union had warned Pakistan against disastrous consequences, should that country persist in its warlike course "in total disregard of international counsel for peaceful political means of resolving its problems." This Soviet diplomatic pressure is to be seen in the context of what was happening along the Indo–East Pakistani border in the last weeks of November. On the twenty-third, large numbers of Indian troops crossed into Pakistan. Five days later, Defense Minister Ram announced at a public meeting in Calcutta: "When the Pakistanis started creating trouble on the borders, I told my generals to take action. When it became worse, I told them to cross borders to silence the guns. Now they've been told that if it becomes necessary, they can advance as many miles into Pakistan territory as the range of the Pakistani guns." Pakistan declared a state of national emergency. Some Indians expected the Pakistani president to declare war. *New York Times*, November 24–29, 1971.

[35] *Times of India*, December 1, 1971.

[36] *Statesman*, December 2, 1971.

[37] *Times of India*, December 6, 1971.

"impede normalization of the situation in the subcontinent."[38] Both Soviet statements implied that South Asia's close geographical proximity to the U.S.S.R. and its importance for the security of the Soviet state made it a Soviet sphere of influence.

It was reported in the Indian press that Moscow had asked New Delhi to conclude its military operations in East Bengal within a week.[39] Apparently the Soviets were afraid that prolongation of the war beyond a week might lead to intervention by the United States or China or both. In the second week of the war, the U.S. ordered a task force of the Seventh Fleet, including the nuclear carrier *Enterprise,* to move into the Bay of Bengal. The Soviet government dispatched to New Delhi a five-man delegation headed by First Deputy Foreign Minister Vassily Kuznetsov, who remained in the Indian capital until the end of the war, holding daily consultations with Indian officials. On her part, Mrs. Gandhi sent D. P. Dhar, chief architect of the Indo-Soviet treaty, to Moscow for close liaison work with Soviet leaders. Thus was ensured the closest coordination between the two countries during the most crucial phase of the fourteen-day war.

The Soviets' decision to move units of their naval fleet into the Bay of Bengal, which was conveyed to the Indian government on December 15, illustrated more vividly than anything else the changes that had taken place in the U.S.S.R. as a power since 1965. The U.S. government decided on a show of naval power more out of petulance than in accordance with a well-laid-out design to intervene in the conflict.[40]

[38] *Ibid.,* December 19, 1971.

[39] *Statesman,* December 12, 1971. Reports in the Indian press suggest that Moscow proposed sending a high-level official to New Delhi to coordinate the two countries' strategies, but Mrs. Gandhi wanted an Indian official of comparable status to be located simultaneously in the Soviet capital. Soviet impatience with the slow pace of the Indian advance in East Pakistan was evidently coupled with the anxiety that the Indians did not carry the war into West Pakistan once Bangladesh had been liberated. Apparently Mrs. Gandhi had already given the Soviet leaders to understand that she would accept a cease-fire after the liberation of Bangladesh if Pakistan also did the same. See *Times of India,* December 12, 1971. "Kuznetsov, after his arrival in New Delhi on December 12, told Indian officials that the Kremlin was 'impatient with the Indian armed forces for their inability to liberate Bangladesh within the ten-day time-frame-mentioned before the outbreak of hostilities.' . . . Kuznetsov pointed out, according to the secret report, that 'Soviet opposition to a ceasefire becomes more untenable the longer the war goes on in the east.' . . . Kuznetsov delayed his scheduled return to Moscow because he is awaiting special instructions from Leonid Brezhnev . . . regarding India's request that the Soviet Union sign a defense agreement with the Bangladesh government after Soviet recognition of Bangladesh." Jack Anderson, *Washington Post,* December 21, 1971.

[40] Jack Anderson said that the secret White House papers dealing with the two-week war made it clear that the task force was sent into Indian waters as a "show of force." The naval deployment was intended (1) to compel India to divert both ships and planes to shadow the task force; (2) to weaken India's

The "Anderson Papers" reveal that, even in the first week of December, the White House had reconciled itself to the emergence of Bangladesh; it was, however, highly apprehensive that, after the fall of East Bengal, the Indians would carry the war deep into West Pakistan and "make Pakistan defenseless." As Kissinger outlined the Presidential perception, "what we may be witnessing is a situation wherein a country, India, equipped and supported by the Soviets, may be turning half of Pakistan into an impotent state and the other half into a vassal."[41] The news of the movement of the Seventh Fleet task force delayed Kuznetsov's departure from New Delhi. The Indian government reacted to the U.S. move with quiet self-confidence. Jack Anderson claimed that Moscow had assured New Delhi that "it would not allow the 7th Fleet to intervene in Bangladesh," and that it would "open a diversionary action in Sinkiang" in case the Chinese attacked India across the Himalayas.[42] Vessels of the Soviet Pacific Fleet steamed through the Straits of Malacca three days after the U.S. task force. The unilateral Indian cease-fire on December 16 and its acceptance by Yahya Khan rendered the U.S. show of force infructuous. President Nixon, however, claimed that he had sought, and obtained, Soviet cooperation in inducing India not to carry the war into West Pakistan after the collapse of East Bengal.[43] The Indians, on the other hand,

---

blockade against East Pakistan; (3) possibly to divert the Indian aircraft carrier *Vikrant* from its military mission; and (4) to force India to keep planes on defense alert, thus reducing their operations against Pakistani ground troops. "The evacuation of American citizens was strictly a secondary mission, adopted more as the justification than the reason for the naval force." *Washington Post*, December 31, 1971.

[41] *New York Times*, December 16, 1971. Anderson also reported that, after President Nixon ordered the Seventh Fleet to send a task force into Indian waters, plans were made to "arrange provocative leaks in such places as Djakarta, Manila and Singapore of the task force's approach. By the time the ships had assembled in the Malacca Strait, both the Indians and Soviets were well aware they were on the way." *Washington Post*, December 21, 1971.

[42] According to Anderson, Ambassador Pegov told the Indian government that "a Soviet fleet is now in the Indian Ocean and the Soviet Union will not allow the Seventh Fleet to intervene." He also "promised" on December 13 that the Soviet Union "would open a diversionary action" against the Chinese if Peking took any adventurist move." Anderson claimed he was quoting from CIA reports to the White House. *Washington Post*, January 10, 1972.

[43] *Statesman*, December 28, 1971. Mr. Nixon gave the Soviet Union "credit" for "restraint after East Pakistan went down to get the ceasefire that stopped what would inevitably have been the conquest of West Pakistan as well." He was evidently trying to salvage the image of some parallel superpower interests in the South Asian region.

The Soviets no doubt did not want India to conquer West Pakistan, but there is no reason to believe that Mrs. Gandhi had any such intention at all. What the Soviets perhaps feared was that the prime minister might be under strong pressure of public opinion to pursue the war even after the fall of Dacca. According to the CIA, Pegov told the Indian government: "If India should decide to take

maintained that they had held the entire decision-making initiative during the war, and that "at no stage has the Soviet Union intervened themselves or on behalf of anyone else to tell us to do one thing or another or refrain from doing one thing or another."[44]

Whether the cease-fire offer was entirely an Indian initiative or the result of Indo-Soviet consultation, it was a triumph of Soviet diplomacy in South Asia. Nixon, in fact, helped Moscow by telling the world that the Soviet leaders had been partly responsible for the survival of West Pakistan. Moscow sent a cordial message of greetings to Zulfikar Ali Bhutto on his appointment as Pakistan's president, and offered friendly assistance to the new regime. At the same time, Moscow moved fast to consolidate its influence in the newly born state of Bangladesh.

*IV*

The Soviet Union has played a major part in ushering in a new regional subsystem in South Asia. The dominant power in the subsystem is India, which is treaty-bound to the U.S.S.R. How the subsystem works in the years to come will depend largely on the growing pattern of Indo-Soviet relationships; I have described it as a coalition-type relationship in which India's power interests will have to be accommodated within the framework of Russia's interests as a global superpower. Indians hope that the Soviets will now abandon their post-1965 policy to build friendship with Pakistan even at India's cost. Indeed, Indians expect the Soviets to use their influence to induce Pakistan to cooperate with India and Bangladesh to construct a symmetrical relationship within the entire subcontinent. As one Indian analyst has put it:

It is unlikely that the Soviet Union's recommendation regarding the terms of Indo-Pakistan peace [after the 1971 war] and coexistence would be much different from those that India herself might offer. Islamabad has to start from the assumption that Indo-Soviet relations will remain friendly and firm and that Pakistan will have to find a place under the sun without disturbing this relationship. The old Ayub model of foreign policy, wherein Pakistan was trying to turn the Soviet Union as much as China and America against India, is outmoded for obvious reasons.[45]

---

Kashmir, the Soviet Union would not interfere. But India would have to accomplish this objective within the shortest possible time." *Washington Post,* January 18, 1971. It should be added, however, that CIA reports, as quoted by Anderson, often proved to be quite removed from the realities, and it is therefore difficult to determine their credibility.

[44] *Times of India,* December 19, 1971.
[45] Sisir Gupta, "Pakistan's Dilemmas," *Seminar,* February 1971.

India, a more candid commentator has written, expects the Soviet Union to foster and underwrite its power status in South Asia. "The USSR is now at last interested in Indian credibility in South Asia." The "very logic" of the Indo-Soviet treaty "brought India into the game of power. From now on, it would be necessary to seek out spheres of influence to outflank and corner potential adversaries, and to build the kind of political and diplomatic thrust which tastes of major power status."[46] Indians, then, expect the Soviets to project much of their Asian strategy during the seventies through New Delhi, and they hope that, while this will expand Soviet *influence* in South and Southeast Asia, it will also to some extent contain Soviet *power*.

While a viable, friendly India as the dominant regional power should be a desirable goal of Soviet strategy, the kind of compact that the Indian elite expects will grow would depend on (1) their shared perception of common adversaries and (2) a minimum symmetry between the terrain of Indian domestic politics and Soviet development models for the Third World.

The Soviets expect India to share their perception of the United States and China. According to one Indian analyst, "The Soviet Union would like to see India play a prominent anti-US role in the region which would be indirectly aimed at Chinese influence."[47] There are others who believe that Moscow's blandishments are designed to persuade India to play a leading role in the containment of Chinese influence. The confusion stems from the uncertainty in Indian minds as to whether the Soviets are more anti-U.S. or anti-Chinese. For Indians, however, it is, or it has been, easier to be anti-Chinese than anti-American; indeed, most Indians regarded as ideal the situation during the sixties when India was the friend of both superpowers, while Pakistan was befriended by the Chinese. In quantity, U.S. assistance for India's economic development has been more than double the aid rendered by the U.S.S.R.; the U.S. is India's foremost trade partner. Despite the socialist rhetoric of India's economic and social planning, India is well advanced on the road to capitalist development, and Soviet scholars have long given up the hope that it would traverse the noncapitalist path.[48] The lowered American profile in South and Southeast Asia, the steady drying up of U.S. foreign aid funds, and, above all, Nixon's bias for Pakistan during the 1971 conflict have currently brought Indo-U.S. relations to an all-time low, and Indian leaders have been talking in terms of self-reliance, of doing without U.S. aid. The impressive spurt in grain output which resulted from the so-called

[46] Romesh Thapar, "Our Security Scenario," *ibid.*
[47] *Ibid.*
[48] See the present author's *Fulcrum of Asia*, chap. 5.

green revolution has, at least for the time being, liberated India from its decade-and-a-half-long dependence on PL-480 grain shipments.

The future pattern of U.S. relations with South Asia will depend on the initiatives Washington may take once it has accepted the realities that emerged from the 1971 conflict. The United States, as President Nixon made quite explicit in his "State of the World" message to Congress in February 1972, would like India to have a "balanced relationship" with the major powers; an India tilting too clearly toward the U.S.S.R. would be a cause of U.S. concern. Mr. Nixons' own efforts to balance U.S. relations with the U.S.S.R. and China, however, create a certain imbalance of power patterns in South Asia in Indian eyes, for many Indians tend to regard it as the beginning of a Sino-American détente principally aimed at Moscow. If such a détente develops, congruence of Soviet and Indian interests will likely occur. In that situation, it is probable that the Soviet Union and India would jointly operate a diplomacy whose main purpose would be to weaken the détente's impact. This diplomacy would probably have two apparently contradictory thrusts. The Soviets would try to consolidate and steadily expand areas of cooperation with the United States while waging their cold war with China. India would try to slowly improve relations with the Chinese, while maintaining a low-profile anti-U.S. posture.

Prospects for even a limited Sino-American détente have enhanced in Indian eyes the importance of living in peace with China, and the importance has not been markedly reduced by the expansion of Indo-Soviet friendship. Indeed, the political crisis in Pakistan and Nixon's support for Rawalpindi prodded the government of India in 1971 to make some earnest effort to unfreeze Sino-Indian relations.[49] Peking,

---

[49] Efforts to bring about an improvement in Sino-Indian relations were initiated in New Delhi and Peking during 1969 and 1970, especially after Mao sought out the Indian chargé d'affaires at the 1970 May Day rally, shook hands with him, and announced that there were no problems between the two neighbors that could not be resolved peacefully. Contacts were established in Moscow, Kathmandu, and other places. At a meeting between the Indian and Chinese ambassadors in Moscow, the question of reassigning the ambassadors who had been withdrawn after the 1962 conflict was discussed. *Patriot*, August 26, 1971. In August, Swaran Singh told Rajya Sabha (upper house of Parliament) that "India was 'ever prepared to create conditions' for talks with China if there were a 'favorable response.'" *Ibid.* In early September, the Indian envoy in Peking, B. Mishra, was recalled to New Delhi for consultations. The *Times of India* reported on September 4, 1971, that "there are reasons to believe that Mr. Mishra left Peking soon after he was assured that the Chinese Government would be interested in having a dialogue on the bilateral issues with India." That Peking made this gesture immediately after the conclusion of the Indo-Soviet treaty was considered significant. "According to informed sources, the signing of the treaty might perhaps have prompted Peking to have an early dialogue with India." India was invited to the Afro-Asian table tennis tournament in Peking in November; the team included at least one senior official of the foreign office. It became clear,

too, was not entirely unresponsive. It did not take too dim a view of the Indo-Soviet treaty when it was signed,[50] but its stance hardened, however, when the Indian army moved into East Bengal. The Chinese feared not so much an accretion to India's status in South Asia as a sharp acceleration of Soviet power and influence. The Soviet Union had supported the Indian intervention in East Bengal, said the Chinese delegate at the U.N., because it wished " to further strengthen its control over India and thereby to contend with the other superpower for hegemony in the whole of the South Asian subcontinent and the Indian Ocean and at the same time bolster India and turn it into a subsuperpower . . . as its assistant and partner in committing aggression in Asia."[51] India, however, did not match the Soviets' anti-Chinese polemics; there was a reluctance in New Delhi to play up the Chinese role

---

however, that progress toward a dialogue was slow in coming and that the process of normalizing relations would be long and difficult. "The border question, it appears, has not figured in any detail in the probings so far, and may not be a substantive point of discussion in the initial stages, if and when contacts are resumed." *Statesman*, September 1, 1971.

[50] An AFP dispatch from Peking at the end of August said that "even privately Chinese officials carefully refrain from any remarks which could be seen as reflecting their views on the Indo-Soviet treaty which they insist is still under study." *Hindustan Times*, September 1, 1971. In early September, a member of a visiting Chinese trade mission to Guyana remarked that Peking did not perceive the treaty to be a friendly act. *Indian Express*, September 5, 1971. In October, Han Suyin, the Belgian confidant of Chou En-lai, arrived in Delhi from China and, in a candid article in a major Indian newspaper, quoted an unnamed Chinese official "whose position and words command attention" in presenting a Chinese perception of the subcontinent. Referring to the treaty, the Peking official was quoted as saying:

> Viewing the treaty as India's affair, we prefer not to comment. But this does not mean that we are not aware of the military clauses of the treaty which actually put India in a position of inferiority. What it amounts to is this: That at the moment the USSR has got troops stationed on certain borders, poised in what may be construed as threatening attitude. India was not informed of these troop movements; yet by this treaty India's agreement to these troop concentrations has been tacitly given. This already placed India in the position of agreeing to a situation created after the fait accompli. This position of inferiority should perhaps worry the Indian people. It certainly does not worry the Chinese people. Each country must make its own experience of what is good and what is bad. We have had our experiences in the past and we hope that the Indian people will not be made use of.

*Indian Express*, October 20, 1971. Indian analysts showed a certain understanding of the Chinese fears and suspicions. On September 1 an editorial in *Hindustan Times* said that "there is equal reason for the Government of India to signal Peking that the Indo-Soviet treaty is not to be regarded as anti-Chinese." Girilal Jain wrote that the Chinese "cannot but be haunted by the fear that if Soviet power comes to be established in the Indian Ocean and the Himalayas, India may reopen the question of Tibet." *Times of India*, September 1, 1971.

[51] *New York Times*, December 16, 1971. The Chinese delegate's speech was released in Peking as an official statement of the government.

in the conflict. On the Chinese side, too, verbal attacks on India were muted soon after the war.

India and other nations of South Asia appear to realize that they are caught inextricably in the Sino-Soviet cold war. While the smaller South Asian nations—Afghanistan, Nepal, and Ceylon—are anxious to remain nonaligned in this cold war, the problem for India is how not to get too involved in it and still remain in Moscow's friendly embrace. In fact, the first task of India's foreign policy in the seventies is to manage its friendship with the U.S.S.R. and at the same time steadily move toward normalization of relations with China. The U.S.S.R., however, is unlikely to be pleased at a dramatic or radical improvement in Sino-Indian relations while their own relations with Peking remain in deep-freeze.[52] If Sino-Soviet relations further deteriorate and lead to more violent clashes, the Soviets would expect India to side with them against the Chinese.

While the Soviet Union can be seen as hoping to stabilize the South Asian subsystem around a strong and dynamic India, Indians are cautiously looking forward to Peking's recognition of their country as the dominant power in the region, from which should stem, in the near future, a modus vivendi for the two neighbors to coexist as peaceful competitors for influence and power in Asia.[53] Meanwhile, the Soviets appear to be hopeful that U.S. disengagement in Asia and Chinese hegemonic aspirations would generate among the nations of Southeast Asia an urge for "genuine neutrality." By this the Soviet leaders mean that these nations would exit from the American military alliance system while individually and collectively refusing to be drawn into the Chinese power orbit. Moscow perceives in Southeast Asia objective conditions that favor the region's neutralization; what hinders progress is the adherence of some of the governments to the "US military bloc."[54] A neutralized Southeast Asia linked in inter-regional cooperation with South Asia appears to be a major plank of the currently unspelled Soviet concept of collective Asian security. The present phase of Soviet strategy appears to be based on the assumption that, whatever may be the strategic ambitions of Peking, China lacks the power parameters to realize these ambitions; nor is its own house in very good

[52] The Soviet embassy advertisement referred to in note 27 said that the Indo-Soviet treaty made room for "a certain degree of normalization" in Sino-Indian relations.

[53] Some Indian analysts came out with the thesis that the real reason for the impasse in Sino-Indian relations was that India could not face China as an equal. The Indian victory against Pakistan altered this situation. In any dialogue with China, India must insist that Peking recognized its "primacy in the subcontinent." See Jain, "The Triangular Balance."

[54] V. Kudriatsev, "Southeast Asia at the Crossroads," *Izvestiia*, January 6, 1972.

shape. The United States is the superpower that needs to be eased out of its dominant position in Asia. The structure of Asian stability that the Soviets seem to foresee is to rest primarily on four pillars: restoration of the status quo ante in the Middle East and a peace guaranteed jointly by the two superpowers; a South Asia which leans upon Soviet influence, if not power; a Southeast Asia whose neutralization is guaranteed by the two superpowers, as well as by China, Britain, and France; and Japan collaborating on equal terms with all of its three great neighbors as a more or less neutralized military power.

Soviet strategy in Asia leaves room for pragmatic conciliation with recalcitrant realities. Perhaps the most recalcitrant realities are the newly independent societies, which, after decades of stagnation, have been pressed into the destabilizing process of development. The Soviets have hitherto perceived conflicts among and within these nations almost entirely as results of the imperialist powers' bid to dominate their economies and control their political actors. In recent years, however, Soviet scholars have identified a process of increasing *internal* polarization in many of the Third World societies, a polarization between the forces of reaction and those of progressive social change. At the present stage, "social and class aspects are becoming predominant in many countries of Asia, Africa and in a number of Latin American countries. In its policy with respect to the young independent states, the Soviet Union, supporting their struggle against imperialism and for national liberation, attaches special importance to the struggle *in* these countries against the exploiting classes and against fedual and capitalist relations."[55] The Soviet concept of security takes cognizance of conflicts and contradictions not only between the new nations and imperialism but also between the forces of progress and reaction within these nations.

Over the past decade and a half the Soviets have invested a substantial portion of their resources in a select group of Third World societies. In the profile of Soviet aid to the developing nations, South Asia occupies a very important position. Between 1955 and 1967, ten African, seven Asian, and six Middle Eastern nations received Soviet aid, but the bulk of it went to four states, India, Egypt, Iraq, and Afghanistan. (Afghanistan alone, with $238.9 million, got more than the ten

---

[55] "The main feature of the struggle for national liberation at the present stage of the general crisis of capitalism is that in many instances it has in practice been developing into a struggle against the whole system of exploitative relations of production, feudal and capitalist alike. [In a considerable number of countries which have not been following the path of noncapitalist development] a stubborn struggle [is] taking place between the forces of progress and those of internal reaction which is supported by imperialism." V. Rymalov, "The Weakening Position of Imperialism," *International Affairs*, 1971, no. 8.

African countries put together—$136 million.)[56] India has so far received $1.3 billion in Soviet economic aid.[57] While the U.S.S.R. is India's second-largest trade partner (after the U.S.), "India is the major trade partner of the USSR among the developing countries of Asia."[58] Since 1965 the U.S.S.R. has supplied 65.0 percent of the total arms trade in the subcontinent as against a mere 0.5 percent by the United States; the bulk of these has been taken by India.[59] The Soviets have at the same time been assisting India to build a modern defense industry.

What introduces an ambivalence in the Soviet stance toward the South Asian nations is the dual competition Moscow wages at the same time against the United States and China. The first accounts for anti-imperialist radicalism, the second for a concern for stability that is often mistaken by the ruling classes as a commitment to the existing status quo. As noted, the elite in South Asia, especially in India, perceive the Soviet Union to be more concerned with the stability of the existing societies than with radical, far less revolutionary change, while the Soviet leaders regard stability to be essentially the result of "progressive social change." This informs Soviet involvement with the developing nations with a certain unpredictability. The imperatives of containing Chinese power and influence induce the Soviets to seek viable allies in Asia, but the drift and scale of the politics of the developing societies would seem to breathe into Russian minds doubts about the viability of the ruling classes.

This can be illustrated by the Soviets' analysis of the "root causes" of the Indo-Pakistani war of 1971. Pakistan's insecurity, according to a *Pravda* analyst, stemmed from the alliance that was formed from 1958 to 1968 between a small group of indigenous industrialists, financial magnates, and big landlords and the "imperialist states, above all the US, which involved Pakistan in the aggressive military blocs of SEATO and CENTO." In 1968 a mass upsurge against this alliance began with a demand for the democratization of Pakistan's political life and the promotion of an independent foreign policy. "The movement assumed particularly large proportions in East Pakistan where

[56] Robert S. Walters, *American and Soviet Aid* (Pittsburgh, Pa.: University of Pittsburgh Press, 1970), app. B.

[57] "Indo-Soviet Treaty and Economic Cooperation," *Economic Times* (Bombay), August 22, 1971. In 1970, 11 percent of India's exports were from Russia. Over 8 percent of Soviet imports from India were nontraditional, including engineering goods. The Soviets have built sixty-six development projects in India, which is more than they have built in any other nonsocialist country.

[58] A. Kalugin, "Eighteen Years of Soviet-Indian Trade," *Soviet Review*, no. 67 (1971).

[59] *Times of India*, February 5, 1972.

general democratic calls were reinforced by demands for autonomy within the framework of a single state." The failure of the rulers of Pakistan to accommodate this demand and their determination to suppress it by military force tore the country asunder.[60] Between 1967 and 1970, Soviet scholars articulated considerable doubts about the Indian bourgeoisie's capability to function as a viable ruling class.[61] These doubts, however, yielded to a fresh renewal of hope following Mrs. Indira Gandhi's nationalization measures and her impressive victory in the parliamentary elections in March 1971. Since then, Soviet sights in India have gone up as a result of the leftward thrusts of Mrs. Gandhi's socioeconomic programs.[62] The Indo-Soviet treaty has enlarged the field of Soviet and East European involvement in India's development; hardly any ministry of the Indian government is now left out of the orbit of collaboration. In the 1972 elections to the state assemblies, the ruling Congress party formed an electoral alliance with the Moscow-oriented CPI.[63] There is, then, some evidence that under Indira Gandhi's leadership, the Congress party has initiated a measure of collaboration with the Moscow-oriented Communists. While this situation falls short of the CPSU's and CPI's strategic goal of the national democratic state, it would appear to lend some ideological muscle to Moscow's friendship for India. A similar situation is developing in Bangladesh.

For the next few years, therefore, the Soviets probably have little cause to worry about the stability of South Asia, and they can be expected to increase their investment in this region, if only to insulate it from China. Their stance may change, however, if Mrs. Gandhi fails to tackle India's worsening problem of massive poverty, and if the CPI(M) and the Maoist groups, who reject the Soviet assessment of the Congress party as a progressive force and are pitted against it, succeed in building up a sizable militant agrarian movement around

[60] For a collection of articles written by Soviet publicists, analysts, and scholars on the crisis in Pakistan, the Indo-Pakistani conflict, and Bangladesh, see *Soviet Review*, January 18, 1972.
[61] Bhabani Sen Gupta, "Moscow, Peking, and the Indian Political Scene after Nehru," *Orbis*, 12 (1968): 534-62.
[62] "New winds are blowing across India. Those who had assumed that India would irrevocably take the capitalist road were quite wrong. Tata and Birla may be the show pieces of Indian capitalism, but they are no more characteristic of Indian capitalism than a couple of modern skyscrapers in a cottage community." G. Mirsky, "Tendencies in the National Liberation Movement Today," *International Affairs*, 1971, no. 8. By "those" the writer evidently means Soviet scholars and analysts who perceive India to be a capitalist country.
[63] Mrs. Gandhi's Congress party had electoral pacts with the CPI in Bihar, Punjab, Rajasthan, West Bengal, and Assam. Mrs. Gandhi's own Council of Ministers includes several former CPI leaders, such as Minister for Heavy Industry Mohan Kumaramanglam and Minister of State for Education Nurul Hasan.

the rural poor, who constitute the bulk of the Indian population.[64] Further removed from the present time lurks the other question that sometimes gnaws at the Indian elite mind: What would be the Soviet stance toward India if and when Moscow arrived at a détente with Peking?

## V

In South Asian eyes, the Soviet Union emerged as an Indian Ocean power during the Indo-Pakistani war of 1971. By their naval movements in the Bay of Bengal, the Soviets gained a significant psychological victory in South and Southeast Asia, particularly because official sources in the United States and China articulated the fear that the success of the Indian intervention in East Bengal, with Soviet political and material support, would vastly enhance Soviet influence in the Indian Ocean area.

An important dimension of the Soviet Union's emergence as a global power is its bid to earn equality with the United States as a world naval power. Students of Soviet military strategy are familiar with the post-Stalin debates that have been going on in Russia on the role to be assigned to the navy in the expanding Soviet military apparatus.[65] In recent years the "naval lobby" would seem to have wrested from the government and the Communist party a greater recognition of the navy's importance in the power equation with the U.S., and a larger portion of the defense budget for building a strong navy capable of operating on the high seas. It may still take the Soviets several years to build a navy capable of taking the strategic offensive. It may not even be the policy of the government to acquire the attack-carrier strike forces that are essential in the present age to contest for command of the high seas. The current phase of Soviet naval expansion is probably designed to achieve what George Fielding Eliot has described as a "sea-denial weapons system" rather than a "sea-control weapons system."[66] This sea-denial weapons system is what the Soviets appear to be extending to the Indian Ocean.

The Soviet argument for building a naval presence in the Indian Ocean runs as follows. The enormous wealth of the Indian Ocean nations attracted European imperialist powers to the region and led to

[64] For an account of militant peasant movements in India under Communist leadership in recent years, see the present author's "Peasant Mobilization by Indian Communists," *Problems of Communism*, 21, no. 1 (1972); and his *Communism in Indian Politics* (New York: Columbia University Press, 1972).

[65] Robert Waring Herrick, *Soviet Naval Strategy: Fifty Years of Theory and Practice* (Annapolis: U.S. Naval Institute, 1968).

[66] George Fielding Eliot, *Victory without War, 1958–1961* (Annapolis: U.S. Naval Institute, 1961), p. 108.

its subjugation, with Britain seizing the lion's share of the colonies. World War II ended the phase of British domination, which was replaced by an Anglo-U.S. partnership. By inventing the "notorious and false" theory of a power vacuum, the United States succeeded in the post war years in "militarizing" the Indian Ocean area. Although this "militarization" is primarily and ostensibly designed to contain Communist power, it is also aimed at circumscribing the independence of the new nations and keeping them under control. The Soviet Union is a great Eurasian state. The important world routes of sea communication provided by the Indian Ocean offer "convenient connections between parts of Soviet territory" separated by vast expanses of land. Moreover, the U.S.S.R. has extensive trade and economic relations with many nations of the Indian and Pacific oceans. "Naturally therefore it uses sea routes, which are sometimes the only possible routes, for peaceful cooperation with its partners."

Soviet warships cruise the waters "where, in the opinion of the Soviet Government, it is necessary to ensure security of important communication lines and freedom of navigation." The Soviet government perceives an American threat to free navigation in the Indian Ocean. Since 1966, the U.S., with British collaboration, has been building major naval bases in the Indian Ocean area, using such strategically important islands as the Seychelles and Diago Gracia. The U.S., in building up its offensive forces in the seventies, "intends to lay emphasis not on the ground but on the sea as a launching pad for missiles and hydrogen bombs." Polaris and Poseidon missiles launched from pads in the Indian Ocean easily threaten the security of vast portions of the U.S.S.R. "In the American strategists' opinion, the coordinated action of the three fleets—the 7th, the 6th and the new Indian Ocean fleet—would enable them to launch, in case of need, a 'nuclear offensive' on a global scale." While this nuclear militarization of the Indian Ocean is directed "first and foremost" against the U.S.S.R. and other socialist nations, it is also a threat to the developing littoral nations. "While 'leaving' the Asian-African territory, they [the imperialist powers] remain in Afro-Asian waters. In other words, only the form of their military presence is changed, not its essence and goals." The Soviet Union does not wish a situation to develop in which the navies of the great powers will be stationed far away from their shores for a long time. But the problem can be solved "only on an equal basis."[67]

The Soviets' desire for parity with the United States on the high seas was reflected in Moscow's and Washington's abstention on the Cey-

[67] S. Kozlov, "The Indian Ocean: Myth and Reality," *Soviet Review*, October 26, 1971.

lonese resolution adopted by the 1971 session of the U.N. General Assembly declaring the Indian Ocean as a zone of peace and calling for international consultations to implement that declaration.

The question that poses itself in the seventies is whether the U.S.S.R. would succeed in establishing a community of security interests in the Indian Ocean region with India and other littoral nations. The Soviets are aware of the competition that exists between their own and India's strategic interests in the Indian Ocean, and to this are added the competitive claims of Indonesia, Japan, and China.[68] As long as Indians perceived that the Soviet navy was balancing U.S. naval power in the Indian Ocean and that the two were jointly keeping China out of it, New Delhi's tacit approval of a Soviet naval presence was tempered by the ritualistic demand that the Indian Ocean be declared a peace zone and by a firm refusal to allow Moscow base facilities there. While these strains are still to be found in the Indian stance, the perception of converging Sino-American interests to contain Soviet power may soften resistance to Soviet blandishment to secure a formidable naval presence. In other words, depending on the thrust of U.S. and Chinese policies and India's response to them, the Soviets may be able to persuade New Delhi that safeguarding Russian security interests by erecting a strong Soviet naval presence in the Indian Ocean would mean the safeguarding of South Asia's security interests as well.

There are other factors that may work toward this end. The role played by the Indian navy during the 1971 war has exalted its position in the eyes of the elite. There will now be an insistent demand for a stronger Indian naval arm. The Soviet Union is already helping India build naval ships and submarines; the Indian submarine fleet is mostly of Soviet make. The anti-Soviet prejudices articulated by a number of Indian naval officers can now be expected to change to emulation of the army's large-scale adoption of Soviet weaponry.[69] In short, conditions seem to be emerging for Indo-Soviet naval cooperation within the framework of the Indo-Soviet treaty. The Soviets may come forward to help India acquire aspects of a regional naval power. While this would predictably whet Indonesian and Chinese jealousies, it might well prove to be a successful political measure by which to impress the less ambitious (and less potentially capable) littoral states with the impor-

[68] In November 1971, Indonesia, Malaysia, and Singapore jointly rejected a Japanese proposal to dredge the Straits of Malacca to ensure the safe transit of large tankers. The three coastal states told Japan that the straits fall within their territorial waters and are within their jurisdiction. *Statesman*, November 18, 1971.
[69] See the present author's "The Indian Ocean: An Indian Evaluation" (Paper circulated at the Georgetown University Indian Ocean Conference held in March 1971) for a detailed discussion of India's perception of the Indian Ocean and of the U.S. and Soviet presence in those waters.

tance of Soviet friendship. That, I have suggested, is a major motivation of the Soviets' South Asian strategies, which remain poised in the early seventies for cautiously bold measures to expand the global aspects of Soviet power.[70]

[70] A conference of Soviet scholars on international affairs, held in the wake of the Twenty-fourth Congress of the CPSU, came to the conclusion that the present phase of the struggle against imperialism calls for the "greatest diplomatic art, combining precision and calmness with boldness in the delivery of strikes, circumspection and resolution." "The 24th Congress of CPSU and International Issues," *International Affairs*, 1971, no. 8.

# 6

## THE SOVIET UNION AND THE MIDDLE EAST

### John C. Campbell

The growing Soviet presence in the Mediterranean, the Middle East, and the Indian Ocean has produced in the West a variety of explanations and reactions. The latter range from alarm to vague concern to complacency. The former may flow from a general view of Soviet policy in the Brezhnev era (and before) or from a specific preoccupation with interests that are obviously affected—Western defense, concern for Israel or for the Arabs or for a settlement between them, access to Middle East oil, or whatever.

If a Soviet grand strategy exists, one must assume that the separate pieces of Soviet policy here and there in the Middle East are logically related to it. It is unrewarding to proceed from theory—from the sacred texts of Leninism on the inevitable triumph of communism or the pronouncements of party congresses and leaders about national liberation movements and progress on the road to socialism in the Third World, or even from some mechanical concept of the balance of power. One has to look at specific developments in the Middle East itself to see where this "presence" is, of what it consists, and against whom it is directed; what the commitments and the means to back them up are; what risks are being taken and where their limits are. Finally, one has to try to measure the importance of the region, in Soviet eyes, in relation to other Soviet interests, foreign and domestic.

In contrast to Europe, where the Soviet leaders have chosen a policy of stabilization and détente, the Middle East has presented a shifting political scene in which the U.S.S.R. is engaged in an active political and military competition with the United States which both sides frankly admit is dangerous to world peace. In contrast to Southeast Asia, where the Soviet leaders, although virtually compelled to support North Vietnam and oppose the United States for reasons of solidarity with a Communist state and of competition with China, have limited their involvement, the Middle East has witnessed such a heavy concentration of Soviet effort and such deep Soviet involvement as to suggest that the leaders in Moscow see vital interests at stake. In contrast to their game in South Asia, where they chose to back India—the

Reprinted by permission from *Problems of Communism*, September–October 1972, where it appeared as "The Communist Powers and the Middle East: Moscow's Purposes."

stronger party—and made notable gains at small risk, in the Middle East they have sided with Arab states of proven weakness and instability.

The inevitable question is: Why? Before attempting to deal with it, we should have before us a brief (if necessarily oversimplified) description of the position that the Soviet Union has attained in the Middle East. What has it gained in military positions, political influence, and general prestige? How solid is the foundation on which these gains rest?

The recent action of Egypt, in requesting the withdrawal of most of the Soviet military advisers and experts, appears to have posed that last question in stark form. This dramatic move and the circumstances surrounding it are not yet sufficiently clear to enable us to reach firm conclusions on their meaning. As an expression of nationalism, it can hardly be overestimated. Some call it a historic turning point, a basic shift in the balance of power, indicating that the Soviet position in the Middle East has passed its apogee and henceforth can only decline. Others pass it off as a temporary setback, or even as a sly game of collusion. Probably neither interpretation is correct. Rather than attempt rash prediction, it seems wise to look at these recent events in the context of the whole pattern of Soviet relations with the Middle East.

## The Military Picture

The Soviet military presence has consisted mainly of ships on the high seas, naval and air facilities, bases, advisory missions, military supply programs, and, until recently, limited combat forces in Egypt. (Thus far we do not know whether all those forces are being permanently withdrawn, along with other "advisers," at Egypt's request; if so, the Soviet presence is diminished, though by no means ended.)

The growth of Soviet naval strength in the Mediterranean from practically nothing in the early 1960s to a permanent squadron which at times has numbered more than sixty ships has been the most spectacular advance.[1] This squadron has the use of facilities for repair in certain Egyptian and Syrian ports and has perfected techniques of refueling and replenishment at sea. However, the effect of the increase of the Soviet naval force on the military balance has not been decisive, for

[1] Michael Salomon, *Méditerranée rouge* (Paris: Robert Laffont, 1970), pp. 87–95; Lawrence L. Whetten, "The Military Consequences of Mediterranean Super Power Parity," *New Middle East* (London), November 1971, pp. 14–25; J. C. Hurewitz, "Changing Military Perspectives in the Middle East," in *Political Dynamics in the Middle East,* ed. Paul Y. Hammond and Sidney S. Alexander (New York: Elsevier, 1972), pp. 72–85.

the Soviet squadron is inferior to the U.S. Sixth Fleet in striking power and could not last long in a direct test of strength, though such a test is neither sought nor likely to take place. Nonetheless, the Soviet squadron has compelled American and NATO naval forces to take account of it. Soviet and Western writers have argued that its mere presence may rule out unilateral moves by U.S. forces, such as the landings in Lebanon in 1958.[2] Above all, it proclaims to all nations that the Mediterranean is not an American lake, that another great power is there. The effects have been evident not only on Arab states but on the political calculations and policies of NATO countries, of Yugoslavia and Albania, and especially of states like Cyprus and Malta, former strongpoints of the Western defense system.[3]

In the Indian Ocean, the trend has been similar, although there the wide expanses of water and the near-absence of naval power exercised by anyone make for a less concentrated rivalry and a more attenuated connection between warships and political influence. This is not to say that American authorities have not been concerned about Soviet naval visits to the Persian Gulf or East Africa, and especially about possible Soviet bases in India following Moscow's strong support of India against Pakistan and the bilateral security treaty of August 1971, or that Soviet authorities have not been concerned about the U.S. submarines in the Indian Ocean which are capable of launching nuclear missiles into Soviet territory.[4]

The new Soviet naval strategy, of course, is not chopped into geographical segments. The forces in the Mediterranean and the Indian Ocean serve the general aim, pursued since the early 1960s, of making the Soviet Union a global naval power capable of flexing its muscles on all the world's seas. In that context, too, it is worth mentioning some physical barriers. The Mediterranean is a highway to the oceans; how-

[2] See A. K. Kislov, "SShA v Sredizemnomore: Novye realnosti," *SShA* (Moscow), April 1972, pp. 35–36; Bernard Lewis, "The Great Powers, the Arabs, and Israelis," *Foreign Affairs*, July 1969, p. 644; Hurewitz, *loc. cit.*, pp. 79–80. However, Admiral Elmo Zumwalt, U.S. Chief of Naval Operations, believes that the Sixth Fleet could still act as it did in 1958 (*U.S. News and World Report*, September 13, 1971, pp. 72–77), and much has been made of its influence on the outcome of the Syrian-Jordanian crisis of 1970.

[3] On the balance of forces and its consequences, see E. Novoseltsev and David Prygov, "SShA i Sredizemnomore," in *SShA: Regionalnye problemy vneshnei politiki*, ed. Yu. P. Davydov and V. S. Rudnev (Moscow: Nauka, 1971), pp. 56–59.

[4] Geoffrey Jukes, "The Soviet Union and the Indian Ocean," *Survival* (London), November 1971, p. 371; Oles Smolansky, "Soviet Entry into the Indian Ocean: An Analysis" (Paper presented at the Center for Strategic and International Studies, Georgetown University, March 18–19, 1971), pp. 6 and 8; Yurii Tomikin, "Indiiski Okean v aggressivnykh planakh imperializma," *Mirovaia ekonomika i mezhdunarodnye otnosheniia* (Moscow), August 1971, pp. 20–22, 27.

ever, it is an inland sea with narrow openings. Between it and Soviet home ports in the Black Sea lie the Turkish Straits, long coveted by Russian governments but now firmly in the physical possession of the Turks. At the moment, both the Soviet Union and Turkey are observing the Montreux Convention. But the Soviets cannot be sure of Turkey's cooperation in all circumstances; thus, the Soviet naval position depends uniquely on Soviet relations with Turkey.

At the eastern end of the Mediterranean, the exit to the Red Sea and Indian Ocean has been closed since 1967; the Suez Canal serves not as an international waterway but as an antitank ditch between two armies. The Soviet Union undoubtedly would like to see the canal reopened. However, it has not pursued an active policy to that end, for the simple reason that it could not bring about Israel's withdrawal except on terms that were unacceptable to its Egyptian ally. The U.S. proposal for an "interim solution" to the Arab-Israeli conflict—whereby Israel would move back from the canal to another defensive line in the Sinai and allow the canal to be reopended for all ships, including its own—would suit Soviet maritime and strategic interests, but this proposal is now festooned with all the intractable issues which have made a permanent settlement impossible and on which neither great power chooses to push its local ally to accept a compromise. So the Soviets are denied the direct route that they would like to have in moving ships between the Mediterranean and the Indian Ocean.

The western end of the Mediterranean has a wider gate than the eastern end. However, Western positions at Gibraltar and Rota afford the means of surveillance, and Western air and naval capabilities provide the means of control.

One can foresee possible additional gains in the Soviet military position: more surface ships and submarines in the Mediterranean, more naval and air facilities along the North African littoral, the neutralization of Cyprus and Malta as bases available to Western forces, perhaps a reopening of the Suez Canal, the use of bases along the Red Sea, and stronger forces in the Indian Ocean. But it is hard to see such gains upsetting the military balance in those regions or permitting Soviet forces safely to engage in military interventions, unless the United States were deliberately to choose a policy of withdrawal or unless there were a total change in the political balance on which American interests so largely depend. We must presume that the Soviet political leaders know these things, despite the loud talk of their admirals about fighting the imperialists on all the seas.

## Political Strategy

For these reasons the essence of the Soviet Union's policy, and of the gains it has made, is primarily political. Political success in the

Arab world in the period of Nikita Khrushchev opened the way for the development of military positions by his successors, and those positions, besides being useful for further political gains, continue to require an adequate political foundation for their very existence.

Soviet political strategy in Stalin's last years was extraordinarily passive in the wake of his failure to break into Iran, Turkey, Greece, and the Mediterranean during the period at the close of World War II. After his death, it emerged along two main lines. The first was to reduce Western commitments and influence in the countries on the Soviet Union's southern borders, Turkey and Iran. This policy had its periods of threat and subversion, as well as of détente, and sometimes it combined all three; but by the mid-1960s the watchwords were normalization and cooperation. The second line was to support Arab nationalism and radical Arab regimes in their conflicts with the Western powers and with Israel. Here the successes were more spectacular, and the gains made at Western expense were more serious.

These were not separate policies. Moscow is often given great credit for having "leapfrogged" the Western-allied "northern tier" to establish Soviet influence in the Arab world, where the West was vulnerable. Yet the Soviet leaders were not so taken with their successes in Cairo and Damascus that they failed to keep in their vision the Middle East region as a whole. Where there were differences within the Soviet leadership about how far to go in commitments to Arab states—and there were such differences, certainly during Khrushchev's last year in power and probably on subsequent occasions[5]—the state of relations with Turkey and Iran was not an irrelevant consideration. Brezhnev and his colleagues, in scaling down Khrushchev's far-flung adventurism in the Third World to concentrate particular attention on the Middle East, have shown their awareness of that fact, as will be demonstrated in the following discussion of Moscow's bilateral relations with Iran, Turkey, and the Arab states.

## Turkey

What political gains have the Soviets made in Turkey? Under the banner of normalization, they have drawn the Turks away from rigid conformity with American policies and strategies. In many ways, they were knocking at an open door, for the Turks not only were already questioning the need for policies of cold-war firmness at a time when their allies in Western Europe were preaching and practicing détente, but were looking askance at American policies, which included withdrawal of missiles from Turkey, decreasing levels of military and eco-

[5] Nadav Safran, "How Long Will Sadat Last? Moscow's Not-So-Secret Wish," *New Middle East*, March/April 1972, p. 7.

nomic aid, and an unwillingness to support Turkey's position in the dispute over Cyprus. Even so, the Soviets were quick to move.

On the diplomatic front, the two nations have exchanged numerous high-level visits since 1964. The Soviet Union has repeatedly proclaimed its respect for Turkish independence and its agreement with the principle that no settlement of the Cyprus question should ignore the rights of the Turkish community there (a principle that Moscow has not found inconsistent with its continued support of Cyprus's President Makarios). The two nations have concluded several economic agreements, including some which provide for the Soviets to supply plants and equipment on liberal terms of credit.[6] In 1970, the Turkish government agreed to allow the Soviets to move arms over Turkish roads to Syria and Iraq, an extraordinary concession that would not have been dreamed of a few years before.

Nevertheless, there is no Soviet military aid program, no military cooperation. Moscow has gained no influence over the basic foreign policy of Turkey, which continues its solidarity with NATO. And Turkey's internal troubles have not proved easy to turn to Soviet advantage.

Since the overthrow of the Menderes government in 1960, Turkey has been unable to stabilize its political system. The interim military regime handed the running of affairs back to the politicians under a democratic constitution, but feuds and factionalism deprived successive governments of stability. Meanwhile, the vociferous Turkish Labor party, helped by many leftist intellectuals, had some success in discrediting the government and turning discontent against the United States and its military presence—that is, its installations and personnel stationed on Turkish territory and its ships and sailors visiting Turkish ports. The growing trend toward violence—especially by terrorists of the extreme left, who provoked counterviolence from the extreme right—finally induced the senior military officers to step in and, without abrogating the constitution, rule through governments that are basically responsible to them alone. The generals worry about possible subversion by Communists, Maoists, Palestinian-trained terrorists, Kurdish nationalists, or anyone else, and they see a link between terrorism at home and plotting abroad.

No one has produced evidence to connect Moscow with these activities, but good relations do not flourish in such an atmosphere. It

[6] George Lenczowski, *Soviet Advances in the Middle East*, (Washington, D.C.: American Enterprise Institute for Public Policy Research, 1971), p. 52. Through 1969, Soviet economic aid to Turkey totaled $376 million. U.S., Department of State, *Communist States and Developing Countries: Aid and Trade in 1970*, September 22, 1971, p. 4.

should be, and probably is, evident to the Soviet leaders that, while prudence might dictate that they always be ready to capitalize on a breakdown of authority in Turkey, their public line has been the right one—that the Soviet interest for the foreseeable future is in an independent Turkey which will in due course assert its full independence of NATO and of Washington. A Turkey moving toward neutralism might be much more subject to Soviet pressures and blandishments— in a situation where Moscow would also enjoy a broader scope for maneuver in the Middle East as a whole.

*Iran*

In Iran, Soviet policy has been similar to that vis-à-vis Turkey, though the pattern and the circumstances have differed. Ever since his victory over Muhammad Musaddiq in 1953, the shah has been the real ruler of the country. His frankly pro-Western policies and Soviet tactics of threat and subversion for many years fed upon each other. Yet there were occasional signs, even in the 1950s, of Soviet awareness of an alternative course.

In 1958, after the Baghdad Pact had lost one of its original members (Iraq) and had been reconstituted as the Central Treaty Organization, the United States decided to conclude bilateral security agreements with each of the remaining Middle Eastern members. For Turkey and Pakistan, already in the Western alliance system through NATO and SEATO respectively, this was not so important a step. For Iran, it was, for it marked Teheran's initial acceptance of a formal treaty link with the United States which resembled an alliance, though the obligations were loosely defined. Moscow took this occasion to try to move Iran back from its Western alignment toward a more neutral position and offered to sign a nonaggression pact. The shah seriously considered the offer, somewhat to the embarrassment of his American friends; however, he ultimately decided to sign the agreement with the United States.[7] The circumstances of the time, especially the rising Soviet influence in Iraq and elsewhere in the Arab world, were such as to emphasize Iran's need for continued American support. But the episode was instructive. It showed both Moscow's capacity for flexibility in dealing with Iran and the shah's wakening confidence in his ability to maneuver between the great powers.

By the mid-1960s, Iran had established a remarkable record of political stability and economic advance, thanks largely to oil revenues and to the shah's political skills. In 1967, the American technical and eco-

[7] Richard W. Cottam, *Nationalism in Iran* (Pittsburgh, Pa.: University of Pittsburgh Press, 1964), pp. 239–42.

nomic aid program came to an end by mutual agreement that it was no longer necessary. The United States, however, continued to supply a large part of Iran's modern military equipment (on a credit rather than a grant basis), and American-Iranian relations remained good. The shah was nevertheless ready for the initiatives which began to come from the post-Khrushchev regime in Russia. As in the case of Turkey, these initiatives included high-level visits, warm expressions of friendship, and specific economic proposals. The most important of the agreements reached covered Soviet aid for construction of a steel plant at Isfahan and of the northern part of a gas pipeline from the main Iranian oil fields to the Soviet border (the southern part was to be built with Western help), and the eventual delivery of large quantities of natural gas through this pipeline to the Soviet Union. In addition, Iran purchased about $100 million worth of Soviet military equipment (mostly vehicles, since aircraft and tanks continued to come mainly from the United States and Great Britain).

Was all this a great success for Soviet policy? The answer, of course, depends on what Moscow was seeking to achieve. Normalization of relations modified Iran's image of the U.S.S.R. as an enemy constantly threatening attack and carrying on subversion, and Soviet diplomacy could now have more direct influence in Teheran. Yet the gain resulting from the loosening of Iran's close ties with the United States was bought at the price of strengthening Iran's independent stance against pressure from all outside powers, including the U.S.S.R. The shah was firm in his conviction that Iran must play the leading role in its own area, that of the Persian Gulf, and he has vigorously asserted Iran's right to do so against outside powers and against Arab states, especially those radical states, like Iraq, which have close ties with Moscow. Thus, the Soviet diplomatic game in Teheran did not open up an avenue to the Gulf, either through Iran or around it.

## Egypt

In the Arab world Soviet advances have been striking in some countries, modest or barely visible in others. To speak generally of Arab attitudes toward the U.S.S.R., or Soviet policies toward the Arabs, tends to distort rather than to clarify.

Egypt has been, and remains, the centerpiece of the Soviet position in the Middle East. The country's size, geographic location, and influence on other Arab states were as apparent to Moscow as to Western capitals. That the breakthrough came there, with the famous "Czech" arms deal of 1955, is a matter partly of historical circumstance, partly of design. The state of Egypt's relations with the Western world had brought that country's leaders to the decision to turn to the U.S.S.R. for support at a time when the latter was looking for just such an opportunity. Since that time, Moscow—despite Egypt's loss of two wars against Israel—has steadily continued its military deliveries, provided economic aid, and increased its political commitment.

The process has been marked by a number of crucial decisions. There is no doubt that the Soviets encouraged Gamal Abdel Nasser to provoke the crisis of 1967 with Israel.[8] When the result was a disastrous war instead of an easy political victory, they scarcely hesitated in making the same choice as was made in 1956—to replace Egypt's lost military equipment and build up its armed forces again. Backing a loser, and one which might lose again if the war were renewed, had its compensations: increased Egyptian dependence on Moscow as Cairo's only supplier of advanced weapons, availability of military facilities in Egypt, and a public role as defender of the Arab cause that brought advantages throughout the Arab world. A further step forward came in the spring of 1970, when, in response to Nasser's desperate appeal for protection against the Israeli air force, which dominated Egyptian skies, the Soviets made the unprecedented and daring move of stationing their own missile ground crews and air-combat pilots in Egypt. It was a sign of how badly Nasser needed the Soviets, and of how essential they deemed him—and Egypt—to their position in the Middle East.

While the Soviet leaders left no doubt of their desire to avoid a direct military confrontation with the United States, they must have known that a clash between their armed forces and those of Israel would carry that risk. Nevertheless, they calculated—correctly, as it turned out—that the risk was one that they could safely take, despite strong words from the White House. Similarly, they did not hesitate to join Egypt in violating the terms of the cease-fire of August 1970 by moving missiles into the Suez Canal area, for again they judged that the United States and Israel would not respond with military force.

But the Soviet leaders did not abandon their caution. Having established a military position which helped stabilize the cease-fire, they worked to consolidate their influence in Egypt. They knew how to restrain themselves and saw the need to restrain the Egyptians from renewing the war.

[8] The entire question of Soviet intentions and actions in the period immediately preceding the outbreak of war still lacks a definitive interpretation. On this point, see Charles W. Yost, "The Arab-Israeli War: How it Began," *Foreign Affairs*, January 1968, pp. 306–11; Walter Laqueur, *The Road to Jerusalem: The Origins of the Arab-Israeli Conflict, 1967* (New York: Macmillan, 1968), pp. 178–83; Nadav Safran, *From War to War: The Arab-Israeli Confrontation, 1948–1967* (New York: Pegasus, 1969), pp. 274–85.

The potential weakness of the Soviet position in Egypt, of course, lay mainly in the unpredictability of that country's conduct in a situation of status quo with Israel, which the Egyptians found unacceptable but were powerless to change. Though the Soviet Union was "big brother," it could suffer the disadvantages of that role if it had to couple fraternal help with frequent attempts to restrain and control Egyptian policy. Soviet leaders have made plain, by the nature of the weapons that they have and have not provided, the attitudes of their military advisers, and the counsel of their diplomats, that they look first to their own interests. As a consequence, an element of tension has run through the Soviet-Egyptian relationiship. For example, both Cairo's push toward war and its angling for peace through talks with the United States have disturbed Moscow, just as direct Soviet talks with the Americans on the Middle East caused distrust in Cairo. A further complication has been the personal friction between Russians and Egyptians that inevitably accompanied the ever-growing presence of the former in the latter's country.

Perhaps the least predictable of all elements is whether or not Cairo will continue indefinitely to have a regime which will follow the Soviet lead in foreign politics. With Nasser, the Soviets had a good working relationship, based not only on his usefulness to them but also on his solid position at home. However, they always confronted the dilemma of how much to depend on personalities and how much to encourage the development of political and social institutions which would provide continuity. In trying to cope with this problem, they displayed a relative lack of interest in the local Communists, who were politically impotent, and a desire to see the Arab Socialist Union become a solid party organization, a political engine which could both run the state and organize mass support for consistent long-term policies—first and foremost, cooperation with the Soviet Union. Their entrenchment in the Egyptian economy provided another means to that end.

Nasser's death shocked Moscow, for it replaced the known with the unknown. Anwar el-Sadat was no carbon copy of Gamal Abdel Nasser. He did not qualify as an inspirational leader of the Arab world; he did not have unquestioned control in Egypt; and he was not "Moscow's man," groomed to succeed Nasser. Indeed, he soon made those who better fitted that definition, notably Ali Sabry, his victims in an internal power struggle. Moreover, events quickly proved that the Arab Socialist Union, despite all the effort that had gone into building it, did not constitute an element of strength for either the regime or its enemies. Sadat has no guaranteed hold on power, and he continues to be under popular pressure for action against Israel and for improvement at home. More than Soviet leaders like to contemplate, the U.S.S.R's position in Egypt can be at the mercy of Egyptian politics.

It was probably internal political pressure, along with frustration at not getting the weapons he wanted, that brought Sadat to demand the withdrawal of the Soviet military personnel in July 1972. The Russians are not fully informed on internal struggles in Egypt. Certainly, they cannot control them. All they can do is hope that any individual or group which holds power, or comes to power, will see the national interest served by continuance of the Soviet connection.

## Syria

The Soviets' handling of Syria has followed the pattern for Egypt fairly closely, but with differences that flow from the dissimilarities in their strategic importance and political situations. Shortly after the U.S.S.R.'s 1955 decision to send arms to Egypt, Moscow undertook a similar, but smaller, program for Syria, which also had a radical nationalist regime, disputes with the West, and a militant policy toward Israel. Syria had, in addition, a more effervescent politics, which gave the local Communists greater opportunities for maneuver. Indeed, it was partly the threat of the Syrian Communists, acting for the Soviet Union, or at least exploiting the rise of Soviet influence, that motivated the Ba'ath and military leaders to offer up Syrian independence to Nasser to form the United Arab Republic in 1958. For three years, Syria proved a source of irritation in Moscow-Cairo relations, as Nasser showed a firm intention not to tolerate Communist activities in his "northern province" any more than in Egypt itself. Syria's breakaway in 1961 was therefore welcomed by the Kremlin—even though the coup returned "bourgeois" politicians to power—for it brought Syria back to its traditionally unstable politics and again gave both Moscow and the local Communists freedom of maneuver.[9]

Palace revolutions put Syria under the control of the Ba'ath's "international command" in 1963, of its more radical "regional command" in 1966, and of a somewhat more moderate leadership in 1970, as successive groups of leaders took the road to exile. Throughout these changes and the underlying instability they reflected, the Soviet Union showed a notable steadiness of policy. Stressing the theme of solidarity against the "Western imperialists" and "Zionist aggressors," the Soviets have maintained their role as protector of Syria's independence and provider of arms and aid for development. Preaching the doctrine of union of

[9] Walter Laqueur, The Struggle for the Middle East (New York: Macmillan, 1969), pp. 84–94.

all "progressive" and "democratic" elements, they have steered clear of too close an identification with particular military and political factions, so as not to compromise their ability to work with whomever comes to power.

At certain points in time, Moscow's special concern for Syria has seemed even greater than that for Egypt. In 1957, the U.S.S.R. threatened dire consequences to Turkey and the Western powers if they should tamper with Syria. In the period 1958–1961, it showed that it was willing to risk spoiling relations with Egypt for the sake of pursuing operations of its own in Syria. In 1966, it pressed Egypt to give Syria greater protection against Israel, and in the following year it helped provoke the June crisis by magnifying Israeli threats of action against Syria.[10] In the closing moments of the Six-Day War, it warned that it would act to prevent a further Israeli advance toward Damascus. After the war, it chose to overlook Syria's deviation from the Soviet line in rejecting United Nations Resolution 242, which laid down the principles for a political settlement, including Israel's withdrawal from occupied territories and the right of all states in the area to live in peace within "secure and recognized boundaries." In 1970, when King Hussein's army was liquidating the forces of the militant Palestinian organizations in Jordan, Moscow apparently called a halt to Syria's intervention, which threatened to provoke action by Israel.

This extraordinary sensitivity about Syria is easier to describe than to explain. Despite Syria's military and political weakness, perhaps because of it, Moscow seems determined to take all the risks of maintaining a position of pre-eminence there. That position helps to put the squeeze on Turkey; it checks Israel; it keeps the Soviet Union associated with Arab nationalism, in which Syria historically has had a special role. If nothing else, it shows the Soviets' determination to stay the course in the Middle East.

## Iraq

Since 1958, Iraq has been just about as unstable as Syria, a prey to the ambitions of would-be leaders among the shifting cliques of officers and politicians. It has been less consistently friendly to the Soviet Union than Syria, for the local Communists have at times been a political factor of importance. Some Iraqi regimes (Kassem's in 1959 and that of the Ba'ath in 1963, for example) have dealt with them by

---

[10] In diplomatic exchanges with Israel after the Syrian-Israeli armed clash of April 7, 1967, Soviet diplomats took a sharp and threatening stance which revealed both a concern for Syria and a desire to teach Israel a lesson on the dangers of playing with fire "in an area near to the borders of the Soviet Union." See Avigdor Dagan, *Moscow and Jerusalem* (London: Abelard-Schuman, 1970), pp. 202–8.

execution and massacre. Even though the course of Soviet-Iraqi relations was bound to feel the impact of these events, Moscow did not propose to leave any openings for the return of Western influence. While the moderate Bazzaz government of 1965–1966 might have created an opening or two, it proved too weak and too brief to get started in that direction. In any event, the Soviet Union and its allies in Eastern Europe established themselves as Iraq's main partners in trade and aid shortly after the revolution of 1958, and so they have remained.

The Kurdish question increasingly posed a problem for the Soviet Union, as it always had for Iraq. As long as Iraq had a pro-Western regime, the Soviets found it useful to encourage Kurdish nationalism against the regime, and they offered Mullah Mustafa Barzani, the principal but not unchallenged Kurdish leader, a haven in the U.S.S.R. When the monarchy was overthrown in 1958, Barzani returned to Iraq as a putative partner in the new nationalist and pro-Soviet regime. However, he proved to be neither a Soviet agent nor a passive junior partner of Kassem, but a Kurdish nationalist. He engaged in a decade of fighting against the Iraqi army under a succession of Baghdad regimes and was never conquered.

Moscow did not denounce Barzani, but it continued to furnish arms which the Iraqi army used to fight him. While the Soviet line varied with the changing circumstances in Soviet-Iraqi relations, in general the U.S.S.R.'s support for self-determination for the Kurds took second place to maintenance of cooperation with Baghdad.[11] Consequently, the Russians greeted with relief the conclusion of an agreement between the Ba'ath government and Barzani in 1970 which ended the fighting and accepted the principles of autonomy for the Kurdish areas and Kurdish participation in the central government.[12] Yet recent reports indicate the unraveling of this agreement and the unwillingness of Barzani, despite Soviet urging, to have his Kurdish Democratic party join a united front with the Ba'ath and the Communists.

The Kurdish question is by no means a side issue, especially after the Iraqi government's nationalization of the Kirkuk oil field of the Western-owned Iraq Petroleum Company and its turn to the Soviet Union for help in working the field, which lies in the Kurdish area. Moscow has found that it does not maintain its position simply by providing arms and making declarations denouncing Israel. It is inevitably involved, as the partner of successive regimes whose actions it does not control, in all the complexities of Iraqi politics.

[11] Laqueur, The Struggle for the Middle East, pp. 98–101.
[12] A. Y. Yodfat, "Iraq—Russia's Other Middle Eastern Pasture," New Middle East, November 1971, pp. 28–29.

Similarly, in the realm of international politics, Iraq may serve as a conduit for the extension of Soviet influence into the area of the Persian Gulf, but can this happy outcome take place without Soviet involvement in Iraq's disputes with Iran, with which the Kremlin has labored hard to repair relations? Or can it take place without commitment to the cause of radical revolution in the sheikhdoms on the Arab side of the Gulf, which would antagonize Iran and a number of Arab states as well?

## Other Arab States

A decade ago, the prevailing Western view was that the Arab states were roughly divisible into two categories, radical and conservative. In the former camp were those discussed above, which had governments born of revolution or *coup d'état*, vaguely socialist in their internal policies, and anti-Western and pro-Soviet in their foreign policies. In the latter were states ranging all the way from traditional monarchies and sheikhdoms in the Gulf area to more modern types, such as Morocco and Jordan, whose governments were generally evolutionary in their approaches to domestic change and were oriented toward the West in international affairs. The cold war between these two groups appeared as real as the cold war between the superpowers, and often the two interlocked.

Because revolutions continued to take place, and because they often added members to the radical group at the expense of the conservative group, it seemed that the tide of history was with the former and that it was only a matter of time before the entire Arab world would be composed of states professing socialism in one form or another and living in close cooperation with the U.S.S.R. Soviet leaders appeared to think so. At least, they said so often enough, as did their experts in ideology and in international affairs. The radical Arab regimes certainly thought so. They fed on success, and the triumph of the FLN in Algeria in 1962, the republican revolution of 1962 in Yemen, the radical takeover of 1969 in Aden, the seizure of power by Jaafar Nimeri and his group in the Sudan in 1969, and the republican revolution of the Young Officers in Libya in 1969 seemed to prove the case beyond a doubt.

However, the past ten years have provided some salutary lessons, especially for those whose interpretation of events is governed by supposed laws of history or of revolutionary change. Some of the conservative regimes showed unexpected strength and a capacity to adapt to new conditions. Some of the radical ones proved unable to turn theory into practice. Some governments, such as those of Lebanon and

Tunisia, fell in between the radical and conservative camps and stayed there. National interests and the personal ambitions and rivalries of individuals made a mockery of supposedly uniform patterns of political and social development. Nor was there any automatic correspondence between progress of "the revolution" in the Arab world and the degree of cooperation with the Soviet Union. Libya had the most radical revolutionaries of all, and they held Moscow at arm's length. Though American influence generally declined after the Six-Day War in 1967, it remained strong in Jordan and Saudi Arabia and did not disappear elsewhere.

### The Middle East as Seen from Moscow

I have made the point that the facts of Soviet conduct toward individual Middle East states are more significant than any general theory or approach to the region as a whole. Of course, modes of thinking about the role of colonial and former colonial peoples in the struggle against imperialism—going back to Lenin and the early years of the Comintern—infuse Soviet thinking about policy toward the Middle East, as toward other areas of the Third World. One can take any arbitrary starting date—say 1960, to keep the discussion in the recent era—and trace the evolution of doctrinal pronouncements from the Statement of the Moscow Conference of Eighty-one Parties down to the most recent speeches of Leonid Brezhnev, statements that have been elaborated at each stage by authoritative writers in the journals of the party and of the academic institutes.

Several concepts have had their innings: the "national democratic" state, "revolutionary democracy," the "popular union of progressive forces," "taking the non-capitalist path," and so on.[13] Each has been trotted out to describe a historical process and to provide a rationale for Soviet strategy. These formulations are directed primarily to a Soviet audience, then to Communist parties and radical movements throughout the world, and finally to the leaders and peoples of the Third World. At home, the Soviet system lives on ideological justification and cannot dispense with it. In its external extension, those Communist parties which it largely controls, it must furnish a combination of guidance and encouragement (especially when it is short on real support). To the aspiring nationalists of the Third World, in this case mainly the Arabs, the Soviets feel the need to press home the argument that nationalism and socialism are allies in a common struggle.

[13] Charles B. McLane, "Russia and the Third World," *Studies on the Soviet Union* (Munich), 6, no. 3 (1967): 73–90; Jaan Pennar, "The Arabs, Marxism, and Moscow: A Historical Survey," *Middle East Journal* (Washington, D.C.), Autumn 1968, pp. 438–47.

Moscow's rather consistent sacrifice of local Communists for the sake of good relations with national regimes has often been cited as proof of its cynicism, or its realism.[14] The most flagrant case of all was Soviet acceptance, with relatively little fuss, of the Nimeri regime's execution of Communist leaders and destruction of the influential and well-organized party in the Sudan. Yet it has been no easy matter to handle these situations. Nikita Khrushchev, one of the greatest realists of them all, chafed under the waves of nationalist rhetoric and burst out publicly, on the occasion of his visit to the Aswan Dam in 1964, to stress the primacy of class over national solidarity.[15] It was never comforting to the Soviet leadership either to witness the impotence of the local Communist cadres or to look away when they were persecuted. And, despite sad experience, the Soviets continued to try to use them: as independent parties sharing power with others and exercising a beneficial influence in local radical regimes (Syria and Iraq); as individuals allowed to move into official front organizations (Egypt and Algeria); or in the old familiar role of subversive agents in countries where they had to operate underground.[16]

George Lenczowski has pointed out that analysts of Soviet policy have no need to expend much time and thought wrestling with the familiar question whether great-power interests or ideological drives underlie Soviet policies, since the contradictions tend to be temporary and are more apparent than real. "Ultimately, a dynamic Soviet state interest to expand and dominate is complemented by Communist ideology and vice versa."[17] Applied to the long run, the proposition is unexceptional. The more immediate question concerns the temporary period of difficult choices, which has gone on for many years and may last for many more. During the process of making their advances into the Arab world, the Soviets have made many decisions which throw light on their motives and their strategy. Perhaps one can judge that record by looking at how they have handled a number of important questions: Arab nationalism and unity, the conflict with Israel, and oil.

[14] Laqueur, *The Struggle for The Middle East*, pp. 173–80. For specific instances involving the Communists in several countries, see John C. Campbell, "The Soviet Union and the Middle East: 'In the General Direction of the Persian Gulf,'" Part II, *Russian Review* (Stanford, Calif.), July 1970, pp. 248–53.

[15] *Pravda* (Moscow), May 18, 1964; Mohamed Hassanein Heikal adds flavor to the story by describing the private conversations Khrushchev had with Nasser, Iraq's President Aref, and Algeria's President Ben Bella during his visit. See *Les Documents du Caire* (Paris: Flammarion, 1971), pp. 114–18.

[16] George Schopflin, "Russia's Expendable Arab Communists," *New Middle East*, June 1972, pp. 20–21.

[17] *Soviet Advances in the Middle East*, pp. 2–3.

## Arab Nationalism

Arab nationalism, in the forms it took in the early years after World War II, held no attractions for the Soviet Union. Those national leaders who were governing newly independent states formerly under British or French control were seen as tame nationalists still bound to the West by a network of military and political ties. Moscow supported the Jewish drive for an independent state in the late 1940s as a means of getting the British out of Palestine, yet it did not simultaneously cultivate Arab nationalism in order to achieve the broader goal of getting the British out of other Arab states. It continued to be well-disposed toward Israel for the next few years, and, although that relationship began to go sour by late 1950 (largely because of Israeli policies, which, in Moscow's view, bent Israel's declared neutrality too far to the Western side),[18] it was not until several years later, well after the new military regime took power in Egypt, that the Soviets discovered in Arab nationalism a natural ally. In the United Nations, they began a consistent policy of support for the Arab side against Israel early in 1954; the following year, Nasser's search for arms offered them the grand opportunity to take up a great-power role in the Middle East.

From the time of this historic breakthrough to the present, the Soviets' relationship with the Egyptian government and other Arab governments of a similar type has been dominated by the efforts of both sides to put it to practical use in pursuing their own respective aims. These aims have coincided in some respects; in others, they have not. Beneath the tactical benefits of cooperation and the clouds of official and unofficial rhetoric on the common struggle for national liberation and socialism against the "imperialists" and the "Zionist aggressors" lay fundamental differences.

Some were ideological. Without relying on the well-worn argument that Islam serves as a barrier to communism and to Soviet domination (actually a dubious proposition), one must take account of the gulf between the various brands of "Arab socialism" and the "scientific socialism" practiced in the Soviet Union. Arab leaders, even the most radical ones, have not tried to build the type of political system that exists in the U.S.S.R. and Eastern Europe, and they probably could not succeed if they did. The Soviet Union has no intention of forcing them to do so. It is sufficient to praise them for having set out on the "noncapitalist path" in the direction of socialism. In Moscow's restricted list of eight or so Third World nations which have reached an

18 Dagan, op. cit., pp. 36–60.

advanced stage in this evolution, Arab states make up about half the total: Egypt, Algeria, and Syria are always on it, and now Iraq seems to qualify. But the fundamental differences remain and are not forgotten on either side.

The question of Arab unity tends to sharpen them. The Soviet government has never endorsed the concept of one "Arab nation," which even for Arabs has more emotional than real political content. Difficult as it is to deal with a patchwork of more than a dozen separate Arab states, it is safer and more rewarding than associating Soviet policy and prestige with a vague and unpredictable movement, the leadership of which must be in Arab hands. Even the limited attempts to unite two or more like-minded Arab states have evoked Soviet distrust. Moscow accepted with ill grace the union of Egypt and Syria in 1958 and showed no enthusiasm for the proposed Egyptian-Syrian-Iraqi union which was under negotiation in 1963. Although the Soviets gave lip service to greater unity among Arab states to wage the struggle against "imperialism" and though it publicly welcomed the formation of the federation of Libya, Egypt, and Syria in 1971 (which Sudan had refrained from joining because of problems with its own Communist party), they had their reasons for suspecting this grouping of anti-Communist and potentially anti-Soviet, as well as anti-Israeli, inspiration.

On more concrete subjects, the disparity in aims is but thinly camouflaged. The Soviet Union and the radical Arab regimes have worked together to reduce the positions and influence of the Western powers, but, where the Soviets have wished to move into the resulting "vacuum, the Arab regimes have said, "There is no vacuum because we, sovereign Arab states are there." The picture is likely to be a mixed one as long as Western power, in one form or another, remains in the region. Egypt, Syria, and others have some unfinished business with Israel and feel the need of the Soviet presence for security, for the recovery of lost territory, or for eventual victory. For its part, the Soviet Union is still in a cold war against the United States in the Middle East. The Soviet leaders feel a continuing need for military power and bases and for local allies in order to carry on their effort.

Suppose that the Soviet Union succeeded in reducing American influence to zero. Would the Arab states face that prospect with equanimity? Their entire experience since independence shows that they do not wish to be left alone with only one outside power. Their conduct today, even as the conflict with Israel turns them toward Moscow, betrays their need to have some counterbalancing weight on the scales. Anwar el-Sadat's response to American diplomatic initiatives in

1970 and 1971 recalled Nasser's tactic of profiting from great-power rivalries. Algeria, in maintaining ties with France and increasing trade with the United States, has shown that it wants alternatives to the Soviet connection. Even the anti-Western regimes in Syria and Iraq do not want an exclusive relationship with the U.S.S.R. just as Turkey and Iran do not want such a relationship with the United States. Thus, the radical Arab states have an interest in the continuation of the Soviet-American cold war, just as the Soviet Union has an interest in the continuation of the Arab-Israeli conflict. Neither seems to wish to see the other's conflict with its principal antagonist end either in victory or in reconciliation.

## Moscow and the Arab-Israeli Conflict

The core of the Middle East crisis of recent years, of course, has been this very question of Moscow's involvement on the Arab side against Israel and the consequent danger of a Soviet-American clash. This involvement is not a simple matter of guaranteeing the existence of Egypt or of Syria; rather, it is an elaborate game in which the Soviets have exploited the Arab need of their support in order to establish positions in the region—positions from which they do not intend to be dislodged. They have no overpowering interest in the attainment of specific Arab objectives. For example, they are not for the destruction of Israel.[19] One may surmise that, despite their declarations, they are less than fiercely intent on Israel's withdrawal from every inch of territory beyond the old armistice lines. They are interested, above all, in playing on the conflict to their own advantage. Such a course, to be sure, involves dangers: the Egyptians may kick over the traces and renew the war, facing Moscow with an agonizing decision of whether to see the 1967 war repeated or to plunge in and risk a clash with the United States.

This is the context in which one must try to answer the familiar question: Does the Soviet Union really want an Arab-Israeli settlement? Its diplomatic notes and public statements say without equivocation that the goal is a political settlement based on U.N. Resolution 242. Soviet publications have been fairly specific in describing the terms of official proposals, which rest on the basic points of Israeli withdrawal from occupied territories and Arab acceptance of the sovereign existence of Israel. Among the other terms, which generally elaborate points of the U.N. resolution, are provisions for stages in the

[19] See, for instance, Premier Kosygin's speech before the United Nations General Assembly, June 19, 1967, *New York Times,* June 20, 1967.

Israeli withdrawal and for four-power guarantees of the security of both sides under the settlement.[20]

The Soviet terms and those which the United States has had in mind for a comprehensive settlement have not been so far apart that negotiations could not conceivably iron out most of the differences. Yet the efforts to this end in bilateral Soviet-American talks in 1969 ended in failure and recrimination, and the subsequent four-power talks at the U.N. got nowhere. In retrospect, it looks as if the Soviets did not intend these undertakings to succeed—because Moscow was not prepared to go beyond what Nasser found acceptable, and because it knew that Israel would insist that each territorial settlement (whether with Egypt, Syria, or Jordan) be negotiated by the two states directly concerned. It also knew that the United States would not be willing to join the Soviet Union and others in pressing or imposing on Israel a settlement which was not freely negotiated. (Needless to say, some might likewise charge the United States with not really wanting a settlement because of its partiality to Israel.)

The U.S.S.R. sees itself as occupying the high ground and feels no real pressure to force the Arab states to make some compromise which Israel might be brought to accept. It is better for the Soviet position in the Arab world for Moscow to play the friend and protector. It is better, too, so far as world opinion is concerned, for the Soviets to stick to the principle of Israeli withdrawal from conquered territory, for this principle is generally accepted not only in the Third World but by many governments allied to the United States. By its refusal to withdraw completely, Israel has put itself in the position of frustrating the Jarring (U.N.) mission, even after Egypt formally accepted the idea of a signed peace agreement with Israel.

The Soviets can calmly accept the absence of a settlement while proclaiming their desire for one. They have profited by the American-initiated cease-fire, and they can contemplate with satisfaction the failure of the diplomatic efforts of the United States, which really wants a settlement, to move Egypt and Israel in that direction—to the damage of its relations with both.

The continuing conflict has obvious risks for the Soviets. After all, their pro-Arab stance has not given their Egyptian and Syrian friends what the latter want—recovery of lost territories. Yet they have succeeded rather well in finding the right measure of commitment without overcommitment. In a new crisis, Moscow might have to swing to cooperation with the United States in order to control events and pre-

---

[20] For example, Evgeny Primakov, "The Way to a Just and Lasting Peace," *Pravda*, October 15, 1970 (official English translation in *New Middle East*, November 1970, pp. 46–47).

vent the worst. But the situation seems too favorable for the U.S.S.R. to embark now on such a course of preventive diplomacy.

As regards the left, Moscow has shunned anything more than occasional verbal support of the more radical elements, such as the Palestinian guerrilla organizations or the firebrands in Syria who would drag the Soviet Union into war if they could. As a price, it has had to accept the growth of Chinese influence among these elements and a barrage of Chinese propaganda linking the "Soviet social imperialists" with the old-style Western "imperialists" as enemies of Arab liberation.[21]

## Oil and Soviet Policy

Recent developments concerning Middle Eastern oil bear upon my general theme and have raised some old questions in new guise. Does the Soviet Union's entry into a series of deals with oil-producing states reflect its own energy problems, its desire to win points with Middle Eastern nations, or a comprehensive strategy to assault the West where it is most vulnerable?

For years, Soviet publications have been filled with stories of the great oil monopolies, their exploitation and repression of the peoples of the Middle East, and their close ties with official Washington and London. From Musaddiq's nationalization of the Anglo-Iranian Oil Company in 1951 to el-Bakr's takeover of the Iraq Petroleum Company in 1972, Soviet voices have applauded every local move to cut down the power and profits of Western companies. But the actions taken by the Soviet government itself to speed this process or to profit from it have been modest.

The first Soviet move was the arrangement with Iran in 1966 for the import of Iranian natural gas. This was followed by a series of deals with Algeria, Egypt, Syria, and especially Iraq, providing generally for Soviet technical help in exploration and operations in exchange for payment in oil.[22] They did not make much of a dent in the position of the big companies, although the pattern and prospects of Soviet cooperation may have contributed to the Iraqi decision to nationalize the IPC.

We should not overlook the valid economic reasons for limited imports of Middle Eastern oil by the U.S.S.R. The Soviets' internal demand curve for energy will go up sharply in the coming years, and domestic production may not keep up with it, except at high cost.

---

[21] See the *Jen-min Jih-pao* (People's Daily) editorial, translated in *Peking Review*, June 9, 1972, p. 10.

[22] John A. Berry, "Oil and Soviet Policy in the Middle East," *Middle East Journal*, Spring 1972, pp. 157–58.

Moreover, Moscow's East European allies are already importing oil from the Middle East. To such economic considerations must be added the obvious political benefits of relationships with local states clearly based on government-to-government agreements, technical aid, and commercial deliveries—in clear contrast to the traditional oil concessions.

The Soviet role is unquestionably expanding as the producing countries and the Western companies move from one crisis to another. But can it expand indefinitely? Scare stories to the effect that the U.S.S.R., either by itself or in concert with radical local forces, can control the oil resources of the Middle East are based neither on a sober assessment of the situation nor on the record of Soviet conduct. Moscow could do so only by seizing the oil (which can be ruled out) or by providing an alternative to the Western companies for transporting Middle Eastern oil to, and selling it in, its natural markets in Europe and Japan, a job which is beyond Soviet capabilities and which the producing countries might well be able to do for themselves.[23]

In oil matters, the Soviets have taken, if anything, an even more circumspect approach than in other aspects of their policy in the Middle East. The watchword is still opportunism, a readiness to take advantage of developments while not seizing them by the forelock. While the West may be greatly vulnerable because of its dependence on Middle Eastern oil, the oil-producing countries are equally vulnerable because of the dependence of their national economies on Western markets, and the Soviets may have learned a lesson from their earlier underestimation of the forces of local nationalism.

### Back to Grand Strategy

Do these many strands of policy make a whole fabric? If they do, it is not one in which a single design is dominant. One can pick out certain themes of ideology and of action, but no exponent or observer, friendly or unfriendly, has been convincing in putting these together as a consistent grand strategy. Nevertheless, it falls into focus somewhat better with a wide-angle lens.

Since World War II, the Soviet Union has been more than a state with a theory of world revolution and an apparatus for subversion. It has been the center of an imperial system, trying to hold together a string of satellite and client states, expanding its power further outward, and competing with other such systems. As the old empires of the European powers declined, the American system became Moscow's natural and only serious rival. By the 1960s, another rival had

[23] John C. Campbell and Helen Caruso, *The West and the Middle East* (New York: Council on Foreign Relations, 1972); Berry, *loc. cit.*, pp. 149–60.

appeared—China. The competition with the United States has been global, but its vital center has been Europe. The competition with China has been largely in Asia, but its side effects have been felt throughout the Third World and wherever leftists gather together under the banner of Moscow or of Mao. In both cases, the struggle has been coated with ideology and propaganda, but the realities of power remain easily visible.

Can the Middle East, then, be said to be a vital area for Moscow, which looks west and east before it looks south? Not as an end in itself, but perhaps so in its relevance to those main rivalries, for it offers opportunities for a Soviet sphere of influence which would be useful in asserting a world role and in blocking both the Americans and the Chinese. The latter cannot now mount a real challenge in the Middle East in terms of power, but politically and ideologically they are already providing real competition in southern Arabia and elsewhere.

Such a "sphere" would not have to be one of total domination, with puppet Communist governments sitting in all the state capitals of the region. It is a matter of going as far as Soviet power, economic ties, and diplomacy can go in making the U.S.S.R. the primary outside power, the arbiter of the relations of individual states with other outside powers and with one another. The aims are not easy to define, because they are not absolute; they operate on a sliding scale, moving up or down in relation to the changing possibilities.

The beginnings of what might be called a treaty system throw some light on overall Soviet strategy as it exists at his juncture. In 1969, Leonid Brezhnev put forward the idea of a collective security system for Asia in which local states would presumably join with the U.S.S.R. for the greater security of all.[24] The response was hardly audible, and there has been little clarification of the broad plan from Moscow since that time. But the Soviet government seems to be providing the bricks and mortar for such a system in the form of roughly similar treaties with individual states. The fact that three of them were prepared for Middle Eastern states—concluded with Egypt (1971) and Iraq (1972) and still being discussed at length with Syria—indicates that the idea has greater application there than in Asia generally. That the other is with India indicates the Soviets' double purpose, the link between the anti-American and anti-Chinese aspects of their policy.

The treaties with Egypt and with India arose from specific circumstances in Soviet relations with those two countries: with Egypt when Sadat had arrested Ali Sabry and wished to reassure the Soviet leaders,

---

[24] *Pravda* and *Izvestiia*, June 8, 1969 (English text in *Current Digest of the Soviet Press* [Columbus, Ohio], July 2, 1969).

who in turn wanted to nail down Egypt's continued collaboration; with India when the latter needed a great power's support as war with Pakistan approached. Yet the fact that the Soviets on both occasions were ready with draft texts in hand shows these documents to be more than creations of the moment. Subsequent negotiations with other states confirm that conclusion. Moscow's purpose seems to be to capitalize on the strength of its position to gain a more formal basis for the continuation of that position.

The fifteen-year treaties with Egypt and Iraq do not constitute straightforward alliances with automatic obligations to take military action. The key clauses provide, in case of threat or acts of aggression, for consultation on coordinating policies to eliminate the danger.[25] In that respect, they resemble the U.S. security agreements of 1959 with Iran, Turkey, and Pakistan. The comparison is instructive, for it reveals a Soviet intention not to be satisfied with the nonalignment of these countries but to align them on the Soviet side. Other clauses of the treaties, covering continuing military aid and other forms of collaboration, look to the consolidation of an alignment—or, if you like, dependence—which cannot easily be broken. Moscow no doubt realizes, of course, that the durability of such treaties depends on the durability of the parties' mutual interests.

In the exchanges surrounding Egypt's demand for the removal of Soviet military advisers, incidentally, neither side called into question the Soviet-Egyptian treaty. Egypt's well-advertised reaffirmation of nonalignment did not go that far. The fact that the Soviet-Iraqi treaty entered into force at that very time, however, throws some light on Moscow's motivation in spreading its alliance system, seeking alternatives, and not putting all its eggs in the Egyptian basket. For their part, the Syrians have proven unexpectedly wary. Damascus' line seems to be that relations with the U.S.S.R. are so firm and cooperative that there is no need to enshrine them in a formal treaty.

The Soviet leadership, as we have seen, has not been bothered by inconsistency in thought or in conduct when a concrete gain was to be made. They have swallowed with no more than verbal protest the decimation of local Communist parties by "national bourgeois" or "pseudo-socialist" regimes, which they have found it useful to cultivate. They have survived violent shifts in relations with individual leaders and governments. Yet they have surely learned from experience that even their own adaptability does not dispel the uncertainty of developments in the Middle East and the obstacles to their control over them.

[25] Texts of treaties in *New Middle East,* July 1971, pp. 40–41, and June 1972, p. 42.

Those in the West who aspire to a general agreement with Moscow to reduce tensions and dangers in the Middle East are not likely to get a positive response as long as the Soviet leaders are convinced that they are still moving forward in the region at acceptable cost. The needs of the domestic economy, which have their champions, have not curbed the policies adopted by the leadership as a whole. Neither do we see signs of controversy about the inconsistency of pursuing strategic arms limitation with the United States and détente in Europe while carrying on an arms race and a cold war in the Middle East. Setbacks there may cause the Soviets to reconsider the extent of their involvement and commitments. Even then, the outcome is likely to be a unilateral course of gradual retrenchment and stabilization, with choices being kept open, rather than agreement on a common course of cooperation with the United States.

# 7

# THE SOVIET UNION AND LATIN AMERICA

## Roger Hamburg

American preoccupation with foreboding events in Asia and the Middle East has led to a relative slighting of a modest but developing Soviet interest in, and concern with, Latin America. The Castro regime, of course, is a notable exception to this and has been subjected to intensive scrutiny by several scholars,[1] but Soviet involvement in the rest of the hemisphere has only recently begun to receive the attention that it may soon warrant.[2] The events in Chile and Peru in particular, and possibly the Bolivian and Uruguayan cases in the long run, demonstrate that Latin America is not to be disregarded either academically or officially in assessing Soviet "third world" policy. It is the purpose of this essay to supply a partial corrective to this perceived deficiency with a review of Soviet policy in the area.

Leonid Brezhnev in his report to the Twenty-fourth Congress of the CPSU noted that "important changes" were "taking place in the life of a number of countries of Latin America," especially the Allende victory in Chile, which was "supported by the working people of other countries of Latin America." The governments of Peru and Bolivia were cited as "struggling against bondage to the American monopolies."

A. N. Kosygin's report on the Five-Year Plan to the Twenty-fourth Congress called for "further expansion of the USSR-foreign economic ties with the developing countries of Asia, Africa, and Latin America." Such an expansion would satisfy the requirements of the Soviet economy more fully and would strengthen the national independence of the states of Asia, Africa, and Latin America and "the overall struggle against imperialism and for peace and social progress."[3]

These remarks were only the latest evidence of the Soviets' interest and concern in improving their diplomatic and economic posture in the area. After the nadir reached at the flash point of the cold war,

---

[1] Hugh Thomas, *Cuba, or the Pursuit of Freedom* (London: Eyre & Spottswood, 1971), is the most recent and perhaps most definitive example.

[2] The July/August 1970 issue of *Problems of Communism* was directed to the Latin American Marxist left, but even it provided little with regard to the overall Soviet position toward the area. See also the review article by Yale Ferguson, "Moscow and Peking in Latin America," *ibid.*, 20, no. 3 (May/June 1971): 72–76, which analyzes recent studies that deal with Sino-Soviet relations in Latin America.

[3] Report by Comrade L. I. Brezhnev, General Secretary of the Central Committee, on March 30, 1971, *Pravda*, March 31, 1971, reprinted in *Current Digest of the Soviet Press* (hereafter cited as *CDSP*), 23, no. 16 (May 18, 1971): 10.

179

during which many Latin American states suspended diplomatic relations either because of Soviet interference in their countries[4] or to satisfy U.S. sensitivities after the Guatemalan debacle of 1954, the Soviet Union now exchanges ambassadors with sixteen Latin American states. In 1970 the first Soviet ambassadors to Bolivia and Ecuador arrived at their missions. In April 1970 the Soviet Union and Venezuela re-established diplomatic relations. On December 21, 1970, *Izvestiia* reported that the Soviet Union and Costa Rica had agreed to put their diplomatic relations, which had previously been established, at the embassy level. On December 19, 1970, it was announced that diplomatic relations between Guyana and the Soviet Union would begin immediately, and by the end of 1970 the Soviet Union had established diplomatic relations with all South American states except Paraguay, and with Cuba and Costa Rica in Central America.[5] This was the culmination of the process begun under the Khrushchev regime, which had become involved in the Cuban relationship and in an economic-diplomatic offensive that resulted in the re-establishment of relations with the Quadros regime in Brazil in 1961. Quadros' successor, Goulart, was deposed in 1964, at least in part because he was deemed to be too closely linked with the Soviet Union.[6]

Trade and credit arrangements in the area, while still small in terms of overall Soviet foreign trade and trade with the developing areas as a whole, appear to be increasing, with frequent announcements of trade agreements, actual or contemplated, being made in the Soviet press.[7] The Soviet Union is selling tools, automobiles, trolley cars, trac-

[4] For a brief review of pre-1953 Soviet policy in Latin America, see Stephen Clissold, ed., *Soviet Relations with Latin America, 1918–1968: A Documentary Survey* (London: Oxford University Press, 1970); see also Luis E. Aguilar, "Fragmentation of the Marxist Left," *Problems of Communism*, 19, no. 4 (July/August 1970): 1–12. For a historical survey of Latin American communism, see Robert Jackson Alexander, *Communism in Latin America* (New Brunswick, N.J.: Rutgers University Press, 1957).

[5] U.S., Department of State, Bureau of Intelligence and Research, *Educational and Cultural Exchanges between Communist and Non-Communist Countries in 1970*, August 30, 1971, p. 107; A. I. Sizonenko, "God 1970: Itogi I Perspektivy Sovetsko-Latino-amerikanskikh otnoshenii," *Latinskaia Amerika*, 1971, no. 1, pp. 101–2; "On Soviet–Costa Rican Relations," *Izvestiia*, December 27, 1970, reprinted in *CDSP*, 22, no. 52 (January 26, 1971): 32; "Joint Communiqué on the Establishment of Diplomatic Relations between the U.S.S.R. and Guyana," *Pravda*, December 19, 1970, reprinted in *CDSP*, 22, no. 15 (January 19, 1971): 29; Jose Ramon Estella, "Un Acercamiento Cauteloso," *Visión* (New York), 39, no. 12 (June 19, 1971): 22.

[6] On Khrushchev's relations with Cuba and Brazil, see Roger Hamburg, "The Soviet Union and Latin America, 1953–1963" (Ph.D. diss., University of Wisconsin, 1965), chaps. VI and VIII.

[7] Witness the remarks of Walter Meneses, director of the Bolivian state tin smelting company: "Establishment of trade relations with the Soviet Union and the other socialist countries is especially important for Bolivia. Our output is no

tors, television sets, and a wide variety of industrial products in exchange for coffee, wool, leather, cotton, cacao, bananas, and other products, primarily raw materials and food stuffs. Soviet trade and credits, it is alleged, are offered on terms that are more favorable than those provided by the world banks, and this gives Latin American states a chance to improve their bargaining position with the United States.[8] Soviet trade provides new customers for Latin American nations, which can conserve scarce foreign exchange in straight barter deals.

Soviet moves are often designed to take advantage of a state's desire to display "independence" of the United States and they emphasize development of the "state sector," which is often attractive to many in industrializing nations. The small volume of trade in Latin America is explained as a consequence of U.S. domination—a desire by the United States to exploit Latin America's vulnerable monocultural position in order to dictate unfavorable trade terms. Economic relations with the Soviet Union would, it is alleged, greatly limit the possibility of such "monopolist dictates" and would exert a "definite influence on the prime function of the world market" for Latin American exports.[9]

It is possible to render both a positive and negative assessment of the future prospects for Soviet-Latin American trade. The past record reveals recurrent patterns that show the limitations of such trade or any great increase in credit arrangements. Latin American nations have often found themselves with credits or trade surpluses that they could not use because of a paucity of goods on the Soviet side. Nor is the situation much better on exports from the Latin American point of view. Exports of agricultural products or raw materials to the Soviet

---

longer subordinated exclusively to the requirements of the Western market. We can choose the most advantageous offers and pursue an independent economic policy." Cited in A. Karmen, "Demand of the Times," *Izvestiia*, January 25, 1971, reprinted in *CDSP*, 23, no. 4 (February 23, 1971): 22. See also Sizonenko, *op. cit.*, p. 104, on the possibility of trade agreements with El Salvador; and "Favorable Prospects," *Pravda*, February 11, 1971, reprinted in *CDSP*, 23, no. 6 (March 9, 1971): 31. For figures on trade and credit, see U.S., Department of State, Bureau of Intelligence and Research, *Communist States and Developing Countries: Aid and Trade in 1970*, September 22, 1971, esp. p. 23; and *idem*, *Communist States and Developing Countries: Aid and Trade in 1971*, May 15, 1972, p. 8 (which details increasing aid commitments to Chile and Peru in 1971) and pp. 26–27. *Soviet Business and Economic Report*, 1, no. 2 (June 26, 1972): 5–6, describes the volume and commodity composition of Soviet trade with Latin America; see also *ibid.*, no. 7 (September 4, 1972), p. 7.

[8] Estella, *op. cit.*, pp. 23–24.

[9] V. V. Rymalov, *SSSR i Ekonomicheski Slaborazvitye Strany* (Moscow: Izdatel'stvo Ekonomicheskoi Literatury, 1963), p. 149; *idem*, *Ekonomika i Vneshniaia Torgovlia Stran Latinskoi Ameriki* (Moscow: Izdatel'stvo Mezhdunarodnye Otnoshenia, 1966), p. 199. See also B. Gvozdarev, "Latin America and the Modern World," *New Times*, 1971, no. 33, p. 222.

Union and socialist states will always remain peripheral. In the case of Brazil, for example, "commerce with the socialist area will always be supplementary and accessory. It will never replace links with traditional markets and suppliers in North America and Western Europe. In only rare individual cases can it be considered an acceptable alternative to well-established business connections to which our agriculture and industry have been geared for years."[10]

But Latin American states must sell their goods and are in a chronically unfavorable economic position. Despite the often shoddy quality of the Soviet goods that are usually available, especially to private importers,[11] and Latin American sensitivity to becoming dependent on Soviet suppliers, the Soviet Union and Eastern Europe could become attractive for several reasons. From the Soviet point of view, consumer goods imported from Latin America are more in line with Soviet quality and may be more acceptable in some cases than the better products of the United States and Western Europe. In Latin American eyes the protectionist policies of the industrial West would seem to offer a rather bleak future for Latin American exports, particularly in the United States. Despite the fact that President Nixon exempted Latin American nations from the 10 percent cut in foreign aid under his economic program of late 1970, he did not exempt them from the 10 percent surcharge on most exports to the United States. Even if this surcharge is modified, powerful domestic forces in the United States will probably result in a form of protectionism that is disturbing to Latin Americans, who have come to depend on the U.S. market. As they are increasingly cut off from markets elsewhere, the Soviet Union and the Eastern European countries may look increasingly attractive to them.[12]

But the past record of the Soviet Union and other considerations to be discussed in connection with Chile do not augur well for Latin American states. The Soviet Union and Eastern Europe may supple-

[10] Jo. de Meira Penna, "Brazilian Relations with Eastern Europe," in "The Soviet Union and Latin America," *Studies in the Soviet Union*, 8, no. 2 (1968): 84. Brazilian goods, Penna argues, are of a luxury variety, part of the world's dessert which cannot find extensive markets in Eastern Europe.

[11] Hirschman contends that, given the spotty Soviet record in the past, more active economic relations with Latin American states might lose rather than gain influence. A. C. Hirschman, *Soviet Bloc–Latin American Relations and United States Policy*, Rand-RM-2457-1 (revised in May 1967), p. 9.

[12] *Ibid.*, p. 17. See also, "Nixon Spares the OAS from Foreign Aid Cuts," *Chicago Sun-Times*, September 14, 1971; John Adams Moreau, "Latin America Faces Sobering Realities," *ibid.*, September 20, 1971; William C. Binning, "The Nixon Foreign Aid Policy to Latin America" (Paper presented to the Annual Meeting of the American Political Science Association, Chicago, Ill., September 7–11, 1971), p. 18.

ment other markets for Latin American states and be used as a wedge against an excess of protectionism elsewhere, especially in the U.S. Congress, but whether Congress will in the future be as receptive to the "red scare" on the economic side is open to doubt. With heavy commitments elsewhere and more traditional partners in the developing areas, the Soviet Union and its allies are in no position to replace the United States and/or Western Europe and probably have no such intention. They can hope to garner some gratitude and good will, as well as create expectations of future benefits, and the inevitable increases in trade in the area will *appear* spectacular because they have started from such a low base. But the prospect of economic "domination" by the Soviet Union or political dependence fostered by trade or aid, outside the Cuban context, is highly unlikely.

Another aspect of Soviet involvement is in the cultural sphere—the exchange of artists of all sorts, sports figures, and political figures between Latin America and the Soviet Union. This may result in a more favorable Soviet image in places where it had previously been regarded warily, or even with hostility. There has been some increase in the number of such exchanges recently, as well as in binational exhibitions and a slight increase in the number of Latin American youths studying in the Soviet Union. A statement by Chilean Minister of Education Maximo Pachecho is an example of the type of psychological and political dividend that Soviet leaders hope to derive from their achievements in education and the arts. Pachecho expressed the opinion that the Soviet educational system "fostered ethical values in the young that go to form high moral principles . . . respect for labor, a keen sense of solidarity and social justice, honesty, loyalty and love for their country." He also commented favorably on Soviet scientific training.[13]

A dispatch in the *New York Times* indicates another area of increased Soviet involvement, but one where information is generally unavailable in published sources outside the intelligence community. The number of Soviet intelligence personnel of all varieties stationed in Latin America has increased significantly recently, and their quality has improved greatly. This is inevitable because one never knows how many secret police and intelligence operations are intermingled with "cultural officials" and "economic experts," who will presumably be in

[13] "Fruitful Cooperation," *New Times,* 1970, no. 12, p. 15. For figures on Latin American students in the U.S.S.R. and Eastern Europe and cultural exchanges and agreements, see U.S., Department of State, Bureau of Intelligence and Research, *Educational and Cultural Exchanges between Communist and Non-Communist Countries in 1970,* August 30, 1971, pp. 107–13; see also *idem, Educational and Cultural Exchanges between Communist and Non-Communist Countries in 1971,* August 31, 1972, pp. 95–103.

Latin America in increasing numbers as cultural and economic programs grow in scope.[14] On a related point, evidence has come to light
of Soviet and North Korean collaboration in training 150 Mexican students at the Patrice Lumumba University in Moscow for purposes of
guerrilla insurgency. This resulted in a severe rupture with a Mexican
government which has maintained amicable relations with both the
Soviet Union and Cuba, even in periods of maximum tension with the
OAS and the Inter-American System.[15] While it is wrong to exaggerate
the importance of this in terms of "penetration" or "subversion"—lurid
terms whose exact meaning is never made precise—there is fresh evidence that the published record and public action of the Soviet Union
have always hidden varying amounts of clandestinity, even at moments
of putative "coexistence." One is reminded of the early Soviet decision
to work with both a legal and illegal apparatus, and Soviet diplomacy
has manifested this duality in varying degrees, perhaps more conscien-
tiously than in the case with other nations.

One area of interest that is available for the public record is the
increasing attention and concern shown by Soviet academicians for the
history, culture, geography, economics, and politics of the respective
Latin American states. No longer is Latin America lumped indiscrimi-
nately with the "peoples of the East." The founding of the Latin
American Institute in the Soviet Academy of Sciences in 1961 has re-
sulted in an ever-increasing output of books and monographs on Latin
America by Soviet authors and scholarly colloquia. In 1969 the insti-
tute began publishing the first periodical devoted exclusively to Latin
American affairs, *Latinskaia Amerika*. Victor Volskii, head of the Latin
American Institute, voiced his hopes for the future of Soviet Latin
American studies thus:

[14] Benjamin Welles, "Soviet Intelligence Role in Latin America Rises," *New York Times*, December 8, 1970.

[15] Conrad Manley, "Guerilla Plot in Mexico Linked to Soviet Cultural Institute," *Christian Science Monitor*, April 1, 1971. The Mexican-Russian Institute for Cultural Exchanges had granted the scholarships in Mexico. The Soviet cultural
attaché, Boris N. Voskoboinikov, attacked the failure of the Mexican government
to reward any scholarships to Russians for study in Mexico according to the terms
of the Mexican-Soviet cultural exchange, which provided for a mutual exchange of
students. Presumably the Mexican government will be in no great haste to change
its behavior. See also Roland Evans and Robert Novak, "Mexican Plot Puts Entire
Soviet Latin Effort in Jeopardy," *Milwaukee Sentinel*, March 28, 1971. In Bolivia
there were charges that documents had been obtained that pointed to the involvement of Soviet embassy personnel with guerrilla groups bent on overthrowing the
Banzer government and charges that some Soviet officials had been mobilizing
certain peasant groups. See James Nelson Goodsell, "Bolivia Jars Kremlin's Hemisphere Inroads," *Christian Science Monitor*, April 5, 1972. Some of this, of course,
may simply be internal political maneuvering by a beleaguered regime, but such
Soviet invol•ement would not be unprecedented.

The main task of Soviet Latinamericanists in the next few years is to raise the quality and increase the quantity of basic research on the root problems of the social-economic political and cultural development of Latin American countries. The demand for such research in our country is very great. It must provide a key to understanding rapidly developing processes, to serve as a base for their scientific interpretation. A deep immersion in the process provides the possibility of being mistaken less frequently in estimating their specific periods, allowing sharply to distinguish quantitative changes, the rapid growth or crisis of this or that current phenomenon, from qualitative jumps from changes in the nature of the phenomena themselves and their mutual connections.[16]

The relationship between these studies and the policy-making process is somewhat imprecise, as it is in the United States.[17] One can argue, however, that some of these works may become a part of the perceptual equipment of policy makers, if only through popularization, and in this way may subtly affect policy choices. This, in turn, may enhance the greater conceptual sophistication and dimunition of ideological distortion that some observers have seen developing recently in the Soviet view of international relations.[18] Of course, sensed domestic political needs or bureaucratic pressures may prevent such "rational" features from predominating in policy decisions and outputs.[19] Nevertheless, it is important to study available Soviet analyses of Latin American developments, especially when they are published in major periodicals such as *World Economics and International Relations* or *Latin America,* to get some idea of the information and analyses available in the Soviet academic-political establishment. Also, as will be shown in this study, a rough correspondence between Soviet statements and actions can be established.

Soviet analyses of Latin American developments tend to follow two courses. One is the usual nationalist analysis, which portrays Latin

[16] V. V. Vol'skii, "Sovetskaia Latinoamerikanistika: Nekotorye Itogi i Zadachi," *Latinskaia Amerika,* 1971, no. 3, p. 14.

[17] For a description of the difficulties of tracing the influence of civilian academicians and their work on military policy decisions in the United States, see Ernest May, "The Influence of Ideas on American Foreign Policy: Ideas about Military Strategy" (Paper presented at the Annual Meeting of the American Political Science Association, Chicago, Ill., September 7–11, 1971).

[18] William Zimmerman, *Soviet Perspectives on International Relations, 1956–1967* (Princeton: Princeton University Press, 1969).

[19] For a study that attempts to determine when factional differences within the party leadership had an effect on policies toward the underdeveloped world, see C. Grant Pendill, Jr., "'Bipartisanship' in Soviet Policy-Making," in *The Conduct of Soviet Foreign Pol cy,* ed. Erik P. Hoffman and Frederic J. Fleron, Jr. (Chicago: Aldine-Atherton, 1971), pp. 61–75.

America struggling against "Yankee imperialism" and the "plundering" of natural resources, oil reserves being a case in point.[20] When broadly disseminated, this has the advantage of appealing to all sections of the population and all shades of opinion, which castigate the "Colossus of the North" for reasons both real and fancied. Communist parties can easily join in this denunciation and cloak their other appeals.

The Soviet Union has been handicapped, however, by not having available to it any "nationalist populist" regimes in Latin America, regimes that are non-Communist but acutely anti-American. While anti-Yankeeism and resentment of the United States have been exploited, a regime analogous to Castro's in his pre–Marxist-Leninist phase has been lacking.

There is recent evidence that this may be changing.[21] Events in Peru, and until quite recently in Bolivia, seem to have brought to the fore what one commentator calls "military Nasserist" regimes.[22] In both nations, Communist parties have been weak and ineffectual. But particularly in Peru a new leadership headed by army officers has taken power. These soldiers, who disdained the role of politicians or revolutionaries, moved to pre-empt by authoritarian means traditionally leftwing and nationalist issues, including control of domestic capital, agrarian reform, nationalization of water supplies, the extraction, refining, and sale of petroleum products, and the progressive nationalization of telecommunications.[23] But the public was to be left out; there would be no mobilization and institutionalization of the public by

[20] Soviet correspondents, for example, condemn "U.S. economic aggression" directed against the oil industry of Venezuela and charge that the U.S. government retaliated against Venezuela because of her condemnation of the U.S. intervention in the Dominican Republic and threatened to "deprive aid from the government of any country which refused dutifully to support it." G. Zafesov, "Ianky Grabiat Venesuely," *Pravda,* July 1, 1965. See also Nathan A. Haverstock and Richard C. Schroeder, "Oil in U.S.–Venezuelan Waters," *Milwaukee Journal,* June 7, 1970.

[21] James Nelson Goodsell, "Andean Nations Forging Leftist Bloc," *Christian Science Monitor,* November 20, 1970.

[22] "On an extremely vague and theoretical level the term has been applied to any military group whose objectives are a combination of radical independence and the reconquest of national identity, national development, and social progress." Ataturk, Peron, Middle Eastern military socialists, and the "new" Latin American military men would be placed under the "Nasserist" label. Howard J. Wiarda, "The New Development Alternatives in Latin America: Nasserism and Dictatorship with Popular Support" (Paper presented at the Annual Meeting of the Pacific Coast Council of Latin American Studies, University of California, Santa Barbara, November 6–7, 1970), p. 12.

[23] Luigi R. Einaudi, *Revolution from Within? Military Role in Peru since 1968,* Rand-P-4676, July 1971, pp. 7, 13; Kenneth Benton "Peru's Revolution from Above," *Conflict Studies* (London), no. 2 (January 1970), p. 14. The changes outlined are from the reform program defined by General Juan Velasco Alvarado in his "Message to the Nation," July 28, 1969.

means of elections, however manipulated. This was to be truly a "revolution from above."[24]

The reaction of Soviet commentators and media to the reforms of the new Peruvian regime was one of guarded approval. The "coming to power of a progressive government in Peru and the increasingly determined resistance to the dictates of U.S. imperialism on the part of Bolivia" attested to the different ways in which Latin America was passing to "true independence." Proposals directed against foreign capital investment by Colombia, Bolivia, Peru, Chile, and Ecuador were approved. U.S. refusal to sell weapons to the Peruvian military, which "broadened the circles of disaffected officers," was exploited, as were the Peruvian decisions to refuse to receive Nelson Rockefeller, to expel the U.S. military mission from the country, and to establish diplomatic and trade relations with the U.S.S.R. and other socialist states. The nationalization of the International Petroleum Company and other "progressive measures" of the Alvarado regime were applauded. In concrete policy terms, the Soviet Union offered trade credits to Peru to build a fishing port.[25]

But Soviet analysts displayed obvious reserve in evaluating the true significance and permanent character of these reforms, deriving as they did from an authoritarian but reforming autocracy. While some steps might lead to a "democratic, agrarian, anti-imperialist revolution," it was necessary to bring in the "energetic and thorough action of the working masses themselves, their progressive political organization."

In like vein one commentator emphasized what was critical. In order to block the "intrigues of domestic reaction and imperialism" and to accelerate reforms, the Peruvian Communist party must create "political groupings" which could support the Alvarado programs but clearly maintain the party's independence. Since the Peruvian population was presumably not fully mobilized by the Alvarado regime, its combina-

[24] "Chile, Peru, Bolivia Differ with Each Other and Fidel," *Latin American Week*, as published in the *Milwaukee Journal*, December 6, 1970.

[25] "In Support of the Struggle of the Latin American Peoples," *Pravda*, January 26, 1971, reprinted in *CDSP*, 23, no. 4 (February 23, 1971): 12; Oleg Ignatev, "Against the Dominance of the Monopolies," *Pravda*, December 29, 1970, reprinted in *CDSP*, 13, no. 52 (January 26, 1971): 31; P. Pavlov, "Peru: Dva Gody Preobrazovanii," *Latinskaia Amerika*, 1971, no. 1, p. 69; Al'fredo Abarka, "Peru: Agrarnaia Reforma v Deistvii," *ibid.*, 1970, no. 1, p. 114; "Peru Sets an Example," *New Times*, 1969, no. 42, p. 7; "Favorable Prospects," *Pravda*, February 11, 1971, reprinted in *CDSP*, 23, no. 6 (March 9, 1971): 31; "Visits and Talks," *Pravda*, August 18, 1970, reprinted in *CDSP*, 22, no. 34 (September 22, 1970): 22. See also "New Trends in Peru's Economy," *New Times*, 1972, no. 22, pp. 26–27; and "Soviet-Peruvian Cooperation," *ibid.*, no. 27, p. 7.

tion of authoritarian reform and eschewal of popular mobilization, except in an oratorical, noninstitutional sense, could be used against it.[26]

The general secretary of the Peruvian Communist party stated the case succinctly: one had to carry "anti-imperialist and anti-oligarchic transformation" to a conclusion. It was necessary to struggle together with an "ideologically heterogeneous [government] which needs to preserve the unity of the armed forces." The future of the revolution does not depend on the government alone but on the "actions of the masses and especially of the political role of the proletariat and its party."[27]

But the Communists in Peru are hardly in a position to achieve their act of political adroitness by supporting reforms while wresting the political initiative away from governmental control.

Peru, at least, seems to offer the prospect of a stable autocracy which is instituting reforms. Bolivia, by contrast, seems more like the chronically unstable Middle Eastern regimes with which the Soviet Union has been bedeviled in the last few years. The "military Nasserists" in Bolivia, first under General Alfredo Ovando Candia and then under General Juan Jose Torrez, nationalized Gulf Oil and carried out policies that were not unlike Peru's. But Bolivia has had many changes of government since it won its independence from Spain, and the pattern has held true to form, with the Torrez regime being overthrown by a three-man military junta headed by Colonel Hugo Banzer Suarez.[28]

Soviet statements and policy initiatives seemed to reflect a cautious evaluation of the unstable Bolivian situation. The Ovando victory was assessed as a "political revolt without the participation of the vanguard and without the direct participation of the action of the masses," the

[26] V. Larin, "Latinskaia Amerika: Sotsial'noe mnogoobrazie i puti razvitiia," *Mirovaia ekonomika i mezhdunarodnye otnosheniia* (hereafter cited as *MEMO*), 1971, no. 3, p. 105; Pavlov, *op. cit.*, p. 69.

[27] Jorge del Prado, "The New State Means New Forms of Struggle," *Pravda*, June 25, 1971, reprinted in *CDSP*, 23, no. 28 (July 20, 1971): 9–10. For further evidence of the arms-length treatment of the Alvarado regime by the Peruvian Communists, see R. Acosta, "Latin America: The Ideological Front," *World Marxist Review*, 15, no. 4 (April 1972): 48; L. Padilla, J. LaBride, and E. Sousa, "Latin America: The Anti-Imperialist Struggle and the Armed Forces," *ibid.*, 14, no. 3 April 1971): 27; and U.S., Department of State, Bureau of Intelligence and Research, *World Strength of the Communist Party Organizations*, 1972 ed., p. 155; or Alvarado's statements which attack the left more than the right, indicating that Alvarado is "known to believe Peru's small Communist Party is potentially more dangerous to his nationalist, reformist government than the country's conservatives." Joseph Novitskii, "Peru's President Details His Goals—Says Military Regime Seeks 'Parliamentary Democracy,'" *New York Times*, July 29, 1971.

[28] See Malcolm W. Browne, "A Leftist General Rides the Bolivian Tiger," *Christian Science Monitor*, October 11, 1970; Lawrence Whitehead, "The Coup in Bolivia," *World Today*, 26, no. 11 (November, 1970); and "Junta Takes Over Bolivian Rule," *Chicago Sun-Times*, August 23, 1971.

"Achilles heel" of the "revolutionary process." "Only the masses themselves," it was observed, "could guarantee a consistent forward movement, blocking the return of counterrevolution." Without one of the
"progressive social parties" supporting it, the Ovando government
lacked a "broad social basis." The army was split into "conservative
elements" and "nationalistically inclined officers," which perhaps foreshadowed what eventually occurred, the victory of the rightists,
although Bolivia's gyrations are hardly over.[29]

The Soviet government conducted trade negotiations with the
Bolivian regime but avoided any deep commitment by party or state
officials, preferring, no doubt, to wait until events in Bolivia had
hardened into a definite pattern.[30]

The common feature in the Peruvian and Bolivian cases is the absence of a strong, cohesive, institutionalized opposition on the left
which could support revolutionary actions instituted from above and
control the revolutionary process itself. Nationalism alone, as one
Soviet commentator observed, is "not enough to achieve progress and
liquidate dependence on imperialism."[31] In the past several years increased reservations have been expressed about the reliability of
"third world" nationalists. Events in the Middle East, for example,
caused one Western observer to question what the Soviet government
had "bought" with its largesse of economic and military aid; in Leninist terms, who was being manipulated by whom? Consequently,
greater emphasis is placed on "proletarian and semi-proletarian
strata."[32] This is especially relevant to Latin America, which is in some
respects distinguished from the Afro-Asian world.

[29] I. Ershov, "Boliviia: Smena pravitel'stva ili smena politiki?" *MEMO*, 1970,
no. 6, p. 115; and Iu. A. Fadeev, "Boliviia: Vybor puti," *Latinskaia Amerika*,
1970, no. 4, p. 97. For speculation on possible leftward movement in the future,
see Juan de Onis, "Bolivian Rightists on Top but a Long Struggle Looms," *New
York Times*, August 29, 1971. For a post-mortem Soviet comment which blames
the Torrez debacle at least in part on American complicity, see P. Orlov, "The
Events in Bolivia," *New Times*, 1971, no. 35, p. 15.

[30] See the text of a Soviet-Bolivian trade agreement in "Torgovoe Soglashenie
Mezhdu Soiuzom Sovetskikh Sotsialisticheskikh Respublik i Respublikoi Bolivii,"
*Venshniaia Torgovlia*, 1971, no. 1, p. 57; and a survey of Soviet foreign trade in
1970 in V. Klochek, "Vneshniaia Torgovlia SSSR v 1970 Godu," *ibid.*, no. 6, p. 17.

[31] Fadeev, *op. cit.*, p. 97.

[32] Robert O. Freedman, "The Soviet Union and the Middle East: The High Cost
of Influence" (Paper presented at the Annual Meeting of the American Political
Science Association, Chicago, Ill., September 7–11, 1971). For further discussion
on this point, see Roger Hamburg, "Soviet and Chinese Revolutionary Strategy:
Comparison and Evaluation at the Present," *Asian Studies* (Quezon City), 6, no.
3 (December 1968). See also Edward Taborsky, "The Communist Parties of the
'Third World' in Soviet Strategy," *Orbis*, 11, no. 1 (Spring 1967); and *idem*, "The
Class Struggle, the Proletariat, and the Developing Nations," *Review of Politics*,
24, no. 3 (July 1967). A recent Western analysis of Soviet affairs argues that a

John Martz has observed that the majority of Latin American countries would fit into the "non-Western category but at least a few would
appear largely Western in political culture and economic development;
Argentina, Chile, Costa Rica, Uruguay, and possibly Mexico."[33] Soviet
commentators echo this observation in the second part of their analysis,
arguing that, while some Latin American states are not far removed
from the status of colonies, others, such as Argentina and Mexico,
closely resemble czarist Russia in the relationship between industry
and population. As in prerevolutionary Russia, the rate of urbanization
is expected to outrun the rate of industrialization and the capacity of
the political and social system to meet the demands raised. This is the
classic "revolution of rising expectations," in which the rate of industrialization in a political system lags behind the demands placed on
political institutions. Communist strength is often greatest in societies
in the "middle stages" of industrial development—above the primarily
agricultural phase, but below the stage of "mature" industrialization.[34]

Chile, the third of the nations of the "Andrean triangle," is a society
that displays the above characteristics. Most significantly, a Communist
party whose leadership is able to exploit these features holds sway—a
situation that is unique in Latin America and the non-Communist
world as a whole, with the exception of Italy.[35]

On September 4, 1970, in a three-man electoral race, Salvador

---

revised "two camps" doctrine has been appearing in Soviet statements on "third
world" nationalism; this is a sharp departure from Khrushchev's "camp of peace."
R. Judson Mitchell, "The Revised 'Two Camps' Doctrine in Soviet Foreign
Policy," *Orbis*, 16, no. 1 (Spring 1972): 29.

[33] John D. Martz, "The Place of Latin America in the Study of Comparative
Politics," *Journal of Politics*, 28, no. 1 (February 1966): 77.

[34] Larin, *op. cit.*, p. 91. This argument is developed more extensively, with
quotations from relevant Soviet sources, in Roger Hamburg, "Urbanization, In-
dustrialization, and Modernization in Latin America: Soviet Views," *Studies in
Comparative Communism*, 5, no. 1 (Spring 1972): 1–20. On industrialization and
modernization in prerevolutionary Russia, see "Russia before Soviet Power,"
Chapter 2 of David Lane's *Politics and Society in the USSR* (New York: Random
House, 1970); Norton T. Dodge and Charles K. Wilber, "The Relevance of Soviet
Industrial Experience for Less Developed Economies," *Soviet Studies*, 21, no. 3
(January 1970): 330–49; and Charles K. Wilber, *The Soviet Model and Under-
developed Countries* (Chapel Hill: The University of North Carolina Press, 1970);
or Chilean President Allende's remarks that, while Russia's circumstances of 1917
and Chile's of the present were "very different," the future challenge is similar.
Backward Europe could face up to advanced Europe. Today, nations with large
populations could "break out of their backwardness and attain the most advanced
level of contemporary civilizations." Salvador Allende, quoted in Regis Debray,
*The Chilean Revolution: Conversations with Allende* (New York: Vintage, 1971),
p. 170.

[35] Sandra Powell, "Political Change in the Chilean Electorate, 1952–1964,"
*Western Political Quarterly*, 23, no. 2. (June 1970): 376; and Hamburg, "Urbanization, Industrialization, and Modernization in Latin America."

Allende Grossens, veteran Chilean Socialist leader, won by a narrow plurality over a member of the outgoing Christian-Democratic party and a Conservative candidate. Allende headed a coalition of the left in which the Communist and Socialist parties formed the backbone and pledged to create "a nationalist popular, democratic and revolutionary government that will move toward socialism," but without totalitarian rule.[36] After confirmation by the Chilean Senate in early November, Allende moved to put his program into effect. Opinions differ as to the character, motivation, and likely path of evolution of the Allende regime, but all would agree that something extraordinary has occurred.[37] A Marxist government, albeit by a narrow plurality, has taken power in a major Latin American state which in Latin American terms is relatively highly developed economically. Chile, however, is afflicted with glaring structural inadequacies and rather typical economic and social inequities. As a political system it has traditionally high stability, but is confronted with inflation, a shortage of capital, and the assorted ills of industrializing societies. Allende is attempting to apply his mix of Marxist solutions to Chile's problems. This includes extensive nationalization of firms partly owned by U.S. interests and a mixed socialist-capitalist system, with some small business remaining in private hands, at least according to published statements.[38]

Soviet commentators are not reticent in presenting the meaning and broader significance of the events in Chile and in highlighting the role of the Communist party in the Allende victory, although they carefully hedge the latter. This is done presumably to avoid a "backlash" effect in Chile or elsewhere. The Chilean experience, it is argued, proves the "impossibility of carrying out the so-called revolution from above"

[36] Joseph Novitski, "Allende, in an Interview, Rejects Totalitarian Rule," *New York Times*, October 4, 1970.

[37] For a grim assessment of the Allende regime and the alleged role of Soviet diplomatic officials and intelligence agents in the election, see "How Communists Took Power in Chile," *U.S. News and World Report*, December 21, 1970, p. 33. For a somewhat less apocalyptic, but still pessimistic, view of the chances for Chilean democracy in the aftermath of the Allende victory, see Western Harris Agor, "Is Chile Still Free? A Test," *Freedom at Issue*, 1971, no. 8, p. 1. For a more "neutral" assessment which offers possible paths of evolution, see Michael J. Francis and· Hernan Vera-Godoy, "Chile: Christian Democracy to Marxism," *Review of Politics*, 33, no. 3 (July 1971). For a sympathetic view of the Allende regime, especially the prospects for the survival of some kind of democratic "pluralism" in Chile, see E. J. Hobsbawn, "Chile: Year One," *New York Review of Books*, 17, no. 4 (September 23, 1971). This article is particularly recommended for its analysis of the relationships among the different currents on the left, and of the potential strengths and weaknesses of the Allende regime.

[38] James Nelson Goodsell, "Chilean Take-overs Test US Commercial Stake," *Christian Science Monitor*, November 27, 1970; idem, "Allende Tailors Socialism to Meet Chilean Conditions," *ibid.*, November 21, 1970; and idem, "Andean Nations Forging Leftist Bloc."

which the preceding Christian-Democratic regime attempted. One commentator argues that it vindicates the unity-of-action theme advanced by the Chilean Communist party:

By utilizing moments of instability that inevitably appear as reforms are carried out, by developing a mass movement for the realization of promises, by constantly expanding and deepening their demands, the revolutionary parties can accelerate the movement forward, develop the struggle already for a change in the character of power, and begin revolutionary transformations. Social strata, which yesterday were still a remaining bulwark of reformism, can in such conditions become supporters of revolutionary actions.[39]

In addition, the crucial role of the 12,000 "Committees of Popular Unity," which had prominent Communist participation and were active throughout the country, especially in the main industrial center, where the population is located, has been noted. These committees were useful in Allende's pre-election campaign. The United States, which intervened covertly in the 1960s through the Alliance for Progress or overtly in the Dominican Republic, could no longer contain the "new advance of anti-imperialist forces" of the 1970s. Unity of the leftist forces could prevent such intervention in the future:

The revolutionary democratic forces won the commanding heights of power in a determined struggle. This is a great victory, inasmuch as the question of power is the main question of any revolution. Unprecedented possibilities open before the anti-imperialist, democratic movement of Chile—to embody the programme of deep economic and social reforms, to begin the construction of a new society.[40]

The Allende victory was "an event of historical significance, not only for Chile, but for all of Latin America," because for the first time a candidate of the left bloc who supported basic "anti-imperialist, anti-monopolist and agrarian reform" was elected president "in conditions of a relatively free democratic election." This confirms "the complete falsity of the opposition of democracy and communism and shows that the alternative to democracy emerges as anti-communism."[41]

[39] I. N. Zorina, "Chili: Novyi Etap Istorii," *Latinskaia Amerika,* 1971, no. 1, pp. 12, 14.
[40] *Ibid.,* pp. 18, 19, 21, 22.
[41] I. N. Zorina, "Chili: Pobeda narodnogo edinstva," *MEMO,* 1971, no. 11, p. 85. Jordan notes that high Soviet officials, including A. P. Kirilenko of the Soviet Politburo and V. G. Korionov of the Central Committee, attended the conference at which Allende was endorsed in October 1965. David C. Jordan, "Marxism in Chile: An Interim View of Its Implications for US Latin American Policy," *Orbis,* 15, no. 1 (Spring 1971): 334.

The broader implications of the Allende victory and strictures against a premature euphoria were spelled out even more explicitly in a series of statements by a leading Soviet specialist on the developing areas, Professor R. Ul'ianovskii. Ul'ianovskii warned against a tendency by the "radical-democratic intelligentsia . . . to underestimate the difficulties in building socialism." The support of socialist states and the rallying of all "patriotic and consistently anti-imperialist forces" was vital. It was imperative to activate the working people and working class and create "an advanced political organization" to help them develop class consciousness and defend political decisions. Chile was a most convincing example of this, for there "the people's front of two basic parties, the Socialists and the Communists, is truly a strong nucleus of the entire working people, who have embarked upon a path of profound social changes."[42]

In an important article in *Kommunist*, the main party theoretical journal, Ul'ianovskii described the "noncapitalist path of development," which involved a lengthy coexistence of the state and private sectors of the economy. The critical criteria are a "steadfast anti-imperialism and a progressive domestic policy," the carrying out of agrarian reform, and the creation of a growing state sector in industry, "gradual occupation of the dominant positions in the basic branches of production, nationalization of financial and banking concerns, mineral wealth, means of transport and communications, broad economic planning, with the expansion and strengthening of the state sector, and the restraint of capitalist tendencies." A certain sphere of the economy would be left to middle and small private entrepreneurs. While nationalization has great significance, the critical factor is the "capability, depending upon the state sector, of directly and effectively utilizing the private capitalist and small goods sector in the interests of the national economy."[43]

The new Chilean governing coalition has been embraced enthusiastically by party and government officials and has received prominent coverage in the Soviet press. Alexander Shelepin received a delegation of the United Center of Chilean Workers at the Central Council of

[42] Professor R. Ul'ianovskii, "When the Chains Have Been Cast Off," *Izvestiia*, April 28, 1971, reprinted in *CDSP*, 23, no. 17 (May 25, 1971): 38.

[43] R. Ul'ianovskii, "Nekotorye Voprosy Nekapitalisticheskogo Razvitiia," *Kommunist*, 1971, no. 4, pp. 108, 110, 111, 112. For an application of the Chilean approach to Uruguay, see I. Zorina, "Chili: Pobeda Narodnogo Edinstva," p. 86; and V. Tikhemenev, "A Broad Front of Progressive Forces," *Pravda*, February 12, 1971, reprinted in *CSDP*, 23, no. 6 (March 9, 1971): 31. "The Popular Unity government has made it clear that the economy should rest on three types of property—state, mixed, and private. It has also reassured the middle strata that they would be granted credits and allowed free enterprise, and that their property would be immune." R. Campusano, "Latin America: The Ideological Front," *World Marxist Review*, 15, no. 4 (April 1972): 55.

Trade Unions. N. S. Patolichev, the Soviet minister of foreign trade, received the Chilean ambassador to talk about Chilean trade and economic relations in connection with a visit to Moscow by a Chilean economic mission. Sharif Rashidov, a candidate member of the Politurbo of the Central Committee of the CPSU, headed a delegation which attended the Twenty-third Congress of the Chilean Socialist Party, emphasizing the close cooperation of the Socialist, Communist and other leftist parties in Chile.[44]

Prominent press coverage was given in Soviet media to the visit of Chilean Foreign Minister Clodomiro Almeyda Medina, who sought to increase the amount of credits granted to Chile by the Soviet Union, purchase machinery and equipment, and set up a Soviet trade mission in Chile and a Chilean trade mission in the Soviet Union. He was quoted to the effect that the Soviet government "supports the policy of the Popular Unity bloc and understands the goals the Chilean government has set itself. We intend to cooperate on questions of the preservation of peace, disarmament and the easing of tension in the international sphere." He also engaged in talks with Prime Minister Kosygin, and a joint communiqué expressed the conviction that the "expansion of trade, economic, scientific, technical and cultural cooperation will facilitate better understanding between the peoples."[45]

On the party level Brezhnev met with a delegation of Chilean Socialists and discussed the activity of the Chilean Socialists and other parties in the Popular Unity coalition. The latter would carry out transformations leading to the "construction of socialism." Brezhnev called for a strengthening of the alliance of Socialists and Communists and the ties between the Soviet Communist party and the Chilean Socialist party.[46]

[44] "Delegation received at Central Council of Trade Unions," Pravda, May 4, 1971, reprinted in CDSP, 23, no. 18 (June 1, 1971): 33; "Minister of Foreign Trade N. S. Patolichev Receives Guillermo del Pedregal Herrera, Ambassador to Soviet Union from Republic of Chile," Pravda, May 7, 1971, reprinted in CDSP, 23, no. 18 (June 1, 1971); and "Chilean Socialist Party Congress Opens," Pravda, January 30, 1971, reprinted in CDSP, 23, no. 5 (March 2, 1971): 32.

[45] "A. N. Kosygin Talks with Chile's Minister of Foreign Affairs," Pravda and Izvestiia, May 29, 1971, reprinted in CDSP, 23, no. 22 (June 29, 1971): 1; "Chile's Minister of Foreign Affairs in Moscow," Pravda, May 29, 1971, reprinted in CDSP, 23, no. 22 (June 29, 1971): 1; and "Joint Soviet-Chilean Communiqué," Pravda and Izvestiia, May 30, 1971, reprinted in CDSP, 23, no. 22 (June 29, 1971): 1–2. For an account of a visit by a high-level Soviet aid mission to Santiago, see Juan de Onis, "Soviet Experts Assisting Chile: High-Level Mission Arrives to Develop Aid Programs," New York Times, January 27, 1972. See also James Nelson Goodsell, "Chile Seeks More Soviet Funds: Allende Will Confer in Mexico, Russia," Christian Science Monitor, December 4, 1972.

[46] "Meeting in the CPSU Central Committee with Delegation of the Chilean Socialist Party," Pravda, June 2, 1971, and Izvestiia (June 2–3, 1971), reprinted in CDSP, 23, no. 22 (June 29, 1971): 3.

Allende granted an interview to Soviet television in which he expressed a desire to strengthen and expand commercial and cultural exchanges with all nations of the world, "and especially with the countries of the socialist camp, above all the Soviet Union."[47]

But comments by Soviet officials and Chilean leaders also contained a note of caution. A too pronounced highlighting of the role of the Communist party in the Allende coalition might have adverse internal effects in Chile and in the United States, whose reactions Soviet leaders scrutinized carefully. While citing the "outstanding contribution" that the Communist party had made, a Soviet commentator emphasized that the Allende victory was the "fruit of the policies and efforts not of a single party but of all the parties in the people's bloc"; Brezhnev, in his report to the Twenty-fourth Congress, emphasized that the victory was brought about by "constitutional means"; and Allende's insistence that his government "will continue to work intensively in order to move Chile towards Socialism within democratic legality" was in the same vein.[48]

The U.S. reaction to the Allende victory was equivocal[49] but clearly made Soviet commentators nervous. A remark made by President Nixon to the effect that, if Chile should "do something" in its own country or in its foreign policy that Washington did not like, the

[47] "Interview with the President of Chile," *Pravda*, March 1, 1971, in *CDSP*, 23, no. 9 (March 30, 1971): 21. For a detailed exposition of Allende's views on Cuba and the course of the revolution in Chile, see the text of an interview with Regis Debray in "Allende habla con Debray," *Punto Final* (Santiago), 5, no. 126 (March 16, 1971). This has been translated as Debray, *The Chilean Revolution: Conversations with Allende*; see esp. pp. 73–74, 77, 84, 88, 113, 117.

[48] "In Support of the Struggle of the Latin American Peoples," *Pravda*, January 26, 1971, reprinted in *CDSP*, 23, no. 4 (February 23, 1971): 12; "Report by Comrade L. I. Brezhnev, General Secretary of the Central Committee, on March 30, 1971," *Pravda*, March 31, 1971, reprinted in *CDSP*, 23, no. 16 (May 18, 1971): 10; *News from Chile* (Chilean Embassy, Washington, D.C.), May 14, 1971, p. 1.

[49] Benjamin Welles, "U.S. Declines Chile's Invitation for Visit by Warships— U.S. Ambassador to Chile Opposes Visit." *New York Times*, February 28, 1971. The U.S. rebuked Chile for its decision to resume diplomatic relations with Cuba. But see also the U.S. decision to lease a seagoing tug to Chile in *News from Chile*, July 1, 1971. For "tough" U.S. actions directed against Chile, see "Tough U.S. Stand on Expropriations—Says Countries That Fail to Give Compensation Can Lose Foreign Aid," *New York Times*, January 20, 1972; and "U.S. Puts Pressure on Chile," *Christian Science Monitor*, July 26, 1972. Columnist Jack Anderson charged that ITT, with the reported assistance of the CIA, was seeking to prevent the inauguration of Allende, but Secretary of State Rogers insisted that the U.S. government had not acted "in a wrongful manner." "I.T.T. Is Accused of Having Tried to Influence U.S. Policies in Latin America," *New York Times*, March 23, 1972. But see Martin Kondracke, "High Level U.S. OK to Thwart Allende Told," *Chicago Sun-Times*, March 22, 1972. President Nixon did ask for $1,114,000 in military assistance to Chile, which demonstrated that a cautious administration policy was still in effect. *New York Times*, March 23, 1972.

United States would "act appropriately" was attacked as "intervention in internal affairs,"[50] even though Mr. Nixon may have intended it solely for nervous domestic critics.

The cautious way in which both Moscow and Washington approached the Chilean question is illustrated by the interplay between statements, both public and private, and actions. A Nixon aide said that the administration was "determined to play it straight. If the Allende government wants to nationalize or confiscate foreign investments, the first move is up to them. But we intend to give them no pretext or justification." At the same time, Soviet diplomats reportedly told Chilean diplomats that Soviet representation at the Allende inaugural would be "not spectacular," to avoid any implication that Chile under the new regime was moving into the Soviet orbit.[51] Conversely, the Soviet press denied a *Washington Post* story that the Soviet Union was preparing to set up a military base in Chile.[52]

The comments of Luis Corvalán, the general secretary of the Chilean Communist party reveal several things. First, the United States was put on the ideological and moral defensive through Corvalán's emphasis on the fact that the election took place through constitutional means. Second, Chile would not be adverse to receiving continued U.S. credits. Third, any U.S. pressure, either diplomatic or economic, would harm the United States in the hemisphere as much as it would Chile.

If the United States cuts off aid it will not be good for the United States. Furthermore, we are not against receiving aid from the United States for specific purposes and under conditions respectful of the dignity and needs of Chile. We have reached power by free elections, which is the recipe that the United has proclaimed. We

[50] Vitaly Borovsky, "Untenable Attempt," *Pravda*, April 21, 1971, reprinted in *CDSP*, 23, no. 16 (May 18, 1971): 39.

[51] Benjamin Welles, "Nixon to Send High Aide," *New York Times*, October 28, 1970. On pressure on Mr. Nixon from U.S. copper companies to take a harder line, see Charles Bartlett, "Constitutional Image of Chile Leader Hurt," *South Bend Tribune*, June 17, 1971. David Jordan quotes President Nixon to the effect that the United States would tolerate the Chilean position as long as it "does not violate the principles of the inter-American system, by interfering in the affairs of their neighbors or by facilitating the intervention of non-hemispheric power." If Chile crosses this line, it "cannot expect to share the benefits of inter-American cooperation." President Richard M. Nixon, *United States Foreign Policy for the 1970's: Building for Peace* (Washington, D.C.: Government Printing Office, 1971), p. 54, cited in Jordan, *op. cit.*, pp. 334–35.

[52] R. Tuchnin, "Another Lie," *Izvestiia*, February 28, 1971, reprinted in *CDSP* 23, no. 9 (March 30, 1971): 20.

plan to nationalize copper of course. We do not plan to take copper out of the dollar area.[53]

Neither Corvalán nor the Soviet leadership wanted either a complete cutoff of Chile's traditional markets or a domestic flight of capital and entrepeneurs which would leave a vacuum that the Soviet Union, already pressed by other commitments, would have to fill. This was reflected in Corvalán's remarks in an interview published in *Pravda*. In regard to selling copper in the world market the Popular Unity government would "take no unilateral steps aimed at a reorientation with respect to foreign markets." Chile would continue to sell copper to the United States, but, if necessary, the Chileans "even in the capitalist world would not lack for markets for our copper." In addition, Chile had re-established relations with Cuba and the People's Republic of China. It intended to make use of the Soviet credit and to conclude economic agreements with the Soviet Union and the socialist states.[54]

Whether Chile can proceed to create a socialism that combines Marxian economics and democratic institutional forms is difficult to determine. Formidable obstacles loom on both left and right, and the Soviets' presence and encouragement are not good harbingers for the future. If such a development did take place, it would have implications for East-West relations far beyond the confines of U.S.–Soviet–Latin American relations.

One of the foremost supporters of the Allende candidacy was Fidel Castro, whose own road to power and subsequent transformation into a Marxist-Leninist would appear, on the surface at least, to diverge substantially from the Chilean experience. Before the elections, Castro

[53] Mervin K. Sigale, "Top Chilean Communist Favors Continued U.S. Aid," *Chicago Sun-Times*, November 8, 1970. Dr. Allende has voiced criticism of the moves of U.S.-owned subsidiaries directed against Chilean nationalization, but has adopted a "conciliatory" position toward them in practice. See "Allende Criticizes Nixon—Says Chile Can Dictate Her Own Laws," *New York Times*, January 20, 1972); and "Chile Says She will Pay 84.6 Million to Kennecott," *ibid.*, February 26, 1972; or Allende's remarks "Mr. Nixon is President of the United States and I am President of Chile. I shall have nothing derogatory to say about Mr. Nixon as long as Mr. Nixon respects the President of Chile. If they break with their obligation, if once again they cast aside the principles of self-determination and non-intervention, they will meet with a reply worthy of a people and its representative."

[54] "Unity is the Guarantee of Victory: A Talk with Comrade Luis Corvalan, General Secretary of the Communist Party of Chile," *Pravda*, April 17, 1971, reprinted in *CDSP*, 23, no. 16 (May 18, 1971): 38. He also stressed that "we came to power through elections and are carrying on revolutionary transformations in conformity with the Constitutional norms and laws of Chile." Allende told workers' meetings that Chile could not depend on the Soviet Union and other Communist countries for many imports. "Chile Says She will Pay 84.6 Million to Kennecott," *New York Times*, February 26, 1972.

proclaimed that he did not necessarily favor violence in Chile. "We're going to suppose that elections [in Chile] may result in a triumph for the left. This occurrence and a Chilean revolution will depend on who directs the leftist movement. I believe that conditions in Chile are different from those of Cuba and I believe things can't be done there as they were here. Here we made a revolution by open struggle, arming a small group of men to wage guerilla war." Chile could proceed to socialism "by the path of fulfilling the election law, by the path of victory in the elections." Chile is a Latin American state where the political struggle is "developing within constitutional bounds and for that reason I repeat, in this concrete case, in Chile in 1970, socialism can win out in elections."[55]

The question of Castro and Cuba must be of paramount concern in any survey of Soviet relations with Latin America. Castro's falling into line behind Soviet support of the Allende regime in Chile is instructive because it seems to illustrate the increasing rapprochement between the Soviet Union and Cuba which some observers have professed to see in recent years. Since the death of Guevara in Bolivia, the Cubans, while not explicitly reducing their commitment to supporting Latin American revolutionary movements, have nevertheless toned down their rhetoric, perhaps because they feel that such movements, as traditionally formulated, offer diminishing returns or because of the dismal condition of the Cuban economy. Also, the new revolutionary wave in Latin America, which is not a consequence of violence, may be attractive to the Cubans. These factors may result in a limited agreement with the Soviet Union concerning its policy toward Latin America unless the present governments in Peru and Chile turn sharply to the right or are overthrown.[56]

---

[55] Malcolm W. Browne, "Castro, on TV, Helping Marxist in Chilean Election," *New York Times*, August 23, 1970; and James Miguel Varas, "Chili: Antikommunizm Poterpel Porazhenie," *Latinskaia Amerika*, 1970, no. 6, p. 213. For Soviet approval of improved Cuban-Chilean relations, see Commentator's Column, "Solidarity Strengthens," *Pravda*, August 7, 1971, reprinted in *CDSP*, 23, no. 32 (September 7, 1971): 13–14. Castro visited Chile from November 10 to December 4, 1971, and his reaction to the Allende victory was quite colorful and dramatic: "How could we look upon such a victory? With sadness? Mortified because an electoral victory had been scored, without arms? We would have to be considered cretins, a bunch of cretins, a bunch of stupid, vile, miserable characters for anyone to expect such an attitude from revolutionaries." Yet his old skepticism about the efficacy of the electoral process re-emerged as he departed. He said that there was "no case in history in which the reactionaries, the exploiters, the privileged members of a social system, resign themselves to change, resign themselves peacefully to change." "No Revolution is Ready-Made" and "Who Has Learned the Most?" in *Fidel in Chile . . . Selected Speeches* (New York: International Publications, 1972), pp. 119, 204.

[56] Daniel Tretiak, *Cuban Relations with the Communist System: The Politics of a Communist Independent, 1967–1970*, Westinghouse Corporation Advanced Studies Group, ASG Monograph no. 4 (Waltham, Mass., 1970), pp. 46–49.

The Soviet Union may quietly back urban and rural revolutionary movements, depending upon time and place and circumstances in which international complications and commitments are unlikely to result.[57] In this sense they are not totally opposed to the Cuban emphasis on guerilla warfare, but it is *not* a component part of their approach, and it differs in several respects from the Cuban position. Certainly the Soviet position on the choice of violent and/or non-violent means for the seizure of power has always been more equivocal than is sometimes suggested. This question will be explored in greater detail below.

The almost total dependence of the Cuban economy on Soviet largess continues, and requires Cuba to shape its policies toward Soviet requirements. Castro was quoted as admitting that "in the final analysis we must say with all justice, that the aid was decisive for us."[58] The backing of the Allende regime can be interpreted both in this light and in the understandable desire of the Castro regime to break out of its formerly isolated position in the hemisphere and strengthen its position toward the United States.

On the question of Cuban-American relations, the expressed Soviet and Chilean "go slow" attitude in internal movement leftward and in severing relations with the United States economically is instructive. There are recurring reports that the Soviet Union is unhappy with its continuing aid burden and the chronic crisis in the Cuban economy, so unhappy that it might apply pressure to remove Castro as Prime Minister of the country and replace him with a more orthodox Communist who would be a more effective administrator.[59] An improvement of relations with the United States, with Castro keeping his party leadership and control of the armed forces, could conceivably ease the Soviet aid burden as well as ameliorate an irritant in American-Soviet relations. While the Castro regime has shown little official interest in

---

[57] Welles, *op. cit.*

[58] A. D. Bekarevich, "SSSR-Kuba: Leninskie Printsipy Proletarskogo Internatsionalizma," *Latinskaia Amerika*, 1970, no. 1, p. 30. As of 1970, State Department estimates were that the Soviet Union was spending about $1.4 million a day in Cuba and that Castro in his speech of April 22, 1970, mentioned the figure of $1.4 billion in total military assistance and $3.2 billion in economic assistance. See the testimony of Deputy Assistant Secretary of State for Inter-American Affairs Robert H. Hurwitch in U.S., Congress, House, *Cuba and the Caribbean: Hearings before the Subcommittee on Inter-American Affairs of the Committee on Foreign Affairs*, 91st Cong., 2nd sess., 1970, p. 18.

[59] Hugh O'Shaughnessy, "Soviets Reportedly Seeking to Oust Castro as Premier," *Chicago Sun-Times*, August 1, 1971. For a brief discussion of degeneration in the Cuban economy and loss of support from many formerly sympathetic quarters in Europe, see "Worldgram," *U.S. News and World Report*, October 11, 1971, p. 62. Despite the economic burden, continued support of the Cuban regime apparently remains a priority of Soviet foreign policy for ideological and "great power" reasons. The current formula seems to be to continue to embrace Castro, whose

improving such relations, some quarters argue that Castro may be seeking to explore the possibility of an eventual détente with the United States, counting on the presence of the new Chilean government, American weariness with a decade of interventionist policy in Asia, and guarded hints of rapprochement from Washington.[60]

Whatever interest the Soviet Union might have in eventually reducing its economic burden in Cuba and in putting the Cuban economy in some kind of order, there is no indication of any military disengagement from the islands or from the Caribbean area as a whole. The Soviet military presence in the area brought about the missile crisis of 1962. An increased military (especially naval) deployment which has fewer entangling implications than the former under some circumstances is not incompatible with partial economic disengagement. It might come as a reminder to the United States not to misinterpret the latter.[61] It could be argued that a similar process of increasing the Soviets' military presence in the Middle East is intended to put pressure on Israel for a diplomatic settlement by denying it certain military options, but is not intended to provoke it.[62]

----

popularity in Cuba is apparently still high, but to maneuver him in lock step with Soviet foreign policy in exchange for aid to the Cuban economy. The latter is to be integrated more closely than ever to the Soviet economy and under closer Soviet tutelage. While visiting the Soviet Union in the summer of 1972, Castro expressed confidence in the "principled" Soviet policy of peaceful coexistence, adherence to a policy of "realism," not "dogmatism," and stressed internal economic construction within Cuba, thereby downplaying any Cuban hemispheric role. See John Adams Moreau, "Frustrations Mar Cuba's Relations with Soviets," *Chicago Sun-Times*, January 2, 1972; V. Volkov, "Cuba Builds," *New Times*, 1972, no. 26, pp. 14–15; P. Orlov, "The Soviet Union and Cuba," *ibid.*, no. 28, p. 5; Juan Cobo, "Fidel Speaks to the People," *ibid.*, pp. 8–9; and Charlotte Saikowski, "Kremlin Leaders Give Cuba Boost out of Isolation Chamber," *Christian Science Monitor*, June 28, 1972. See also "Dinner in the Kremlin: Comrade Fidel Castro's Stay in Moscow, in a Fraternal, Cordial Atmosphere," *Pravda*, June 28, 1972; and "Soviet-Cuban Friendship Grows Stronger," *ibid.*, July 7, 1972; both reprinted in *CDSP*, 24, no. 27 (August 2, 1972): 13.

[60] For Cuban coldness on the official level, see James Nelson Goodsell, "Talk of Cuban-U.S. Ties Dampened," *Christian Science Monitor*, August 5, 1971. But see also *idem*, "Warmup Volley for US and Cuba?" *ibid.*, September 17, 1971. The official U.S. position is cool; see Hurwitch in *U.S. News and World Report*, October 4, 1971, p. 62. For a cogent argument for improved U.S.-Cuban relations, see Edward Gonzales. "The United States and Castro: Breaking the Deadlock," *Foreign Affairs*, 50 (July 1972): 722–38.

[61] For a discussion of possible Soviet policy options in Cuba, see Desmond P. Wilson, Jr., "Projection and Policy Options in the Soviet-Cuban Relationship," *Orbis*, 12, no. 2 (Summer 1968).

[62] David Jordan suggests that the Soviet naval deployment in the Caribbean may be linked to the Middle East in a tit-for-tat way. The Soviet Union may hope to get enough influence for an exchange. The Soviets would quietly offer to neglect the Caribbean if the U.S. tacitly ignored the Middle East (except for Israel) and the Eastern Mediterranean. They may hope to gain predominance in the Middle East and eventually parity in the Western Hemisphere. Jordan, *op. cit.*, p. 334.

Whatever the case may be, a task force with a nuclear-powered submarine, two conventionally powered submarines, a submarine tender and guided missile cruiser, a missile-equipped destroyer, and an oil tanker came to the Caribbean in May 1970. This was the second Soviet naval visit to Cuba, the first having occurred in July 1968. The Soviet task force entered Cuban territorial waters and stopped at the port of Cienfuegos; it was the first time a nuclear-powered submarine had visited a Cuban port. Later, two of the vessels visited Havana. This followed the first visit of a Soviet defense minister to Cuba (November 1969) and the first landing outside the Soviet Union of the TU-A5 "Bear" reconnaissance aircraft, in April and May of 1970.[63]

The U.S. press was filled with reports of the Soviet naval presence in the Caribbean in the fall and winter of 1970–1971, and especially with concern that nuclear submarines were to be serviced in Cuban ports.[64] The Nixon administration apparently did not object to a "show-the-flag" port-of-call visit, but it opposed the construction of a military base. Whatever its military value for defense of the island, which may have been aimed against the Cubans themselves without any ominous external implications,[65] it was agreed that such a base would have high "prestige" value for future Soviet commitments in the area. An "agreement" not to service vessels armed with nuclear missiles in or from Cuban ports was reached and thereby defused the "symbolic" importance of the issue, at least temporarily.[66]

[63] Testimony of Deputy Assistant Secretary of State for Inter-American Affairs Robert A. Hurwitch, in *Cuba and the Caribbean*, p. 28; and Assistant Secretary of Defense for International Security Affairs Warren Nutter, *ibid.*, pp. 104–5. Nutter testified that Soviet assistance had given Cuba "the best equipped forces in Latin America," but that they had neither the air- nor sealift to mount operations outside Cuba. Manolo Reyes, Latin news editor of television station WTVJ in Miami, Florida, reported the presence of two Soviet military convoys without Cuban troops and the presence of Soviet MIG planes on an open field in Cuba. *Ibid.*, p. 164.

[64] George W. Ashworth, "Washington Keeps Tabs on Soviets in Caribbean," *Christian Science Monitor*, November 7, 1970; Chalmers W. Roberts, "Soviet Flotilla to Arrive in Cuban Ports Monday," *Chicago Sun-Times*, December 6, 1970; James Nelson Goodsell, "Soviet Ships Prowl Caribbean—Guatemala, Honduras, Nicaragua Grow Uneasy," *Christian Science Monitor*, August 28, 1970.

[65] In his account of the interaction between Moscow and Washington on the issue, George H. Quester, "Missiles in Cuba, 1970," *Foreign Affairs*, 49 (April 1971): 493–506, contended that the naval build-up was simply a Soviet desire to provide a Polaris-type, second-strike deterrent that was less vulnerable to land-based missiles, like similar American forces, and that it was connected with SALT. The strong Washington response, he argued, was possibly due to domestic "nervousness" and a desire to prove American resolution in the face of unfavorable developments in Latin America (Chile) and a reaffirmation of American resolve world wide, especially in the Middle East.

[66] Benjamin Welles, "Soviet's Removal of Vessel in Cuba is Awaited by US—Submarine Support Ship is Expected to go as Result of an Understanding—Nuclear Arms at Issue—American Officials Hopeful Soviet Talks Resolved Dispute over Issue," *New York Times*, November 15, 1970. The agreement renewed the U.S.

It is doubtful that the Soviet Union seeks to convert any Latin American states, even Cuba, into offensive military bastions against their neighbors in the hemisphere. Such a move might only trigger the American offensive action it is designed to deter. At present, as far as is known, the Soviet Union has no military aid programs in Latin America outside of Cuba. It is possible that Soviet arms instructors or technicians might appear in Latin America in the future, along with military hardware, especially in "sympathetic" Latin American states. It is conceivable that recent conversations among Soviet Minister of Defense Marshall Grechko, Commander in Chief of the Soviet Air Force P. S. Kutakhov, and Commander in Chief of the Chilean Air Force Lieutenant General Cesar Ruiz Danyau might portend such a development.[67]

The new Soviet naval developments in the Caribbean probably served a variety of military, diplomatic, and psychological purposes. They were the result of a general naval building program, the consequences of which have been increasingly evident in the Brezhnev-Kosygin regime. This has been seen in the increasing presence of Soviet naval forces in Indian, Mediterranean, and Caribbean waters and in greater Soviet aggressiveness in commercial maritime policy.[68]

New Soviet naval developments do not involve any attempt to achieve traditional "command of the seas"; there has apparently been no policy decision to mount a general challenge to Western naval forces. Instead by "invading the ocean preserves of the imperialists," the Soviets have attempted to deny absolute control of the oceans to any opponent. This is as much psychological as military; as strategic

---

commitment not to invade Cuba in return for a Soviet agreement not to put offensive weapons in Cuba and not to base missile-carrying submarines, store nuclear weapons, or establish repair and servicing facilities anywhere in the Western Hemisphere. The Soviet Union officially denied that there was ever an intention to set up such a base. V. Matveev, "Version or Diversion," *Izvestiia*, October 10, 1970, reprinted in *CDSP*, 22, no. 4 (November 10, 1970): 14–15. For an account of a later Soviet naval visit to Cuba, see "Sub Visit to Cuba Called Soviet Presummitry," *Chicago Sun-Times*, May 19, 1972; see also Lynn Darrell Bender, "US Cuban Policy: Subtle Modifications and the Implications of the American-Soviet 'Understandings,'" *Journal of International and Comparative Studies*, 5 (Spring 1972): 50–67.

[67] Wynfred Joshua and Stephen P. Gibert, *Arms for the Third World: Soviet Military Aid Diplomacy* (Baltimore: The Johns Hopkins Press, 1969), pp. 91–95; "Friendly Talk," *Krasnaia Zvezda*, June 29, 1971, reprinted in *CDSP*, 23, no. 26, (July 27, 1971): 22. See also an account of a visit by a Soviet military delegation, headed by Kutakhov, to the Chilean Air Force Academy to become familiar with the facilities and operations. *Izvestiia*, September 22, 1972, reprinted in *CDSP*, 24, no. 38 (October 18, 1972): 27.

[68] For two of the large number of official and nonofficial sources on this question, see *The Changing Strategic Naval Balance: USSR vs. USA*, prepared at the request of the House Committee on Armed Services, 90th Cong., 2nd sess., December 1968; and *The Soviet Drive for Maritime Power*, prepared for the Senate Committee on Commerce, 90th Cong., 1st sess., December 1967.

parity it may be meant to convey the idea that certain U.S. commitments, if extended, could be dangerous. While it is not being used for
direct intervention in local military conflicts, the Soviet deployment
may be beginning to occupy a position where it can "make an impression, inspire confidence, and have an influence on the military political
situation in countries distant from the USSR, first and foremost, in the
'third world' countries." A "denial" capability used for such political-
strategic purposes is most immediately relevant to the Mediterranean
but is also pertinent to the Caribbean.[69]

The Soviet navy may just be "showing the flag" in the Caribbean
and does not intend to use naval forces for the broader purposes of
"coercive diplomacy." Certainly the Soviet Union has increasingly indicated by word and deed that it is indeed a global power with military
instruments that are generally considered indispensable to that role.
What better place is there to project such a role than in the United
States' "backyard"?

A more ambitious Soviet course can be posited—that present and
future political developments in the Caribbean and Latin America
(Peru, Chile, and so on) might warrant a naval buildup analogous to
that in the Mediterranean. Thus, this naval development might have
consequences beyond any concrete issue of U.S.–Cuban–Soviet relations, and it might be designed as a naval backdrop to what is perceived as a developing "revolutionary situation" in Latin America.
The use of American naval forces for reverse purposes is known to the
Soviet Union, and the lesson may not be lost on Soviet strategists. A
prominent British specialist on Soviet military affairs has surmised that
Soviet military planners might hope that another Central or South
American area, farther away from U.S. territory than Cuba, for example, would become available for support facilities for Soviet naval
activity perhaps Chile,[70] despite vociferous Soviet denials of such an

---

[69] John Erickson, "The Soviet Weapons Build-up, 1965–1970/71: Roles and
Capabilities" (pp. 95, 109), and Joseph S. Baritz, "The Soviet Armed Forces:
Improved Capabilities and Changing Roles" (p. 133), in *The Present Stage of
Soviet Global Expansion: Sources, Goals, and Prospects*, U.S. Army Institute for
Advanced Russian and East European Studies, Fifth Annual Soviet Affairs Sympo-
sium, Garmisch, Germany, April 20–22, 1971.

[70] John D. Hayes, "The Soviet Navy in the Caribbean Sea and Gulf of Mexico,"
*Interplay*, 4, no. 1 (January 1971): 8, Drew Middleton, "Russ Building Caribbean Fleet?" *Milwaukee Journal*, February 21, 1971; Malcolm Mackintosh,
"Russia's Defense: A Question of Quality," *Interplay*, 4, no. 2 (February 1971):
16. Mackintosh comments that Soviet Navy doctrine apparently does not antici-
pate the launching of landings on well-defended coasts. Perhaps "Soviet political
action will still be expected to pave the way effectively for intervention overseas."
The Egyptian involvement might act as a precedent, overcoming barriers to
setting up bases overseas. *Ibid*, p. 17. See also James D. Theberge, ed., *Soviet
Seapower in the Caribbean: Political and Strategic Implications* (New York:
Praeger, 1972).

intention.[71] Presumably, "agreements" made with the Nixon administration could be interpreted "ambiguously."

Soviet support for guerrilla *movements,* as distinguished from leftist *regimes,* will probably remain shadowy, ambiguous, and highly circumstantial. The question of relations with movements that are considered to be to the "left" of current Soviet policy is a recurring problem. Reference is made to both the Chinese role in Latin America and, more significantly, the character and role of "home-grown" urban guerrillas such as the Tupamaros in Uruguay and groups like them elsewhere in Latin America.

The Soviets' responses to "third world" developments are partly determined by their need to respond to rival Chinese policy initiatives and especially to ideological pronouncements which may appeal to revolutionaries of various stripes.[72] There was an echo in Latin America of the split among leftists and Communist parties that arose after the Sino-Soviet dispute of 1960. Many were impatient with the Soviet "gradualist" approach toward winning political power. The Chinese emphasis on violence and armed struggle and excoriation of the Soviet position as nonrevolutionary and revisionist, as well as the stress on the revolutionary role of the peasants, found some support. There were Chinese sympathizer groups in several countries and pro-Chinese splinter parties in Peru, Brazil, and Colombia.[73]

The prevalance of anti-imperialist sentiments among Latin Americans as a result of experience in dealing with the United States and West European countries is a key Chinese asset, especially the lingering fear of U.S. intervention in the domestic affairs of Latin American states. Also, the propensity of Latins to settle political differences by armed force may predispose them to follow the path of armed struggle advocated by the Chinese in the past. The political radicalism of Latin American university students may also redound to the benefit of the Chinese. The desire for land reform and greater diplomatic and economic flexibility could benefit the Chinese as well as the Soviet Union.

But the People's Republic of China is far away, without an overseas intervention capability and the capacity of the Chinese to supply arms and other material to admirers in Latin America is quite limited. In addition, Latin American culture is largely Western or South European and is quite distinct from the Chinese. There are Chinese colonies in

[71] See note 53.

[72] A point made by Alvin Z. Rubinstein in "Assessing Soviet Power in the Third World," *Asian Affairs,* no. 58 (February 1971), p. 10.

[73] Aguilar, *op. cit.,* pp. 3–4. For Soviet attempts to attribute partial responsibility to the pro-Chinese Communist Party of Brazil for the overthrow of the Goulart government in 1964, see Hamburg, "The Soviet Union and Latin America," chap. VIII. Chinese support has generally been more verbal than active.

Peru, Cuba, and other Latin American states, but these show little enthusiasm for identification with the erstwhile motherland. Presumably, no cultural or religious groups are available for proselytization.

As for Chinese-encouraged "people's wars," it is less likely than before that the United States would intervene to furnish the Chinese a foil with which to transform a civil war into an "anti-imperialist" one, although this cannot be excluded. Of course, there is considerable doubt that rural-oriented insurgencies could ever reach that point, especially if there is no major international conflict like the one which facilitated the Chinese rise to power in Asia.[74]

Yet the Chinese are just beginning to strengthen relations in Latin America, as evidenced by the establishment of relations with the Allende government in Chile.[75] It is conceivable that a Chinese turn to a more "pragmatic" foreign policy orientation might find a sympathetic echo in Latin America, where governments might find a three-sided U.S.-Soviet-Chinese rivalry useful for economic and other purposes.

The influence of the "Castrista" left has declined primarily because of guerrilla failures, the death of Che Guevara in 1967, and the fact that the Castro victory in Cuba, like the victory of the Maoists in China, was the result of exceptional circumstances that are not likely to be repeated elsewhere. In addition, the partial rapprochement of Castro with the Soviet Union has dimmed his lustre somewhat as an independent revolutionary center, as has his partial softening of revolutionary rhetoric. Castro's bitter dispute with China on both the governmental and the ideological plane has also partially neutralized rival claimants from the "governmental left" of the Soviet Union.[76]

Many of Castro's disagreements with the Soviet approach have been perpetuated in new revolutionary constellations which apparently have

[74] The analysis of the Chinese position in Latin America is taken from Cecil Johnson, *Communist China and Latin America, 1959–1968* (New York: Columbia University Press, 1970), pp. 286–302. See also *idem*, "China and Latin America: New Ties and Tactics," *Problems of Communism*, 21 (July–August 1972): 53–67.

[75] Henry S. Hayward, "Chile Puts Name on Growing List," *Christian Science Monitor*, January 8, 1971. See also George Ginsburgs and Arthur Stahnke, "Communist China's Trade Relations with Latin America," *Asian Survey*, 10, no. 9 (1970): 803–19; and Henry S. Hayward, "Peking's Selective Loans," *Christian Science Monitor*, October 14, 1971.

[76] Aguilar, *op. cit.*, pp. 6–10, is quite useful for his discussion of differences between Castro and Latin American Communist strategies on the proper method for seizing power and for Castro's later de-emphasis of armed revolution. For a discussion of acrimony between the Chinese and the Cubans, see Tretiak, *Cuban Relations with the Communist System*, pp. 2, 25–39; and *idem*, "Soviet and Chinese Policies toward Cuba and Cuba's Response" (Paper delivered at the Annual Meeting of the American Political Science Association, Los Angeles, 1970), pp. 11–12.

only loose organizational contact with either the Cubans or the Chinese. As has been the case with Castro and Debray, the emphasis in these groups is on guerrilla fighters and armed force rather than on the crucial role of Communist cadres, the building of political consciousness, and creation of the proper organizational forms among the masses. The Soviet position does not involve an eschewal of violence as such, but finds the activity and doctrine of these groups dangerous nonsense, echoing Lenin's warnings about "left-wing infantilism" and "Blanquism," terrorism divorced from the existence of an "objective revolutionary situation."[77] Soviet commentators, for example, attack "left extremism" in Chile as presenting "a great danger," even though it was dealt a serious blow by the Allende victory. They attack the "ultra left" for forcing revolutionary progress and for the sins of "voluntarism" and "subjectivism," which the "forces of reaction" could use for their own purposes.[78]

Prominent among the new, "home-grown" Latin American guerrilla movements are those which combine Castro's emphasis on armed revolution with the Soviets' emphasis on the cities—the urban guerrillas. This phenomenon is the result of both the failure of the Castro-Guevarist rural strategy and the rapid growth of Latin American cities. The most attention-gathering of these groups recently has been the Tupamaros in Uruguay. The urban guerrilla strategy was expressed succinctly by Carlos Marighella, the late Tupamaro leader. "The urban guerrilla's reason for existence, the basic condition in which he acts and survives, is to shoot." The urban guerrilla seeks to place the government on the defensive, create a general sense of insecurity, and above all "turn political crisis into armed conflict by performing violent actions that will force those in power to transform the political situation in the country into a military situation. That will alienate the masses, who, from then on, will revolt against the army and police and blame them for this state of things. "Beyond this they are vague on the

[77] On differences that existed between the Soviet position and that of Debray and others, see Hamburg, "Industrialization, Urbanization, and Modernization in Latin America." Debray has recently moved toward the Allende and, obliquely, Soviet position. See Harry Raymond, "Debray Shifts toward Allende Views," *New York Times*, February 9, 1972.

[78] Zorina, "Chili: Novyi etap istorii"; A. F. Shulgovskii, "Latinskaia Amerika i opyt respublik Sovetskogo Vostoka," *Latinskaia Amerika*, 1970, no. 3, p. 86. On the necessity for a close tie between peasant organization and Communist parties, see A. D. Galkina, "Sovremennye Krest'ianskie Organizatsii Latinskoi Ameriki," *ibid.*, no. 1, p. 62. For a discussion of *one* of these guerrilla groups in Chile, see James Nelson Goodsell, "Leftist Guerrilla Band 'Stalks' Chilean Regime," *Christian Science Monitor*, March 15, 1971. For Allende's statements attacking unauthorized land seizures and the activities of the "lunatic fringe left," see Hobsbawn, *op. cit.*, pp. 24, 29.

type of society they would want to create but are opposed to the Peruvian formula of revolution from above and coexist only uneasily with the Allende government."[79]

The Tupamaros are the products of an overwhelmingly urban society whose appeal is to middle-class youth and white-collar workers whose economic expectations have not been met. The latter has resulted from inflation, a decline in agricultural productivity, a drop in the price of wool, and great fluctuations in the price of meat—all these in one of Latin America's traditionally stable democracies.

The Tupamaros have specialized in political kidnapping, which has attracted international attention particularly when foreign diplomats were abducted. They have been successful in establishing a network of secret agents within the administration and armed forces. They may have been able to bulid up support through the use of armed propaganda, the selective application of terror, and a sustained campaign to discredit individual members of the government.[80]

The declared Communist reaction to this group is not surprising in view of the fact that the *Frente Amplio*, which has prominent Communist participation, has specifically endorsed the Chilean road to power. The Uruguayan Communists, in the person of General Secretary Rodney Arismendi, praised the guerrillas for their "courage and sincerity" but insisted that "we will make the revolution by other means." A recent Soviet publication was more categorical in its denunciaton, attacking the Tupamaros as "petty bourgeois pseudo-revolutionaries" and "rollicking, loud-mouthed thugs" who pursue "gangster tactics."[81]

It is natural that the Soviets would mistrust groups they did not control, especially in a society where it is hoped, no doubt, that a Chilean-type coalition would come to power. The effect of the Tupamaros may

---

[79] Carlos Marighella, cited in Robert Moss, "Urban Guerrillas in Latin America," *Conflict Studies*, no. 8 (October 1970), p. 7. For other general surveys, see R. F. Lamberg, "Latin America's Urban Guerrillas," *Swiss Review of World Affairs*, 20, no. 3 (June, 1970); and Priscilla Clapp, "Urban Terrorism in Latin America: The Politics of Frustration and Fury," *Christian Science Monitor*, May 5, 1971.

[80] Robert Moss, "Uruguay: Terrorism versus Democracy," *Conflict Studies*, no. 14 (August 1971), pp. 4, 6, 7, 9.

[81] Rodney Arismendi in *L'Unita* (Rome), January 16, 1971; and D. A. Kunaniev, "Uruguay—So Near and Yet So Far," *Prostor* (journal of the Kazakhstan Writers Union), March 1971, cited in Robert Moss, "Urban Guerrillas in Uruguay," *Problems of Communism*, 20, no. 5 (September–October 1971): 22. Veliz argued that it was possible that the Tupamaros would participate in the November 1971 electoral coalition. Claudio Veliz, "The Chilean Experiment," *Foreign Affairs*, 49, no. 3 (April 1971): 443. For a Soviet comment on the Uruguayan presidential election, in which the Soviet-supported Frente Amplio finished third, but improved its standing from past elections, see V. Tikhmenev, "After the Uruguay Elections," *New Times*, 1972, no. 1, p. 12.

be contradictory, however. On the one hand it would seem to make the Communists vulnerable to suppression, the very eventuality that the Tupamaros profess to seek. On the other hand the Communists might appear to be a respectable alternative, in the same way that the Soviet Union may have benefited in its drive for improved diplomatic and other ties by Castro's activities of recent years. Generally, though, the existence of a "fractionated left," particularly one with strong internal roots, complicates the task of Soviet policy.

In attempting to estimate Soviet goals and influence in Latin America, some caveats must be kept in mind. The questions of whether or not the Soviet Union intends to expand, and whether it seeks an expansion of control or only increased influence, make a difference to the final policy the United States adopts. The military means, the amount of violence, and the frequency of application also are significant, as is whether these are adopted for offensive or defensive reasons.[82]

In like vein, Rubinstein, in analyzing U.S. specialists' treatment of Soviet "third world" policies, found a chronic tendency to equate Soviet "inputs (trade, military aid programs, and so on) with "outputs" (influence) without proving that the inputs actually brought about changes in the actual behavior of the target country. Aid, trade, and diplomatic support were treated either as influence or precursors of influence. Input and output were linked almost as cause and effect.[83]

It is "not by chance" that the neutral term "policy" has been used in this essay rather than the term "influence," or the far more lurid and misleading "penetration," or the even starker "subversion." Even "policy" creates difficulties, for it, too, may imply a single policy or a clearheadedness about means and ends which students of foreign policy and bureaucratic behavior in general know is terribly misleading, if not altogether false. Nevertheless, one can take the different policy instruments discussed and attempt to delineate possible goals and chances for success or failure.

In the cultural field it would seem that a key Soviet goal is to obtain a more positive response from elite audiences in the various Latin American states that may have been the case previously. People responding in this way would at least implicitly be more receptive to Soviet diplomatic or other overtures because they would be less likely to attribute them to sinister motives. The emphasis on Soviet achieve-

[82] William Welch, American Images of Soviet Foreign Policy (New Haven: Yale University Press, 1970), pp. 41–42.

[83] Alvin Z. Rubinstein, "US Specialists' Perception of Soviet Policy toward the Third World (Paper presented at the Annual Meeting of the American Political Science Convention, Chicago, Ill., September 7–11, 1971), pp. 4–6, 11.

ments in the arts, education, science, and sports would seek to convey an image of a "selfless" society not necessarily pursuing political advantage singlemindedly but seeking unselfish cooperation among peoples. This type of "people-to-people" diplomacy is, of course, also practiced by the United States and other political systems. A side effect of cultural programs and one that cannot be ignored is that an increasing number of persons are inevitably stationed in the host country to administer them. Such personnel may be used for purposes other than those for which their visas were granted, and traditionally the Soviet Union has not been remiss in taking advantage of opportunities offered. Even so, it is highly unlikely that they would "take over" any society by this route. If high level "penetration" did occur, consequences within the society concerned might be unfavorable for the Soviet Union. The Soviet Union and Latin American states need only look at Sudan or other political systems where a conspicuous Soviet presence made the Soviet Union and local Communists vulnerable to local policy upheavals.[84] Chile is the obvious Latin American case to watch in this connection. But political systems are not so easily "subvertible," especially in areas that are still far removed from the main center of Soviet power. Latin America is not low, and is not likely to become, the Eastern Europe of the late 1940s, even if the worst were to happen in Chile from an American point of view.[85]

Foreign aid and trade can lead to influence in four ways, by pro-

---

[84] The exact Soviet role in the events in Sudan is murky. What is clear is that there was sizable economic and military assistance to the Ja'Afar Nimeria regime. The Sudanese Communists opposed Nimeri's plan to join an Arab federation of Egypt and Libya. Nimeri cracked down on the Communists, but was supplanted in a coup that received support from some Soviet press organs. Nimeri subsequently recovered power and accused the Communists of being behind the coup, a charge that Egyptian sources echoed. The Nimeri retaliation, which included the execution of the general secretary of the Sudanese Communist party, and which took on an increasingly anti-Soviet tone, was sharply denounced by the Soviet press. Soviet disillusionment with "third world" nationalists was even more strongly in evidence thereafter. See Robert O. Freedman, "Soviet Foreign Policy toward the Middle East since Nasser," in *The Soviets in Asia,* ed. Norton T. Dodge (Mechanicsville, Md.: The Cremona Foundation, 1972), pp. 81, 83, 87, 90; and David Morison, "Moscow and the Problems of Third World Communists: The Lessons of Sudan," *Mizan,* 13, no. 3 (December 1971): 112; "New Sudanese Regime Acts to End Curbs on Reds," *New York Times,* July 21, 1971; Raymond H. Anderson, "Cairo Team Reported Sent to Sudan," *ibid.,* July 22, 1971; *idem,* "Sudan Coup Raises Question on Arab-Red Ties," *ibid.,* July 25, 1971. For some Soviet sources, see Dmitri Volsky, "Changes in Sudan," *New Times,* 1971, no. 30, p. 11; and a Tass statement condemning the suppression and execution of Communists, *Pravda,* July 28, 1971, reprinted in *CDSP,* 23, no. 29 (August 17, 1971): 3–4.

[85] Williams argues that the Christian Democratic movement may act as a barrier to the spread of Soviet influence. Edward J. Williams, *The Political Themes of Inter-American Relations* (Belmont, Calif.: Duxbury Press, 1971), pp. 51–55.

moting good will and solidifying friendly relations, making the recipient country dependent upon the donor, cultivating a natural ideological ally over the long run, or obtaining military advantages.[86]

Except for, and possibly because of, Cuba, it is highly unlikely that Soviet foreign aid or trade in Latin America will make the recipient country dependent upon the donor. In the case of Chile and Peru, for instance, Soviet trade and aid have been modest and, while it may increase, neither the Soviet Union nor the recipient governments seem to want to terminate Western aid, and certainly they do not want to replace it with Soviet aid on a large-scale basis. The Soviet Union will act as opportunity warrants to purchase Latin American goods and surpluses, particularly as protectionism in the Common Market and U.S. economy increases. It will also sell an increasing, though still modest, quantity of Soviet goods, industrial and otherwise, to Latin American states. This may eventually be true for the People's Republic of China, too, according to their requirements and capabilities. But many "third world" countries have shown a considerable ability to play off one donor against the other, particularly (in the past) in the U.S. Congress. Latin America is no exception. But Latin American needs are great, and U.S. trade and aid policy should not be dictated by any apocalyptic assessment of the Soviets' ability to "subvert" Latin American economies.

Solidifying friendly relations or cultivating a natural ideological ally over the long run appears to be both a more realistic goal of Soviet aid and trade in Latin America and a possible means of affecting the behavior of the host country. The intention to help build up the state sector and other linkages of Soviet aid and trade with political and psychological appeals has had, and will continue to have, a receptive audience in an area which appears to be moving to the left economically and politically. But this increase in influence may be glacial in impact, and any attempt to wield it too precipitously and crudely for obvious political purposes is likely to be resisted. The very visibility of Soviet aid officials and a Soviet economic (or cultural) presence may redound to the latter's disadvantage if the position of the host government deteriorates and foreigners are available as scapegoats. More "businesslike" Soviet economic dealings with "third world" recipients, based on durable mutual advantage, may be more effective than "gifts" or other devices used for obvious political purposes.[87] 'Gratitude" be-

[86] David Bein, "The Communist Bloc and the Foreign Aid Game," *Western Political Quarterly*, 18, no. 4 (December 1964): 785–87.

[87] For recent evidence of a more "businesslike" Soviet relationship toward the "third world," see Elizabeth Valkenier, "New Trends in Soviet Economic Relations with the Third World," *World Politics*, 22, no. 3 (April 1970). Long-term considerations and the need to import oil to reduce the East European drain on

tween nations is usually a most evanescent phenomenon and cannot survive changed conditions. Soviet advantages in aid and trade in Latin America to this point may have resulted from the very unfamiliarity and novelty of the Soviet presence. If this presence were to continue to grow appreciably, the Soviet Union's past record would indicate that they have not discovered a unique and foolproof way to convert aid to influence.

The fourth use of aid, to obtain military advantages, pertains at the moment only to Cuba. The great risks here are overcommitment to an area that is still far removed from the center of Soviet military power, and the fact that, even in Latin America, regional rivalries might develop by which improved relations with one country could be achieved only at the cost of a deterioration of relations with another.[88] Soviet leaders probably know only too well that similar political orientations of states do not guarantee an absence of rivalries. Such rivalries could develop in Latin America if one state industrialized more quickly than others and/or if sharp ideological rivalries developed. The effect of Soviet and American (and Chinese?) military aid efforts might be to bring Latin America into the world political arena with a linkage between great power rivalries and tensions among individual Latin American states. Chile and Peru immediately come to mind. In Peru the highly nationalistic military regime might turn to Soviet aid as a riposte in a period of increasing tension with the United States, an eventuality the Nixon administration has sought to avoid. Possible inter-American military rivalries are a question for the future, but economic rivalries might be be reflected in increased military tensions among states.

Internal political developments within Latin American states, refractory generals, unpredictable political coalitions, and problems on the left all point to the difficulty that any great power has in attempting to translate policy instruments into influence. Chile, where the Allende regime has gone through cabinet crisis and faces hostility and suspicion from left and right, attests to the uncertainty of political situations even in a country where events seem to favor the Soviet Union at the present time. Open civil war there could pose new dangers to Soviet interests.[89]

---

Soviet oil reserves might provide a solid economic basis for trade with Venezuela. See "Thirst for Oil Jumbles Communist Bloc Patterns," *Christian Science Monitor*, June 18, 1970.

[88] Rubinstein, "Assessing Soviet Power in the Third World," p. 11.

[89] "Cabinet Crisis in Chile: 4 Quit," *Christian Science Monitor*, August 8, 1971; "Fifth Chile Minsiter Resigns," *ibid.*, August 11, 1971; and Hobsbawm, *op. cit.* Statements by Soviet commentators and Chilean Communists seem to reflect an awareness of the dangers contained in the Chilean situation, especially the inflation, strikes, and the apparent polarization of left and right. They attack local

Finally, there is the military question itself. The increased Soviet projection of forces in the Caribbean area may portend danger of "confrontation" with the United States. The Soviet Union might attempt to use its naval forces as an "inhibitory" or "denial" force to affect any future American inclination to intervene in what are perceived to be highly unfavorable developments in Latin America (a "successful" national liberation war or an internal move that is too far to the left). Present U.S. policy would seem to seek to avoid such moves, if at all possible, but a greater American propensity to intervene might develop in the train of a nationalistic "backlash" after America's involvement in Vietnam has ended. The national disillusionment with Vietnam might simply harden into a determination to avoid "unsuccessful" interventions. Certainly the anxiety displayed in Washington in 1970 at the movement of Soviet ships and submarines in the waters in and around Cuba indicates that the United States is still nervous about Soviet movements and intentions in that part of the world. It may perceive that such issues have a high potential for creating a strong domestic reaction.

Latin America has recently evidenced a turn to the left, as witnessed by developments in Peru, Chile, and perhaps Uruguay, Bolivia, and elsewhere. The Soviet Union, continuing the policies of the Khrushchev years, has sought to capitalize on these developments as best it can to move Latin American states closer to its position on international issues, or at least to a position that is more "independent" of the United States. In the latter goal it seems to have acted congruently with the interests of many Latin American states and the post–World War II trend in the "third world."

Recently, more ambitious objectives and greater developments of policy instruments seem to have characterized Soviet policy in the area. Chile is a prime example, although the Soviet economic and military stake is not yet extensive. Such policies have run up against, and will

---

"reaction" and "foreign" (U.S.) interests, especially the copper companies, but admit that major economic errors have been made and that some of the "middle sectors" of the Chilean population, and even working-class women, have been needlessly antagonized. They express confidence that a threat of violence from the right will be met successfully by their own, but they seem afraid that events might move out of their hands; the far left might provoke a showdown. See the articles in *Latinskaia, Amerika*, 1972, no. 2, pp. 9–66, esp. 66. 46–47, 52. See also M. Kudachkin, "Chile: Years of Struggle and Victories," *New Times*, 1972, no. 12, p. 13; and V. Listov, "Chile: Concerns and Hopes," *Pravda*, January 27, 1972, reprinted in *CDSP*, 24, no. 4 (February 23, 1972): 22. Joaquin Gutierrez, "The Destinies of Chile," *New Times*, 1972, no. 42, pp. 18–21, is a "self-critical" analysis of the Chilean situation with a minimum of ideological distortion. For an interesting analysis of the problems of the Allende regime, see Paul E. Sigmund, "Chile: Two Years of 'Popular Unity,'" *Problems of Communism*, 21 (November–December 1972): 38–51.

almost inevitably continue to run up against, the recalcitrant facts of life in nations that lie along the periphery of the Soviet Union and the United States. Vietnam stands out as an example for all who care to observe and learn. But the Soviet Union is not in an isolationist mood and will continue to take advantage of whatever "openings" are perceived in Latin America, with the hope or expectation that events are in its favor. Such a Soviet policy might seem a fitting riposte to U.S. efforts to improve relations with the People's Republic of China, President Nixon's "bridge-building" trip to Rumania, and the general U.S. interest in Eastern Europe, but the Soviets must also consider the effects this might have on improved relations with the United States, which presumably is a prime objective of Soviet foreign policy.

# 8

## SOVIET ECONOMIC RELATIONS WITH THE DEVELOPING NATIONS

*Elizabeth Kridl Valkenier*

Lively and expanding economic relations with the former colonial territories of the West constitute one of the hallmarks of Soviet policy in the Third World in the post-Stalin period. Before World War II there were a few isolated instances of Soviet credits and factory construction in Turkey and Afghanistan, but these never developed into a large-scale program. After the war, preoccupied with reconstruction and the cold war, the Soviet Union failed to work out positive policies in Asia and Africa. Instead of backing nationalist regimes, Moscow vigorously supported the Communist parties of the new states in their bid to wrest power from the bourgeois leaders, whom both regarded as mere Western puppets. Indicative of Moscow's hostile attitude to the middle-class regimes was its refusal to contribute to the U.N. Technical Assistance Program when it came into being in 1948.

Though some signs of reassessment were discernible before 1953, it was only after Stalin's death that the hostile policy was definitely abandoned. Almost overnight the Soviets stopped castigating nationalist statesmen, such as Nasser and Nehru, as imperialist lackeys or fascist usurpers and began courting them as heroic leaders of their downtrodden people. By the time the Bandung conference of nonaligned nations convened in 1954, the U.S.S.R. was playing the role of the friend of nationalist governments and supported them vis à vis the West.

To be effective, the new policy of rapprochement had to be attuned to the aspirations of the former colonies. Besides rendering diplomatic support against the West, the most persuasive stance the U.S.S.R. could assume was to back the insatiable desire of these countries for economic independence by granting them economic and technical aid for development.

There is little doubt that political objectives were dominant in the Soviet aid program and trade drive undertaken in 1953–1954. When Bulganin and Khrushchev went on their goodwill tour of the Asian capitals in 1955, their lavish offers of a steel mill here and a shipyard there were gestures designed to curry political favor and support. The two leaders knew the economic potentials, as well as the requirements, of Soviet industry, which by then had almost wholly recovered from the devastations of the war, but what they had in mind was manipulating the aspirations of the new states, not coordinating aid with the needs of Russia's expanding economy.

The sudden Soviet penetration into areas where the West had long held sway created a pervasive uneasiness, especially in the United States. The new policy was not viewed as a shift from Russia's hitherto prevailing autarky to participation in the international economy. It was regarded by most observers as yet another Soviet effort at subversion designed to steer the new nations in the direction of economic, political, and diplomatic radicalism, an effort that was to be capped eventually by Soviet dominance of the new nations' domestic and foreign policies. The more gloomy Kremlinologists predicted that the showy and costly projects were meant to promote economic imbalances that would facilitate Communist takeovers.

The first reactions in the West were lacking in balanced judgment. But there was little in the propagandistic pronouncements that accompanied Moscow's efforts to inaugurate aid and trade programs that could have led observers to consider it a rationally designed venture to promote economic development among the recipients, bring tangible economic gains to the donor, and at the same time win friends and clients in the Third World. The West had to compete against lavish gifts of hotels and sports stadiums, huge credits for steel works, generous purchases of surplus commodities, all of which were announced with a barrage of extravagant claims on behalf of radical protosocialist economic policies and with nasty attacks against the "imperialist powers." Extensive nationalization, the development of heavy industry, and expansion of the state sector with Soviet aid were pictured as assuring a straight and speedy road to prosperity, independence, and progress, whereas Western policies, it was said, would keep the former colonies in perpetual dependence as raw-material suppliers to the capitalist world.

Two decades have passed since the U.S.S.R. reversed its policy of economic isolation. The change was first heralded by a dramatic gesture at the United Nations, when the Soviet Union for the first time contributed to the Technical Assistance program in August 1953. This step was soon followed by credits and trade agreements with Afghanistan (1954) and India (1955). Since then, what seemed like hasty and haphazard gestures has become a network of ever-expanding, quite complex, and economically advantageous commitments.

Though mere figures cannot convey the full extent of Soviet economic involvement in the Third World, they do sketch its growth over the years. In 1955 the U.S.S.R. could boast of but two economic cooperation agreements; by 1971 it had economic and technical assistance pacts with forty developing nations—eighteen of them in Asia, twenty in Africa, and two in Latin America. Under the terms of these agreements the U.S.S.R. has thus far granted about $7 billion in credits for the construction of more than 700 projects, about half of which are already in operation.[1]

The Soviets like to boast that almost 70 percent of their aid finances the development of heavy industry. Actually the range of activity is much wider; the Soviets have contracted to build 120 schools, to set up about 150 agricultural, irrigation, and soil improvement projects, and to construct some 60 consumer goods and food-processing plants, as against 55 steel mills and machine-building plants, 30 factories and shops in ferrous and nonferrous metallurgy, and 31 electric power stations.[2]

About 10,500 Soviet technicians are working on Soviet aid projects; close to 1,500 technical personnel from the developing nations are receiving advanced training in the U.S.S.R. each year, and about 12,500 students from Asia, Africa, and Latin America are studying in Soviet universities, medical schools, and technical institutes.[3]

As for trade, in 1955 the U.S.S.R. traded with eighteen developing nations but had interstate agreements with only nine. Today Russia trades with over sixty new states, in most cases on the basis of treaties. Since 1965, Moscow has been increasing its long-term trade agreements (ranging in duration from three to fifteen years), and by now it can boast of more than a dozen such agreements. Trade with this group of states accounted for 5.0 percent of Soviet foreign trade in 1955, and by 1971 the figure had reached 13.5 percent. During the past five years, the growth of this trade has averaged over 11 percent annually, which exceeds the growth of Soviet foreign trade as a whole.[4]

Machinery and equipment figure prominently in Soviet exports, accounting for 37.5 percent of Soviet exports to the Third World. In 1969 these countries purchased 24.0 percent of all Soviet machinery exports.[5] Industrial raw materials—oil, petroleum products, ferrous metals, lumber—and foods, such as sugar, also make up a substantial portion of Soviet exports, constituting about 40 percent of the total.[6]

[1] *International Affairs*, October 1970, p. 16; *New Times*, January 20, 1971, p. 18; U.S., Department of State, Bureau of Intelligence and Research, *Communist States and Developing Countries: Aid and Trade in 1970* (Washington, D.C.: Government Printing Office, 1971), p. 6.
[2] *Vneshniaia torgovlia*, April 1970, pp. 21–22.
[3] Department of State, *op. cit.*, pp. 10, 12, 13.
[4] *Vneshniaia torgovlia*, March 1971, pp. 13–14, and June 1971, p. 17; *Ekonomicheskaia gazeta*, no. 24 (June 1971), p. 20.
[5] *Vneshniaia torgovlia*, March 1971, p. 14.
[6] Department of State, *op. cit.*, p. 42.

In return for their machinery and raw materials, the Russians get consumer goods (especially clothing and foods) and raw materials—such as rubber, natural gas, or copper—which are in short supply either at home or among the European satellites.[7] In the Soviet press these days, much is being made of how the U.S.S.R., unlike the West, is increasingly purchasing manufactured goods from the nascent industries of the Third World nations. (These imports account for almost 20 percent of the total.) Indeed, this is the case, but it is readily explained by the fact that the long-forgotten Soviet consumer is at last getting some attention and that, to meet the growing domestic demand, the production of an insufficiently developed Russian light industry has to be supplemented by imports.

Behind these figures, which indicate a considerable expansion in aid and trade, lies a much more interesting story of the evolution of a well-reasoned and organized program. It is a pattern of economic relations which is increasingly geared to be economically more effective abroad and commercially more beneficial to the U.S.S.R. Moreover, much of it is carefully integrated with definite strategic designs that serve not the political aims of international communism but the power objectives of the second strongest nation in the world. Nowadays, the patterns and objectives of Soviet aid and trade are a far cry from what they were said to be in the West during the early years of their inception. In many ways it is a much less sinister and a much simpler story. But in other respects it is a program of portent, presenting many serious challenges with its purposefulness.

## I

Since about 1964–1965, Soviet economic relations with the Third World have definitely lost their haphazard and politically motivated character. They have become better integrated and economically more justifiable. Probably the last spectacular example of Khrushchev's flamboyant style of dispensing aid was his grant in 1960 of a further $250 million credit to Indonesia, even though none of the projects under the terms of the 1956 credit of $100 million had been completed and many had not even been started. The following year, after evident failures in Cuba and Indonesia, the Khrushchev regime substantially reduced aid commitments and started looking for ways to realize definite returns on its investment.

Speaking before the Twenty-second Congress of the CPSU in Octo-

---

[7] Almost 80 percent of Soviet imports from the developing nations consist of consumer goods or primary products for their manufacture. *Vneshniaia torgovlia*, June 1971, p. 17.

ber 1961, Anastas Mikoyan informed his audience that it "will be necessary to make use of foreign trade as a factor in economizing in current production expenditures and in capital investment."[8] Although he did not specifically refer to it, trade with the Third World was of concern to the government. At about this time the Presidium of the Academy of Sciences set up a research group in the Institute of the Economy of the World Socialist System to devise indices of the effectiveness of economic relations with the newly independent states.

Very little of the ongoing re-evaluation leaked out into the open at first, and only a few general references to the contribution that foreign economic relations could make to domestic development appeared in print. It seems likely that Khrushchev was opposed to any public airing of the U.S.S.R.'s interest in a fair return on all the money and resources poured into the former colonies. He tirelessly proclaimed that Russia valued trade with the developing nations primarily for political reasons and considered it a burdensome obligation to give them economic aid. (By contrast, nowadays, Soviet aid officials frequently lecture the less developed nations that the Soviet awareness of its "international duty" does not entitle them to pose excessive unilateral demands which do not "create any sound basis for developing mutually advantageous relations.")[9] Understandably, then, it was only after his fall from power in October 1964 that detailed and practical policy proposals began to appear openly.

First an article, and then an entire book, based on the findings of the research group set up by the Academy of Sciences was published.[10] Basically, these economists proposed a precise economic rationale for Soviet dealings with the developing nations through an integration of the allocation of aid with the expansion of trade. They viewed aid-giving primarily as an alternative to domestic investment and argued that it would be cheaper for the U.S.S.R. to import certain goods and materials than to produce them at home. Similarly, they proposed that the East European states replace some of the raw materials they obtained from the Soviet Union by imports from Africa and the Middle East. They advocated closer economic integration between donor and recipient, which would involve the joint extraction or processing of various natural resources, as well as the joint production of some industrial goods, based on long-term aid and trade commitments.

[8] *Pravda*, October 22, 1961, p. 8.
[9] V. Smirnov, "Vazhnyi faktor v ekonomicheskom progresse razvivaiushchikhsia stran," *Vneshniaia torgovlia*, March 1971, pp. 13–18.
[10] L. Zevin, "Vzaimnaia vygoda ekonomicheskogo sotrudnichestva sotsialistiches-kikh i razvivaiushchikhsia stran," *Voprosy ekonomiki*, February 1965, pp. 72–83; G. M. Prokhorov, ed., *Problemy sotrudnichestva sotsialisticheskikh i razvivaiush-chikhsia stran* (Moscow, 1966).

Integration of aid and trade into the planned development of the U.S.S.R. and some of its major economic partners has proceeded apace since 1965. The leadership gives increasing prominence to this problem. At the Twenty-third Congress of the CPSU in April 1966, Kosygin remarked briefly and vaguely that cooperation with the new states enabled the U.S.S.R. to "make better use of the international division of labor."[11] Five years later he treated the same subject much more fully before the Twenty-fourth Party Congress. Said Kosygin:

Our trade and economic cooperation with many [developing nations of Asia, Africa, and Latin America] are entering a stage at which one can begin to speak of stably founded, mutually advantageous economic relations. Our cooperation with them is based on the principles of equality and respect for mutual interests, . . . and is acquiring the character of stable distribution of labor. . . . At the same time, by expanding trade with the developing countries, the Soviet Union will gain the opportunity of satisfying more fully the requirements of its own national economy.[12]

Economists are making ever more ambitious proposals. For example, A. P. Karavaev, a member of the Soviet Far East Export Council, has drawn attention to the contribution that trade with Latin America could make to the development of Siberia. "Deliveries of goods from Latin America . . . can effect a significant economy in transport costs. At present, many food and raw material items are conveyed to these regions by road . . . over distances of 5,000 to 10,000 kilometers."[13]

The prospects for the expansion of economic relations seem bright, especially since the assortment of goods the U.S.S.R. is interested in is growing steadily. During the first years of the new policy based on greater integration, the needs of heavy industry were chiefly stressed. But now, with the new five-year plan—which for the first time departs from the orthodox principle of the preponderance of heavy over light industry as regards rates of growth and which promises significant improvements in living conditions to Soviet citizens—there is considerable interest in increasing the share of consumer goods, as well as of raw materials for their production, in imports from the new states.

Already in 1968, Soviet purchases of fresh fruit from the developing nations amounted to 527,000 tons (as compared to 133,000 in 1955), while clothing and underwear imports were valued at $689 million (compared to $56 million in 1955). According to Soviet experts, dur-

[11] *Pravda*, April 6, 1966, p. 6.
[12] *Ibid.*, April 7, 1971, p. 6.
[13] "Problemy sotrudnichestva v basseine Tikhogo Okeana," *Latinskaia Amerika,* January 1971, pp. 214–18.

ing the next fifteen to twenty years, consumer goods, ranging from tropical foodstuffs to textiles and footwear, will assume a much larger share in Russian imports and will contribute substantially to the growth of Soviet trade with the Third World.[14]

Several new departures in Soviet economic relations with the Third World in recent years demonstrate the efforts to introduce elements of integration and profitability.

Relations with the major aid recipients and trade partners are now being based on *coordinated planning*. Permanent bilateral economic commissions have been set up with India, Iran, the U.A.R., Algeria, Morocco, Afghanistan, and Iraq. These commissions, besides affording regular consultations, also work out long-range plans. Thus, the Soviet-Iranian commission has undertaken to work out twelve- to fifteen-year projections for increased economic collaboration and trade based on the two countries' natural resources, as well as other economic and technical potentials.[15]

In addition to innovating these regularized channels for bilateral planning, the U.S.S.R. has finally moved off dead center and agreed to formalize multilateral exchanges among the Communist bloc nations and the new states. Since the early 1960s, East European economists have persistently advocated the advantages of coordinating and integrating the bloc's economic relations with the Third World. Faced with Soviet immobility, most East European states have pursued this path on their own. For example, the 1969 trade agreements of Poland, Hungary, and Rumania with India envision trilateral import arrangements and transferability of funds.[16] Only in 1968 did Soviet specialists begin to discuss the advantages of multilateral clearing accounts within the bloc.[17] Finally, at the July 1971 meeting of the Council of Mutual Economic Assistance, the U.S.S.R. agreed to introduce by the end of the 1970s a convertible ruble to settle accounts with other Communist states as well as with the developing nations.[18]

[14] Lev L. Klochkovsky, "U.S.S.R. Trade Partner," *International Forum*, December 1970, pp. 18, 21.

[15] These groups also help to coordinate aid and trade agreements with the implementation of the recipients' development plans.

[16] *Weekly India News*, November 22, 1968, p. 3.

[17] V. Savelev, "Obmen mezhdu razvivaiushchimisia i sotsialisticheskimi stranami," *Ekonomicheskie nauki*, January 1968, pp. 58–64.

[18] Bernard Gwertzman, "Red's Trade Bloc Seeks to Expand Its Global Role," *New York Times*, August 8, 1971. Even though there has been no discussion of this in the Soviet press, some sort of a multilateral approach must have been in operation under the auspices of the CMEA for quite some time. The U.S.S.R. and its European allies have participated in a number of large aid projects in Third World states; Middle Eastern oil extracted with Soviet aid is being sold to Eastern Europe; and in May 1971 a CMEA delegation started negotiations with the Economic Council of the Arab League on some unspecified projects.

Another novel approach is the *joint production* of raw materials. Geological prospecting figures prominently among Soviet aid projects, and the discovery of valuable deposits usually results in additional aid for their extraction and commercial exploitation (in some cases even in Soviet marketing of the product). In return, the Russians receive as payment a share of the output. After Soviet geologists discovered rich natural gas deposits in Afghanistan, an agreement was signed in October 1963 for aid in extracting the gas and constructing a pipeline to the Soviet border. In May 1967, just before the pipeline was opened, Afghanistan agreed to supply the U.S.S.R. with 58 billion cubic meters of natural gas through 1985 to repay the debts incurred in this venture and to finance additional imports from the Soviet Union.[19]

In cases where the U.S.S.R. has not helped to locate a nation's natural resources, it is willing to accept raw materials in exchange for aid in their exploitation. In April 1971 the Soviet Union granted Iraq a loan of 200 million rubles to finance a refinery, two pipelines, and several industrial projects; the loan is to be repaid entirely in crude oil produced by the Iraqi National Oil Company.[20] Similarly, the Soviet Union will be repaid for the construction of a bauxite mining enterprise near Kindia, Guinea, with two million tons of bauxite annually over the next thirty years.[21]

At first the Soviets admitted that the additional supply of natural gas from Iran and Afghanistan helped them to alleviate the fuel shortage in the Central Asian republics.[22] Now there is discussion of how imports from the Third World will enable the U.S.S.R. and its European satellites to meet projected increases in the consumption of fuels and raw materials in the next fifteen to twenty years.[23]

Another advantage the Soviet Union derives from the additional fuel imports is that this frees considerable amounts of natural gas produced in European Russia for export to the West in exchange for scarce industrial products, such as the large diameter pipes obtained from Austria in June 1968. As for the oil, it might be sold through the refining and marketing companies the Soviets are setting up in Western Europe or it might be diverted to Eastern Europe in order to free more Soviet oil for hard-currency transactions in the West. Moreover, Soviet experts have calculated that, given the cost of extracting natural gas

[19] *Izvestiia*, May 25, 1967, p. 3.
[20] Radio Baghdad, April 11, 1971.
[21] Radio Moscow, December 9, 1970.
[22] *Kommunist* (Erevan), September 8, 1968.
[23] L. Zevin, "Voprosy povysheniia ustoichivosti i effektivnosti ekonomicheskikh sviazei SSSR s razvivaiushchimisia stranami," *Planovoe khoziaistvo*, July 1971, pp. 17–26.

and petroleum in the U.S.S.R., imports in certain cases can be cheaper than home production.[24]

Cooperation in *industrial production and manufacturing* has had a slower and more difficult start. Thus far it has taken the simple form of repayment with the finished products of the plants set up with Soviet assistance and credits. In this way the U.S.S.R. gets canned meat from Guinea and valuable high-quality cotton yarn from the U.A.R. and Uganda. However, the Russians would like to see more production specifically geared to their own domestic needs. Since 1967 they have been negotiating with India on specialization and coordination in the more complex branches of industry, such as petrochemicals and fertilizers, which would involve more intricate and closer relations between the contracting parties than merely exporting part of the production to the Soviet Union. But not much headway has been made. So far India has set up only a shoe factory with production specifically adapted to Soviet standards and designs. The five-year trade agreement, concluded in December 1970, calls for an annual 15 percent increase in trade, mainly through India's increased export to the U.S.S.R. of such items as surgical instruments, pharmaceuticals, electric motors, and aluminum cables produced in Soviet-assisted projects. As for "new avenues of industrial cooperation," these are undergoing exploratory negotiations.[25]

For the past five years, Soviet economists have been urging the formation of *mixed companies* as a more advantageous form of utilizing credits—a way that would earn profits and at the same time assure the U.S.S.R. of a steady supply of needed raw materials and industrial goods. However, they face strong opposition from the political leadership. It has been a cardinal ideological tenet for so long that the U.S.S.R., unlike the West, renders "disinterested" aid and does not seek to hold any assets on the territory of other countries or to derive profit at their expense that any proposal which undermines this principle is hard to accept. Therefore, the practical and legal aspects of partnership have hardly been discussed in print. One recent article argued that the Soviet Union should take fewer profits for its share in a joint enterprise than would a Western partner, but that at the same time it should obtain an unspecified "fair" return on its investment. Furthermore, the author envisioned partnerships of limited duration, with the Soviet share being gradually bought up by the assisted country.[26] Interestingly, the East European states are not constrained by

---

[24] *Ibid.*, p. 23.

[25] *Weekly India News*, January 8, 1971, p. 1.

[26] Iu. Shamrai, "Problemy sovershenstovovaniia ekonomicheskogo sotrudnichestva sotsialisticheskikh in razvivaiushchikhsia stran," *Narody Azii i Afriki*, August 1968, pp. 10–13.

similar ideological niceties and since about 1966 have been busy in Asia and Africa setting up joint ventures ranging from sugar refineries to copper mines.

Until recently the Soviets have been willing to set up joint companies only to promote trade. There is a joint shipping line with Singapore, and another one with Australia is under discussion. Several joint trading companies have been established—notably in Ethiopia, Nigeria, Iran, and Morocco—to facilitate the sale of Soviet goods. But these efforts to increase trade by utilizing local middlemen firms have not been noticeably successful. For example, the Soviet-Nigerian company for the sale and servicing of motor vehicles has sold only about 2,500 Soviet cars and trucks since its formation in 1968.[27]

Faced with such results, Moscow seems to have at last overcome its ideological reservations and to be willing to venture into the field of investment. The five-year trade agreement with India, mentioned above, is the first to include clauses that provide for setting up joint projects, as well as for joint marketing, in third countries.[28] Serious negotiations are under way with Malaysian businessmen concerning joint investment in various enterprises, especially for the production of industrial equipment.[29]

Other evidence of Soviet interest in more profitable relations with the developing nations is the increasing number of *commercial contracts*. Until 1966, sales of Soviet machinery were almost exclusively financed by intergovernmental loan agreements. Since then the Soviet Union has been trying to sell its products on the customary trade basis and has been eager to grant commercial credits for the purchase of Soviet equipment and know-how both to foreign governments and to individual firms. These commercial credits carry a 4.0 percent per annum interest and are usually repayable in from five to eight years, whereas the aid loans carry a 2.5 percent interest and are repayable in from ten to twelve years after the completion of the project.

## II

A marked Soviet interest in the promotion of sustained and balanced development among aid recipients is another novelty in the changing pattern of economic relations. The U.S.S.R. is now definitely interested in long-range stability and growth and has abandoned its original conviction that a few large projects in the public sector would automatically inaugurate prosperity and progress, detach the former col-

[27] Radio Moscow, March 10, 1971.
[28] Radio New Delhi, December 26, 1970.
[29] Radio Kuala Lampur, October 1, 1970.

onies from the West, and create dependence on the Communist bloc.

Blind trust in the efficacy of the state sector dominated Soviet relations with the Third World until about 1962. Soviet economists and aid officials were almost exclusively concerned with expanding public ownership, and the performance of the public sector was judged in terms of its size. Three methods for strengthening the state sector were advocated by Soviet advisers and encouraged by Soviet aid projects: industrialization, nationalization of foreign and domestic private property, and expansion of economic ties with the Soviet bloc.

Those were the days when Moscow granted generous credits for steel mills, machine-building plants and other import-replacing industries, often without any regard for either the size of the domestic market or the availability of resources. Aid officials were guided primarily by the "political effectiveness" of the projects, by the desire to build up the public sector into the dominant "progressive" force in the economies of the recipients. Their political convictions relieved the Soviets of any worry about whether their projects engendered real growth or represented optimal investment choices.

Moscow's advice and generous credits encouraged the adoption of radical and ambitious policies by many of the aid recipients. In the absence of full documentation it is impossible to argue that the Russians were actually responsible for such measures as Mali's withdrawal from the franc zone or Guinea's nationalization of domestic trade. But, given the presence of numerous Russian advisers in both countries and their views at the time on development strategy, it can be assumed that these radical measures were undertaken at least with the approval of Communist experts.

Signs of stocktaking and reappraisal on the part of the Russians began to appear in 1963, when high aid officials started to visit the larger aid recipients to check on the progress of the assistance programs. (Previously, missions had been sent only to check on the completion of individual projects.) The headlong expansion of the public sector began to be questioned. Instead of granting new credits for new projects, the Russians began to insist on completing projects already started, as well as on assuring their efficient operation. Thus, despite broad hints from Modibo Keita about his country's expectation of assistance for the next development plan (scheduled to start in 1964), the team of Soviet experts who visited Mali in April 1963 did not recommend additional credits. Instead, the two countries agreed on the adoption of unspecified measures "to increase the efficiency and speed up work" on numerous aid projects.[30]

[30] Agence France-Presse, May 4, 1963.

By 1965, several factors made it both easier and mandatory for the Soviets to reconsider their penchant for a centralized economy and to start demanding that the aid recipients take various measures to put their house in order.

Khrushchev was ousted in October 1964. Among the contributing causes was his largess in granting credits despite the mounting economic difficulties of the regimes on which he lavished aid and the scandalous delays in the completion of many large projects he promoted.

Next, several radical regimes collapsed, beginning with Ben Bella's in June 1965. In each case, the new regime cited the chaotic economic conditions brought about by overambitious government schemes among the main reasons for the coup. Yet these very policies had been extolled by the Soviets as signifying the choice of the noncapitalist path and had been encouraged with generous aid until 1963.

At about the same time, Moscow began to face the problems of repayment. The Soviets were especially shrill in claiming that their aid, particularly for the large industrial projects, would prove more effective in generating income than Western credits for infrastructure. But, instead, Indonesia sought a rescheduling of debt repayments as early as 1963, and Egypt was unable to begin repayments in 1964.[31] Similarly, in 1965, Mali's interest payments had to be cancelled and its debt repayment deferred.[32]

Lastly, by about 1965, Soviet experts began to discuss in print entirely new theories of growth based on far less radical assumptions about the capabilities and goals of Third World development. With growing urgency they criticized the economically unjustifiable radical reforms and advocated the maximum application of economic criteria.[33]

As a result of these factors, Moscow is now giving quite different advice to its clients. The top leadership never misses an opportunity to deliver a lecture on the need for a pragmatic approach, hard work, and greater efficiency. For example, at the 1967 celebrations of the fiftieth anniversary of the October Revolution, Brezhnev limited his remarks about the Third World to a disquisition on how "constant efforts to advance the economy" were necessary to guarantee progress.[34] The Soviet popular and specialized press is quite explicit these days in its

---

[31] Marshall Goldman, *Soviet Foreign Aid* (New York: Praeger, 1967), pp. 13, 72.

[32] N. Kovrygina, "Gosudarstvennyi i chastnyi sektor v ekonomii Mali," *Mirovaia ekonomika i mezhdunarodnye otnosheniia,* January 1967, p. 130.

[33] Elizabeth Kridl Valkenier, "Recent Trends in Soviet Research on the Developing Countries," *World Politics,* July 1968, pp. 644–59. Subsequent changes in Soviet development economics are covered by David Morison, "U.S.S.R. and Third World: Questions of Economic Development," *Mizan,* December 1970, pp. 124–52.

[34] *Pravda,* November 4, 1967, p. 3.

denunciations of "leftist extravagances," unrealistic projects, and other economic miscalculations which have brought ruin instead of the planned independent socialist economy to such countries as Ghana and Mali.[35] And Soviet experts, who are becoming increasingly involved in drawing up long-range economic cooperation plans with individual countries, as well as national development plans for these states, are now offering advice that is much less doctrinaire and quite understanding of the economic factors in generating growth.

On *planning*, the once-popular views that the nationalization of production and the neutralization of market forces were the necessary prerequisites for successful direction of the economy have definitely been abandoned. We can safely assume that Soviet experts no longer urge upon the Afro-Asian nations a crude and stereotyped imitation of the Soviet experience of the 1930s, as they did for India's Second Five-Year Plan. Instead, the Soviet New Economic Policy experience is now being discussed as a possible model for the developing nations.[36]

But it should not be assumed that every aid decision or counsel on planning will be offered with only cost-and-profit considerations in mind. Soviet development literature recognizes that, especially on the macro level, profit cannot be the only criterion for investment, since social gains and future goals are often of overriding importance. However, there is no doubt that Soviet experts now recognize the organizational role of costs, as well as the dynamism of the profit motive, and will try to prevail on African and Asian regimes to take them into consideration in national development plans.

Current Soviet views on the roles of the *state* and private sectors are closely related to the changed outlook on planning. Economists no longer argue that the larger the public sector the better the economy. What interests the Russians these days is performance, not size.

There is frank discussion of the ills that afflict the state sector: overextension, burdensome bureaucracy, corruption, and deficit operations. However, we should not infer that the Soviets are going to turn their backs on public ownership as the proper organizational form. It still remains a cardinal tenet in Communist development theory. The recent criticism does not mean that the Russians will advise countries such as India and the U.A.R. to dismantle the public sector; rather, it indicates that they are now searching for ways to make it function more efficiently.

Thus, far, two approaches are apparent. One method is to make careful preparations so that the state sector is not hampered by limited

[35] A. Kiva, "Kapitalizmu net," *Aziia i Afrika segodnia*, March 1971, pp. 8–11.

[36] N. Shmelev, "Stoimostnye kriterii i ikh rol' v ekonomike razvivaiushchikhsia stran," *Mirovaia ekonomika i mezhdunarodnye otnosheniia*, June 1968, p. 51.

administrative resources. In Algeria, for example, the Soviets no doubt favor the eventual nationalization of the oil industry. But in the meantime they are being instrumental in the preparation of what might be called an organizational infrastructure by setting up a large Petroleum Training Institute in that country, by training Algerian engineers in the U.S.S.R., and by building up an Algerian tanker fleet.

The other method is to extend additional aid and technical services to existing state enterprises. When Kosygin visited India in 1968, he was so upset by the poor performance of the Soviet-aided projects in the public sector that he was reported to have strongly advised Mrs. Gandhi to concentrate more on the internal economic situation and to cease worrying about external threats.[37] He also promptly dispatched teams of Soviet experts to the scene. As a result of several inspection missions, the 1966 credit agreement was revised in December 1968 and some Soviet funds were diverted for "raising the efficiency" of large industrial projects.[38]

The other side to recognition of the pitfalls of excessive and premature public ownership is an appreciation of the contribution *private business* can make to the economic welfare of the new nations, provided it does not assume the predominant position. R. A. Ulianovskii, a prominent economist whose specialty is Asia and who is deputy chairman of the Central Committee's department dealing with the Third World, has completely reversed his former stand in favor of nationalization of domestic trade and services and has begun extolling the useful role played by the small trading and industrial bourgeoisie.[39]

This new attitude toward the small enterpreneur is reflected in stray items. There have been reports from Kabul that Russian advisers told the Afghan government to expand private enterprise.[40] And the Soviet press approved steps taken by the U.A.R. in 1969 partially to free the private sector from rigid controls and to promote private investment in industry.[41]

Despite occasional thunderings about the need to oust "monopoly capital," the Soviets now recognize the contribution of *Western investment* to the development of the Third World, as well as the unreadiness of the new states to dispense with the Western presence altogether. What the Soviet Union now favors is not wholesale expulsion

[37] *Hindu Weekly Review,* February 12, 1968, p. 1.

[38] I. Temirskii, "Moscow and Delhi," *New Times,* February 5, 1969, pp. 10–11.

[39] "Nauchnyi sotsializm i osvobodivshiesia strany," *Kommunist,* 1968, no. 4, pp. 92–106; "Nekotorye voprosy nekapitalisticheskogo razvitiia," *ibid.,* 1971, no. 4, pp. 103–12.

[40] Drew Middleton, "East Meets West in Afghanistan," *New York Times,* May 28, 1967.

[41] *Pravda,* January 27, 1969, p. 4.

but arrangements that recognize the sovereignty of each nation over its natural resources and leave as large as possible a share of the profits at home. In this area, too, the Russians are likely to advise their partners against hasty nationalization. Speaking in 1967 before the Second International Congress of Africanists in Dakar, V. G. Solodovnikov, a prominent economist specializing in the developing nations, recalled how earlier in the year at the Economic Commission for Africa conference he had urged changing the conditions under which foreign capital was invested—mainly reinvestment and limitations on profits—in the hope that such modification "would considerably weaken the tendency toward nationalizing private property."[42] And, to judge from the newspaper comments on agreements between the developing nations and the big Western companies, the Soviets now fully support arrangements that involve reasonable compromise.

Two other issues of development economics—*agriculture* and *industry*—also have been liberated from the doctrinal approach, both in theory and in practice. The agrarian problem is now seen in terms of output, not exclusively in terms of ownership or management. Therefore, radical land reform is no longer indiscriminately advocated. Some experts note that reforms could reduce farm output, and have cautioned that "carrying out land reform requires careful preliminary analysis and weighing of all the possible economic factors." They are against the subdivision of large estates farmed by extensive methods, for their fragmentation would "impair the organization of labor . . . and the crop rotation. Their profitability would decrease."[43] Other specialists approve the setting up of cooperative and state farms only when adequate administrative personnel and machinery are available to assure full production.[44] Since state management is no longer regarded as the answer to productivity, the Russians no longer stress establishing state farms in order to introduce radical organizational concepts and schemes. Instead, they help set up research and experimental stations to improve and increase the yields.

This concern for farm output has been marked by an entirely different attitude on aid to agriculture. It used to be passed over in silence. Only recently have aid officials begun to speak of it as an important contribution to development. The fact that the U.S.S.R. built

[42] V. G. Solodovnikov, "Some Problems of Economic and Social Development of Independent African Nations," *II International Congress of Africanists* (Moscow, 1967), pp. 5, 8–9.

[43] R. Andreasian and A. Elianov, "Razvivaiushchiesia strany: Diversifikatsiia ekonomiki i strategiia promyshlennogo razvitiia," *Mirovaia ekonomika i mezhdunarodnye otnosheniia*, January 1968, p. 32.

[44] V. G. Rastiannikov, "Prodovol'stvennia problema v razvivaiushchikhsia stranakh," *Narody Azii i Afriki*, January 1967, pp. 41–42.

or is committed to some 150 projects in irrigation, land reclamation, and so on (that is, one-fifth of all aid projects), is often mentioned nowadays and is publicized almost as much as aid to industry.

Industrial production is no longer the cynosure of economic development. Its heyday is definitely over. In discussing the strategy of development, many specialists warn that the impairment of a proper balance between industry and agriculture "creates bottlenecks in the economy, causes excessive stress, and in the long run leads to worsening of the general condition of economic growth." The U.A.R. is blamed for "overstepping in the direction of industrialization." India's troubles are diagnosed as due to "inadequate attention to agriculture" and "faulty industrialization policy."[45]

Now, before the U.S.S.R. undertakes a costly industrial project, several careful feasibility studies are undertaken. Take the case of Nigeria's request for a steel mill in 1968. The Soviet Union lent a sympathetic ear, but after several surveys and feasibility studies it committed itself only to prospecting for the raw materials which eventually might make the production of steel economically feasible.[46]

In countries such as the U.A.R. and India, where the easy availability of Soviet credits through the early 1960s had encouraged over-ambitious industrialization programs, there are definite signs of Soviet restraining influence. Here, the Soviet reaction to (and role in) the changes Cairo had to institute in its second development plan are instructive. The 1965–1970 plan called for a greater emphasis on industry than the first one had. In late 1965 it was revised to extend two years longer in order to reduce the annual level of investment. But in 1966 a mounting economic crisis prompted Nasser to seek the advice of the International Monetary Fund (IMF), whose team recommended a stiff austerity program to bring the economy into balance. Because there were disagreements in the government over the IMF's report, Nasser asked a top-level Soviet team for advice. Interestingly enough, according to Western reports, the team's recommendations were roughly the same as those of the IMF.[47] And the following month the seven-year expanded plan was scrapped for a three-year stabilization program designed to complete projects already started and to promote those that promised the earliest profitability. At that time no printed comments in the U.S.S.R. indicated the Soviet position. But when it became possible to write with greater candor about the economic prob-

[45] Andreasian and Elianov, *op. cit.*, pp. 30–31.

[46] *Vneshniaia torgovlia*, October 1970, p. 56.

[47] Hedrick Smith, "Cairo, Squeezed, Slashing Budget," *New York Times*, October 22, 1966.

lems of the larger creditors, the seven-year plan was criticized severely and the three-year plan was given a very favorable treatment.[48]

Significantly, one of the high Soviet aid officials, D. Degtiar, brought out a book in 1969 which stresses that it has become important to give aid not just for the construction of industrial enterprises but also to make them function to their full capacity in the quickest time possible. Accordingly, he advocates full preliminary feasibility studies, the training of skilled personnel while the project is under construction, and a planned marketing of the finished product.[49]

### III

Whereas the growing use of aid to serve Soviet economic needs is something that only a few Western experts foresaw in the early days of the program,[50] nobody doubted that it would serve the Soviets' power drive. But the pattern of aid serving strategic purposes that has emerged in the last ten years exceeds the predictions about the U.S.S.R.'s efforts to establish its presence and influence abroad.

In general, attention was focused on the military aid program as the chief, if not exclusive, means of gaining strategic footholds in faraway lands. The significance of skillfully placed and coordinated aid projects, such as airfields, improved port facilities, or road-building, in creating an infrastructure that could serve Soviet military power all over the globe has, however, been overlooked. Moscow has offered and continues to offer arms assistance whenever the West refuses to do so, in order to acquire a foothold—the Nigerian civil war provides a clear-cut example. But for a more lasting and assured basis of influence, the U.S.S.R. relies on an ever-expanding network of airports, harbors, and communication facilities. The drive first started in the Near East and around the shores of Africa. It has expanded into the Indian Ocean, and more recently the Russians have begun to extend feelers on the shores of Latin America.

A well-coordinated network of air routes first emerged in North and West Africa between 1961 and 1965. In most cases, aid projects and trade deals preceded the signing of an air pact. The sale of Soviet airliners to the fledgling Ghanaian civil aviation company paved the way for an air link between the two nations. In Guinea, where there was no suitable airport, the reconstruction of an old airfield was fol-

---

[48] Ob"edinennaia Arabskaia Respublika (Moscow, 1968), p. 157.

[49] Plodotvornoe sotrudnichestvo (Moscow, 1969).

[50] Joseph Berliner's Soviet Economic Aid (New York: Praeger, 1958) was one of these few exceptions.

lowed by the opening of an air route to Moscow. Subsequently, the Soviet TU-114 service to Havana was more conveniently routed through Conakry rather than through Murmansk. In 1965 the Russians started constructing a modern jet airport in Yemen, which has since served to link Moscow with East Africa—Kenya, Uganda, and Tanzania.[51]

Asia and beyond was the next step. The original air routes to India, Burma, and Indonesia were expanded in 1964 to include Pakistan and Ceylon. In the past three years Malaysia and Singapore have been added. A draft air agreement was initiated with Thailand in February 1971, two months after the signing of the first trade agreement ever between the two countries. Currently, negotiations for a direct air connection with Australia are under way.[52]

Aeroflot planes will soon be flying to Peru and Chile. It has been noted in the Western press that the eagerness with which the U.S.S.R. offered to airlift its aid to the victims of the Peruvian earthquake in 1970 was at least partly motivated by a desire to test the feasibility of flying a long direct route to Lima.[53]

The Soviets claim that air routes help to invigorate economic relations with distant lands. But airports in the developing nations have also been used by the U.S.S.R. for other purposes. During the Cuban missile crisis, Russia unsuccessfully tried to refuel its planes in Conakry en route to Havana with personnel and supplies. North African airports were used by the Soviets to airlift arms to the Congolese rebels in 1961. And since the Arab-Israeli war, Russian long-range bombers have started paying "friendly visits" to the U.A.R. and Syria.

The appearance of the Soviet navy in the Mediterranean in 1964 was an unexpected shock to most observers. Since then, and especially since the 1967 Middle East crisis, Soviet ships have cruised regularly around the Arabian peninsula, around Africa, and in the Indian Ocean. Years of patient preparation of naval facilities and the gathering of intelligence under the guise of economic aid preceded the dramatic appearance of the Soviet fleet in distant seas.

In 1958, the Soviets undertook to construct a Red Sea port for Yemen. Since then they have been modernizing ports, building shipyards, and developing commercial fishing for nations stretching from Singapore to Senegal.

Certain Soviet activities prior to the Cuban missile crisis of 1962 in-

[51] Elizabeth K. Valkenier, "Soviet Air Routes Lace Africa," *Christian Science Monitor*, February 9, 1965.

[52] V. Rosen, "Golden Routes of the 20th Century," *New Times*, May 9, 1970, p. 41.

[53] "Soviet Airlift to Peru Halted," *New York Times*, August 26, 1970.

dicate that there can be a direct connection between this type of economic assistance and military operations. In that summer the Russians tried to camouflage their stepped-up military traffic by publicizing the technical aid they had granted to Havana. They claimed they were busy enlarging the Cuban trawler fleet, locating new fishing grounds, and building a new fishing port in the Atlantic to be used jointly by the two nations. After the Khrushchev-Kennedy confrontation over the offensive missile sites, nothing more was heard of the ambitious plans for the joint fishing port aside from the delivery of a floating dry dock for Havana's harbor in the fall of 1964.

Sinister objectives, as in the case of Cuba, are not the sole purpose of Russian maritime aid. But its pattern does suggest definite strategic aims along important sea routes to facilitate the world-wide operations of the Soviet navy.

Take the matter of ports. With an eye to securing easier access to the Indian Ocean, Moscow began to acquire a foothold south of Suez in 1958 by making improvements in the harbor at Hodeida in Yemen. Four years later the Russians began working on a deep-water port at Berbera in Somalia; and in May 1967, just before the outbreak of the Arab-Israeli war, they undertook to build a fishing port for the U.A.R. Located in the Gulf of Suez, it was to serve as a base for joint Soviet-Egyptian deep-sea fishing in the Mediterranean, the Red Sea, and the Indian Ocean.

On the West coast of Africa, Guinea received Soviet assistance in reconstructing the port at Conakry under the terms of the 1959 aid agreement. With the harbor dredged, Soviet warships could dock at Conakry when they took to cruising the African waters ten years later.

The construction of shipyards in Iraq and at Alexandria has extended the reach of Soviet sea power. Red fleet units now regularly visit Alexandria, where they maintain their supply and repair facilities. Bassra became a port of call in May 1968, when the Russian navy appeared for the first time in the Persian Gulf.[54]

The development of commercial fishing (a prominent item in the overall Soviet aid program), especially in states that do not receive Russian military aid, serves as a strategic wedge. Work on such projects, resulting as it does in the extensive use of the ports and coastal waters, establishes a Russian presence in those nations and facilitates the gathering of intelligence. Often what starts as permission for Soviet trawlers to dock at a certain port in return for assistance in developing that nation's ocean fishing eventually expands into provi-

[54] Elizabeth K. Valkenier, "Soviet Aid Forms Strategy Pattern," *Christian Science Monitor*, May 21, 1969.

sions for naval facilities for the Red Fleet. Thus, the agreement with Mauritius in August 1969 for the construction of a modern fishing fleet was followed by several visits of Soviet warships to Port St. Louis. Seemingly without much effort and publicity, the U.S.S.R. added yet another port of call for refueling and supplying its growing Indian Ocean fleet.

It will be interesting to see what results from the Soviet-Peruvian talks on cooperation in ocean fishing that were initiated in June 1971. This move suggests that, having secured extensive refueling, repair, and landing facilities in the Mediterranean, around Africa, and in the Indian Ocean, Moscow has now begun to work on the Pacific area. Thus far, under the terms of the September 1971 agreement, the Soviets have undertaken to build a huge fishing center in northern Peru.[55]

An interesting adjunct to this drive to establish the Soviet presence along important air and maritime routes is the effort to secure overland connections with the Middle East and the Indian subcontinent through transit agreements and the completion of all-weather road networks. In return for a loan to repair a stretch of the highway system in Eastern Anatolia, the U.S.S.R. has signed a road pact with Turkey that permits Soviet trucks to cross into Syria and Iraq.[56] Similar transit agreements have been signed with Iran and Pakistan. In turn, Pakistan has concluded transit agreements with Iran and Turkey but not with India (despite considerable Soviet pressure). In Afghanistan, the Soviet-built highways that connect the northern and southern sections of the country are now being used as a direct transit route between the U.S.S.R. and Pakistan.[57] This network enables the U.S.S.R. to overcome some of the inconveniences caused by the closing of the Suez Canal. And, in the case of Pakistan, it has cut the time of delivery of Soviet goods from six weeks by sea to four days by road.[58]

As in the case of air routes, the Soviets comment only on the economic advantages of the new overland trade routes. But the possibility that these transport facilities may some day be used to deliver supplies for military purposes cannot be discounted.

## IV

A review of Soviet economic relations with the Third World over the last two decades is of interest not merely because of the quite con-

[55] "Soviet Set to Build Peru Fishing Center," *New York Times*, September 7, 1971.
[56] Alfred Friendly, Jr., "Soviets and Turkey Sign a Road Pact," *ibid.*, October 21, 1970.
[57] *Pravda*, February 28, 1971, p. 6.
[58] Radio Moscow, June 20, 1970.

siderable growth of Soviet aid and trade with these nations.[59] What is important is the solidification of relations into settled patterns. But, because the Soviets are now increasingly regarding aid and trade as forms of investment and are advising their partners to take market forces and the question of profitability into consideration, one should not jump to conclusions that the U.S.S.R. will now undertake ventures on strictly economic grounds, or that there is convergence, or that one should feel relaxed about the Soviet challenge.

The measures now taken or advocated by the Russians to resuscitate the economy of the new states, it should be remembered, are aimed as much at preserving the good name of socialism as at assuring their clients' economic viability. Moscow is trying to correct the malfunctioning of the state sector and to improve the methods of state control not in order to lessen the influence of "socialist" economics but to improve its chances and popularity.

Moreover, even when the Soviet Union enters into profitable ventures in the Third World, it does so on terms that differ from those of the West, and the difference does not pass unnoticed by the developing nations. As an example, one can cite their demand that Western companies enter into "Soviet-type" agreements on petroleum explorations, whereby the companies must rest content with service contracts rather than with concessions on oil lands, or with the offers of crude oil, instead of cash, for their services.

Many other aspects of the new Soviet policy answer the needs and aspirations of the developing nations. The willingness and ability to extend long-term aid, to correlate aid with trade, to intermesh planning, and to import manufactured goods respond to the needs of the new nations for long-range program aid on a continuing basis and for expanding markets for their nascent industries.

Closer economic cooperation, involving as it does measures of integration, is bound to bring the developing nations into the Soviet orbit. In the case of Iran, advantageous aid and trade agreements have easily erased years of hostility and have put an end to Iran's once exclusively pro-Western orientation. The case of Algeria shows that, where extensive economic aid has been sensibly planned and implemented, the overthrow of a pro-Soviet regime does not lead to the collapse of an alliance. Even though the pro-Communist ideologues no longer have a say in Algerian politics, Soviet planners and experts continue to be

[59] Even though the new states taken altogether conduct less than 3 percent of their trade with the U.S.S.R. and about 5 percent with the Communist bloc, individual countries, such as the U.A.R., India, Pakistan, Syria, and Afghanistan, conduct more than 20 percent of their trade with the Soviet Union. Department of State, *op. cit.*, p. 41.

active in Algeria's economic life, and the country has not become noticeably more pro-Western. In short, a well-coordinated and well-executed economic program has in many respects successfully replaced political infiltration as a method of Soviet penetration in the Third World.

# 9

# THE SOVIET UNION, THE UNITED NATIONS, AND THE DEVELOPING STATES

*Richard W. Mansbach*

In recent years, international organizations in general, and the United Nations in particular, have increasingly been subjected to systematic study by scholars of international politics.[1] There are two closely related reasons for this. In the first place, international organizations—notably those with a global character—appear to mirror many of the properties of the international system itself.[2] The second reason is that such organizations offer a fund of readily accessible data which, if the initial assumption is correct, permit the scholar to observe the process and change of several of the system's central emergent properties, such as the number of participant actors, goal cleavage, and influence distribution.[3] The increasingly sophisticated quantitative work being done on such questions as group voting, voting cohesiveness, U.N. issues, delegate interaction, U.N. participant attitudes and beliefs, and the like, reflect less of an effort to understand the organization itself in institutional terms, as was the case with much of the earlier research on international organizations, and more of a systematic effort to infer hypotheses about the international system and international politics in general.

[1] See Chadwick F. Alger, "Research on Research: A Decade of Quantitative and Field Research on International Organization," *International Organization,* 24 (1970): 414–50.

[2] See Stanley Hoffmann, "International Organization and the International System," *ibid.,* pp. 389–413; Oran R. Young, "The United Nations and the International System," *ibid.,* 22 (1968): 902–22; and Inis L. Claude, Jr., *The Changing United Nations* (New York: Random House, 1967).

[3] "Influence," as I employ the concept, suggests the ability to lead others to behave as they would not have done autonomously. As Rupert Emerson claims, influence "is a property of the social relations: it is not an attribute of the actor." Emerson, "Power-Dependence Relations," *American Sociological Review,* February 1962, p. 32. Influence *distribution* refers to the distribution of this ability among actors; it is generally inferred from the actors' possession of important base resources that could be used to establish an influence relationship. See J. David Singer and Melvin Small, "Capability Distribution and the Preservation of Peace in the Major Power Sub-System, 1816–1965" (Paper delivered at the Sixty-sixth Annual Meeting of the American Political Science Association, Los Angeles, September 1970). While capability analysis remains an unsatisfactory means of measuring influence distribution, deducing it from outcomes remains even more difficult. Nevertheless, it is possible to deduce influence by utilizing U.N. voting data, specifically success in obtaining positive outcomes of voting on the "winning side."

While certain U.N. procedures, such as equal voting in the General Assembly, tend to distort the nature of selected system properties, there is little doubt that the world organization offers a fertile field in which to explore many of the evolving characteristics of the contemporary international system—for example, movement away from attitudinal bipolarity and the increase in the number of autonomous actors whose needs, views, and policies are substantially unlike those of "older" actors.[4] For example, we have been able to trace the development of a "North-South" value cleavage in the international system through U.N. data based on status, economic, and racial questions.[5] The emergence of these "Third World" states and their vociferous participation in political life have altered assumptions concerning the bipolar nature of the system and have had a profound impact on the behavior of the major cold war competitors. Indeed, the U.N. provides an excellent focus for studying changes in this behavior and for observing the way in which growing interdependency relations between the United States and cerain Afro-Asian states and between the Soviet Union and other "neutralist" states have affected the most critical interdependency relation—Soviet-American relations. With the admission of the People's Republic of China into the U.N. orbit, we are now able to follow the three-cornered game among the superpowers as they vie with one another for dominant influence in the Third World and compete with one another, often by proxy. The U.N. is thus a *barometer* or indicator of changing structural properties, a *forum* in which the superpowers seek to increase their influence among the uncommitted, a *stake* in the bimodal East-West conflict, and, on occasion, an autonomous international *actor*.

## Soviet Perceptions of International Organization

It would be difficult to fathom Soviet behavior in the U.N. toward the Third World without a prior understanding of the development of Soviet attitudes and expectations about the role of that and other international organizations. The evolving Soviet attitude toward the U.N. has been critically influenced by a complex interaction between ideological predilections towards international organizations and underdeveloped states and perceptions of the way in which such organiza-

[4] See, for example, Robert L. Rothstein, "Alignment, Nonalignment, and Small Powers: 1945–1965," *International Organization*, 20 (1966)): 397–418.

[5] See, for example, Bruce M. Russett, *Trends in World Politics* (New York: Macmillan, 1965), pp. 55–105; and *idem, International Regions and the International System* (Chicago: Rand McNally, 1967), pp. 498–99.

tions and states reflect the major structural properties of the international system. In general, the U.S.S.R. is selective in its support of, and participation in, international organizations. Organizations that mirror a "correct" international distribution of attitudes and capabilities are arenas in which the U.S.S.R. is prepared to participate actively. Those that are perceived to be dominated by capitalist states or their allies are either ignored, assailed, or obstructed. Two factors in particular appear to have persuaded Soviet leaders of the value of active participation in the U.N. system. The first is the emergence of new actors that are either pro-Soviet or anti-Western; the second is the re-evaluation of "neutralist" states as being autonomous of their former colonial rulers and thus potential targets of Soviet penetration.

Until the 1960s, Soviet perceptions of international organization were conditioned by a negative appraisal of influence distribution in the international system during a protracted era of transition from capitalist to socialist dominance, a period during which antagonistic socio-economic blocs must coexist. As a Polish observer declared, "In the opinion of the Socialist states restrictive membership policies, because they do not reflect the actual pattern of forces in the world, endanger the effectiveness of the universal international organizations."[6] For example, Soviet views of the League of Nations, particularly before 1934, were based on an assumption that the organization was dominated by implacable enemies of the Soviet state. Indeed, during the early period of the League, the U.S.S.R. sought to align itself with selected Afro-Asian states, such as Afghanistan, Turkey, and Persia, against the dominance of the League powers. The League represented "capitalist encirclement" and "international imperialism." Thus, Alexei Rykov, chairman of the Council of People's Commissars, declared in 1925 that

> the League of Nations is a little business undertaking that deals in peoples; it passes over them, as it sees fit, in the form of mandates, to the so-called states of high culture, which defend their mandate rights by force of arms and mercilessly enslave the peoples under their tutelage. For this reason, the East would naturally regard us as traitors if we were to stand behind the counter of this shop.[7]

[6] Wojciech Morawiecki, "Institutional and Political Conditions of Participation of Socialist States in International Organizations: A Polish View," *International Organization*, 22 (1968): 498–99.

[7] Cited in Xenia J. Eudin and Harold H. Fisher, eds., *Soviet Russia and the West, 1920–1927: A Documentary Survey* (Stanford: Stanford University Press, 1957), p. 321.

However, even when structural conditions do not seem to favor Soviet goals, the U.S.S.R. has been prepared to make use of international organizations to facilitate the creation of defensive alliances based on complementary interests. As Alexander Dallin aptly expressed it, "It is the problem of a state with a 'two-camp' world view trying to operate in a 'one-world' organization."[8] Thus, the Soviet entry into the League in 1934 represented a shift to "popular front" tactics at a time when the U.S.S.R. was prepared to seek capitalist allies to increase Soviet security against Nazi Germany.

The initial Soviet view of the United Nations was that its single task was to maintain peace and security and that it should serve neither as an agency with economic and social goals nor as a bridge to resolve the socioeconomic differences that separate the two camps. "It has been the original Soviet position," noted Leland Goodrich, "that the organization should be exclusively devoted to that task [the maintenance of international peace and security], and that it should not be concerned with the promotion of international cooperation in deal-ing with economic and social problems."[9] The basic Soviet position corresponded to the perception that, despite gains accruing from World War II the world was still dominated by capitalist forces, and that, while a "temporary truce" would be advantageous to the U.S.S.R., con-flicts with the capitalist camp could be expected. The world, in Stalin's view, was divided into "two camps," and the smaller states and Afro-Asian participants were at best "bourgeois nationalists" and at worst dominated by wealthy capitalist states. In any event, the independent Afro-Asian actors and the emerging nationalist political parties were perceived as undependable allies.

As reciprocal suspicion degenerated into cold war, the U.S.S.R. in 1946–1947 adopted an increasingly intractable "leftist" orientation. Only nations that were ruled by a "dictatorship of the proletariat" guided by a Communist party directly responsible to Moscow were deemed "friendly." As the Hungarian Communist party's official publication bluntly expressed it, "He who is loyal to the Soviet Union only conditionally and with reservations, is not a communist."[10]

In a system increasingly dominated by tight bipolarity, the United Nations began to reflect the major global cleavage between East and West. As Stanley Hoffmann has suggested:

[8] Alexander Dallin, *The Soviet Union at the United Nations: An Inquiry into Soviet Motives and Objectives* (New York: Praeger, 1962), p. 6.

[9] Leland M. Goodrich, *The United Nations* (New York: Thomas Y. Crowell, 1959), p. 23.

[10] *Szabad Nep,* July 1, 1948.

Since international organizations provide procedures for cooperation or for the temperate pursuit of conflict, it is obvious that their effectiveness depends on the degree of moderation of the international system. A revolutionary system wracked by inexpiable power rivalries and ideological conflicts is one in which international organization is reduced to impotence as a force of its own and to the condition of a helpless stake in the competition of states.[11]

Indeed, the Soviet Union initially sought to gain greater influence in the councils of the U.N. and to divide the enemy camp. Thus, it attacked South African *apartheid,* supported the Indonesian independence movement, and denounced Franco's Spain. In addition, the Soviet Union and its allies opposed Great Britain in its quarrels with Egypt and Sudan and assailed French policies in Morocco, Tunisia, Syria, and Lebanon. However, Soviet positions were generally radical and impractical, and the U.S.S.R. refused to support compromises which even Afro-Asian nationalists favored. For instance, it opposed terms for an Indonesian peace settlement which even Indonesian nationalists were prepared to accept.

The debates on the Iranian issue seemed to convince the Soviet Union and its allies that they formed a relatively permanent voting minority in a hostile General Assembly and Security Council. On these conditions, the provision for a veto in the Security Council probably enabled the U.S.S.R. to remain a member of the U.N. "The Socialist states, since they are a numerical minority and understandably wish to secure a better defensive position for themselves, often feel that a simple majority vote is not adequate when important issues are concerned."[12] Thus, one quantitative study of voting outcomes in the Security Council concluded that "the three Western permanent members of the Security Council have been most successful in securing adoption of the draft resolutions they have sponsored; the 'Southern bloc' has been the second most successful; and the Soviet Union, which has never been successful, was last."[13] During the first phase of the U.N., the U.S.S.R. could safely depend on the votes of only five supporters—Ukraine, Byelorussia, Poland, Yugoslavia, and Czechoslovakia. Soviet deportment, however, and the generally obstructionist tactics which the U.S.S.R. employed probably contributed to the opposition to its proposals. Indeed, many of its proposals were merely

[11] Hoffmann, *op. cit.,* p. 390.
[12] Morawiecki, *op. cit.,* p. 499.
[13] James E. Todd, "An Analysis of Security Council Voting Behavior," *Western Political Quarterly,* 22 (1969): 66.

propaganda gestures and were so vague or divisive that they could not be acted upon seriously.

As a consequence of its minority position, the Soviet Union insisted on strict interpretation of those Charter provisions which protected minority rights, notably the principle of great power unanimity in the Security Council. Of Stalin's attitude, Edward Stettinius observed, "He would never agree to having any action of any of the Great Powers submitted to the judgment of the small powers."[14] Largely in order to defend itself against what it perceived to be a hostile majority in the Security Council, the U.S.S.R. was "responsible for 103 of the 109 vetoes cast by late 1965, or almost 95 per cent of the total."[15] Indeed, despite the fact that it withdrew from certain of the organization's agencies and participated only marginally in others, the Soviet Union's willingness to remain in the United Nations between 1947 and 1960 is partly explicable as an attempt to prevent the U.N. from being mobilized into an anti-Soviet alliance. The veto power provided the U.S.S.R. with the necessary means to achieve this objective.

A second major component of Soviet attitudes toward the U.N. was that the organization should not aspire to supranational status. Again, this partly reflected a defensive response to structural conditions. From the Soviet perspective, an enlargement of U.N. powers meant at best a reinforcement of the status quo and at worst a stepped-up and organized assault on Soviet security. In game theory terms, Soviet leaders viewed the international context from a zero-sum perspective and pursued a maximum strategy in preventing an extension of U.N. powers. As Inis Claude has observed:

> The urge to enlarge the functions and powers of an international agency is characteristic of majority mentality; the demand for restriction and inhibition, the outlook of a minority. Viewed from the minority position, effectiveness is a euphemism for majority domination. From the vantage point of the majority, the protective tactics of the minority represent perverse obstructionism. In the present international system, states are not so much committed to supporting or opposing a strong and active United Nations, as to enhancing their ability to promote internationl action favorable to their interests, and to prevent international action unfavorable to their interests.[16]

[14] Edward Stettinius, *Roosevelt and the Russians* (Garden City, N.Y.: Doubleday & Co., 1949), p. 112.

[15] John G. Stoessinger, *The United Nations and the Superpowers* (New York: Random House, 1965), p. 5.

[16] Inis L. Claude, Jr., *Swords into Plowshares: The Problems and Progress of International Organization*, 3rd ed. (New York: Random House, 1964), p. 130.

While prepared to accept an extension of organizational powers in organizations such as COMECON, in which Soviet views predominate, the U.S.S.R. sees little reason to "upgrade" organizations in which they occupy a minority position. The "outlook of a minority" is succinctly and frankly expressed by Morawiecki:

> The Socialist states, in particular, have displayed thus far, and probably will continue to display, a tendency to resolve those institutional questions near the lower level of possibilities. This rather cautious attitude reflects their fear that, since they are a numerical minority, their risks are greater at a higher level of resolution and their past experience confirms this. For this reason the Socialist states naturally maintain a more critical attitude than some other states in regard to the powers of international organizations.[17]

Soviet opposition to an extension of U.N. powers was and is reinforced by the doctrine of peaceful coexistence. To the extent that an international organization reflects the principles of peaceful coexistence, the U.S.S.R. is willing to participate in its activities and remain a member. Such an organization can, in fact, provide a substitute for more integrative institutions based on Western models or norms. One of the core principles of the coexistence doctrine is the legal (not political) equality and sovereignty of states. Fearful of Western efforts to violate Soviet sovereignty, the U.S.S.R. has consistently opposed supranational aspirations outside the Soviet bloc as manifestations of class interests that are repugnant to Marxism-Leninism. Supranationalism is perceived as a violation of state sovereignty and, in organizations such as the U.N., as a legal façade for intervention in Soviet bloc affairs. Soviet behavior in the U.N. at the time of the Hungarian revolution of 1956 and the Czechoslovak invasion of 1968 suggest the intensity with which Soviet leaders adhere to this view. As Russett has shown using factor analysis, the Soviet bloc has opposed supranationalism in the U.N. more consistently than any other group.[18] In light of the global division into antagonistic socioeconomic systems, the U.S.S.R. perceives supranationalism in an organization consisting of capitalist and Communist states as being ideologically improper and impossible. Ideological "bipolarity" precludes "unipolar" organizational forms.

As the participants in international organizations are states, the legal character of these organizations is international not supranational. These organizations are the institutional instruments for the inter-

---

[17] Morawiecki, *op. cit.*, p. 496.
[18] Russett, *International Regions,* p. 77, Table 4.4.

national collaboration of sovereign states. They do not, nor can they, act as an "international administration" standing above the states.[19]

Alexander Dallin succinctly summarized the Soviet outlook when he argued:

> A large complex of the Soviet attitude toward the United Nations may be subsumed under the sovereignty syndrome. It is a characteristic fusion of politics and principle, the protective device of a minority power, the legal basis for a keep-out attitude, and an appealing slogan in dealing with the new and small states. . . . The primary purpose behind Soviet insistence on "sovereignty" has been to maintain maximum freedom of action and to eliminate outside interference. Given its bipolar view of world (and UN) affairs, Moscow assumed that any restriction of sovereignty was bound to benefit the stronger bloc, which would use such restrictions to meddle in the affairs of its enemies. One may speculate that a Soviet bloc in command of a working majority in the United Nations would choose to abandon the "sovereignty weapon" and seek to exploit the resulting opportunities for its own political benefit.[20]

Soviet doctrine still holds that the contemporary era is one in which the forces of "imperialism" are declining, and the U.S.S.R. is unlikely to encourage the creation of integrated or powerful organizations in which capitalist states play a large role.

Soviet history views international law and organization as expressing and reflecting the will of the dominant socioeconomic bloc. In the conditions of a divided world, it claims the existence of two forms of law and organization. However, the relative weakness of the Soviet regime during much of the twentieth century and Soviet perceptions of the destructive nature of modern warfare, articulated most forcefully since the Twentieth Congress of the CPSU in 1956, persuaded Soviet leaders that major war was to be avoided and that competition between the two blocs should remain within the confines of "peaceful coexistence."[21] Under these circumstances, the U.S.S.R. views the U.N. as being marginally useful in preventing Soviet-American conflict and in providing an arena in which nonviolent conflict can be waged. Initial

[19] D. B. Levin and G. P. Kaliuzhnaia, eds., *Mezhdunarodnoe Pravo* (Moscow, 1964), p. 269, cited in Bernard A. Ramundo, *Peaceful Coexistence: International Law and the Building of Communism* (Baltimore: The Johns Hopkins Press, 1967), p. 160.

[20] Dallin, *op. cit.*, pp. 45, 48.

[21] For the evolution of Soviet views on war, see Raymond L. Garthoff, *Soviet Strategy in the Nuclear Age* (New York: Praeger, 1962).

Soviet attitudes toward U.N. intervention in the Congo and Cyprus, for example, suggested that the U.S.S.R. was prepared to permit U.N. interposition in the Third World in order to prevent the opening of new "fronts" at the peripheries. Moreover, after 1956, the U.N. appeared increasingly useful to the U.S.S.R. for exploiting antagonisms between imperialist states and the postcolonial or colonial areas. In the Soviet view, this cleavage remains a fundamental one. Indeed, it has become even more salient since Khrushchev articulated the revised Soviet position on the Third World as constituting a "zone of peace."

In summary, the U.S.S.R. perceives its participation in the United Nations as a means of exploiting the Third World–Western cleavage and of competing with the West within the limits set by peaceful coexistence. Moreover, its participation is viewed defensively as preventing Western mobilization of the world body against the U.S.S.R. Changing Soviet behavior in the U.N. has been largely tactical and has reflected an altered perception of international structure—notably the distribution of capabilities and the emergence of new participant actors that are not aligned with the West. As we shall see, the post-Stalinist leadership concluded that Soviet participation in the world body need no longer be exclusively defensive and obstructionist. By the late 1950s, the U.N. had become a means by which the Soviet Union could further its own specific interests and, therefore, an avenue for offensive tactics as well. This shift in emphasis was reflected in the Soviet Union's blustering performance in the General Assembly in 1960 and 1961, in its demand for greater representation in U.N. organs, and in the increasing participation of Soviet representatives in the U.N.'s social and economic agencies.[22]

On questions of sovereignty, peaceful coexistence, and even supranationalism, Soviet views have tended to converge with those of many Third World actors. Many of the "neutralist" states also perceive the U.N. as a means of preventing conflict between the superpowers which might lead to their involvement and of keeping the bloc leaders out of their regional quarrels. While it is difficult to find any precise meaning for the doctrine of "nonalignment" advocated by many Afro-Asian states, it is clear that they abjure participation in the cold war and seek to concentrate on resolving problems of economic development and political stabilization. Moreover, although most of these states at one time or another have paid lip service to the U.N. as a means of dissolving blocs and lessening cold war tensions, they are *not* averse to the

[22] See Alvin Z. Rubinstein, *The Soviets in International Organizations: Changing Policy toward Developing Countries, 1953–1963* (Princeton: Princeton University Press, 1964).

organization's providing a forum for East-West competition. At one level, the Afro-Asians cannot afford to permit the cold war to end. At worst, this would entail a Soviet-American agreement to police their affairs and regulate their behavior; at best, it would mean that they could be ignored and that their political leverage might disappear. As Rothstein has contended:

> The unaligned Small Powers require the presence of both antagonists in order to retain their maneuverability. . . . The lesser units in any bipolar or quasi-bipolar system prefer the dangers and advantages of bipolarity to the disadvantages a hegemonial system offers.[23]

While the Afro-Asian states prefer to avoid the costs of alignment, they are not averse to taking vociferous positions on cold war issues. Indeed, this fact distinguishes them from traditionally neutral states such as Switzerland. In the U.N. they are able to take such positions, play each side against the other, enhance their value to the superpowers, and make their own demands heard. With few resources to offer the superpowers, their voting strength in the U.N. takes on added importance as a means of extracting benefits from one or both sides. As Jawaharlal Nehru candidly admitted in 1954:

> When there is substantial difference in the strength of the two opposing forces, we in Asia, with our limitations, will not be able to influence the issue. But when the two opposing forces are fairly evenly matched, then it is possible to make our weight felt in the balance.[24]

Soviet emphasis on sovereign equality and opposition to supranationalism has coincided with Afro-Asian inclinations. While the Afro-Asian states are prepared to press for an extension of U.N. authority into certain areas—notably in dispensing economic assistance and intervening in certain "domestic" quarrels, such as the race questions in Rhodesia and South Africa—their fear of neocolonial intrusion and their determination to obtain international status and respectability have cooled their enthusiasm for radically altering the structure of the world organization. Even on questions of economic assistance, the Afro-Asian states recognize that bilateral aid from the superpowers is easier to obtain and is given more quickly, and often on better terms, than multilateral aid. Rhetoric to the contrary notwithstanding, these

[23] Rothstein, op. cit., p. 403.
[24] Cited in Coral Bell, "Non-alignment and the Power Balance," in Components of Defense Policy, ed. Davis B. Bobrow (Chicago: Rand McNally & Co., 1965), p. 69.

states, notably larger ones such as India, are concerned lest their political leverage be lessened by a U.N. distribution of economic resources. In effect, a competitive bipolarity is perceived as serving the economic interests of the nonaligned. As Rubinstein has declared:

> This professed neutralist commitment to the principle of channeling economic aid through the UN . . . is in sharp contrast to the views expressed by neutralist officials in private conversations. . . . In general, the neutralists are not convinced that any relaxation in the Cold War would be translated into wholehearted Great Power support for a UN economic development fund.[25]

While the doctrine of nonalignment is at best made up of several diffuse principles, it is based on the idea that states should pursue policies of coexistence and mutual respect for sovereignty. However, the Afro-Asians' view of sovereign equality diverges from the Soviets' view to the extent that the former argue for the principle of political as well as legal equality. As Rubinstein has suggested of Yugoslavia, a leader of the Third World:

> Unlike the Soviet Union, Yugoslavia predicates its conception of peaceful coexistence on the assumptions that the small nations can exert an influence on world development and must actively seek to do so, and that for lasting political agreements to emerge the two blocs must consider the interests of the developing countries.[26]

Thus, the U.S.S.R. seeks to influence the nonaligned, but is totally unwilling to permit them to guide Soviet foreign policy or intrude into Soviet-American bargaining.

In summary, then, while developments such as rapid decolonization and the creation of the United Nations Conference on Trade and Development (UNCTAD) have enhanced the value of the U.N. to the Third World, many of these states have been loathe to see an increase in the organization's authority at the expense of their freedom of maneuver, particularly where regional or local interests are at stake. In the years immediately after attaining independence, the Afro-Asians were more amenable to U.N. "activism" in order to protect themselves from the superpowers and to provide psychological, technical, and economic props for their new regimes. As Clark, O'Leary,

[25] Rubinstein, *The Soviets in International Organizations*, pp. 49, 55. For an alternative view, see Robert E. Asher, "Multilateral versus Bilateral Aid: An Old Controversy Revisited," *International Organization*, 16 (1962): 697–719.

[26] Alvin Z. Rubinstein, *Yugoslavia and the Nonaligned World* (Princeton: Princeton University Press, 1970), p. 316.

and Wittkopf have shown, however, with the passage of time the new states have increasingly opposed efforts to expand U.N. activities in the direction of supranationalism.[27] They jealously guard the marks of sovereignty so painfully attained. As such states become economically and politically viable and less dependent on particular outside states, they may decreasingly view the extension of U.N. authority as a necessary condition for the maintenance of independence. For them, as for the U.S.S.R., the U.N. will continue to provide a forum in which to present their demands and make their presence felt. Utilizing the decolonization and race issues, the Third World states have been able to make the superpowers modify their positions and have made their own status a persistent and central subject of international attention.[28]

## The New Members of the United Nations

"Nonalignment" is the typical response of the emerging Afro-Asian states.[29] Their lack of economic and military resources and political cohesion threaten to make them "pawns" in the conflicts of the superpowers, and they are exceedingly vulnerable to systemic and external influences. In any discussion of states that profess this foreign policy, we must recognize that they are, in fact, a loosely knit group with a diversity of backgrounds and specific objectives.[30] As President Julius Nyerere of Tanzania has observed, "All that the non-aligned nations have in common is their non-alignment; that is, their existence as weak nations, trying to maintain their independence, and use it for their own benefit in a world dominated politically, economically, and militarily by a few big powers."[31] Although the nonaligned countries are bound together by certain common interests, local conflicts, boundary disputes, and problems of nascent nationalism separate them.

[27] John F. Clark, Michael O'Leary, and Eugene R. Wittkopf, "National Attributes Associated with Dimensions of Support for the United Nations," *International Organization*, 25 (1971): 21.

[28] See David A. Kay, "The Politics of Decolonization: The New Nations and the United Nations Political Process," *ibid.*, 21, no. 4 (1967).

[29] Fifty-four states participated in the third conference of nonaligned states, held in Lusaka, Zambia, in 1970.

[30] For the theory and practice of nonalignment, see J. W. Burton, ed., *Nonalignment* (New York: Heineman, 1966); Cecil V. Crabb, Jr., *The Elephants and the Grass: A Study of Nonalignment* (New York: Praeger, 1965); Laurence W. Martin, ed., *Neutralism and Nonalignment* (New York: Praeger, 1962); and Rubinstein, *Yugoslavia and the Nonaligned World*. Much of the following discussion of nonalignment is based on Raymond F. Hopkins and Richard W. Mansbach, *Structure and Process in International Politics* (New York: Harper & Row, 1973), pp. 190–95.

[31] Cited in H. Hveen and P. Willets, "The Practice of Non-Alignment" (Paper read at the Social Science Conference, University of Dar es Salaam, December 27–31, 1970), p. 3.

National identity and territorial nationalism in these states are frequently fragile and fragmented. Indeed, the phobic accusations alleging attempts by outside powers to divide these countries can be more accurately understood as manifestations of this weak nationalism. In general, their political systems are weak and lack historical precedent, shared expectations for behavior, or a historical accumulation of legitimacy. Their frontiers are often defined in ways that cut across common ethnic, linguistic, or religious groups. As a result, border conflicts and sectional cleavages are important foci of their attention.

The "nonalignment" which unites the Third World refers basically to a rejection of *permanent* involvement in the cold war on either side. Third World states seek trade and aid from both sides in order to acquire the capital necessary for developing their own resources. They cannot adopt a foreign policy of isolationism, because of their economic and political vulnerability; in most cases, they have no wish to adopt such a policy, because they intensely desire to make use of the symbols of independence and acquire recognition and status as autonomous actors. In some cases, an active foreign policy is perceived as necessary for enhancing domestic unity and developing a sense of nationalism. Thus, nonalignment has not prevented these states from taking public positions on particular cold war issues. Nyerere summed up the general attitude on the question of activism versus passivity when he declared:

> We shall deal with each problem as it occurs, and on its own merits. We shall neither move from particular quarrels with individual countries to a generalized hostility to members of a particular group, nor to automatic support for those who also happen to be, for their own reasons, quarrelling with the same nations. We wish to live in friendship with all states and all peoples.[32]

Nonalignment, which Prime Minister Nehru of India labeled "positive neutralism," has been justified as a strategy to prevent East-West conflicts from spreading to the Third World. It emerged from the Afro-Asian movement that originated at the time the U.N. was founded in 1945. At the Bandung conference of 1955, five principles were adopted by the nonaligned: (1) mutual respect for one another's territorial integrity and sovereignty; (2) mutual nonaggression; (3) mutual

[32] Julius K. Nyerere, "Tanzanian Policy on Foreign Affairs," Ministry of Information, Dar es Salaam, 1967. See also *idem, Freedom and Unity* (New York: Oxford University Press, 1967); *idem, Freedom and Socialism* (New York: Oxford University Press, 1968); Kwame Nkrumah, *Africa Must Unite* (London: Heineman, 1963); and *idem, Neo-Colonialism: The Last Stage of Imperialism* (London: Thomas Nelson & Sons, 1965).

noninterference in one another's affairs; (4) equality and mutual benefit; and (5) peaceful coexistence. In effect, these were the themes
which the Soviet Union pressed in the United Nations after 1956.

Many nonaligned states view the U.N. as a valuable institution in
which to enhance their status, protect their independence, and press
their claims upon the large states. Moreover, owing to their general
lack of bureaucratic and fiscal resources to fund embassies and the
unavailability of qualified diplomats and foreign policy personnel to
staff them, they find the U.N. a vital means through which to conduct
foreign relations. Many of the Afro-Asian states regularly press to increase the budgets of the U.N. and its functional agencies. However,
because their voting strength exceeds their resources and because they
are the chief benefactors from the redistribution of wealth and services
that such agencies undertake, this policy seems more self-serving than
supranationalist.[33] Finally, as we have seen, there is a discernible decline in supranational identities among elites in the underdeveloped
areas as they move away from the independence struggle.

### Changing Soviet Policies toward the Third World in the United Nations

Soviet attention toward the Third World over time, as revealed in
the total number of Soviet comments made about these areas in the
U.N., does *not* provide any pattern (see Table 9-1). Even before
Stalin's death, the U.S.S.R. sought to exploit differences between the
developed West and the underdeveloped territories of Africa and Asia.
However, the geographical focus of Soviet attention has shifted. After
1960, for instance, tropical Africa became more salient to the U.S.S.R.
as more African states attained independence and joined the U.N. Of
greater importance was the shift in the treatment of the Third World
by the U.S.S.R. Increasingly, Soviet remarks were directed toward
supporting Third World initiatives and resolutions and proposing positive programs rather than simply denouncing Western policies.

One of the earliest indications of the change in Soviet attitudes
toward the Third World was the unexpected announcement by the
Soviet delegate to the Economic and Social Council in July 1953,
shorty after Stalin's death, that the U.S.S.R. was prepared to contribute to the Expanded Program of Technical Assistance (EPTA).
This reversal of policy indicated that Stalin's successors were con-

---

[33] See Ali Mazrui, "The United Nations and Some African Political Attitudes,"
*International Organization,* 28 (1964): 499–520; and Benjamin Meyers, "African
Voting in the United Nations General Assembly," *Journal of Modern African
Studies,* 4 (1966): 213–28.

Table 9-1

Soviet, Byelorussian, and Ukrainian Comments on the
Third World in the U.N. (Combined), 1950–1968

| Year | Number of Comments |
|------|--------------------|
| 1950 | 46 |
| 1952 | 119 |
| 1954 | 58 |
| 1956 | 50 |
| 1958 | 30 |
| 1960 | 63 |
| 1962 | 40 |
| 1964 | 40 |
| 1966 | 50 |
| 1968 | 93 |

Source: *Yearbook of the United Nations*, 1950–1968 (New York: Columbia University Press).

sidering abandoning some of the more costly features of Stalin's "two-camp" image which had heretofore prevented the U.S.S.R. from exploiting discontent in Africa and Asia and creating allies among the emerging nationlist elites in those areas. In addition, Soviet economic and military capability had increased so that an active foreign policy beyond the Soviet periphery was feasible. Soviet efforts to woo the Afro-Asians in the U.N. were accompanied by increased bilateral aid to these countries as well, which culminated in a massive loan to India for the construction of a steel mill at Bhilai and large-scale arms shipments to Egypt in 1955.

The shift in Soviet tactics toward the Third World is illustrated by the case of SUNFED. In 1951, proposals by a number of economically underdeveloped states culminated in the idea for a Special United Nations Fund for Economic Development (SUNFED) to provide continuing large-scale capital investment for the Third World on a multilateral basis. Both the United States and the Soviet Union greeted the proposal with ill-disguised hostility. The Soviet delegate claimed that SUNFED would merely permit further Western penetration of the Third World and provide greater opportunities for increased capitalist influence in Africa and Asia. Lacking the support or encouragement of either superpower, SUNFED was doomed. In 1953 and 1954, however, Soviet opposition to the plan eased considerably, and by July 1955 the U.S.S.R. dropped all its reservations to the proposal. Although the Soviet delegate demanded certain modifications in the original proposal, his support for the idea placed the United States in a difficult position, isolating it from the growing Afro-Asian membership in the U.N. that enthusiastically embraced the plan. The Soviet position earned the U.S.S.R. political capital at little cost; Soviet leaders were aware that the United States would probably continue to oppose SUNFED and that, in the event of a shift in American policy, the U.S.S.R. could shape the outcome sufficiently to ensure its full participation.

> Support for SUNFED served a Soviet purpose at a particular period: it lent credibility to Moscow's championing the cause of rapid heavy industrial development for underdeveloped countries; and it helped dispel the widespread skepticism among them that had been the lingering consequence of Stalin's lack of interest in UN aid programs. The shift to support for SUNFED . . . was a change which did not require any basic modification of objective or attitude, though it did portend the subsequent reappraisal of the importance of underdeveloped countries for Soviet foreign policy and the way in which the interests of the Soviet Union could coalesce and complement those of these countries.[34]

At the Twentieth Congress of the CPSU in February 1956, Nikita Khrushchev publicly abandoned Stalin's "two-camp" thesis. "The forces of peace," he declared, "have been considerably augmented by the emergence in the world arena of a group of peace-loving European and Asian states which have proclaimed non-participation in blocs as a principle of their foreign policy."[35] The world, according to Khrushchev, was no longer simply bipolar but had become more complex with the addition of a third bloc, a "progressive" group of neutralist states that had freed themselves or were in the process of freeing themselves from Western tutelage. The ideological modification was neither as precipitous nor as extreme as it appeared. Stalin himself in 1952 had begun to explore the possibility of modifying Soviet attitudes to facilitate an extension of Soviet influence into the underdeveloped areas.[36] The U.S.S.R. viewed the new bloc as a stake in what remained fundamentally a bipolar contest with zero-sum implications, and Soviet leaders perceived this new group as moving away from the Western, and closer to the Soviet, sphere of influence. By 1956 the Soviet Union was abandoning the remnants of a "sectarian" dogmatism, which permitted it to seek allies only among Communists in Africa, Asia, and Latin America, in favor of a "popular front from above" tactic, in

---

[34] Rubinstein, *The Soviets in International Organizations*, pp. 101–2.
[35] *Pravda*, February 15, 1956.
[36] See Marshall Shulman, *Stalin's Foreign Policy Reappraised* (Cambridge, Mass.: Harvard University Press, 1963).

which it was prepared to look for allies and sympathizers among the new nationalist leaders, many of whom espoused some form of socialism.

Changes in U.N. membership suggested a new distribution of influence in the world body. The first major enlargement occurred in December 1955, when Molotov's proposal for the "package" admission of sixteen new members was accepted. While only four of these were Soviet allies (Bulgaria, Rumania, Hungary, and Albania), five were Afro-Asian states that had little stake in East-West quarrels (Jordan, Libya, Laos, Cambodia, and Ceylon). Previously, the U.S.S.R. had cast 55 vetoes on membership questions; now it perceived a growth in membership as adding, if not Soviet allies, at least states whose history made them naturally unsympathetic to the West. In Soviet eyes, the U.N. was becoming less of an appendage of Western foreign policy as new states, dominated by the "nationalist bourgeoisie" insteal of by "bourgeois imperialists," entered. Consequently, Soviet behavior in the U.N. shifted on issues ranging from multilateral economic assistance to disarmament and anticolonialism. Between 1956 and 1966, forty-six new members entered the U.N. Of these, thirty-four were African states and six were Asian. The U.N. thus began to reflect a new international distribution of attitudes and resources and was increasingly perceived by Soviet leaders as a forum in which to increase Soviet influence in the Third World and weaken the West at least on the world's peripheries. The U.S.S.R. sought to take advantage of "the emerging anti-colonial consensus in the UN" and consistently voted against colonialism.[37] Since 1955, it has sought to align itself with the Afro-Asians whenever possible on colonial and other issues and has tended "to vote with the African group (and each of its subgroups) more frequently than does the United States."[38] The U.S.S.R. began to find itself increasingly on the side of the majority in the General Assembly. However, this was not so much because Third World states adopted a pro-Soviet position but because the U.S.S.R. supported Afro-Asian initiatives.

After 1956 the Soviet Union's behavior in the U.N. appeared to redound in its favor. While continuing to pursue defensive objectives, the U.S.S.R. began to undertake offensive initiatives as well. Unhampered by previous colonial interests in Africa or Southern Asia, not interdependent with unpopular states such as Portugal or South Africa, and with a model of rapid economic and social development

---

[37] See Edward T. Rowe, "The Emerging Anti-Colonial Consensus in the United Nations," *Journal of Conflict Resolution*, 8 (1964): 209–30.

[38] Thomas Hovet, Jr., *Africa in the United Nations* (Evanston, Ill.: Northwestern University Press, 1963), p. 181.

which was attractive to many Afro-Asian leaders, the Soviet delegates in the committees and agencies of the U.N. sought to identify themselves with anticolonialism and anti-imperialism. Moving away from previously held positions on certain issues, the U.S.S.R. began to advocate General Assembly predominance in selected cases, the political and legal equality of member states, and a flexible interpretation of the Charter on issues such as *apartheid* and Rhodesia. Majoritarianism, previously scorned and denounced by Soviet representatives, was extolled in the late 1950s and early 1960s as a means of eradicating colonialism and ending Western economic and political domination in the Third World.

The evolution in Soviet perceptions of the U.N. and of the Soviet role in that organization which began after Stalin's death reached a climax at the fifteenth session of the General Assembly. In his speech to the Assembly in September, Khrushchev demanded major changes in the organization and administration of the U.N. "We deem it wise and fair," he declared, "that the United Nations executive agency consist not of one person, the Secretary-General, but of three persons." Each of the three would represent one of the major blocs of states, and each would have a veto over the initiatives of the other two. The "troika" proposal indicated that the U.S.S.R. was confident that it would receive the support of the nonaligned in the U.N. and that the world balance of forces had shifted sufficiently to permit it to take initiatives in the organization rather than simply to respond to those of other groups of states. In essence, Khrushchev was demanding that the U.S.S.R. be granted coequal status with the United States as *primus inter pares* in the U.N. In addition, the proposals reflected the revised Soviet appraisal of the international system. International institutions, according to the U.S.S.R., had to reflect international "realities." While the crisis in the Congo precipitated the Soviet proposals, they reflected a careful tactical shift based on increasing Soviet optimism and perceptions of strength.

As Triska and Finley have suggested, Khrushchev "seemed to be returning to certain of Lenin's views, for instance those concerning the proper behavior of a communist minority in a parliamentary situation."[39] According to Lenin, when Communists find themselves in a minority, they should *not* sever their ties from the masses but should form a disciplined and united group. At the same time, they should seek to acquire sympathizers or allies from among the majority. Although the "troika" proposals were defeated, the high level of Soviet

[39] Jan F. Triska and David D. Finley, *Soviet Foreign Policy* (New York: Macmillan, 1968), p. 362. For an analysis of the U.N. based on an analogy to parliamentary politics, see Russett, *Trends in World Politics,* pp. 55–66.

participation in U.N. work since the early 1960s suggests that the U.S.S.R. has become relatively satisfied with U.N. activities in contrast to its negative perceptions of U.N. behavior in the 1950s.[40]

### The U.S.S.R. and the Third World in the United Nations: Soviet Success or Failure?

Evaluating the relative success of Soviet policies in the U.N. in terms of increased influence within the Third World is a complicated task. "Success" might be variously regarded as "being on the winning side" in votes, mobilizing the U.N. to take favorable action on issues vital to a state, preventing adversaries from achieving outcomes favorable to them, or developing influence relationships *within* the organization that can be translated into influence relationships *outside* its formal structure. Soviet payoffs based on any of the above criteria are unclear. The United States continues to be the single most influential member of the U.N., although its influence appears to have substantially declined in the 1960s and 1970s. Thus, the United States can no longer count on "mechanical majorities" in the various agencies of the world organization. However, the changes that have occurred in issues and membership within the U.N. have lessened Western interest in mobilizing the organization to further its interests. Indeed, the growing American-Soviet détente after 1962, the increasing role of the People's Republic of China, the loosening of both major blocs, and the rise of states that have little direct interest in the cold war have made Soviet-American competition in the U.N. less of a zero-sum contest than it was in the 1950s.

In terms of "being on the winning side," *both* the U.S.S.R. and the United States tend to be members of minority coalitions more often than most U.N. members. Research done on the ninth, fourteenth, and seventeenth sessions of the General Assembly show that both superpowers are notably unsuccessful in voting with the majority in comparison to other members.[41] In contrast, selected African and Asian states find themselves consistently in voting majorities. The nature of winning coalitions in the General Assembly seems to be issue-specific, as Table 9-2 suggests. As Plano and Riggs have declared, "Given the present complexion of the Assembly, a country which votes anti-

[40] Clark, O'Leary, and Wittkopf found that the Soviet Union was high on what they term the "system-conforming factor," an indicator of an actor's socialization into the system. *Op. cit.*, pp. 12–13.

[41] See Catherine Senf Manno, "Majority Decisions and Minority Responses in the UN General Assembly," *Journal of Conflict Resolution,* 10 (1966): 1–20.

Table 9-2

Roll-Call Voting Alignments on Six Issues in the Twentieth General Assembly, 1965

| Issue | Vote (yes-no-abstain) | Prevailing Coalition | Opposing Coalition | Abstentions | Position of U.S. | Position of U.S.S.R. |
|---|---|---|---|---|---|---|
| Anticolonialism | 74–6–27 | Africa 32<br>Asia 18<br>Lat. Am. 11<br>Soviet 11<br>W. Eur. 2 | W. Europe 4<br>S. Africa 1<br>U.S. 1 | Asia 3<br>Lat. Am. 10<br>W. Eur. 14 | No | Yes |
| Convention on racial discrimination | 62–18–27 | Africa 32<br>Asia 16<br>Lat. Am. 3<br>Soviet 10<br>Cyprus 1 | Lat. Am. 13<br>W. Eur. 4<br>U.S. 1 | Asia 8<br>Lat. Am. 3<br>W. Eur. 15<br>Congo (Dem. Repub.) 1 | No | Yes |
| Korea | 61–13–34 | Africa 14<br>Asia 10<br>Lat. Am. 18<br>W. Eur. 18<br>U.S. 1 | Africa 2<br>Soviet 10<br>Cuba 1 | Africa 18<br>Asia 13<br>Finland 1<br>Jamaica 1<br>Yugoslavia 1 | Yes | No |
| Pacific settlement | 48–27–8 | Africa 28<br>Asia 9<br>Soviet 10<br>Cuba 1 | Asia 5<br>Lat. Am. 5<br>W. Eur. 16<br>U.S. 1 | Asia 3<br>Lat. Am. 2<br>W. Eur. 2<br>Nigeria 1 | No | Yes |
| Financing UNEF | 44–14–45 | Africa 8<br>Asia 11<br>Lat. Am. 9<br>W. Eur. 16 | Soviet 10<br>Lat. Am. 4 | Africa 22<br>Asia 10<br>Lat. Am. 8<br>W. Eur. 3<br>U.S. 1 | Abstain | No |
| Tibet | 43–26–22 | Africa 4<br>Asia 8<br>Lat. Am. 18<br>W. Eur. 13 | Africa 9<br>Asia 5<br>Soviet 11<br>Cuba 1 | Yugoslavia 1<br>Africa 6<br>Asia 8<br>Lat. Am. 2<br>W. Eur. 6 | Yes | No |

*Source*: Jack C. Plano and Robert E. Riggs, *Forging World Order: The Politics of International Organization* (New York: Macmillan, 1967), p. 159.
*Key to Regional Designations*: Africa = African states; Asia = Asian states, except Mongolia; Lat. Am. = Latin American states; Soviet bloc (including Mongolia) and Yugoslavia; W. Eur. = West European states, Australia, Canada, and New Zealand.

colonial, underdeveloped, and moderately pro-western will generally be in the majority."[42]

Despite the difficulty of analyzing relative success in the U.N., there is a general perception among scholars and statesmen that Soviet influence has declined, since the admission of large numbers of Afro-Asian states.[43] As we have seen, the perception of waning American majorities has been accompanied by increasing Soviet optimism and activism in the U.N. The extent to which American observers perceive Soviet gains in the Third World is revealed in a survey conducted among scholars and American State Department specialists by Alvin Rubinstein. According to Rubinstein, "There was overwhelming agreement among all categories of specialists that Soviet influence increased during the 1955–1959 period; with the exception of Soviet specialists . . . , the same held true for the 1965–1969 period."[44] The first period coincides with the admission to the U.N. of large numbers of Third World states; the second coincides with the upsurge in the Middle East controversy. As to why they felt that Soviet influence in the Third World was highest in the most recent period, many respondents mentioned "the tendency of Third World countries to follow the lead of the U.S.S.R. in international affairs, especially in the United Nations."[45] Two-thirds of all respondents believed that U.N. voting patterns were reliable indicators of relative influence in the Third World, and nine of fourteen Foreign Service Officers believed this to be the case, which indicates the extent to which this view is held in the State Department.

Thus, since the 1950s, there has been growing American concern that the Soviet Union was reaping handsome dividends from its behavior in the U.N. American observers have frequently alleged that many Third World states, despite their professions of neutralism, do not behave "evenhandedly" and seem prepared to excoriate American policies without fear of retribution, while they are unwilling to take "principled" stands against Soviet policies. One scholar reported that a high-ranking American State Department official commented of India, "We [the United States] have to use all our persuasion to make them [the Indians] even listen to us. But they seem to run for their lives if the Russians do so much as thump the table."[46] Yet India's

[42] Jack C. Plano and Robert E. Riggs, *Forging World Order: The Politics of International Organization* (New York: Macmillan, 1967), p. 158.

[43] See, for example, Claude, *The Changing United Nations*, p. 39.

[44] Alvin Z. Rubinstein, "U.S. Specialists' Perception of Soviet Policy toward the Third World" (Paper delivered at the Sixty-seventh Annual Meeting of the American Political Science Association, Chicago, September 1971, p. 3.

[45] *Ibid.*, p. 5.

[46] Swadesh Rana, "The Changing Indian Diplomacy at the United Nations," *International Organization*, 24 (1970): 62, n. 47.

position becomes more comprehensible when viewed in terms of that country's sensitivity about its colonial past and America's resistance to India's participation in major conferences. When in July 1958, for instance, Khrushchev suggested a summit conference to deal with the Middle East question, he declared that "the representative of India in the person of Mr. Nehru should take part in the Security Council meeting." Secretary of State Dulles's response showed marked insensitivity to Indian feelings. He said, in part, "Of course, one would have to consider whether if you invited India . . . you would not have to invite so many more countries and the conference would become particularly unmanageable."[47] Regardless of the merit of the respective positions, the Soviet suggestion held strong appeal for the Indians, while the American response appeared to denigrate India's international role and equated that country with the smallest states of Africa and Latin America. In return, Indian behavior often seemed ill-considered and prejudiced to American observers, particularly when Krishna Menon represented India in the U.N. While prepared to condemn the United States for its behavior in Vietnam and the Dominican Republic, India resorted to similar tactics in seizing Goa in 1960 and attacking Pakistan in 1971. Indian voting on issues such as Hungary, the Article 19 controversy, and its abstention on the August 1968 Security Council draft resolution condemning Soviet intervention in Czechoslovakia seemed "unfair" and hypocritical to many Americans.

While most Third World states purport to be neutralist in the cold war, their U.N. voting sometimes belies this claim. Many of them have shifted their support from issue to issue without supporting either side consistently. However, some Third World states have consistently supported one side or the other, even on cold war issues. Thus, through the twenty-first session of the General Assembly, states such as Ghana, Guinea, Mali, Somalia, Tanzania, Uganda, Algeria, and Egypt (after the tenth session) voted heavily with the Soviet Union on cold war issues, while states such as Togo, Upper Volta, Iran, Lebanon, Jordan, Cameroun, Cyprus and Rwanda took pro-American positions. In rare cases such as those of Sierra Leone, Kuwait, and Tunisia, professed neutralism was consistently reflected in U.N. voting.

Several recent efforts have been made to shed further light on the relative support received by the United States and the Soviet Union from the Third World in the U.N.[48] Stephen Gibert investigated the

---

[47] Cited in *ibid.*, p. 63.

[48] See Edward T. Rowe, "Changing Patterns in the Voting Success of Member States in the United Nations General Assembly, 1945–1966," *ibid.*, 23 (1969): 231–53; *idem*, "The United States, the United Nations, and the Cold War," *ibid.*, 25 (1971): 59–78; and Stephen P. Gibert, "Soviet-American Military Aid Com-

relationship between U.N. voting outcomes and bilateral military assistance. He did not, however, look at the effect of changes in U.N.
membership. Viewing the amount of military aid as an independent
variable and U.N. voting as a dependent variable, Gibert concluded:

> The results indicate a strong relationship between military aid policy
> and attitudes, as expressed in UN voting, on political and security
> issues. The Soviet government has tended to be "rewarded" by mili-
> tary aid recipients to a somewhat greater degree than has the United
> States.[49]

The extent to which Third World states supported the U.S.S.R. on
political and security issues (which correspond roughly to "cold war"
issues), however, is far from overwhelming. States which received
military aid *exclusively* from one of the superpowers tended to support
that superpower on political and security issues. Except for Cyprus, for
instance, the ten countries aided exclusively by the U.S.S.R. agreed
with the Soviet Union most of the time. Of the thirty-five states aided
solely by the United States, only six (Burma, Ethiopia, Lebanon,
Saudi Arabia, and Tunisia) exhibited higher agreement scores with the
U.S.S.R. than with the United States. The Soviet advantage appeared
in the case of those states which received military assistance from *both*
superpowers. With the exception of Laos, all nine nations which had
received aid from both tended to agree with the U.S.S.R. on political
and security issues.

The pro-Soviet "bias" of the Third World was more evident in votes
concerning colonial issues. In these cases, all states that had received
military assistance exclusively from the Soviet Union or jointly from
both superpowers had higher voting agreement scores with the
U.S.S.R. than with the United States. Indeed, most of those states
which received assistance from the United States alone also tended to
vote with the Soviet Union on colonial issues. These results led Gibert
to conclude:

> It is clear that the USSR has succeeded in identifying itself with the
> positions of the less developed countries on colonial questions, but

---

petition in the Third World," *Orbis*, 13 (1970): 1117–37. Both Rowe and Gibert
employed a formula used to calculate "scores of voting agreement" on the basis
of the percentage of times states agreed with the United States or the Soviet
Union. The formula was developed by Arend Lijphart in "The Analysis of Bloc
Voting in the General Assembly: A Critique and a Proposal," *American Political
Science Review*, 57 (1963): 909–10.

[49] Gibert, *op. cit.*, p. 1132. For similar conclusions concerning the relationship
between economic assistance and U.N. voting, see Triska and Finley, *Soviet Foreign Policy*, pp. 273–80.

not to the same degree on roll calls involving political and security issues.[50]

Gibert's research suggests that Third World support of Soviet positions on major cold war issues is not as great nor as consistent as some observers have feared. However, it does suggest that to a certain extent U.N. voting reflects patterns of behavior outside the organization (in this case military assistance).[51] Gibert sees Third World voting behavior in the U.N. as a function less of superpower behavior in the organization than of bilateral military assistance. He predicts that

> voting trends in the United Nations suggest that as more countries become recipients of Soviet military aid programs, there will be a tendency for these countries to move closer to the position of the Soviet Union in world politics.[52]

Edward Rowe was concerned exclusively with cold war issues and their relation to membership changes in the U.N. His conclusion was that, "while changes in membership did not produce defeats for the United States on cold-war issues, these changes seriously weakened the United States position by narrowing the margins of United States victories and by reducing the proportion of the membership that the United States could consider highly reliable."[53] On cold war issues, the United States was able to support virtually all General Assembly decisions in contested roll-call votes from the first through the twenty-first sessions of that body; in contrast, the Soviet Union opposed most of them. On other issues, however (notably those of a colonial nature), the United States has found itself increasingly in opposition to General Assembly resolutions. "In other words, despite the losses on cold-war issues, the Soviet Union was able to support more non-cold-war decisions than was the United States during the 1951–1955 and the 1961–1966 periods."[54]

Rowe's data strongly suggest that Soviet "gains" in the Third World have been made largely in non–cold war areas. This leads me to

[50] Gibert, op. cit., p. 1133.

[51] For indicators of international alignments, see Henry Teune and Sig Synnestvedt, "Measuring International Alignment," Orbis, 9 (1965): 171–89. Teune and Synnestvedt found that the most reliable indicators of alignment were military commitments, U.N. voting, diplomatic recognition, and diplomatic visits. Maurice D. Simon found a relatively consistent increase in the number of treaties concluded between the U.S.S.R. and twenty-six selected Third World states between 1954 and 1962. Simon, "Communist System Interaction with the Developing States, 1954–1962: A Preliminary Analysis," Stanford Studies of the Communist System, Research Paper no. 10, January 1966, p. 92.

[52] Gibert, op. cit., p. 1137.

[53] Rowe, "The United States, the United Nations, and the Cold War," p. 77.

[54] Ibid., p. 62.

hypothesize that the trends found by Rowe and Gibert reflect Soviet support for Third World states in cases, such as those concerning Rhodesia and South Africa, when they can behave as a bloc, *rather than an increase in Third World support of Soviet positions. Seen in this light, voting trends do not represent increased Soviet influence in the Third World, although they do reflect Soviet efforts to woo the Afro-Asian states.* Rowe's figures indicate that the United States has remained just as successful in obtaining favorable outcomes on cold war votes as it was in the 1950s and that new member states have had only a marginal impact in determining these outcomes.

These conclusions, however, must be tempered by certain other observations. In the first place, during more recent sessions of the General Assembly the United States has been content with less radically anti-Communist resolutions than it was earlier. Essentially, the United States no longer seeks to mobilize "anti-Communist majorities" and, owing largely to Afro-Asian pressure, is prepared to support less-decisive resolutions. In addition, while the United States has continued to be successful in terms of the absolute number of favorable General Assembly decisions on cold war issues, its margin of victory has declined substantially. Although the decline has not been consistent, it shows a strong negative relationship to the admittance of Afro-Asian states into the U.N. As Rowe declared, "The altered situation during the 1957–1966 period is unmistakeable, with scores sharply and consistently lower than in earlier years."[55] It has become increasingly difficult for the United States to rally two-thirds majorities. Indeed, this was confirmed by America's inability in 1971 to persuade the General Assembly to declare the issue of the seating of the People's Republic of China and the ousting of the Taiwan regime an "important question." Finally, the percentage of states that are "strongly opposed" to the United States on cold war questions has increased precipitously. According to Rowe, almost 19 percent of the members of the General Assembly "strongly opposed" the United States in 1966, as compared to 9 percent during the ninth session. By 1966 just over 49 percent of the membership consisted of "strong supporters" of the United States, as compared to almost 64 percent during the ninth session. During the earlier sessions, "strong opponents" consisted almost entirely of members of the Soviet bloc. However, the Soviet Union and its East European allies are no longer isolated. As Rowe has declared:

> The data presented shows that there have been changes in the degree of support which the United States received from various groups of members divided according to their date of admission. . . .

[55] *Ibid.*, p. 66.

The differences in the distributions of those states which became United Nations members before and after 1955 are striking and clearly support the generally accepted proposition that the newer membership was less strongly oriented toward the United States on cold-war issues.[56]

In the twenty-first session of the General Assembly, 50 percent of the South and Southeast Asian members strongly or moderately opposed the United States on cold war questions, as did over 39 percent of the Black African members and over 38 percent of the Middle Eastern and North African members. Thus, since 1960, the Afro-Asian states have formed the bulk of opposition to the United States in the General Assembly.

## The Soviet Union, the Third World, and the Future

Until Stalin's death, the U.S.S.R. and its allies pursued a defensive strategy in the U.N. With the admission of new Afro-Asian members, whose objectives and attitudes the Soviet Union found congenial, Soviet strategy was altered to achieve maximum influence upon them, divide the West, and support an extension of Soviet policy objectives into the Third World. To a large extent, it appears that the Western position in the U.N. has declined, although it is less clear that the Soviet Union is emerging as a "leader" of the Third World. Rather, the U.S.S.R. is behaving more as a "follower" of the Afro-Asians, particularly on colonial and race issues, in which its stake is marginal. In this way, the U.S.S.R. has been able to exploit tensions between the United States and certain allies, such as Portugal, Great Britain, and South Africa, and between the West and former colonial territories in Asia and Africa.[57]

Turning to the future, I am led to conclude that there are limits to which the U.S.S.R. will be able to exploit Third World discontent. In the first place, the Soviet Union as a status quo actor is bound to oppose Third World attempts to gain decisive influence over outcomes where their interests are at best convergent and often divergent. Indeed, the existing Soviet–Third World alignment is based on convergent, not common, interests. As fear of the West and neocolonialism recedes, and as the Afro-Asians fail to obtain the economic and prestige benefits they seek in the U.N., it is possible that pro-Soviet attitudes will be replaced by a "plague on both your houses" view.

[56] *Ibid.*, p. 68.

[57] The significance of the race issue as a major emerging "international issue-area" should not be underemphasized. See James N. Rosenau, "Race in International Politics: A Dialogue in Five Parts," *The Scientific Study of Foreign Policy* (New York: Free Press, 1971), pp. 339–97.

Moreover, the decline in cold war hostility and the increase in shared interests between the superpowers will provide the Afro-Asians with increasingly less room in which to maneuver and less leverage with which to obtain favors from either of the major adversaries. On issues such as arms control and disarmament, the Middle East, and European security, the Afro-Asians are simply unimportant. While continuing to compete in the Third World, neither American nor Soviet leaders are prepared to risk direct confrontation in these areas. In fact, since their initial surge of enthusiasm for the emerging nationalist leaders of the Third World, the Soviet Union has learned that the interests which they may share with these leaders do not provide the basis for long-term influence or alignment.

Third, the Chinese factor has, and will continue to have, a marked impact on Soviet behavior toward the Third World.[58] Now that the People's Republic of China has entered the U.N., we can expect Soviet objectives in the world body again to become increasingly defensive—but against China rather than the West. Mainland China has a strong racial and ideological appeal to many Third World states, such as Tanzania and Algeria. By 1965 the U.S.S.R. was prepared to argue that in the U.N. "the glacier of history is moving in a direction that does not suit Washington at all."[59] By 1972 this observation also began to characterize Soviet perceptions of the U.N. as a result of Chinese entrance. Security Council debates on the Indo-Pakistani war in December 1971 and the ensuing Soviet vetoes suggest that on specific issues certain Third World states find China a comfortable partner.

Finally, the lessening of the major bipolar cleavage, the emergence of divergent regional and local interests among the Afro-Asians, and the uneven pace of economic and social development within the Third World make the Third World even less of a bloc than it has been in the past. The specter of neocolonialism and the common bond of economic underdevelopment are no longer sufficient to prevent the emergence of parochial concerns that will fragment the Third World and pit some of these states against others, even in the U.N.

There has been a quantum increase in local international conflict throughout the peripheries because the probability of its autonomous local occurrence has increased. The foreign policies of countries in the peripheries are focused on their local subsystems because they

[58] For Soviet-American-Chinese competition in the foreign aid field, see David Beim, "The Communist Bloc and the Foreign Aid Game," *Western Political Quarterly*, 17 (1964): 784–99.

[59] Boris Izakov, "The U.N., Past and Present," *New Times* (Moscow), 1965, no. 49, p. 5.

lack the resources to do more; domestic pressures and demands over-load them, and their international problems, opportunities, and goals are local. Even when many of these countries act in the United Nations . . . , their actions reflect their "local" concerns. The African states press for action on issues of racism in general and of southern Africa in particular. The Arab states press for action in the Middle East. There is, therefore, a long-term structural trend toward inter-national fragmentation.[60]

Under these conditions, Soviet support of certain Third World states will alienate others. Other allies will be sought, including China and Cuba. Perhaps, then, the next five or ten years will witness the emer-gence in the U.N. of a "Fourth" and a "Fifth" World, consisting of groups such as radical supporters of China, conservative African states that are unwilling to take partisan stands on issues such as the Middle East or even South African *apartheid,* and radical or conserva-tive Latin American states. Thus, Soviet opportunities in the U.N. to exploit Third World dissatisfaction with the West will be increasingly circumscribed. In conclusion, politics in the U.N. will become increas-ingly complex, and the great powers will become less able to perceive dominant strategies for themselves.

[60] Jorge I. Dominguez, "Mice That Do Not Roar: Some Aspects of International Politics in the World's Peripheries," *International Organization,* 25 (1971): 178.

# 10

## THE SINO-SOVIET SPLIT AND THE
## DEVELOPING NATIONS

### Jan S. Prybyla

*I*

The long drawn-out and multidimensional dispute between the
Soviet Union and the People's Republic of China is bound to have had
an impact on Soviet and Chinese attitudes toward the developing,
non-Communist nations of Asia, Africa, and Latin America, and just as
surely it has affected the policies of those nations, both foreign and
domestic. The empirical difficulties in documenting this intuitive statement are, however, quite formidable. It is not always possible (even
assuming that one is privy to behind-the-scenes information) to isolate
the particular impact of the dispute on postures of the Soviets, Chinese,
and developing nations toward one another from the vast complex of
influences which bears down on such postures. This may perhaps be
described as the "input" side of the problem. There is, unfortunately,
not very much one can do to thin out this jungle of input influences,
beyond taking the usual precautions not to exaggerate the causal
powers of any single event taken out of context. In the specific case
facing me here, this means placing restraint on a fairly understandable
temptation to attribute to the dispute most shifts in Soviet and Chinese
domestic and foreign policies of recent years, such restraint being
guided largely by good sense. But there is also what one might call
the "output" side of the problem. What special effects am I looking for?
I have chosen to answer this question by means of a discussion of one
broadly defined field of reactions. I have elected to examine the economics of the problem—specifically, developmental aid. Besides my
personal preference for this approach, there are cogent objective arguments which favor such a restriction.[1] Economic development is seen
by leaders of Third World nations as an overriding goal of policy; one
could say the cornerstone of national survival. On the other side, developmental assistance is an important component of the Soviet Union's

---

[1] "Aid," says one Soviet writer, "is a kind of lever on which two antagonistic
forces are pressing." S. I. Tiul'panov, *Ocherk ipoliticheskoi ekonomii: Razvivaiushchiesia strany* (Moscow: "Mysl," 1969), p. 140. Tiul'panov means that the two
antagonistic forces pressing on foreign aid are the socialist states and Western
capital, but the argument may easily be applied to Soviet-Chinese aid efforts.

and China's relations with such nations.[2] It goes without saying that this self-imposed restriction must be handled in perspective: economics, especially in its international and developmental manifestations, is a package deal tied up in political strings. It is political economy *par excellence*. I trust that the other essays in this volume make this abundantly clear and that their collective weight will correct any untoward tendency on my part to lend to economics more than its due share of importance.

Several other limitations of this essay should be pointed out. I will be dealing here only with Soviet and Chinese economic aid and trade policies toward those developing nations which are not "socialist" in the Communist sense of the word. In a way this is a pity, for the economic impact of the Sino-Soviet dispute seems often to manifest itself most succinctly in Chinese-Soviet competition for the allegiance of, and influence in, developing socialist nations (the Mongolian People's Republic, North Vietnam, and North Korea come to mind as excellent examples).[3] To add these to the roster, however, would make the study quantitatively unmanageable and would take it beyond the scope of the present volume. What this essay tries to do is to compare Soviet and Chinese aid practices vis à vis Third World nations in the setting of strained ideological and interstate relations between China and Russia. The origins and detailed substance of the Sino-Soviet dispute are not discussed. It is assumed that the reader is generally familiar with them; hence the problem is relegated to a bibliographical footnote. Only the barest bones of the dispute are specifically mentioned in the text. To sustain the proposition that the quarrel does enter into the complex of Soviet and Chinese economic attitudes toward the developing nations, brief samples are given of what Peking thinks about Soviet aid and trade and what Moscow thinks of parallel Chinese efforts. These mutual insults must, however, be seen in the light of actual aid and trade performance rather than as majestic semantic abstractions. To the Chinese especially, words have a charm and a life of their own, but words have been known to be eaten.

[2] "We have never concealed the fact that such [economic] cooperation is one of the factors in the struggle between the two world systems—socialist and capitalist." V. Sergeyev, "The Soviet Union and the Developing Countries," *International Affairs* (Moscow), 1971, no. 5, p. 26. According to A. Kosygin, the aim of further developing the Soviet Union's foreign economic relations includes the consolidation of the "international positions of the Soviet Union," as well as augmenting the "economic power of the world socialist system." Report on the Five-Year Plan, April 6, 1971, in *Reprints from the Soviet Press*, 12, no. 11–12 (June 11, 1971): 72 (hereafter cited as *RSP*).

[3] See, for example, my "Soviet and Chinese Economic Aid to North Vietnam," *China Quarterly*, July–September 1966, pp. 84–100; and *idem*, "Soviet and Chinese Economic Competition within the Communist World," *Soviet Studies*, 15 (1964): 464–73.

## II

I will first dispose of the words. "Let us," say the Chinese,

tear off the wrappings of Soviet revisionism's so-called "aid" and see what dirty stuff it contains. In providing "aid," Soviet revisionism aims not only at fleecing Asian, African, and Latin American people; what is more important, it wants to dominate the recipient countries politically so as to establish a colonial rule of the new tsars. Its "aid" is adapted to and closely coordinated with its counterrevolutionary global strategy. Since it regards Southeast Asia and the Middle East as important strategic areas for its expansion abroad, it gives priority to these regions in its "aid" program in order to tighten its grip as much as possible. . . . Soviet economic "aid" is tied to all kinds of harsh political conditions. . . . [Soviet revisionism] controls many vital economic sectors in India, including one-fourth of the latter's iron and steel industry, half of its oil refining industry, and one-fifth of its electric power industry. . . . The more the reactionary Indian Government depends on Soviet revisionism's "aid," the more tightly it is controlled politically by the latter. . . . Internationally, the reactionary Indian Government follows Soviet revisionism, serving as a bellwether in opposing China . . . [and] to betray and suppress the Asian, African, and Latin American people's liberation struggle. . . . In Southeast Asia, Soviet revisionism uses its military and economic "aid" directly to serve its vile motive of opposing China and to form, in league with U.S. imperialism, an encirclement of China. . . . By pressing for payments on loans and interest, by selling dear and buying cheap and other contemptible means, the Soviet revisionists have seized large amounts of important materials and natural resources from Asian, African, and Latin American countries. . . . The Soviet revisionists dump old machines and equipment in Asia, Africa, and Latin America, usually at prices 20 or 30 per cent higher than those on the world market. . . . [Soviet revisionism's] "aid" to Asian, African, and Latin American countries consists mostly of items for heavy industry, such as mining, metallurgy, and power plants. This is because the lopsided development of its economy has resulted in large stockpiles of machines and equipment—products of heavy industry—and it is anxiously looking for markets abroad to dump these outdated machines in an effort to extricate itself from the difficulties in production at the expense of the Asian, African, and Latin American people. . . . [The whole affair is based on an] extremely absurd gangster logic [and the] barbarous and sinister undertakings of Soviet revisionism [are dressed up in] lies to fool the people.[4]

[4] "Soviet Revisionist New Tsars Use 'Aid' to Stretch Their Claws into Asia, Africa, and Latin America," *Peking Review*, July 11, 1969, pp. 24–26 (hereafter cited as *PR*).

But the people will not be fooled. "The regressive acts of this renegade clique," for instance, "have educated the Latin American people by negative example, just as all reactionaries have done by their crimes. . . . When that hired poet of the Soviet revisionist clique, Yevtushenko, was sent to carry out criminal activities at the National University of Colombia in February 1968, angry Colombian students shouted: 'We are not your friends!' and 'Soviet revisionist, get out!' "[5]

These samples are typical of the official Chinese statements on Soviet foreign aid which have been issued periodically since 1963. Four themes run through this assessment of Soviet efforts in Third World nations: (1) colonial exploitation based on some rather disreputable profit-and-loss calculation; (2) political domination, a major purpose of which is to get the developing nations to do the Soviet Union's handiwork abroad, this work being aimed at (3) extinguishing the prairie fires of national liberation and (4) isolating and encircling China (all of it in collusion with U.S. imperialism). The reference to the Soviet Union's lopsided development and the consequent alleged dumping abroad of heavy-industry products, which have seen better days, suggests another theme—perhaps the most important in a long-range perspective. The Soviets, the Chinese are saying, do not have much to teach the developing nations in the way of socialist economic construction. Resting as it does on the priority development of heavy industry at the expense of agriculture, their economic model is a historical freak, from which the developing nations can at best learn by negative example. Implied in this downgrading of the Soviet model is an invitation to give thought to the Chinese alternative of priority to agriculture and industries aiding agriculture, the combination of advanced and native technology ("walking on two legs"), respect for local, small-scale industry and labor-intensive projects, producers' "mass democratic consultation," and the whole gamut of recipes for "initial prosperity" which has been developed by China since 1958. The Soviets, the Chinese seem to be saying (and have said explicitly on more than one occasion), are basically "European," out of touch with the character, instincts, drives, and what have you of the non-European, formerly colonial, or semicolonial peoples (which presumably, in an elastic interpretation, include the Latin Americans). This line of argument cannot be dismissed, as the Soviets are prone to do, as merely making virtue of necessity. The Chinese are indeed poor, and they know it. But the advocacy of their way to development is not just an opportunistic rationalization of their present straitened circum-

[5] "Rampant Counterrevolutionary Acts by Soviet Revisionism in Latin America," *ibid.*, June 20, 1969, p. 20; see also "On Soviet Neocolonialist 'Aid,'" *ibid.*, September 12, 1967, p. 41.

stances. It is, one gathers, a deeply held conviction, one which colors the Chinese vision of full communism, and not only the Maoist vision. The new Communist industrial state of Chinese imagination has as one of its characteristics a degree of tolerable poverty: plain living and thinking in unison on a high plane. The vision is profoundly moral (although the morality of it can be disputed). It may well turn out that it speaks more persuasively to the "masses" of the developing nations than it does to those among their leaders who were brought up to believe that noncapitalist economic development means "metal-eating."

Soviet language, as befits an established power, has been more restrained (except for the KGB outlet, the Novosti Press Agency, which befouls the Chinese on their own terms). Judging by Moscow's response, Chinese busybodying in sensitive areas of the developing world is causing anxiety, and Chinese strictures—like the ones I have quoted—cut to the quick: "A speck of rat's dirt will spoil a bowl of rice," as the Chinese say. Soviet criticism of China's economic ventures in the Third World hits, as one would expect, where it hurts most at the moment of impact, but the political mileage the Russians get out of it may yet turn out to be considerably short of expectations. Thus, a fuss is made over the smallness of the Chinese contribution. The Chinese do not deny this, but once in a while they counter—for example, with a whopping $300 million-plus for the Tan-Zam railroad, which at one swoop puts Soviet and East European aid in that area somewhere near last place. The paucity of Chinese aid is, of course, tied by the Soviets to the retarded condition of China's economy, a retardation which is not likely to be remedied by the Maoist penchant for periodic leapfrogging over historical periods and other objective laws. "The volume of aid given by the Chinese People's Republic amounted to only eight per cent of the aid granted to young national states by the Soviet Union and the other Socialist CMEA countries."[6] As I will show later, the logic behind Soviet worries about such pittance rests on the fact that the Chinese do manage on occasion to convert quantitative weakness into qualitative strength. This is what V. Kudriavtsev probably meant when, with a diplomat's double-edged skill, he lectured the Chinese in the following terms:

[6] *Izvestiia*, July 12, 1964. "We have done as much as our capacity permits to help other Afro-Asian countries develop their national economies and to strengthen mutual assistance and cooperation with them. But at present China's economic level is not high. What we have been able to do is limited. . . . What we have so far done falls far short of what we should have done. But we are sincere." Chinese delegate to the Economic Preparatory Meeting for the Second Afro-Asian Conference (Bandung II), *PR*, June 26, 1964, p. 10.

It is natural that the Afro-Asian countries turn their gaze toward the experience of the Chinese People's Republic, especially since the conditions of that country and the other countries of Asia and Africa have many features in common: strong remnants of precapitalist formations; backwardness of the economy, in which the predominant place is held by agriculture; a largely peasant population; and a recent colonial or semicolonial past. It is precisely this that imposes on the leaders of the C.P.R. great moral responsibility before the young independent countries of Asia and Africa. The transfer of experience, one would think, would necessitate a highly cautious approach, one that takes into account the specific features of historically evolved conditions in each country, and also, and not least of all, national pride, which has become especially vulnerable as a result of decades of colonial oppression.[7]

In their pathological impatience, the leaders of the People's Republic of China have betrayed this great moral responsibility before the young independent countries of Asia and Africa in the following respects:

First, the Soviets argue, an indiscriminate transposition of the Chinese doctrine of self-reliance

leads the newly independent states . . . to squander their means and resources. The disruption of their economic relations with Socialist countries and the other highly developed countries, and the failure to utilize their advanced experience can bring the young developing countries nothing but a weakening of their positions in the struggle against imperialist exploitation, the slowing down of the rate of growth of their national economies, and aggravation of their difficulties, grave as they are.[8]

Peddled abroad, the thesis of self-reliance, the Soviets imply, is a combination of an anti-Soviet plot aimed at isolating the U.S.S.R. from its friends in the Third World, and a doctrinal rationalization of China's inability to give nearly as much as the Soviet Union.

Second, especially since the outbreak of the Cultural Revolution, [The Maoist group] has substituted hegemonism for the transfer of objective experience, presenting the Chinese experience as the sole and incontrovertible model for the peoples of all continents. . . . Ignoring Lenin's warning about the diversity of revolutions, the Maoist

---

[7] V. Kudriavtsev, "Dangerous Instigators," *Izvestiia*, April 13, 1968, p. 5.

[8] *Ekonomicheskaia gazeta*, August 22, 1964, p. 19, cited by Milton Kovner in "Communist China's Foreign Aid to Less-Developed Countries," *An Economic Profile of Mainland China* (Washington, D.C.: Government Printing Office, 1967), a report prepared for the Joint Economic Committee of the U.S. Congress, p. 619.

group is attempting to impose itself upon other peoples as a Delphic oracle, spouting truths and tolerating no objections."[9]

This manifestation of "great-power chauvinism" (the Chinese term to describe the Soviets is identical) takes on various forms:

a. "Pressure, flagrant interference in the internal affairs of liberated states, and subversive activities against progressive regimes"[10] have occurred, for example, in Burma, Ceylon, Indonesia, Congo (Brazaville), Kenya, the Central African Republic, and Mali. At its most hysterical, the charge is that "the policy pursued by Mao Tse-tung with regard to developing Asian and African countries is fully in line with the Great-Han 'Celestial Empire' policy of the Chinese feudal emperors. Its substance is that a foreign state must become either a vassal of the 'Celestial Empire' or its enemy."[11]

b. "Unlimited nationalization in the absence of a firmly established state organism of the new type is capable of completely shattering the economy of a country that has already been weakened by the prolonged domination of the colonialists."[12] This, according to the Soviets, is precisely the sort of economic advice the Chinese have been giving the developing nations—all of it, one may add, with paltry sums.

c. "Negative consequences," the Soviets continue,

may also be brought about by ignoring actual conditions during the implementation of the policy of industrialization, especially when fundamental social and economic transformations have not been carried out in rural areas and there has been no rise in agricultural production, which is basic to the economies of the overwhelming majority of the Afro-Asian countries. Excessive haste in the cooperative organization of agriculture may prove equally mistaken. [Memories of Stalin coming back to haunt?] Forgetting the objective laws of economic development merely brings grist to the mill of the imperialists, since it leads the economies of backward countries to catastrophe and then, through various types of "aid," hurls these

[9] Kudriavtsev, op. cit.; cf. I. Trofimova, "The Fallacy of Maoist Doctrines," New Times, 1971, no. 35, pp. 25–26. In her review of E. Korbash's book The Economic "Theories" of Maoism, Trofimova has pointed out the fallacy of both the Maoist doctrine of development in "waves" or "leaps" (which the Chinese are selling abroad) and the Maoist interpretation of self-reliance, which "precludes cooperation with socialist countries."

[10] B. Zanegin, "The Failure of Peking's Foreign Policy," Izvestiia, May 23, 1968, p. 2, reprinted in Current Digest of the Soviet Press, 20, no. 21 (1968): 5–7 (hereafter cited as CDSP).

[11] Wang Ming, China: Cultural Revolution or Counter-Revolutionary Coup? (Moscow: Novosti Press Agency Publishing House, 1969), p. 67.

[12] Kudriavtsev, op. cit.

countries back into the embraces of the same foreign monopolies.[13]

d. Chinese harping on the alleged readiness of developing nations for revolutionary action and violent uprising is, say the Soviets, "in fact . . . irresponsible adventurism."[14]

e. The question of who is encircling whom is predictably answered by the Soviets with charges of Sino-U.S. collusion in Southeast Asia. The Soviets throw complicity with the German Federal Republic into the bargain gratis.[15]

Third, the Chinese pretension to know the peoples of Asia, Africa, and Latin America better than the "European" Soviets is combatted by Moscow with the charge of racism. While posing as champions of oppressed peoples of all colors, the Chinese ruling circles savagely oppress their own national minorities, tens of thousands of whom have had to take the drastic step of seeking refuge in the Soviet Union. Moreover, say the Soviets, China trades with South Africa and Rhodesia.[16]

Fourth, according to the Russians, China's eight-point charter of foreign economic relations (made public by Chou En-lai in Bamako, Mali, during his 1964 African tour) serves the end "of discrediting the disinterested assistance of the Soviet Union and of other socialist countries to young national states."[17] The eight points are a sham: deliveries of aid goods lag behind promises and contractual schedules; the technical level of plant and equipment supplied by China is low, well beneath world standards; Chinese-built factories are designed to make African industry dependent on Chinese raw materials; and so on.

Irresponsibility verging on paranoia, recklessness, a certain primitivism (political as well as technical), obtuseness, unreliability, chauvinistic arrogance wrongheadedness about the Leninist dynamics of history, hypocrisy, and poverty—these are the leitmotivs of the Soviet

[13] *Ibid.*

[14] *Ibid.* The exceptions are Yemen, Sudan, and other places where the correct historical timing for such revolutionary action and violent uprising is divined in Moscow.

[15] Zanegin, *op. cit.* See also Ernst Henry [pseud.], "Bonn-Peking?" *Literaturnaia gazeta*, April 10, 1968, p. 14, and April 17, 1968, p. 15.

[16] For example, see A. Mirov, "Sinkiang Tragedy," *ibid.*, May 7, 1969, p. 15; and G. Rakhimov, "Troubadours of Chauvinism—Maoists Oppress Small Nationalities," *Komsomolskaia pravda*, May 20, 1969, p. 3. On China's trade with South Africa and Rhodesia, see V. Shurygin, "Peking Finds Partners," *Pravda*, June 23, 1969, p. 5; Radio Moscow (June 7, 1971) claimed that deals worth $15 million were concluded between China and South Africa in the first few months of 1971. In 1970, China bought from South Africa gold worth $70 million. *U.S.S.R. and Third World*, 1, no. 6 (June 2–July 4, 1971): 333.

[17] *Izvestiia*, July 12, 1964, cited by Kovner, *op. cit.* The text of the Charter may be found in *PR*, August 21, 1964, p. 16.

attack on Chinese economic efforts in the developing nations. The intensity and density of Soviet verbal output on the subject vary with changes in the political climate in China and the corresponding fluctuations in Chinese assaults on the Soviet Union. But the themes remain the same, and the most basic of them all is China's challenge to Soviet know-how. The mutual recriminations on the subject of aid are, of course, parts of a much larger dispute, the substance of which I cannot go into here.[18] Given the emotionalism and the injured pride, one cannot expect the logic that underlies the Soviet and Chinese arguments to be unimpeachable. The aesthetic level of the verbal exchanges has been quite low. However, as both the Chinese and the Soviets have said, "people will judge their real friends not by their words but by their deeds." This pragmatic reflection imposes on the combatants a certain restraint in the actual implementation of their aid policies. A lot of investment in plant and good will may be lost by a single rash move. The loss is not necessarily irretrievable; it can be made good by the subsequent costly unruffling of feathers and the massaging of nationalist hurt egos—but it is both bothersome and expensive.[19]

For the developing nations the Sino-Soviet quarrel is both a dilemma and an opportunity. The first consists in the delicate problem of how to take sides without getting involved. The acuteness of the dilemma seems to be inversely proportional to the geographical distance which separates a developing nation from the disputants, but the rule is not foolproof. The opportunity lies in turning the quarrel to one's own

[18] A short bibliography of the Sino-Soviet dispute is as follows: G. R. Hudson, R. Lowenthal, and R. MacFarquhar, *The Sino-Soviet Dispute* (New York: Praeger, 1961); David Floyd, *Mao against Khrushchev: A Short History of the Sino-Soviet Conflict* (New York: Praeger, 1963); William E. Griffith, *Albania and the Sino-Soviet Rift* (Cambridge, Mass.: M.I.T. Press, 1964); Robert C. North, *Moscow and Chinese Communists* (Stanford: Stanford University Press, 1963); Klaus Mehnert, *Peking and Moscow* (New York: Mentor Books, 1964); *The Polemic on the General Line of the International Communist Movement* (Peking: Foreign Languages Press, 1965); Harrison E. Salisbury, *War between Russia and China* (New York: Bantam Books, 1970); Walter C. Clemens, Jr., *The Arms Race and Sino-Soviet Relations* (Stanford: Hoover Institution, 1968); Jan S. Prybyla, *The Political Economy of Communist China* (Scranton, Pa.: International Textbook Co., 1970), chaps. 3, 8, 10.

[19] It is reasonable to see in China's 1971 $30 million loan offer to Ceylon conscience money for Chinese-sponsored excesses in Ceylon during the Cultural Revolution. The loan, described by H. A. Gynesekera (Ceylon's minister of planning) as unprecedented for his country "in the annals of economic assistance," was to be given in pounds sterling, a generous gesture on the part of China. It was repayable in twelve years after a three-year grace period. There was no interest. Concurrently, Peking condemned terrorist activity in Ceylon (which had been linked to China), cut the ribbons on the Bandaranaike Memorial International Conference Hall in Colombo, and made assurances that it opposed both ultraleft and right-opportunist violence.

advantage. The eagerness of each side to the dispute to find fault with the conduct of the opponent and to curry favor with the recipients of aid presents the developing nations with some slight leverage and a margin for maneuver. How to use both without offending either side, however, is in itself a dilemma.. It calls for Machiavellian skills, moderation, patience, and other attributes (including a good grip on one's own society), which are not always the most notable attributes of leaders of newly independent states. Apart from living by their wits, the developing nations have little in the way of tangible means with which to pressure the two hardened poker players.

## III

To clear the decks for a comparative study of Soviet and Chinese aid programs in the developing world, one other issue should be laid to rest. There is an interesting concordance of timing. Both the Soviet Union and China began to trade actively with the developing nations and got their aid going at about the same time: the Soviets in 1954, the Chinese in 1956. The role played in this decision by the deteriorating relations between China and Russia has probably been more important in the case of the latter, although, at the time, the Chinese move was widely interpreted as one more emulation of the Soviet example, a sign of international socialist solidarity. With the wisdom of hindsight, one can now say that by mid-1956 it had become abundantly clear to many Chinese leaders that the long-range prospects for cooperation with Stalin's successors were dim unless China was willing to accept a by-product status within the socialist commonweal, like Bulgaria or Czechoslovakia. This, quite understandably, the Chinese were not about to do. China's sudden leap into foreign economics may thus be partly explained as an attempt to stake out independent positions in the outside world, given Peking's pessimistic appraisal of the future course of Sino-Soviet fraternization. The material means available to do this job were, and remain, exiguous. However, with a careful husbanding and geopolitical distribution of resources, the odds were good that the symbol-planting insurance operation would bring in compensation over the long run. All this should not be interpreted to mean that the growing stress on Sino-Soviet relations in the mid-fifties was the key influence on the decision of both China and the Soviet Union to emerge from the Stalinist cocoon. It would have happened anyway—"objectively," as the Marxists say—but it would probably have happened later and more slowly, especially where China was concerned. The looming rift simply speeded things up. Neither the Soviet Union nor China could have for long passed up the opportunities presented by the rotting away of Western colonial empires in Asia and Africa. The U.S.S.R. especially (but China too) "believes that it is entitled to a far greater measure of participation in the evolution and management of the nation-state system lying beyond its immediate borders. The belief is nourished by increments in power, by the nature of great power rivalries, and by the economic needs of an expanding industrial society."[20] The release of economic energy was facilitated in Russia by the demise of the dictator and the completion of postwar industrial reconstruction. It was spurred by restlessness and dissatisfaction with Stalinist rates of capital accumulation on the Soviet Union's European periphery (Berlin in 1953, Warsaw and Budapest in 1956). Domestic circumstances also affected the Chinese decision to "lean to all sides" in the international economic field, although the new approach was not formally given a name until the open break with the Soviet Union in 1960. China's First Five-Year Plan was nearing a generally gratifying end; socialization of industry, trade, and agriculture had been completed; and—at least from the fall of 1956 through the spring of the following year—a pragmatic spirit informed domestic policies. All these considerations had a hand in China's and Russia's respective openings to the underdeveloped south.

## IV

In spite of the profusely advertised differences between the Soviet and Chinese approaches to the developing nations, there exist in practice wide areas of tacit agreement and complementarity in the two antagonists' aid programs.

In practice, the Chinese are not, all things considered, so reckless and pyromaniac as the Soviets picture them, nor are the Russians so grasping and grossly calculating as the Peking press would have us believe—although both do have their moments.[21] While the verbal noise level has risen since aid began in the mid-fifties, both sides have perceptibly come to terms with the size and complexity of the developmental problem and with the limited capacity of any one country, however rich, to make an appreciable dent in that problem. More important, there seems to be in Moscow and Peking a good deal of cold-blooded realism about the political and economic benefits which the donor may expect to draw from aid, and about the short-run costs in-

[20] Alvin Z. Rubinstein, "Soviet Policy toward the Third World in the 1970's," *Orbis*, 15 (1971): 107.

[21] I am talking here of overt, "legitimate" aid, not of the parallel efforts in the developing nations expended by the intelligence departments of both Russia and China, or of any aid-giver for that matter. The two policies have been known to be at odds.

volved in the deal. Although both the Soviet Union and China relish fluid situations beyond the borders of their respective spheres of influence, they have learned in places such as Ghana, Cambodia, and Indonesia that fluidity may go either way. The Soviets are the more dogged but slow learners; they have had the benefit of a geographically more varied experience, larger sums laid on the line, and, in the last few years, a comparatively free-wheeling discussion of the subject in professional literature. The Chinese, hamstrung since 1966 by Chairman Mao's thoughts on this and other matters, and made to execute periodic summersaults of socialist consciousness, have nonetheless digested the message of practical experience and—since the end of the Cultural Revolution—have made proof of hard-nosed pragmatism in their dealings with the developing nations and the Soviet economic presence (or lack of it) in those nations. In spite of provocative flourishes, incendiary language, heroic posturings, Mao buttons, and the lot, they have managed to keep their feet planted in foreign soil right through the cultural upheaval at home. Poverty has been their ally. The high jinks of resident Chinese technicians, advisers, and others have tended to be argued away in Bamako, Dar es Salaam, and elsewhere as a passing, if recurring, disorder of the poor-on-the-make. Moreover, there has always been the prospect of wrenching hard currencies and other desirables from Western legislatures as soon as things were patched up with the Chinese revolutionaries. The prospects have improved whenever the mending process has been extended to the Soviets.

These general reflections are made by way of bringing balance to the inflammatory sentiments recorded in section II of this essay. "Paper," the late Josip Vissarionovich once remarked, "will put up with anything written on it."[22] That these reflections are grounded in fact will, I think, be brought out by an analysis of the data, which follows.

## V

In order not to dam up the stream of argument, the data have been put in the appendices. It is symptomatic of the kind of problem I am faced with that elementary economic arithmetic on what is actually going on is harder to come by these days than *ex cathedra* pronouncements on what goes on. One has to dig deeply into Soviet and Chinese security complexes to get an inkling of the aid picture (the Chinese complex is psychiatrically perfect: no figures are systematically re-

[22] Or, "as the saying goes, 'harsh words will break no bones.'" This gem of folk wisdom comes from G. Arbatov, "The Forthcoming U.S.-China Summit Meeting: Questions Demanding Practical Answers," *Pravda,* August 10, 1971.

leased),[23] and delve into the less than scientific statistical manuals published with a lag by the emerging nations. In this and the subsequent sections I will try to interpret the appendix data from the standpoint of their relevance to the Sino-Soviet dispute.

There is, first of all, the question of magnitude. The simplest thing to spot is, of course, the smaller Chinese aid contribution, a fact which is almost self-explanatory. However, when they think it worth the trouble, the Chinese can come up with tidy sums—for railroad construction, for example. The obvious smallness of China's contribution should be qualified in several less-obvious respects.

First, the types of projects for which China makes loans are comparatively "cheap"—that is, they are labor intensive and employ traditional (capital-saving) techniques. A good part of the capital needed for the execution of the projects is improvised along the way from all sorts of *moyens de bord*. I have in mind here China's road and railway building activities, agricultural melioration ventures (experimental tea, cotton, rice, and rubber plantations), and public health schemes, the last using a mixture of Western and Chinese traditional medicine and a *Feltscher* (or barefoot doctor) approach to health problems in the countryside. There has been a good deal of receptivity in the beneficiary states to this kind of development on the cheap.[24] On the other hand, as was noted in section II (and the Soviets do not deny it), an overwhelming majority of Soviet aid schemes are capital intensive and industry (especially heavy industry) oriented.[25] The Aswan dam, the Bhilai and Bakaro steel mills, the heavy engineering works at Ranchi, oil refineries at Barauni and Koyiali—all in India—and lead and zinc dressing plants (for example, at El Abed, Algeria) are representative of the projects for which the Soviets are best known. Naturally, the sums required will be considerably larger than those needed to dig

[23] The New China News Agency makes public from time to time figures on China's aid offers. These, however, are meager pickings.

[24] The one important exception to the general run of Chinese projects is the heavy mechanical complex at Taxila, near Islamabad, Pakistan. On the distinction between infrastructure and import-substitution schemes and those the products of which pay for aid, see the text below.

[25] The percentage distribution of Soviet economic and technical aid for 1954–1970 was:

| | |
|---|---|
| Industry and power projects | 68.7 |
| Agriculture | 6.2 |
| Transport and communications | 10.0 |
| Geological prospecting | 10.0 |
| Education, culture, public health, sports | 4.2 |
| Housing and municipal economy | 0.4 |
| Other | 0.5 |

Sergeyev, *op. cit.*, p. 30. "Over one half of Soviet aid goes to the construction of enterprises in heavy industry." *Ibid.*, p. 26.

artesian wells, plant rice, and stick needles into the natives. Point eight of the Bamako Charter says that experts sent by China to the aided nations are to live a life the level of which is no higher than that of local technicians. There is no doubt that the cost of the recipients of Chinese technical advice is substantially below the cost of Soviet technical assistance. There is also evidence that the quality of Chinese advice is good, if not consistently so.[26]

Rather than pick—as the Soviets and Chinese are doing—on the unsuitability for the recipient states of this or that project sponsored by the other side, it is more sensible to look at Soviet and Chinese aid efforts as being in many ways complementary. The dovetailing is brought about unwittingly and unwillingly and it has its limits; but it is there. Chinese material aid and advice focus on agriculture, geological prospecting, light industry, road and rail transportation, and public health. The Soviets specialize in heavy and extractive industries, especially metallurgy, machine tool manufacture, power generation and transmission, oil extraction and processing, and coal mining. With few exceptions, Chinese projects tend to be small or medium-sized (textile mills, tannery plants, cigarette and match factories, dry docks for re-

---

[26] According to Radio Moscow (in English for South and Southeast Asia, June 26, 1971),

> in addition to everything, the effectiveness of [Chinese] aid is, in practice, very low. In a number of developing countries where China gave aid in building heavy industry enterprises, as in Pakistan, Cambodia, and others, there were numerous claims made in regard to the quality of the equipment supplied and the production technology. Now, this is not surprising, since the present technical level of China's own industry is such that many experts believe it is hardly in a position to render highly qualified assistance in developing heavy industry.

Moreover, the specialists and workers sent from China to work on aid projects "engaged in propaganda and subversive activities." U.S.S.R. and Third World, 1, no. 6 (June 2–July 4, 1971): 286. Compare this with Radio Lusaka (Zambia), June 29, 1971: "The Chinese in Tanzania and elsewhere prefer to keep themselves very much to themselves. They live together in camps and settlements which few Africans can penetrate. But then the Chinese are deep thinkers, and it is possible that they have decided to pour out aid while at the same time adopting a very low profile regarding politics." U.S.S.R. and Third World, 1, no. 6 (June 2–July 4, 1971): 336. A special correspondent of the London Financial Times reported: "One South Yemeni official told me: 'They [the Chinese road construction crews] have made a very good reputation for themselves as road builders. . . . Their methods are simple, effective, and fast. They are very suitable for countries with scant capital resources.'" China Trade and Economic Newsletter, February 1971, p. 2. Chinese specialists, according to H. Y. Mawle, Zambia's minister of state, "not only work hard, but also pass their technical knowhow to Zambian workers and teach them how to master it." Ibid., January 1971, p. 6. There has also been much patting on the back of Chinese medical teams in various African nations. However, on September 9, 1970, Radio Lusaka (Zambia) complained that the Chinese medical team was not up to Zambian medical registry standards. Far Eastern Economic Review, November 7, 1970, p. 6.

pairing small boats), while the Soviets go in for large-scale projects, but no longer with the old cost-discounting gusto. Careful feasibility studies are now an accepted prelude to Soviet (and increasingly to Chinese) aid commitments. The precise criteria of what is considered feasible differ as they must, but the precondition applies to both Soviet and Chinese aid offers. Soviet studies since the mid-sixties have tended to be oriented toward uncovering economically well-founded schemes, a concept which includes comparative labor cost advantages for the U.S.S.R.[27] I will return to this subject later.

The figures in the appendices represent commitments. Disbursements typically run well below offers: about 60 percent below for Russia and a little less than 70 percent below for China. The reasons are to be sought not just in inflated promises and tight fists when it comes to deliveries. Many potential beneficiaries are often unable to come up with the domestic resources (skilled labor, for one) that are needed to get the aid projects going, or to pay for local costs. This difficulty is not lessened by erratic shipments, faulty assortments, and cost overruns, which reflect parallel situations in the two donor nations.[28] However, the fact that the Soviets normally give only about two-fifths of what they promise, and the Chinese one-third at best, does not invalidate my first observation: that Chinese assistance is much leaner than Soviet aid. It merely brings it down to a lower plane. Nor does it alter the argument about the dialectical complementarity of efforts. But it is sobering to know that all the noise and

[27] In their professional literature the Soviets have in recent years moved away from their earlier view that capital formation was the *sine qua non* of economic development, a universally valid first principle. They now tend to stress the partial substitution of labor resources for capital and training of qualified personnel. In this respect they appear to have converged with Chinese aid practice. However, Soviet writers still regard the direction of quantitative development as of paramount importance, the direction being the old Soviet one (industry, especially heavy industry). See David Morison, "U.S.S.R. and Third World: III. Questions of Economic Development," *Mizan*, 12, no. 3 (December 1970): 127. The concept of labor cost advantage and the need for aid projects to promote the Soviet Union's political aims have been openly mentioned in both the professional literature and official statements since 1962. Given the Soviet Union's indecision about how far economic principles may be allowed to penetrate an administratively run economy, it is not surprising that the notion of what is economically rational or "well founded" remains fluid and indeterminate at present. See L. Sirc, "Changes in Communist Advice to Developing Countries," *World Today*, August 1966; and Elizabeth K. Valkenier, "Recent Trends in Soviet Research on the Developing Countries," *World Politics*, July 1968.

[28] One example will have to do. A report issued by the Indian Parliamentary Committee on Public Undertakings (April 1969) noted that Soviet experts had tremendously underestimated the production costs in the Soviet-aided Indian Drugs and Pharmaceuticals Ltd. project. Vitamin $B_1$, the experts thought, would cost 100 rupees per kilogram. In fact, the cost has turned out to be 1,200 rupees per kilogram.

rudeness is really about piddling magnitudes: for example, $2 billion (Soviet) and $200 million (Chinese) over a ten-year period, or a joint competitive exertion of $220 million a year spread over two continents. The worst quarrels are usually played out at the nerve ends, ostensibly over marginal issues. Economic aid is no exception. For $220 million you could give 110 million Russian women a shampoo and set (no extras) once a year, or buy 3.7 billion U.S.S.R. postage stamps (letter, domestic).

The Soviet gibe that China does not—because it cannot—give enough rests on doubtful moral foundations. Soviet aid transfers (the gross of repayments on earlier loans) average out at about 0.05 percent of the Soviet GNP. Chinese annual expenditures on foreign aid run below 0.01 percent of China's estimated GNP. The Soviets would probably agree that, cast in these terms, the comparison is not all that favorable to them and that it would be best to keep it under wraps. The Russians and their East European allies contend that the 1968 recommendation of the United Nations Conference on Trade and Development (UNCTAD II) to the effect that each developed nation should annually transfer 1 percent of its GNP to the developing nations, does not apply to them: "the Socialist countries have never exploited and do not exploit developing countries and, therefore, do not and cannot have any moral or material responsibility for the economic backwardness of the countries of Asia, Africa, and Latin America."[29] To this the Colombian delegate replied that the socialist states were buying coffee from his country at 40 cents a pound and retailing it at 4 dollars a pound.

There is a subtle convergence here, in spite of the Soviets' fuming about China's rash (anti-Soviet) export to the developing nations of her pull-yourself-up-by-your-own-bootstraps doctrine and the smallness of her aid. It has been described by some outraged beneficiaries as a coming together in stinginess, but that is too facile. (Spokesmen for some developing nations do tend once in a while to have an exagger-

[29] Joint statement by delegations of the U.S.S.R., Bulgaria, Czechoslovakia, Hungary, and Poland at the UNCTAD Trade and Development Board's ninth session, February 14, 1970. The same sentiments were expressed in a letter addressed to the secretary general of the United Nations on September 23, 1970, by the above states plus Mongolia. The Ethiopian delegate to the 1969 UNCTAD Committee on Aid noted that "not all market economy countries which were participating in development work had helped to create the present situation." Sins of commission by some Western nations were thus being compounded by sins of omission by the socialist nations. In 1968 alone the *net flow* of aid resources (strictly defined as government funds made available on concessional terms) from non-Communist developed nations to the Third World amounted to $6.4 billion. This is the same order of magnitude as total Soviet *offers* of aid from 1954 through 1969. The Soviet net flow during that whole period was well below $2.7 billion.

ated idea of the amounts of help they are entitled to receive and of the developed nations' moral responsibility toward them, either because of past wrongs inflicted or by virtue of the simple definition of poverty.) The Soviets and the Chinese both believe that development cannot be imported wholesale. They share the view that the onus rests with the underdeveloped themselves. They feel that foreign aid must pass the twin test of supplementing domestic efforts and benefiting the donor—politically, economically, or both. The Chinese express this "sincerely" in the self-reliance thesis, which, they say, has worked for them. The Soviets, after paying the ritual homage to equal rights, mutual advantage, and noninterference in others' internal affairs, imply very much the same thing as the Chinese. The point of convergence is found in what may best be described as the "capacity argument."[30] The Chinese argue from absolute capacity ("we have done as much as our capacity permits"); the Soviets argue from the margin of a more complex capacity, where opportunity costs have to be closely computed. Aid, the Soviets say, does not come from any sort of dumping of surpluses, but from the very economic guts of the donor. Assistance that is not well justified economically may adversely affect the growth rate of the socialist states, which hold the key to the future. The Soviets—and this is what the Chinese seize upon in their attacks—push their logic as far as accepting coexistence with Western capital for a more or less indeterminate future. The Chinese settle for it in fact, largely because they cannot do much about it, but they make up for the concession with verbal abuse.[31] At a juncture in history when, despite appearances, the possibility of a Sino-Soviet accommodation cannot be excluded, these underlying similarities in Soviet and Chinese positions on developmental aid acquire, it would seem, a special relevance and importance.

Another way in which the Chinese manage to make a little money

[30] The argument starts with some U.N. estimates. These show that, if the developing nations managed to push their GNP growth to 5–6 percent a year while keeping their population increase down to 1–2 percent a year, they would by the year 2000 reach about one-half of the present average West European GNP level, and about one-fifth of the present American level. Since neither Western Europe nor the United States is likely to stand still, the gap in the year 2000 will probably be wider than it is today.

[31] "The developing countries justly demand that the capitalist states and international financial organizations increase the flow of their capital on conditions which meet the interests of the young states." N. Semin, "Equal and Mutually Profitable Cooperation," *Kommunist*, no. 14 (1968), p. 76. "In present-day conditions the flow of foreign capital is objectively essential for the majority of the developing countries. It is naive to think that 'with a Leftist phrase' and by verbal revolutionizing one can achieve the overthrow of imperialism in the West and redistribution of existing resources in the interests of the peoples of the three continents, as they hope in Peking." Tiul'panov, *op. cit.*, pp. 137–38.

go a long way is in the terms on which their aid is offered. Because here both Sino-Soviet competition and togetherness show up succinctly, I will devote a separate section to the subject.

## VI

I have already noted the curious dialectical composition of what on the surface appear to be differences between Soviet and Chinese foreign economic moves. Each apparent difference contains within itself a germ of its opposite. This should naturally warm the cockles of Marxist hearts, yet, judging from the reactions of the two contestants, it does not.

The socialist (Marxist-Leninist) philosophy of foreign aid lays down that grants corrupt the giver and the receiver because gifts inject a superior donor–inferior client element into the relationship between the aider and the aided. Grants may be given in cases of particular distress (plagues, droughts, floods, and the like), but on the whole they should be used sparingly. Besides, such philosophy saves money. Overtly, both the Soviets and the Chinese adhere to this formulation. Over time, grants have constituted a much smaller share of total socialist aid than has been the case with, say, U.S. assistance. However, grants *sensu stricto* accounted for a larger portion of total Chinese aid (roughly 20 percent) than of Soviet assistance (about 5 percent), at least until the mid-sixties. One reason was that Chinese projects were more intimately involved with the soil (hence with the elements), as well as with public health, and thus some of the grants went for drought, flood, and epidemic relief. Budgetary support also played a part. Since the mid-sixties there has been a shift toward loans as an even more dominant vehicle of Chinese aid.

In addition to outright gifts, there is a concealed grant element in Chinese loans that is absent from parallel Soviet efforts. The majority of Chinese long-term loans are interest-free, while similar Soviet credits usually carry an interest rate of 2.5 percent. This interest, the Soviets argue, gives the transactions a "businesslike" touch, without imposing on the debtor. In recent years the Soviet Union has increasingly resorted to shorter-term (from five to eight years) "commercial" credits, which carry a higher rate of interest (3.5–4.0 percent). Although repayment of principal and interest is usually deferred by the Soviets until completion of the aid project, interest begins to accumulate from the date the credit is drawn. The absence of interest charges and their corollaries constitutes the first particle of the grant element in Chinese loans. The second particle has to do with grace periods. The amortization period of the majority of Soviet credits is in the neighborhood of twelve years. No grace period is granted. As a rule, Chinese credits are repayable over ten years (but repayment periods of as much as twenty and thirty years have been negotiated—for example, with Tanzania, Yemen, and Pakistan), and there is normally a grace period of five years or more before repayment is due. This is hard to beat.[32]

There is also the question of the tying of assistance. One should distinguish between what may be termed "simple" and "advanced" tying. Simple tying means that loans and grants are extended for the purchase of goods and services (including technical assistance) in the aid-giving nation only. From the vantage point of the recipient, this in effect means import tying. Simple tying has been practiced by both the Soviet Union and China for reasons that are readily understandable and not necessarily grubby (shortage of foreign exchange, for example). It is a quite common procedure in intergovernmental credit relations.[33] Very few cash transfers are involved. (This, incidentally, has the added advantage of keeping a reign on an occasional compulsion to transfer aid monies into numbered personal accounts in Geneva.) In exceptional cases the U.S.S.R. and China have made loans and grants available in convertible currencies (for example, the 1956 Chinese grant to Egypt was made in Swiss francs, and part of the $200 million credit to Pakistan was reportedly extended in pounds sterling, as was apparently the whole 1971 $30 million loan to Ceylon). The Soviets have also given loans for the procurement of goods in East European states.

Advanced tying refers to the repayment of credits. Two degrees of advancement can be distinguished. While it is commonly specified that repayment is to be made in the commodities of the recipient state (or in local currencies),[34] the first, or lower, degree of advanced tying

[32] It is hard but not impossible. The Agency for International Development (AID), which handles an important part of U.S. assistance, has adopted a minimum forty-year amortization period, with a 2 percent interest rate in the grace period and 3 percent thereafter. A number of OECD nations have accepted an average twenty-five year amortization, with a seven-year grace period at 3 percent interest. In 1967 the average non-Communist loan terms for developing nations were a 23.4-year amortization period, a 5.3-year grace period, and 3.8 percent interest. Over 50 percent of Western aid to the developing nations is in the form of nonreturnable grants.

[33] About three-quarters of Western aid disbursements are tied in this way. Some 40 percent of this tied aid is in the form of outright grants. The Soviets, while practicing the very same thing, have charged that "China made wide use of credits to finance her own exports. According to some estimates, no less than one-third of Chinese credits are meant for these purposes. So it becomes quite obvious that the main purpose of the credits is to ensure widening of exports of Chinese goods to Asian and African markets." Radio Moscow (in English to South and Southeast Asia), June 26, 1971. On the validity of the Soviet charge, see the text below.

[34] There exist a number of agreements under the terms of which repayment of all or part of the loan must be made in convertible currencies.

means repayment in the recipient state's traditional exports (normally raw materials and agricultural produce, and often a single crop such as cotton). In this case the aid is directed toward the promotion of import-substitution projects (for example, cigarette and match factories, steel and textile mills) or social infrastructure (roads, railways, and power generation and transmission). The output of such projects is largely marketed in the recipient state. Over time the Soviet Union (and China too, despite its protestations) has moved toward the second, or higher, degree of repayment tying, one which in Soviet literature is described as "productive cooperation" or "international division of labor of a 'new' kind."[35] In this case the output of the aided project pays for the aid, and the deal itself is made after calculating comparative cost advantages. This is what Kosygin had in mind when at the Twenty-fourth Congress of the CPSU he referred to Soviet

> trade and cooperation . . . entering a stage where we may speak of firmly established, mutually advantageous economic ties. [Soviet] cooperation with [India, Afghanistan, Iran, Pakistan, the United Arab Republic, Syria, Iraq, Algeria, and others], based on principles of equality and respect for mutual interests, is acquiring the nature of a stable division of labor counterposed in the sphere of international economic relations to the system of imperialist exploitation.[36]

This is also what the Chinese have in mind when they attribute to the Soviets an "extremely absurd gangster logic," the object of which is to

[35] For example, E. Borisova *et al.*, eds., *Politekonomicheskii slovar'* (Moscow: Izdatel'stvo politicheskoi literatury, 1964), p. 143. Now, in Chinese eyes, the Soviets can do no right. When they engage in what I have called "first-degree advanced tying," they are accused by the Chinese of "doling out some cranky machines and arms to Asian, African, and Latin American countries [while they] plunder fabulous wealth from them, inflicting untold misery on the people of these countries." "Soviet Revisionist New Tsars Use Aid to Stretch Their Claws into Asia, Africa, and Latin America," *PR*, July 11, 1969, p. 24. "Ninety-five per cent of [the Soviet revisionists'] imported rubber and 92 per cent of imported cotton are carried off from Asia, Africa, and Latin America. Soviet revisionism covets petroleum in the Middle East, copper in Chile, tin in Bolivia, fruit and wine in North Africa, and meat in East Africa." *Ibid.*, p. 26. When the Soviets try second-degree advanced tying, they provide, for instance, " 'aid' for an Asian country to exploit natural gas with the harsh condition that three-quarters of the gas produced be supplied to the Soviet Union." *Ibid.* (The unnamed country is Afghanistan.) The Soviet Union, the Chinese say, has learned how to use second-degree advanced tying in Eastern Europe. There, and now elsewhere, "the Soviet revisionist clique has again and again ballyhooed that 'specialization and cooperation in production' is a 'higher form of socialist division of labor' which can 'accelerate socialist construction.' " In fact, say the Chinese, what the Soviet Union really wants is to turn the ballyhooed states into colonies. " 'Council for Mutual Economic Aid'—Soviet Revisionist Tool for Pushing Neo-Colonialism," *PR*, February 14, 1969, p. 16.

[36] Kosygin, *op. cit.*, pp. 73–74.

"control many vital economic sectors" in the recipient states (see section II above). Although the Chinese have so far concentrated their efforts on infrastructure and import-substitution projects, they, too, have resorted to advanced tying of the second degree, though admittedly on a more discreet scale. Examples of the principle of exporting a product to pay for the project are the Soviet-Afghan agreement of October 1963, under the terms of which the Soviet Union extended a 35 million ruble loan for the development of natural-gas resources and the construction of a pipeline to the Afghan-Soviet border (repayment of the loan was to be mainly in exported gas, some 58 billion cubic meters during 1967–1985); the Soviet credit to Uganda (1969) for the construction of a cotton-goods mill (the loan to be repaid with part of the mill's ouput); and the Soviet aid in building a fruit and vegetable cannery in Guinea. What galls the Chinese, although it does not seem to bother the recipients too much, is that this kind of "new" international division of labor calls for a sizable on-the-spot presence of Soviet advisers during the very process of the recipient states' domestic economic planning. Knowing what they are talking about, the Chinese argue that, with so many experts in such sensitive spots, the Soviets can undertake more than economic planning.

Connected with what I have described as "simple" tying (loans tied to the procurement of goods and services in the creditor state) is the question of motivation. As was noted earlier, the Soviets allege that the Chinese engage in this type of tying in order to stimulate their exports to Third World nations; the Chinese say that the Soviets do it in order to dump their obsolete ("cranky" is the word) machines on the underpriviledged and the unsuspecting, and, with the same gesture, to shrink their junk heaps at home. Even granting that both arguments contain a grain of truth, the fact remains that almost every nation undertakes simple tying and that the motivations are less murky than the Sino-Soviet dialogue suggests. There have been some complaints that with tied Chinese loans the recipient state could buy only towels, carpets, bicycles, glassware, Mao uniforms, and the like, in China, these items being the only ones that are competitive in price and quality by international standards.[37] There have also been reports from Tanzania of banjos, guitars, accordians, and pencils arriving from China as part of the tied-loan developmental package. Such things happen, but they are surely not typical. More interesting is the fact that the Soviet Union, rather than China, has so far used its credits to boost exports to the developing nations. Admittedly, the data on Chinese trade are

---

[37] Report of a Zambian trade mission to China, *China Trade Report,* February 1970, p. 25.

fragmentary, but the conclusion seems well founded.[38] When considering the absolute and relative smallness of China's trade with the developing nations, it should be remembered that China's merchant fleet
is tiny and old, the distances separating China from her African trading
partners are great, and recourse has to be had to the international
charter market, which is considerably expensive. Despite this, the
Chinese have managed to build for themselves a good reputation in
some places; their goods, such as textiles, simple consumer durables,
canned foods, cement, and tea, are welcomed on the old Japanese
principle of "cheap and good."

The Chinese, as was noted in section II, take pleasure in raising the
subject of Soviet price exploitation. The Soviets, they argue, buy cheap
and sell dear, like any revisionist worthy of his salt. Ever since the
1956 troubles in Eastern Europe (during which embarrassing facts
came to light about Soviet pricing policies), the Soviets have been
sensitive to such accusations and defensive on the subject. Taken out
of polemical framework, the problem of pricing in the foreign trade of
centrally planned economies is knotty and thorny.[39] The Chinese and
their trading partners are close-mouthed about their pricing practices,
but, for the record, Peking insists that there should always be a modi-
cum of "justice" to pricing. How exactly this desideratum is to be satisfied is not spelled out. At the first UNCTAD meeting (1964), complaints were made by emerging traders about the Soviet Union's "non-
equivalent exchange." The present Soviet position on the subject, a
hard but fairly realistic one, is expressed in the work by Tiul'panov.
"The expansion of foreign trade between the socialist and the developing countries," he has written, "is not to be achieved on an artificial
basis of 'just prices'—the unprofitability of relations of such kind would
put an end to any increase in trade exchanges—but rather on a normal
economic basis. Since the world capitalist market will for the foreseeable future maintain its predominant significance for the developing

[38] Exports of Soviet machinery to developing nations are almost fully financed
by Soviet credits. Such exports have accounted for about half the value of Soviet
sales to developing nations in recent years. By contrast, only about 10–15 percent
of Chinese exports to Third World states have in those years been credit-financed.
Malaysia is China's largest export market in the less-developed world; it has not
received any Chinese aid. Thus, the Soviet charges cited in note 33 are something
less than accurate. See Kovner, op. cit., pp. 615–16.

[39] See Franklyn D. Holzman, "Soviet Foreign Trade Pricing and the Question of
Discrimination," Review of Economics and Statistics, May 1962; Horst Mender-
hausen, "Terms of Trade between the Soviet Union and Smaller Communist Coun-
tries, 1955–1957," ibid., May 1959; idem, "The Terms of Soviet Satellite Trade:
A Broadened Analysis," ibid., May 1960; and Jan S. Prybyla, "Eastern Europe and
Soviet Oil," Journal of Industrial Economics, 13, no. 2 (March 1965).

countries, it is it which will determine the prices for goods."[40] The Chinese, of course, maintain that Soviet export prices to developing nations are above the going world market prices.

Again, according to the terms by which trade is conducted and aid is offered, there seems to be a core of commonality and complementarity between China and the Soviet Union, a core which is befogged by surface differences and the political noise of the dispute. Egged on by their respective propaganda departments, Chinese and Soviet polemicists do their level best to uncover each other's improprieties and issue dire warnings to those who in the meanwhile are benefiting from the rival's aid.

## VII

The metaphor of the poker players was used earlier in connection with the slight leeway which the Sino-Soviet dispute offers Third World nations. There is one instance in which Soviet and Chinese bidding took on all the trappings of a poker game, and it is worth noting.

In the months preceding the (eventually aborted) second conference of Afro-Asian countries—labeled a "solidarity" conference and, after much haggling, scheduled for June 1965 in Algiers—the Soviet Union and China fell over themselves to pay for what were thought to be forthcoming uncommitted votes. The episode bore some resemblance to old city ward politics. The Chinese at that time were doing their best to keep the Soviets out of the meeting because the Soviets were not Asians ("whites have nothing to do here"), and the Soviets were as strenuously trying to get in. Table 10-1 traces the bidding sequence.[41] Interesting though it is, this particular scramble, spiced with bribes, should not be generalized beyond its time. It occurred at a moment of great polemical tension between the two powers and tended to be seen in both Moscow and Peking as a crucial test of influence. Some of the monies promised were, in the event, never disbursed or at best were paid out in part (for example, to Ghana and Indonesia). When tempers settle at more normal temperatures, the competitive element in aid offers becomes less clear (at least it is more demure), and the pace at which aid commitments are entered into is more relaxed.

[40] Tiul'panov, *op. cit.*, pp. 169–70.
[41] For this discussion I am indebted to Marshall I. Goldman, *Soviet Foreign Aid* (New York: Praeger, 1967), pp. 188–90.

Table 10-1

Soviet and Chinese Aid Offers in the Months Preceding Bandung II

| Recipient | Date | Loan Amount (in millions of dollars) | Offered by |
|---|---|---|---|
| Afghanistan | June 1964 | 39 | U.S.S.R. |
|  | March 1965 | 28 | P.R.C. |
| Algeria | September 1963 | 100 | U.S.S.R. |
|  | October 1963 | 50 | P.R.C. |
|  | May 1964 | 128 | U.S.S.R. |
| Cambodia | November 1964 | 12 | U.S.S.R. |
|  | November 1964 | 10 | P.R.C. |
| Ceylon | February 1964 | 4 | P.R.C. |
| Congo (B) | December 1964 | 9 | U.S.S.R. |
|  | 1964 | 5 | P.R.C. |
|  | 1965 | 20 | P.R.C. |
| Ghana | February 1964 | 22 | P.R.C. |
| Indonesia | 1964 | 50 | P.R.C. |
|  | 1965 | 16 | P.R.C. |
| Iran | July 1963 | 39 | U.S.S.R. |
| Iraq | March 1965 | 140 | U.S.S.R. |
| Kenya | 1964 | 3 | U.S.S.R. |
|  | 1964 | 18 | P.R.C. |
|  | 1965 | 10 | P.R.C. |
| Pakistan | July 1964 | 70 (?) | U.S.S.R. |
|  | 1964 | 60 | P.R.C. |
|  | 1965 | 40 | P.R.C. |
| Senegal | November 1964 | 7 | U.S.S.R. |
| Somalia | August 1963 | 22 | P.R.C. |
|  | January1965 | 3 | P.R.C. |
| Tanzania | June 1963 | 46 | P.R.C. |
|  | August 1964 | 42 | U.S.S.R. |
| Turkey | April 1964 | 168 | U.S.S.R. |
| U.A.R. | May 1964 | 277 | U.S.S.R. |
|  | 1964 | 80 | P.R.C. |
|  | 1965 | 18 | P.R.C. |
| Uganda | December 1964 | 15 | U.S.S.R. |
|  | 1965 | 15 | P.R.C. |
| Yemen | March 1964 | 72 | U.S.S.R. |
|  | May 1964 | 29 | P.R.C. |
| Zambia | February 1964 | 0.5 | P.R.C. |

The bidding revealed by Table 10-1 raised Soviet and Chinese aid offers to levels not reached until then or since. In 1964 alone, when the game was at its closest, Communist aid commitments reached the unprecedented figure of $1.7 billion.[42] After things went sour with the conference (and with Ghana and Indonesia), retrenchment came into vogue.

[42] This figure includes East European contributions.

## VIII

The geopolitical distribution of Soviet and Chinese aid and trade should be mentioned, if only because it has a bearing on the absolute and relative size of each nation's effort.

While the Soviet Union and China give developmental assistance to about 40 nations (compared to some 100 that are receiving Western aid), the bulk of Soviet and Chinese aid is concentrated in a small number of nations. China's major clients are Pakistan, Ceylon, and (off and on) Burma in Asia, Egypt and the Yemens in the Middle East, Guinea (and, off and on, Mali) in West Africa, and Tanzania in East Africa. Help for the Palestinian guerrillas has been provided via Iraq. China's commercial ventures in Latin America have been quite marginal so far, and have been limited in recent years to commodity trade agreements with Chile and Peru.[43] (The Soviets recently made a dent in this area by offering a commercial credit to Brazil.) Of a grand total of Soviet aid offers of roughly $6.8 billion (1954–1969), about three-quarters went to nine nations, led by India, the United Arab Republic, Iran, Afghanistan, and Indonesia. Because of the need to husband its as yet modest resources, China gives aid to fewer nations than does the U.S.S.R. In some instances, however (India is the best example), the reason for withholding aid is more political. In spite of the shifting pattern of relations and preferences, almost every nation that is presently receiving Chinese assistance has at one time or another also received aid from the Soviet Union. To this day there are many nations in which Soviet and Chinese aid programs coexist peacefully and, as has been seen, complement each other.

In the few nations which receive the bulk of Soviet aid, the tendency has been to concentrate on a few large projects, most of which represent the economies' "commanding heights." Until 1967, Chinese aid projects tended to be more scattered and numerous within the main beneficiary states. However, the trend is being reversed, and nowadays the Chinese, too, are prone to focus their assistance on one or two large projects, usually in the area of rail and road transport.

Both the U.S.S.R. and China give their assistance only to the beneficiary nations' state sector.

<hr>

[43] See Economist Intelligence Unit, *Quarterly Economic Review: China, Hong Kong, North Korea,* no. 3 (1971). For earlier Chinese trade contacts in Latin America, see "China and Latin America: Peking's Shopping Bag," *Economist,* October 10, 1964.

## IX

It is, I think, fair to say that the conclusions to which this review of Soviet and Chinese aid policies lead have emerged in the course of the survey. This absolves me from tedious repetition. However, one or two points may usefully be mentioned.

Perhaps the most salient conclusion is that the influence of the Sino-Soviet rift on the two state's aid and trade programs in the Third World has been quite marginal. According to an old Chinese saying, "there is much noise on the staircase, but nobody's coming down." The noise of the dispute has been deafening, but the polemicists' cacophony has not affected all that much the decision-makers' foreign economic policies. The Soviets did what they would have done anyway, as have the Chinese; and, while the mutual recriminations have shown a distinct trend toward greater irrationality, the two verbose contestants' aid policies have grown, if anything, more rational within each state's definition of that term. The temptation to cut off one's nose to spite the other man's face has been kept to a minimum. In China's case it has not been a linear progression, what with Big Leaps and Cultural Revolutions, but even these traumatic domestic experiences have had less of an impact on China's foreign economics than might have been expected. Perhaps the dispute has made both powers more sensitive to the political implications and potentialities of foreign aid. Certainly, at times, aid has been used to fashion those potentialities in a sense which was favorable to the respective bidders. The nervous tension of the propagandists has, now and then, communicated itself to policy-makers; it has speeded things up. But it is difficult to find conclusive proof of the commonly held belief that proletarian abuse has basically affected the substance of proletarian hard-headedness in matters of aid. Hence, the leeway for playing off one contestant against the other has not been very noticeable, except before Bandung II, and then only in the realm of aid promises.

On the whole, the developing nations have benefited from Soviet and Chinese interest in them by reason of the simple fact of multiplication of options. What is "economically well founded" for the economists of, say, AID or a multilateral agency of the U.N. is based on calculations that involve a certain type of economic theory. When these bankers turn you down, you can nowadays go to the Russians, whose notion of economic rationality is often different: sometimes more restrictive, at other times not. At any rate, it is possible to get an extra hearing and to add a dimension or two to the concept of an "economically well-founded" project (the Aswan dam comes to mind). Then, and not necessarily in that order, you can put your case before the Chinese, whose economics contain many criteria of rationality which are alien even to Soviet administrative economics. But one has to be circumspect about making the rounds. In short, the developing nations have, on balance, benefited, not only from the addition of Soviet and Chinese funds to the developmental pool, but from the concurrent broadening of the definition of economic rationality, provided, of course, they have been careful not to mortgage themselves to the point of political insolvency.

## Appendix 10-A

### Communist Offers of Economic Aid to Non-Communist Developing Nations, 1954–1969

*(millions of U.S. dollars equivalent)*

| Recipient Area | Offers by U.S.S.R. | Offers by E. Europe[c] | Offers by China | Total | Percentage |
|---|---|---|---|---|---|
| Africa | 1,015 | 445 | 350 | 1,810 | 16 |
| Asia | 2,955 | 835 | 485 | 4,275 | 39 |
| Latin America[a] | 210 | 415 | — | 625 | 6 |
| Middle East[b] | 2,505 | 1,535 | 160 | 4,290 | 39 |
| Total | 6,775 | 3,230 | 995 | 11,000 | 100 |
| Percentage | 62 | 29 | 9 | 100 | |

Source: *Radio Liberty Dispatch*, September 10, 1969.
[a] Excluding Cuba.
[b] Including the U.A.R.
[c] Excluding Yugoslavia.

Appendix 10-B

Communist (Soviet, East European,[a] Chinese) Economic Aid:
Main Recipients and Total Offers, 1954–1969[b]

(*millions of U.S. dollars at current prices*)

| Recipient | Total Offers | Percentage |
|-----------|--------------|------------|
| India | 1,965 (1) | 17.9 |
| Egypt | 1,810 (112) | 16.5 |
| Iran | 1,050 (0) | 9.6 |
| Indonesia[c] | 755 (124) | 6.9 |
| Afghanistan | 735 (28) | 6.7 |
| Syria | 450 (27) | 4.1 |
| Itaq[d] | 405 (?) | 3.7 |
| Turkey | 395 (0) | 3.6 |
| Parkistan[e] | 385 (100) | 3.5 |
| Brazil | 310 (0) | 2.8 |
| Algeria | 300 (52) | 2.7 |
| Total | 11,000 | 78.0 |

*Source*: As in Appendix A. The author's calculations of Chinese aid are based on New China News Agency reports, press releases, and recipient states' statistics.

[a] Except Yugoslavia.

[b] Chinese offers in parentheses.

[c] Aid projects suspended.

[d] 1971 Chinese loan of $40 million; 1967 Chinese loan of "Indeterminate" amount.

[e] 1970 Chinese loan of $200 million.

Appendix 10-C

Main Recipients of Chinese Aid, 1956–1971

*(aid offers in millions of U.S. dollars)*

| Recipient | Amount |
|---|---|
| Tanzania[a] | 391.5 |
| Pakistan[b] | 300.0 |
| Guinea[c] | 133.5 |
| Indonesia[d] | 123.6 |
| Burma[e] | 92.0 |
| Ceylon[f] | 80.0 |
| Cambodia | 59.4 |
| South Yemen | 57.0 |
| | 1,237.0 |

*Sources*: Partners' statistical manuals, press reports, and New China News Agency dispatches.

[a] Includes about $340 million offered in 1967 for the Tan-Zam railway. Estimates vary from $240 million to $388 million.

[b] Includes a $200 million offer reportedly made in 1970.

[c] Includes a reported 1970 loan offer of $100 million for the Mali-Guinea railway.

[d] Aid projects suspended; less than one-quarter of earlier offers had been used.

[e] About one-third of a 1961 loan offer of $84 million had actually been drawn by 1967, when offer expired.

[f] Includes $39 million offered in 1970 and 1971.

# INDEX

Aden, 166
Afghanistan, 45; Soviet Union and, 25,
26, 123, 124, 215, 221, 222, 285
Africa: Chinese inroads into, 51–52,
64–65; class struggle in, 74–76;
Communist influence in French
colonies of, 22–25; Communist
parties in, 39–40, 53, 58–59;
East European aid to, 67; East-West
competition over, 47, 51, 63, 77;
socialism in, 69–70, 72–74, 76;
Soviet attitude toward nationalism in,
51, 53, 54, 56, 61–62, 65, 66;
Soviet investments in, 229;
united African political movement
(1946), 22–23. See also individual
African nations
Afro-Asian People's Solidarity Organiza-
tion, 54, 68
Afro-Asian "solidarity" conference
(1965), 287
Agency for International Development
(AID), 283n
Agopian, G., 38
Agricultural development, 48, 229–30
Aidit, D. N., 98–99
Air routes, to developing nations,
231–32
Algeria, 45, 57, 166; Communist party
in, 39, 58; Soviet economic aid to,
235–36; and trade with Soviet Union,
68, 173, 221
Allende, Salvador, 191, 192, 194
Alvarado, Juan Velasco, 187
Anderson, Jack, on Bangladesh,
126n, 138n, 139 and n
Anti-Imperialist League, 12–13
Arab-Israeli War, foreign intervention
in, 156, 161, 164, 171–72, 232, 233
Arab Socialist Union, 162
Arbatov, Georgi A., 130
Argentina, 190
Arismendi, Rodney, 207

Asia: American influence-building in,
123; Soviet collective security system
for, 105–7. See also South Asia;
Southeast Asia; individual Asian
countries
Association of Southeast Asian Nations
(ASEAN), 81, 108, 109, 111;
Soviet attitude toward, 112–13
Attaturk, Kemal, 10
Australia, in five power defense
agreement (1971), 110, 111
Avakov, R., 44
Awami League, 128, 129, 135, 136

Baku Congress of Peasants and Workers
(1920), 6–7, 12
Bandung conference (1955), 54,
249–50
Bangladesh: Indo-Pakistani war over,
137–40; national liberation movement
in, 124–25, 136; negotiations over,
133–36
Barzani, Mullah Mustafa, 165
Baskin, V. S., 46
Beloff, Max, 15
Ben Bella, Ahmed, 39, 40, 51, 63
Biafra, 63
Bipolarity, in United Nations, 238, 243,
244, 247
Bolivia: Soviet Union and, 188–89;
U.S. and, 187
Bolshevik Revolution, 2, 5; effect of on
Indian nationalism, 121
Botswana, 66
Bourgeoisie, nationalism and, 17,
18–19, 33, 44, 54, 74, 93–94, 121,
122, 176
Brazil, Soviet Union and, 180, 182, 183
Brezhnev, Leonid, 105, 106, 107, 114,
175, 179, 194
Bukharin, Nilolai I., 3n, 12
Burma: China and, 82, 115, 118; Soviet
Union and, 57, 114–15

Burundi, 65

Calcutta Conference of Southeast
    Asian Youth (1948), 97
Cambodia: China and, 83, 114;
    Sihanouk's attempt at neutrality, 82;
    Soviet Union and, 83–84, 114
Caribbean Sea, naval power in,
    200–203, 212
Casablanca bloc, 57–58
Castro, Fidel: as model nationalist, 56,
    57, 58; relations of with U.S.,
    199–200; support for Allende by,
    197–98
Césaire, Aimé, 24
Ceylon, 44, 232; Chinese aid to, 273n
Chiang Kai-shek, 10
Chile: China and, 197; coalition of
    Communists and Socialists in, 191,
    194, 195; Communist party of,
    190, 195; Cuba and, 197–98;
    nationalization of property by, 191;
    political uncertainty in, 209, 211;
    Soviet Union and, 193–95, 196, 209,
    232; U.S. and, 192, 195–96,
    196–97, 201
China: Africa and, 51–52, 64–65;
    Asian sphere of influence policy of,
    115; Burma and, 12; Cambodia and,
    83; Ceylon and, 273n; cultural
    revolution in, 65, 68, 82, 88;
    D.R.V. and, 87–88; India and,
    122, 126, 142–44; Latin America and,
    204–5; nationalist movement in,
    10; Nixon's visit to, 81, 109;
    reaction of to Soviet aid to
    developing nations, 267–69,
    284–85; revolution in, 19–20; role
    of in United Nations, 255, 263;
    Soviet Union and, 129–31; Thailand
    and, 80, 81; U.S. and, 129–30, 213
Chou En-lai, 65
Claude, Inis, 242
Collective security system, 105–7, 114,
    134, 175
Colonialism: in Africa, 70–71;
    Comintern policy toward, 3, 6–7,
    10–12, 14; effect of Bolshevik
    Revolution on, 2–3; Lenin on, 3–4, 5;
    Marxist doctrine on, 5; national
    liberation movements and, 11, 16–18,
    79, 84, 87; Trotsky on, 3
COMECON, 243
Comintern
—anti-imperialist policy of 12–13
—colonial policy of, 3, 6–7, 9–12, 14
—congresses of: first, 3; second, 3, 6;
    third, 9; sixth, 11–12; seventh, 97, 98

—foreign trade policy of, 8–9
—Indonesian Communist party and,
    96–97, 98
—Manifesto of, 3
—nationalism and, 9–10, 97
Commercial fishing, Soviet policy
    toward, 233–34
—Communist parties: of Africa, 52,
    57–58, 62; of Algeria, 39; of Bolivia,
    186; of Chile, 191, 192; of China,
    131n; Congress of Eighty-one
    (1960), 32; of Egypt, 39; of France,
    24, 52; of Great Britain, 52; of
    India (CPI), 122, 147; of Indonesia
    (PKI), 86, 96, 97, 98, 101, 102, 103,
    104; of Peru, 186, 187, 188;
    of Philippines (PKP), 91, 92, 94, 95;
    proposed establishment in colonial
    areas, 11; role of in socialist regimes
    of developing nations, 39–40; Soviet
    attitude toward local, 4, 36, 176,
    209, 215; of Soviet Union (see
    Soviet Communist party); of Sudan,
    209n; of Syria, 163
Congo, 45, 57, 58
Corvalán, Luis, 196, 197
Costa Rica, 180, 190
CPSU. See Soviet Communist party
Cuba: Castro nationalism in, 56–58;
    Chile and, 197–98; Soviet Union and,
    56, 58, 199–202, 205–6, 232–33;
    U.S. and, 199–200; U.S.-Soviet
    relations and, 199, 201, 211
Cyprus, 156, 158

Dallin, David, 32, 240, 244
d'Arboussier, Gabriel, 22, 24
Degtiar, D., 231
Democratic Republic of Vietnam, 84;
    peace proposal (1971), 89–90;
    Sino-Soviet relations and, 87–89;
    Soviet Union and, 84, 87, 90
Developing nation. See Third World
    nations
D.R.V. See Democratic Republic of
    Vietnam

Economic aid. See Foerign aid to
    Third World nations
Education, of Third World students,
    61, 68
Egypt, 37, 57; and Arab-Israeli War,
    161, 171, 233; and collective security
    treaty with Soviet Union 175, 176;
    Communist party of, 39, 58;
    expulson of Soviet advisers from,
    66; industrialization policy of, 230;
    national democracy in, 57; Soviet

Union and, 1, 51, 63, 160–63, 171, 173, 175–76, 221, 223, 233; and Suez War (1956), 54; suppression of local Communists in, 41n; and union with Syria and Iraq, 170

Engels, Friedrich, 5

Ethiopia: feudalism in, 45; Italian invasion of, 14; Sino-Soviet competition in, 65

Fedorov, V., 79

Feudalism, in Africa, 73–74

Foreign aid to Third World nations
—amount of, Soviet versus Chinese, 279–80, 287–88, 291–93
—by China: Soviet attitude toward, 269–73, 380; types of projects financed, 277–79
—effect of Soviet-Chinese competition over, 266, 273–74, 290–91
—geopolitical distribution of, 289
—grant versus loan, 282–83
—pricing policy related to, 286
—purpose of, 281
—by Soviet Union: agricultural, 229–30; Chinese attitude toward, 267–69, 284–85; for industrial development, 217, 229–30; integration of with trade expansion, 219–20; investments, 145–46, 228–29; joint production of raw materials, 222–24; loans, 218, 225, 226; military assistance, 146, 150, 211–12, 231; political objectives of, 210, 215–16, 225, 266; technical assistance, 217; transportation development, 231–34; types of projects financed, 277–79
—tied loans, 283–84, 285
—by Western nations, 49–50, 283n

French Union, 24, 25

Friedman, L., 37, 41

Gabon, 66

Gandhi, Indira, 135–36, 137, 138, 147

Geopolitics, 120, 124, 127, 131; foreign aid and, 289

Germany, 2, 14

Ghana, 39, 58, 60; air route to Soviet Union, 231; independence of, 54; national democracy in, 45, 57; and trade with Soviet Union, 68

Gibert, Stephen, 258, 259, 260

Goodrich, Leland, 240

Gordon, L., 37, 41

Great Britain: in five-power defense agreement (1971), 110, 111; and trade relations with Soviet Union, 9

Guber, A. A., 16

Guerilla movements: in Cuba, 199; Huks, in Philippines, 91, 92–93; training of Mexicans for, 184; Tupamaros, in Uruguay, 204, 206–8

Guinea, 39, 58, 65; and air link with Soviet Union, 231; independence of, 55; and joint mining operations with Soviet Union, 222; national democracy in, 45, 57; and trade with Soviet Union, 55, 68, 223; Soviet aid to, 233, 285

Guyana, 180

Guzevatti, Ia, 48

Hatta, Muhammad, 97

Highways, foreign aid for building, 234

Hofmann, Stanley, 240–41

Houphouet-Boigny, Felix, 23, 24, 52

Huk movement, 91, 92–93

Ideology
—of developing nations, 39
—of Soviet Union: applied to African nations, 51, 59; changes in, 74–76, 185; effect of nationalism on, 65–66; effect of on policy toward Third World nations, 168–69; establishment of, 69; Khrushchev and, 69. See also Socialism, scientific

Imperialism: Bolsheviks on, 2, 5–6; Comintern on, 12–13; Lenin on, 1–2; renewed Soviet struggle against, following World War II, 18–20

India
—China and, 122, 124, 126, 142–44
—and claim to Portuguese enclaves, 121, 123
—industrialization policy of, 230
—integration of communism and nationalism in, 122
—national bourgeoisie in, 17, 44
—naval power of, 150
—role of in United Nations, 257–58
—Soviet Union and: air route between, 232; Indo-Soviet Treaty (1971), 115, 116, 131, 132–34; under Khrushchev, 121; relations of with Communist party of India, 122, 147; role of in Indo-Pakistani war (1971), 1, 136–40, 146–47; trade relations of, 146, 216, 221, 223, 224
—U.S. and, 126, 137, 138–40, 141
—and wars with Pakistan, 124, 129, 119n, 126, 127, 135–40, 146–47

Indonesia: attitude of toward "neutralization" policy, 109–10; China and, 101–3; and conflict with

Dutch over West New Guinea, 100; national democracy in, 57; reaction of to Soviet collective security proposal, 106; Soviet Union and, 16, 86, 96–105, 116–17, 232

Indonesian Communist party (PKI), 86; Comintern and, 96–97; effect of Sino-Soviet relations on, 101–2; rise of, 98; Suharto and, 103–4; Sukarno and, 98, 102

Indo-Pakistani wars: (1948), 124; (1965), 129; (1971), 119n, 126, 135–40, 146–47

Industrial development, of developing nations, 46–48, 50, 59, 230

International Monetary Fund, 230

International organizations, Soviet attitude toward, 238–41. See also United Nations

International Trade Union Committee of Negro Workers, 14

Investments, in developing nations, 145–46, 228

Iran: Soviet Union and, 25, 157, 159–60, 221, 235; U.S. and, 26, 159–60

Iraq, 44; and collective security treaty with Soviet Union, 175, 176; Kurdish nationalism in, 165; nationalization of petroleum resources in, 173; Soviet Union and, 164–66, 221; and union with Egypt and Syria, 170

Israel: and Arab-Israeli War, 156, 161, 164, 171–72; Soviet Union and, 169

Italy, Soviet trade with, 14–15

Ivory Coast, 66

Jordan, 166, 167

Kautsky, John, 18

Keita, Modibo: Lenin Peace Prize to, 57; overthrow of, 39, 40, 51, 63, 73; Soviet relations with, 62, 225

Kenyatta, Jomo, 53

Khan, Yahya, 128, 131, 135, 136, 139

Khrushchev, Nikita: cooperation of with African nations, 62, 67; on Marx, 69; on nationalism, 85, 168; peaceful coexistence and, 29–31, 54, 70; policy of toward developing nations, 42, 53–54, 87, 157, 219, 245, 252; on role of communism in developing nations, 33, 35n, 42; South Asia and, 27, 121; on United Nations, 254

Kissinger, Henry, 126, 129

Kosygin, A. N., 87, 88, 179, 220, 284

Kuala Lumpur, 79; declaration on

neutralization (1971), 108, 109, 111

Kudriavtsev, V., 112, 136, 269–71

Kurdish movement, 165

Laos, 117

Latin America
—China and, 204–5
—Communist front organizations in, 22
—guerilla movements in, 183, 204–8
—Soviet Union and: cultural and educational influence, 183–84, 208–9; diplomatic relations, 180; foreign aid, 209–12; intelligence operations, 183–84; military deployment, 200–203, 211, 212; political influence, 184–86; trade relations, 180–83, 209–10, 220
—U.S. and, 181, 182, 183
—U.S.-Soviet relations over, 212–13

Latin American Institute, Soviet Academy of Science, 184

Lava, José, 92, 95

League of Nations, 239

Lebanon, 44, 166

Lee, Vladimir, 61

Lenczowski, George, 168

Lenin, Nikolai: on behavior of a Communist minority, 254; on colonialism, 3–5; on imperialism, 1–2. See also Marxist-Leninist doctrine

Lenin Peace Prize, 57, 62

Lesotho, 58, 66

Levinson, G. I., 92

Liberia, 66

Libya, 58, 166, 167

Liu Shao-chi, 19

Magsaysay, Ramon, 92

Malagasy Republic, 45, 58

Malawi, 66

Malaya, 20, 45

Malaysia: attitude of toward "neutralization" policy, 79, 107–8; in five-power defense agreement (1971), 110, 111; Soviet Union and, 224, 232

Mali, 37, 45, 50, 225; military overthrow of government in, 39, 57, 58, 60

Malik, Adam, 106, 107, 108, 109

Marcos, Ferdinand, 79, 94, 95

Marighella, Carlos, 206

Martz, John, 190

Marx, Karl, 5. See also Marxist-Leninist doctrine

Marxist-Leninist doctrine, 36, 74–75, 125n; developing nations and, 43, 46; foreign aid and, 282

Medina, Clodomiro Almeyda, 194
Mexico, 44; guerilla movement in, 184; Soviet Union and, 184, 190
Middle East: Soviet Union and, 153–54, 175; U.S.-Soviet competition in, 153, 170–71, 177. *See also individual Middle East nations*
Mignan, Souron, 22
Mikoyan, Anastas, 219
Military aid, Soviet, 231–34; to Africa, 63, 66; to Egypt, 161, 163, 167; to India, 146, 150; to Latin America, 211–12
Minh, Ho Chi, 9, 87
Mirskii, Georgii, 37, 40, 44
Montreaux Convention (1936), 25, 156
Morawiecki, Wojciech, 243
Morocco, 44, 58, 68, 166, 221

Nasser, Gamal Abdel, 161, 162, 163, 230
National democracy, 72, 85, 167; characteristics of, 32–34, 45, 72; in Philippines, 92–93; in South Asia, 122–23; as transition to socialism, 35, 38, 57, 70, 85. *See also* National liberation movements; Nationalism
National Executive Council (NEC), Thailand, 82
Nationalism: in Africa, 22–24, 51, 53–54, 56, 61–62, 65, 66; Arab, 169–71; bourgeois, 17, 18–19, 33, 93–94, 121, 122, 176; in China, 10; Comintern and, 9–10; in India, 121, 122; Kurdish, 165; in Latin America, 22, 186, 189; socialism and, 38, 167, 168; Soviet policy toward, 21–22, 51, 53, 56, 61–62; Stalin on, 20–21, 53; state versus tribal, 34. *See also* National democracy; National liberations movements
Nationalization of property: in Chile, 191; in Peru, 187; Soviet support for, 225, 228
National liberation movements, 61; in Bangladesh, 124, 136; in Cambodia, 84; in Malaysia, 79; Soviet attitude toward, 123; in Vietnam, 87. *See aslo* National democracy; Nationalism
National United Front of Kampuchea (Cambodia), 83, 84
NATO. *See* North Atlantic Treaty Organization
Natural gas: in Afghanistan, 222; in Iran, 160, 173, 222
Naval power
—of India, 150

—of Soviet Union: in Caribbean Sea, 200–203, 212, 232–34; in Indian Ocean, 148–50; in Mediterranean Sea, 66, 154–56
—of U.S., 148–50, 155
Nehru, Jawaharlal, 121, 122n, 246
Nepal, 45
Neutralism, 31, 52, 77. *See also* Neutralization, of Southeast Asia; Nonalignment, of Afro-Asian states; Peaceful coexistence
Neutralization, of Southeast Asia: ASEAN and, 108, 113; to combat outside military assistance, 122; Indonesia and, 109–10; Kuala Lumpur declaration and, 111; Malaysia and, 79 and n, 107, 110; Philippines and, 109; Thailand and, 81, 107. *See also* Neutralism; Nonalignment, of Afro-Asian states; Peaceful coexistence
New Zealand: in five-power defense agreement (1971), 110, 111
Nigeria, 44, 58; Soviet Union and, 63–64, 66, 68; and war with Biafra, 63
Nimeri, Jaafar, 166, 168, 209n
Nixon, Richard M., visits China, 81, 109, 129
Nixon Doctrine, 117, 118
Nkrumah, Kwame, 40, 51, 53, 62; on African personality, 71; Lenin Peace Prize to, 57; overthrow of, 63, 73
Nol, Lon, 83, 117
Nonalignment, of Afro-Asian states: cold war and, 246, 249; explanation of, 245; Nehru on, 246; Nyerere on, 248–49; principles of, 247, 249–50
North Atlantic Treaty Organization, 155, 158, 159
Nyerere, Julius, 248–49

Oil: agreement on exploration for, 235; Algerian, 228; effect of on Soviet Middle East policy, 173–74; Iranian, 159; Iraqi, 165, 222; Soviet imports of, 222
Organization of African Unity, 58
Ovando, Alfredo, 188, 189

Padmore, George, 14
Pakhtoonistan movement, 122, 123, 124
Pakistan: Soviet Union and, 120, 124, 127–28, 232; U.S. and, 126–27; and wars with India, 124, 129, 119n, 126, 127, 135–40, 146–47
Pan-Africanism, 72

Paraguay, 180
Peaceful coexistence: characteristics of, 30, 243; competition between world powers and, 125, 244, 245; Khrushchev on, 29, 70; neutralism and, 31; Yugoslavia and, 247
Pepper, John, 9
Peru: reforms of Alvarado regime in, 186–88; Soviet Union and, 87, 232; U.S. and, 187
Philippines, 45; anti-Americanism in, 92, 93, 94, 118; attitude of toward "neutralization" policy, 109; bourgeoisie in, 93–94; Communist party of, 91, 92, 94, 95; Huks' guerilla activity in, 91, 92–93; Soviet Union and, 91–96, 114, 118; and trade with Communist nations, 79–80
Podgorny, Nikolai, 128
Population, of developing nations, 48–49
Potekhin, Ivan, 35, 37, 53

Racism, of African nations, 71, 72
Rajaratnam, S., 116
Rassemblement Démocratique Africain (RDA), 23, 52
Razak, Tun Abdul, 107, 108, 113
Religion, in Africa, 70, 71
Revolutionary democracy. See National democracy
Rhodesia, Northern, 15
Rostovskii, S. N., 28
Rowe, Edward, 260, 261–62
Roy, M. N., 3, 10, 11
Rubenstein, Alvin Z., 208, 247, 257
Rykov, Alexei, 239

Sabri, Ali, 162, 175
Sadat, Anwar el: attitude of toward local Communists, 41n; relations of with Soviet Union, 163, 175; relations of with U.S., 170; rise to power of, 162
Saudi Arabia, 167
SEATO. See Southeast Asia Treaty Organization
Senghor, Léopold, 70, 71
Shelepin, Aleksandr, 88, 193
Shmelev, N., 49
Sihanouk, Norodom, 82, 83, 114
Simoniia, N. A., 42, 62
Singapore: in five-power defense agreement (1971), 110, 111; Soviet Union and, 115, 116, 232
Socialism
—in Africa: class differences and, 75–76; religious aspects of, 71, 73

—Arab, 169–70
—in Chile, 191, 194, 195, 197
—in developing nations, 5, 35, 38–39, 60–61
—in Indonesia, 99
—national, 38–39
—nationalism and, 38, 167, 168
—scientific: compared with other forms of socialism, 38–39, 169; failure of in Africa, 43, 69, 72, 73
Solodovnikov, V. G., 229
Somalia, 44, 58, 65, 66
South Africa, Republic of, 52, 58, 66
South Asia: Soviet influence-building in, 119–20, 125–26, 140–41, 143–45; U.S. role in, 120, 142. See also individual South Asian nations
Southeast Asia: China and, 115; neutralization policy for, 79 and n, 81, 107–13. See also individual Southeast Asian nations
Southeast Asia Treaty Organization, 81, 82, 111
Soviet Communist party
—congresses: twentieth, 33, 54, 70, 85, 122, 244, 252; twenty-second, 32, 57, 101, 218; twenty-fourth, 84, 151n, 179, 195, 220, 284
—ideology of, 69. See also Ideology, of Soviet Union
—split in, 1947–49, 18
Soviet-Turkish Treaty of Friendship, Neutrality, and Nonagression (1925), 25
Soviet Union: attitude of toward colonialism following World War II, 16–19; collective security system of, 105–7, 114; foreign aid of, 145–46, 150, 222–27, 229–34, 277–79; geopolitics of, 120, 124, 127, 131; influence-building in Southeast Asia by, 119–20, 125–26, 140–41, 143–45; international organizations and, 238–41, (see also United Nations, Soviet Union and); investment in Third World nations by, 145–46, 228–29; military aid by, 63, 66, 146, 161, 163, 167, 211–12, 231–34; naval power of, 148–50, 154–56, 201–3, 212, 232–34; New Economic Policy of (1921), 8; reaction of to Chinese aid to developing nations, 269–73; spheres of influence of, 120, 123, 125, 141; support for national liberation movements by, 16–20, 123; trade relations of, 1 and n, 14–15, 67–68, 180–83, 209–10, 216–21. See also Ideology, of Soviet

Union; Soviet Communist party
Soviet writers: on anti-American nationalism in Philippines, 92, 93; on Asian and African nationalist governments, 35; on Chinese aid to developing nations, 269–71; on neutralization of Southeast Asia, 111–12; as representatives of changing Soviet attitudes, 27–29; on socialism in developing nations, 38–39, 41–43
Special United Nations Fund for Economic Development (SUNFED), 251–52
Spheres of influence, 120, 123, 125, 141, 175
Stalin, Josef: on Asian-African states, 240; on nationalism, 20–21, 53; neglect of Southeast Asia under, 84
Stettinius, Edward, 242
Straits of Malacca, 110, 139
Sudan: China and, 65; revolution in, 68; Soviet Union and, 209; suppression of local Communists in, 41n
Suez Canal, 64, 156, 161
Suez War (1956), 54
Suharto: ASEAN and, 113; attempt at neutralization by, 109; opposition to, 105; relations of with Soviet Union, 103, 104, 117; relations of with the West, 102–3
Sukarno: overthrow of, 4, 102, 103; PKI and, 98–99; relations of with China, 101, 103; relations of with Soviet Union, 100, 103, 117; revolution by, 97
Supranationalism, in United Nations: Soviet reaction to, 242, 243; Third World nations' reaction to, 248
Swaziland, 66
Syria, 57; Soviet Union and, 163–64, 173, 175, 176; and union with Egypt and Iraq, 170

Tanzania, 248; Chinese aid to, 279n, 285
Tanzania-Zambia railroad, 65, 67
Technical assistance, 215, 216, 217, 250
Thailand, 45; attitude of toward "neutralization" policy, 108–9; China and, 80, 81; Soviet Union and, 80–82, 115
Thanat, Khoman, 81, 82, 108
Thanom, Kittikachorn, 81, 108
Third World nations: Chinese influence on, 64–65, 68; classification of, 44–45; education of students from,

61, 68; efforts to encourage economic stability in, 224–28, 230–31, 235; Marxist-Leninist doctrine applied to, 33, 36, 43, 46; and multilateral relations with Communist bloc countries, 221; national democracy in, 32–35, 57, 85, 92–93, 99, 122–23, 167; nationalism in, 22–24, 51, 53–56, 61–62, 65–66, 121–22, 169–71, 189; nationalist socialism in, 38–39; national liberation movements in, 61, 79, 84, 87, 123, 124, 136; population of, 48–49; regional cooperation in, 47; public-versus private-sector projects in, 224–28; socialism in, 35, 38–39, 60–61, 69–76, 99, 169–70, 191, 194–95. *See also* Foreign aid, to Third World nations; Trade with developing nations, Soviet
Tied foreign-aid loans, 283–84, 285
Tiul'panov, S. I., 286
Touré, Sékou, 55, 57, 62
Trade with developing nations, Soviet, 1 and n, 216, 217; in Africa, 67–68; in consumer goods, 218; establishment of bilateral economic commissions for, 221; integration of foreign aid and, 220; in Latin America, 180–83, 194, 209–10; political reasons for, 219
Transportation development: air routes, 231; highways, 234; shipping, 232–33
Trotsky, Leon, 3
Tunisia, 44, 58, 167
Tupamaros movement, 204, 206, 207, 208
Turkey
—Cyprus and, 158
—relations of with NATO, 158, 159
—Soviet Union and, 215; effect of on foreign policy, 157–59; Montreaux Convention (1936), 25, 156; Soviet-Turkish Treaty of Friendship, Neutrality, and Nonaggression (1925), 25
—U.S. and, 157

Uganda, 285
Ul'ianovski, R., 36, 193
Union of Soviet Socialist Republics. *See* Soviet Union
United Arab Republic. *See* Egypt
United Nations
—bipolarity in, 238, 243, 244, 247
—China and, 255, 263
—enlargement of membership of, 253

—as forum for East-West competition, 245, 248
—as milieu for studying superpowers' behavior, 238
—predicted future policies of, 262–64
—role of in Indo-Pakistani wars, 127, 137
—Soviet Union and: attitude of toward nonaligned nations in, 244–47; changing position of influence in, 250–53; early role of in functions of, 240; minority status of in, 241–43; opposition of to supranationalism in, 242, 243; support of for Third World programs and policies in, 250–55
—Third World nations in: doctrine of nonalignment and, 245–47; effect of on Soviet-American relations, 238, 260–62; future role of in, 263–64; support for Soviet issues by, 253, 259–60
—Troika proposal for, 254
—U.S. role in, 255, 261
United Nations Conference on Trade and Development (UNCTAD), 247, 280, 286
United Nations Technical Assistance Program, 215, 216, 250
United States: Africa and, 65; Chile and, 192; China and, 129–30, 133n, 142, 213; India and, 126; involvement of in Indo-Pakistani War (1971), 132–33, 137, 138–40, 141; Iran and, 159–60; Latin America and, 181, 182, 183; naval power of, 148–50, 155; Pakistan and, 126–27; rivalry of with Soviet Union, 125–26, 199–201, 212–13; role of in South Asia, 120, 142; role of in Southeast Asia, 115; Turkey and, 157
Uruguay, 190; Tupamaros' guerilla movement in, 204, 206, 207, 208
U.S.S.R. See Soviet Union

Varga, Evgenii, 17, 28
Venezuela, 180
Vietnam. See Democratic Republic of Vietnam
Volskii, Victor, 184

West African Common Market, 47
Win, Ne, 82, 117, 118
World Assembly for Peace and Independence of Indochina, 114
World Federation of Trade Unions, 68
World revolution, Communist, objectives of, 4, 8, 12

Yemen, 45
Yew, Lee Kuan, 115, 116
Yugoslavia, on peaceful coexistence, 247

Zambia, 58
Zanzibar, 58
Zarine, D., 43
Zhdanov, Andrei, 16, 17, 18, 97, 100
Zhukov, Evgenii, 17, 18, 28